PC Magazine
Windows 3.1
Graphics Programming

WINDOWS 3.1
GRAPHICS
PROGRAMMING

Ben Ezzell

Ziff-Davis Press
Emeryville, California

Development Editor	Eric Stone
Copy Editor	Kandy Arnold
Technical Reviewer	Stuart Ozer
Project Coordinator	Bill Cassel
Proofreader	Vanessa Miller
Cover Design	Gary Suen
Book Design	Gary Suen
Word Processing	Howard Blechman, Cat Haglund, Kim Haglund
Page Layout	Bruce Lundquist
Screen Graphics Editor	Dan Brodnitz
Indexer	Julie Kawabata

This book was produced on a Macintosh IIfx, with the following applications: FramoMaker®, Microsoft® Word, MacLink®*Plus*, Aldus® FreeHand™, Adobe Photoshop™, and Collage Plus™.

Ziff-Davis Press
5903 Christie Avenue
Emeryville, CA 94608

ISBN 1-56276-055-6
Manufactured in the United States of America

♻ The paper used in this book exceeds the EPA requirements for post-consumer recycled paper.
10 9 8 7 6 5 4 3 2

DEDICATION

More than five centuries past, Henry of Portugal offered a prize,[1] a very generous sum at the time, for the development of a device that could keep time—not on land, but at sea.

The prize offered was important for two reasons. At that time, while clocks were not totally uncommon, all "modern" clocks depended on a pendulum action for their timing. Aboard a rolling ship, however, a pendulum motion was a far-from-satisfactory regulatory mechanism. But, directly as a result of Henry's prize offer, someone invented an ingenious mechanism called an escapement, which performed two tasks. First, the escapement freed timepieces from their wedlock to terra firma. Second, and more important, the escapement freed seamen from their cautious but also quite rational coast-hugging courses.

Thus, less than a century later, a Genoese sea captain begged, cajoled, and persuaded another European monarch to finance a voyage into the unknown—a voyage sailing far from sight of land, deliberately toward the unknown, and guided every bit as much by the sea captain's faith in and reliance on a new, "modern" invention as on his own stubborn disagreement with what was actually common knowledge among the educated of that time.[2] But even if he knew not where he had arrived even after returning, the results—given the benefit of 20/20 hindsight—were still revolutionary.

So it is in many ways with computers: We do not know precisely where we are headed—and may not know even after we arrive—but whatever successes we achieve, whether we realize it or not, owe a great debt to an individual five centuries in his grave.

Therefore, this book is respectfully dedicated, not to the famous (or infamous) Christopher Columbus, but to an insightful individual who recognized a need, prompted an invention, and therefore made possible the first regulated timepiece, without whose modern electronic analogs computers simply would not function:

Henry the Navigator
King of Portugal
1394–1460

---

1. Henry the Navigator, so called for the end results of his prize offer, was reputed to hold this affectionate title in much greater esteem than his inherited title of King.

2. The idea than anyone in the fourteenth century—or even centuries earlier—thought the world was flat is simply a modern myth and is every bit as incorrect as any of the real medieval errors; unfortunately, however, the past has never held a monopoly on ignorance. Where Columbus erred was in doubting the distance to India, which had been calculated with a high degree of accuracy by the Greek philosophers many centuries before the Europeans acquired the capability to venture beyond their tidal estuaries.

CONTENTS AT A GLANCE

TABLE OF CONTENTS

Part 3　　Beyond the GDI

ACKNOWLEDGMENTS

While the author alone is responsible for any faults or flaws that appear in this work, the success of any technical book depends heavily on the efforts of a great many people to whom I wish to extend my sincere thanks as well as all due credit. Responsible individuals include Cindy Hudson, who accepted this project for Ziff-Davis Press; Eric Stone for both his editorial work and his patience; and Bill Cassel, Dan Brodnitz, and Cheryl Holzaepfel, also of Ziff-Davis, for a variety of reasons. Thanks are also due to Nan Borreson, Karen Giles, and Tom Orsi as well as others at Borland International. And, if last, also far from least, very special thanks to Stuart Ozer for his careful and critical technical review. Stuart, while I did not follow all of your suggestions, I assure you all were considered and, whether used or not, were very much appreciated.

INTRODUCTION

As computers become both increasingly sophisticated and increasingly common, the demand for applications that are both graphic and interactive is on the increase. At the same time, developing interactive graphics places an increased demand on both the application environment and the application developer.

But, although the demands on the programmer have increased, using the graphics environment also has offered new opportunities and prompted the development of new tools and new capabilities to meet these demands.

Developing a graphic user interface under DOS was, with few exceptions, a monumental task, requiring the dedicated efforts of a programming team faced with (among other problems) the need to adapt to systems with unknown video resolutions.

But, under Windows, most of the adaptation problems are already handled with the Windows shell. The shell provides both a (relatively) smooth graphic operating environment and an extensive assortment of low-level graphics functions, display windows, control buttons, and scroll bars, as well as the handling and message functions necessary to control this monolithic and almost unwieldy system.

Still, all of these features, however useful, are only the framework for applications—the modular foundations, framing, and subflooring with which to build your own designs, whether these be bungalows or castles in the air. The embellishments—the interior finish, gingerbread trim, balconies, drawbridges, and moats—are left to your own architectural devising. Although these similes are somewhat picturesque, they are not, perhaps, inappropriate—if only because what is being presented in this book is not only a collection of graphics programs, but also a toolbox of graphics features with which to build your own applications.

WHAT'S IN THIS BOOK?

Of course, before building an application, it helps to understand the tools and the materials available. *PC Magazine 3.1 Windows Graphics Programming* begins with the traditional "Hello, World"—although in a new, Windows-compatible guise—in Chapter 1 before moving on to simple dialog boxes in Chapter 2. Chapter 3 looks at application resources and how these are created.

Chapter 4 returns to the principal topic of graphics images, with two programs demonstrating Windows mapping modes and a version of the popular game Life, which offers a firsthand look at the isotropic and anisotropic mapping modes.

However, knowing what modes Windows supports is only half the battle. Therefore, Chapter 5 explains how to query and identify system (hardware) device capabilities with a demo program that provides data on both video and (if any) printer devices.

After identifying the system's hardware limitations, Chapter 6 moves to graphics colors, using a trio of programs to examine Windows's default palette, demonstrate color dithering, and demonstrate palette color creation.

In Chapter 7, screen and image manipulation are introduced with two programs. The first demonstrates screen capture, redisplaying the captured image using the BitBlt and StretchBlt modes; the second shows how to save a captured screen image to a disk file using the .BMP format.

While Chapter 7 introduces Windows's native bitmap format, Chapter 8 examines several other popular image file formats, including a decoder/display program for the very popular .PCX format. Later chapters return to the .BMP image format for general use.

The next two chapters introduce image processing algorithms. Chapter 9 covers image enhancement, smoothing, and edge detection processes, and Chapter 10 introduces conversion processes to change color images to grayscale equivalents for output to a printer.

In Chapter 11, the topic turns to simple animation techniques with two demonstrations showing cursor animation and bitmap animation.

In Chapter 12, a strong feature of Windows graphics is introduced: interactive images. In this chapter, the MapDemo application uses two bitmap images—a map of the entire United States and a map of the New England states—to demonstrate two quite different interactive methods with two very different algorithms for identifying irregular regions.

Chapter 13 concerns two popular topics in the business world: incorporating graphics imagery into business graphs and making business graphs interactive.

Next, Chapter 14 looks at some of the problems and possibilities of using graphics in simulations. This chapter features a demo program that displays a numerical simulation of the life cycle of a forest.

Because Windows is not the ideal environment for all graphics, and because newer graphics hardware requires provisions within Windows for use, Chapter 15 explains and demonstrates Super VGA (SVGA, a.k.a. Extended VGA) video systems and, most important, SVGA 256-color palettes under both DOS and Windows.

Last, Appendix A describes a variety of additional resources for use with image programming, including ZSoft's PhotoFinish and several image compression utilities. Appendix B explains how to install and use the programs on the accompanying disk.

ABOUT THE DISK THAT ACCOMPANIES THIS BOOK

PC Magazine Windows 3.1 Graphics Programming includes a bound-in disk that contains all of the demonstration programs used in the book, plus a selection of images for use with a number of the demo programs. A .TGA conversion program is also included on the disk as a bonus. The TGA2VGA.CPP application provides a means to convert high-color-resolution TARGA (video camera) images to SVGA-compatible display formats. (Note: TGA2VGA.CPP is not discussed in the book but, together with the TGA.H header, does provide the basics for TARGA image handling.) Appendix B contains detailed information about the disk programs.

Part 1

Basics of Windows Programming

CREATING A WINDOWS PROGRAM

WINDOWS MESSAGES AND CHILD
PROCESSES

WINDOWS APPLICATIONS RESOURCES

Creating a Windows Program

W hile some familiarity with Windows programming is assumed later in this book, Chapters 1–3 provide a brief review. Chapter 1 begins with the basics of creating a Windows application and exercising program control through event message handling. It also includes a review of Windows terminology, the use of Hungarian notation, and basic compiler and linker operations. In all chapters, examples concentrate on the Windows version of the Borland C/C++ compiler (TCW 3.0), though any compatible compiler desired may be used.

Traditionally, a program titled Hello.C is the introductory example, and for Windows programming, a similar example—WinHello.C—will be employed. Although the familiar Hello.C generally requires a scant few lines of code, WinHello.C is not quite as brief.

The reasons for this difference are twofold:

▶ First, even the simplest Windows programs accomplish a variety of tasks that are not handled by—nor required of—conventional DOS programs. Because a DOS program does not operate in a multitasking environment, it has complete access to and control of all system resources (screen, keyboard, mouse). A Windows program, on the other hand, has to share resource access with other applications and, therefore, must access these resources indirectly through Windows. This shared and restricted access imposes requirements that a DOS program does not face and requires appropriate provisions within the source code of the Windows program.

▸ Second, an application operating within the Windows graphical environment is required to do more than a parallel application operating within the DOS text environment. At a minimum, a Windows application maintains a display window, an outline, and a menu bar, as well as its own task or function. And, even though the Windows system handles the major portion of these tasks, a few elementary provisions within the program source code are still required.

Initially, this may appear to be a lot of complexity to move a DOS program into Windows, and in fact, if this were the only objective, it would be entirely too much trouble and hardly worthwhile. And, for the sample program Hello.C, the Windows version, WinHello.C, is certainly a futile exercise accomplishing only a little more than its ancestral original (see Figure 1.1). But, in both cases, the point is not what the sample program accomplishes but to demonstrate the rudiments of programming in each situation.

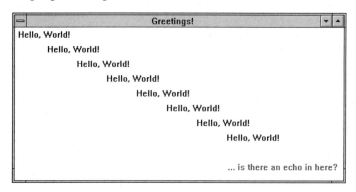

Figure 1.1: Hello, World ... Windows style

And a demonstration of the rudiments of Windows programming is precisely what this chapter is about, beginning with the basis of every program: the WinMain() procedure.

MAIN() VERSUS WINMAIN()

In all traditional C/C++ programs, the main() procedure provides the entry point for the application—the central control point where it all begins. But, in Windows, the main() procedure is replaced by a new procedure titled WinMain().

Granted, the purpose of the WinMain() procedure is essentially the same: providing an entry point and central control for execution. Beyond this, however, the resemblance is limited because the WinMain() procedure has to accomplish a number of tasks that are unique to Windows but are not required by DOS applications.

And there is a second, equally important difference. In a DOS application, the main() procedure is not only the entry point of the application but, in many cases, may include a greater or lesser portion of the program's major provisions. In contrast, in a Windows application, the WinMain() procedure will actually accomplish very little of the application's purpose. Instead, in the Windows application, WinMain() sets initial conditions for the application—principally only those required to notify Windows of the application's presence and requirements—and then passes further control to the Windows system.

In return, to accomplish the application's tasks, Windows calls procedures that are exported by the application, passing temporary control to these subprocedures while handling their responses and communications with the physical system.

Please be aware, however, that the WinMain() procedure is not, in itself, responsible for creating the application's main window. What the WinMain() procedure is responsible for is initiating an application's entry into the Windows environment. Subsequently, it limits itself to accepting messages from Windows (that is, from the environment) and forwarding these to the various exported procedures, such as the *WndProc* procedure—which, incidentally, is primarily responsible for the application's main window.

DECLARING THE WINMAIN() PROCEDURE

Not only is the WinMain() procedure different in purpose from the familiar main() procedure, but it also is declared and called in a quite different fashion.

In DOS, for example, unless command line parameters are expected, the main() procedure would be called as

```
void main( void )
```

or simply as

```
main()
```

In Windows, however, the WinMain() procedure is always called with parameters as

```
int PASCAL WinMain(
           HANDLE hInstance,    HANDLE hPrevInstance,
           LPSTR  lpszCmdParam, int nCmdShow )
{
```

These arguments are not supplied by the user but, instead, are supplied by the Windows system to identify the application instance and its status.

For example, the *hInstance* handle uniquely identifies this specific instance of the application as it executes under Windows while the *hPrevInstance* handle identifies any previous instances of the same application that were also currently executing. Of course, if this is the only instance of the application, the *hPrevInstance* parameter would be passed as null, but when more than one copy of an application is executed at the same time, it is useful—and often essential—to have access to the previous instance, if for no other reason than to share resources and thus conserve memory usage.

The third parameter, *lpszCmdParam*, is rarely—if ever—actually used within the WinMain() procedure but, nonetheless, is passed as a standard calling parameter. Since this argument is not used, however, the compiler will generate the warning message:

```
lpszCmdParam is never used.
```

cautioning you that this argument has not been referenced within the procedure.

Since this parameter is always supplied—and the WinMain() procedure must be written to expect it—you have two choices in dealing with the discrepancy. First, you may simply ignore this warning message as unimportant (which it is) or, second, you can insert a prophylactic directive prior to the WinMain() procedure:

```
#pragma argsused
```

The *argsused* directive, quite simply, directs the compiler to ignore any unused arguments in the following procedure.

The final argument, *nCmdShow*, will be passed presently as a calling parameter to the *ShowWindow* instruction.

NOTE: The source code for the WinHello.C program appears in full at the end of this chapter.

INSIDE WINMAIN()

Beyond the initial declaration of the WinMain() procedure, WinMain() conventionally begins with several variable declarations:

```
static char szAppName[] = "WinHello";
HWND        hwnd;
MSG         msg;
WNDCLASS    wc;
```

The *szAppName* variable is declared as a static array with the application name. This is an optional declaration but is more convenient than subsequent multiple repetitions of the string. The *hwndk*, *msg*, and *wc* variables, on the other hand, are mandatory and will be needed subsequently, beginning with the WNDCLASS (window class) variable, *wc*.

Of these three, the *wc* data structure is the most important because this structure defines the principal properties of an application's main window. Once defined, these properties are essentially static and will not be changed during the application's execution.

If this is the first instance of the application—that is, there are no other copies of this application currently executing—the *wc* variables are assigned initial values and, last, the window class is registered (with the Windows system).

```
if( ! hPrevInstance )
{
    wc.style          = CS_HREDRAW | CS_VREDRAW;
    wc.lpfnWndProc    = WndProc;
    wc.cbClsExtra     = 0;
    wc.cbWndExtra     = 0;
    wc.hInstance      = hInstance;
    wc.hIcon          = LoadIcon( hInstance, szAppName );
    wc.hCursor        = LoadCursor( NULL, IDC_ARROW );
    wc.hbrBackground  = GetStockObject( WHITE_BRUSH );
    wc.lpszMenuName   = NULL;
    wc.lpszClassName  = szAppName;
    RegisterClass( &wc );
}
```

The declaration

```
    wc.lpfnWndProc    = WndProc
```

associates the exported procedure *WndProc* with the application instance's main window. Later, messages processed by the WinMain() procedure will be passed to *WndPro*—or to other exported procedures—where the bulk of an application's task is handled.

Alternatively, if a previous instance of the application is already running, this entire sequence is unnecessary and is skipped. After all, since there is another copy of the program active, Windows already knows the essential details and can avoid wasting memory by, for example, not loading an extra copy of the application's icon image.

Within the WinMain() procedure, however, there are other tasks that must be handled by every instance of the application, and the next step, *CreateWindow*, is one of them.

```
hwnd = CreateWindow(
        szAppName,                // window class name
        "Greetings!",             // window caption
        WS_OVERLAPPEDWINDOW,      // window style
        CW_USEDEFAULT,            // initial X position
        CW_USEDEFAULT,            // initial Y position
        CW_USEDEFAULT,            // initial X size
        CW_USEDEFAULT,            // initial Y size
        NULL,                     // parent window handle
        NULL,                     // window menu handle
        hInstance,                // program instance handle
        NULL  );                  // creation parameters
```

The *CreateWindow* procedure uses the information in the parameter list to create the application's main window. The calling parameter *szAppName* also appeared in the *wc* data declaration and, in part, provides a link between the application instance and the window class registration.

CreateWindow is called with a lengthy argument list—this length is typical of many Windows function calls—and returns a handle (*hwnd*) to the newly created window. The several parameters are identified (above) by comments, and the arguments shown can be used as standard defaults for most applications.

The window-size parameters have been passed as CW_USEDEFAULT, permitting Windows to position and size the new window as appropriate for the existing desktop. Specific arguments can be supplied if necessary.

Also, since this application is assumed to be a parent and has no custom (non-stock) menu nor special creation parameters, the corresponding arguments are specified as nulls. In other applications, one or more of these parameters may be specified differently but, in general, all of these can be taken as generic defaults.

Simply creating an application window, however, is only a part of the task and there are several standard tasks remaining. The first of these are calls to the *ShowWindow* and *UpdateWindow* functions.

```
ShowWindow( hwnd, nCmdShow );
UpdateWindow( hwnd );
```

Creating an application window is an entirely separate task from actually causing the window to be displayed. It is the *ShowWindow* procedure that is used to have the application window displayed, while the *nCmdShow* parameter, which was originally passed to the application by Windows, specifies how the window should be displayed initially: maximized, minimized, or as an icon. And the *UpdateWindow* procedure is equally important because this instruction is used to have the window's client region redrawn.

> **NOTE:** For those unfamiliar with Windows terminology, an application window consists of several parts, each of which may be treated in a partially or completely autonomous manner. At the moment, three principal parts are important: the window frame, or outline, that surrounds the window, the title bar across the top of the window, and, far from least, the client window that is the application's central display.

At this point, the WinMain() procedure has been quite busy establishing the prerequisites for the application and finishing by issuing instructions for the application window to be created and displayed. But, as you may have noticed, thus far the application hasn't actually done anything—which might make you wonder what the application consists of, except, perhaps, a titled frame and an empty client window.

The message loop   The truth of the matter is that, at this time, the application consists of little more than an empty frame and a title bar. Still, WinMain() is not entirely finished; there is a message loop remaining:

```
while( GetMessage( &msg, NULL, 0, 0 ) )

{
   TranslateMessage( &msg );
   DispatchMessage( &msg );
}
return( msg.wParam );
}
```

The message loop shown is also a stock element in the WinMain() procedure and consists of three instructions.

▶ The first instruction, *GetMessage*, is called with a pointer to the *msg* structure and, if there is a message in the queue, returns the message for further handling. The latter three parameters may, in other circumstances, be used to restrict which messages are retrieved, but for the present specify retrieval of all messages belonging to the current application.

▶ After the messages are retrieved, *TranslateMessage* is used to convert virtual-key messages to ASCII characters. The reasons behind this are not immediately relevant and can await further explanation at the appropriate time. For the present, this is stock handling within the WinMain()

procedure and normalizes keyboard messages before they receive further handling.

▶ Last, the *DispatchMessage* function is called and, in brief, sends any retrieved messages on for further handling.

Once the message queue is emptied, the *msg.wParam* component from the last message handled is returned to the Windows system as the WinMain() procedure exits.

It still appears, however, that the application has effectively done nothing and still consists of no more than a frame, a title bar, and an empty client window. In one sense, this is entirely correct. Yet, in another sense, a great deal has happened and there are further events that have occurred despite the fact that they have not been particularly obvious thus far.

But, before we investigate these hidden events, there are a few other aspects of the message loop that deserve attention.

WINMAIN() AS A TEMPLATE

The WinMain() procedure just demonstrated can and will be used, with minor modifications, as a template for further applications. Most of the necessary modifications should be relatively obvious. Indeed, in most cases, simply changing the application's name (*szAppName*) and the window caption label is more than sufficient to adapt the WinMain() procedure to the new application. In other cases, more extensive revisions may be required, but in either situation, essentially the same basic provisions will be required and the general format will remain constant.

EXPORTED PROCESSES

Thus far, you've seen how the WinMain() procedure functions. At the same time, however, the provisions within the WinMain() procedure haven't actually accomplished much except to set up an application window, and none of the code shown thus far does anything specific to the application.

So, where and how does the application accomplish its own tasks?

The answer lies in exported processes—processes that are not called directly by the WinMain() procedure but which are called by Windows.

Before going into the practice of exported processes, there is another topic that requires introduction: the .DEF module.

MODULE DEFINITION FILES (.DEF)

The module definition file, while brief, is an integral element in programming a Windows application. It consists of instructions defining the application's contents and system requirements to be observed by the Link program.

> **NOTE:** Using Borland C/C++ for Windows, the link operation is handled as an integral part of the compiler's Build All operations. When using some other compilers, or when using Make File instructions with a command line compiler, the linker may be referenced separately. In either case, however, the .DEF file provides integral and necessary instructions for producing a Windows .EXE program.

THE WINHELLO.DEF FILE

In general, a .DEF file consists of a dozen or so lines of ASCII text, each line beginning with a keyword and followed by one or more labels or directives.

Optionally, a .DEF file may begin with a header consisting of one or more lines that are identified as comments by the semicolon characters leading each line. In like fashion, further comments may be inserted anywhere within the .DEF file but must consist of lines beginning with the semicolon identifier. Conventional C/C++ delimiters (the // and /* character pairs) are not valid in a .DEF file.

```
;=======================================;
;  WINHELLO.DEF module definition file  ;
;=======================================;
```

While the precise order of the instructions in the module definition file is not critical, a typical .DEF file begins with the NAME field identifying the application name, an optional DESCRIPTION field, which is itself simply a comment for the programmer, and the EXETYPE field, which, for a Windows application, will always be WINDOWS. Of course, applications compiled for OS/2 would revise this last field appropriately.

```
NAME         WINHELLO
DESCRIPTION  "Windows Hello, World Program"
EXETYPE      WINDOWS
```

The STUB field refers to a DOS executable stub program that is appended to the Windows program. If an attempt is made to execute the application program from DOS rather than from Windows, the stub program displays a message and terminates the application rather than permitting the application to hang up the system.

```
STUB         "WINSTUB.EXE"
```

A custom stub program can be used if special instructions are required. Otherwise, the default *WinStub.EXE* program will serve.

Next, the CODE and DATA directives specify how these portions of the executable program will be handled by Windows.

```
CODE        PRELOAD MOVEABLE DISCARDABLE
DATA        PRELOAD MOVEABLE MULTIPLE
```

In general, both the code and data segments are defined as PRELOAD (loaded into memory when the module is loaded) and MOVEABLE (permitting the segment to be moved as necessary so that memory can be compacted). As alternatives, the LOADONCALL option specifies that the segment is loaded only when explicitly needed, and FIXED prevents segment relocation.

For the CODE segment, the DISCARDABLE directive specifies that the segment can be discarded if it is not in use and the memory resources are required for other uses. If the segment should not be discardable, the directive is simply omitted.

The DATA segment has its own directives specifying that no data segment exists (NONE) or that a single data segment is shared by all module instances (SINGLE, valid only for libraries) or that each application instance requires its own data segment (MULTIPLE, valid only for applications).

The HEAPSIZE and STACKSIZE directives define the size of the application's local heap and local stack. The values shown are adequate as standard defaults for most applications.

```
HEAPSIZE     1024
STACKSIZE    8192
```

The instance heap size requires a minimum of 256k and a maximum of 65,536k (the size of a segment). The minimum stack size is zero if no function calls are used (unlikely) but otherwise defaults to 5k. The STACKSIZE statement is not used with Dynamic Link Libraries (DLLs).

In this sample, the final link directive is the EXPORTS statement that is used, in this case, to declare the WndProc procedure as an export and, therefore, available (callable) from Windows or another application.

```
EXPORTS      WndProc
```

In other program examples, the EXPORTS directive may specify more than one procedure (each on a separate line) or may include further arguments, flags, or conditions applicable to specific exported procedures. In still other cases, the IMPORTS directive may specify external procedures that are needed by the present application.

This sample program has used only a few of the link directives, which can be included in a .DEF module definition file. Further details on link (.DEF) directives can be found in the *Microsoft Windows Programmer's Reference* under the heading Module Definition Files.

Following is the complete *WinHello.DEF* module definition file:

```
;=======================================;
;   WINHELLO.DEF module definition file   ;
;=======================================;

NAME          WINHELLO
DESCRIPTION   "Windows Hello, World Program"
EXETYPE       WINDOWS
STUB          "WINSTUB.EXE"
CODE          PRELOAD MOVEABLE DISCARDABLE
DATA          PRELOAD MOVEABLE MULTIPLE
HEAPSIZE      1024
STACKSIZE     8192
EXPORTS       WndProc
```

REACHING THE EXPORTED *WNDPROC* PROCEDURE

Previously, while discussing the message loop in the WinMain() procedure, the point was made that the message loop polled incoming messages (using *GetMessage*), translated the messages (using *TranslateMessage*), and then returned the messages to the message queue (using *DispatchMessage*). But what was not discussed was where the dispatched messages were sent, and what was done with them subsequently.

And, later, in discussing the module definition file, an exported procedure was declared using the title *WndProc* with the comment that this exported procedure could, subsequently, be called directly by Windows.

If you have surmised a connection between these two subjects, you're absolutely correct, because it is the exported *WndProc* procedure that will handle the forwarded messages and will provide the heart of the application's actual task execution. Further, exported and imported procedures act as entry points for secondary program sections.

Individually, an exported procedure may call any number of conventional subprocedures and functions directly—that is, in the same fashion as in conventional DOS programming. In general, only major entry points are declared as export and import, and subprocedures and functions called directly are not declared for export or import.

Before looking at how the *WndProc* procedure operates, of more immediate importance is understanding how the *WndProc* procedure is reached—how Windows is able to call the *WndProc* procedure and how directives and information are passed to the *WndProc* procedure (or to other exported procedures).

MESSAGES AND MESSAGE HANDLING

In conventional programming, procedures and functions are called with one or more arguments (or, sometimes, none) that pass information to the subprocedure specifying the tasks required or providing information required for specific tasks. An identical parameter-passing format is used in Windows—in most cases.

But there are exceptions as well. The principal exceptions are anytime that Windows calls an exported procedure, because in all such cases the export procedure is declared in the same fashion and receives four calling arguments. A typical declaration appears as:

```
long FAR PASCAL WndProc( HWND hwnd,    WORD message,
                         WORD wParam, LONG lParam )
```

The first argument is a window handle—a value identifying the window where the message originated (or where the message was originally sent and then redispatched).

But it is the second argument that is important here: the message parameter. Messages are integer values with predefined meanings and are commonly identified using the message constants, such as WM_PAINT, WM_MOVE, WM_DESTROY, defined in the Windows.H header file.

NOTE: The values associated with each of these message identifiers are unimportant. In all cases, only the mnemonic identifiers will be used.

These messages are simply a comprehensive series of identifiers which will be used as directives to request specific responses and will always be sent individually with subsidiary information passed in the *wParam* and *lParam* arguments. (That is, message identifiers will never be OR'd, AND'd, XOR'd, or otherwise modified or combined, as is often done with flag-byte values.)

The *wParam* (a WORD value) and *lParam* (LONG) arguments accompanying individual messages may be used to provide additional information and may be nulls, secondary messages, values, coordinates, pointers, or even bit flags. The type of information that is contained in these arguments is dictated by the message type identified by the message argument.

When more than one export procedure has been declared, or if import procedures are declared, all communications between these entry points are handled indirectly by posting a message to Windows with the appropriate accompanying arguments. Exported and imported procedures are never called directly.

Admittedly, this is a sketchy explanation of how Windows messages work, but further explanations will wait for demonstration by example rather than explanation by theory. And for an initial demonstration, the *WndProc* procedure is ideal.

OPERATING THE *WNDPROC* PROCEDURE

The *WndProc* procedure is called with four arguments as described above. The first argument, *hwnd*, provides a window handle for directing subsequent operations. The second argument, *message*, was generated in this example by Windows; it identifies the task that should be carried out.

In the WinHello program, provisions are made for only two Windows messages: WM_PAINT and WM_DESTROY, both of which should be anticipated with possible, but rare, exceptions by all applications.

The first of these, WM_PAINT, is a directive instructing *WndProc* that it's time to create (paint, draw, or write) the application's display. Remember, the application's window frame, title bar, and any controls have already been drawn by Windows when the application was initialized. At the same time the application's window is created, Windows issues a WM_PAINT message instructing the *WndProc* procedure to create the actual display.

But this is not the only occasion when a WM_PAINT message will be issued. A WM_PAINT message will be issued anytime an application window has been moved, resized, uncovered (as by another application), or otherwise requires recreation or reconstruction. A WM_PAINT message also will be issued in response to a call to the *UpdateWindow* function. With the WM_PAINT message, the *wParam* and *lParam* arguments are null (unused).

The second standard directive, WM_DESTROY, is issued when an application window is closed (from the main menu) or when the *DestroyWindow* function is called. This message provides the application with an opportunity to execute any clean-up and shut-down provisions that may be required.

Responses on closing an application window could include querying the termination; writing, or closing output files; passing closing messages to other applications with interrelated operations; or anything else necessary for a clean termination. Or, if no responses are necessary, simply call the *PostQuitMessage* function and exit gracefully.

What is not required—except under very unusual circumstances—is any provision for erasing the application and its client (display) window, since this particular task is handled automatically by Windows.

RESPONDING TO WINDOWS MESSAGES

The heart of the *WndProc* procedure, as with any message-handling procedure, is a *switch..case* statement with case provisions for all messages to be handed directly. Any messages that do not receive specific handling instructions will be handled by a default provision.

In its simplest form, the message-handling *switch..case* statement will look something like this:

```
switch( message )
{
   case WM_PAINT:
        hdc = BeginPaint( hwnd, &ps );
        ... detailed drawing provisions ...
        EndPaint( hwnd, &ps );
        return( 0 );
   case WM_DESTROY:
        PostQuitMessage( 0 );
        return( 0 );
}
return( DefWindowProc( hwnd,   message,
                       wParam, lParam ) );
}
```

In the truncated example above, the case responses to both the WM_PAINT and WM_DESTROY messages end with the instruction *return (0)*, providing an immediate return and avoiding any other responses to these messages.

When provisions are not made for a message response, the *DefWindowProc* procedure (which is provided by Windows, not by the programmer) is called using the same four parameters that the *WndProc* procedure originally received. The result is that the message and its accompanying arguments are returned to Windows for default handling, for whatever response Windows may provide.

Because many, if not most, of the possible messages are likely to be totally irrelevant to a specific application or may even be very unlikely to occur, requiring every application to respond to all possible messages would be cumbersome and unnecessary. Therefore, the *DefWindowProc* provision simply transfers both the message and the responsibility back to the Windows system, where the event message may be handled if a response is appropriate, or ignored if not.

Future samples will, in most cases, handle many more messages than the two shown here. In all cases, however, both explicit responses to selected messages and default handling for all other messages are equally important.

The actual mechanisms provided in response to the WM_PAINT message are not the topic at this time. However, the appropriate code for the display shown in Figure 1.1 appears in the program listing at the end of this chapter, and the mechanisms used will be discussed in later chapters.

APPLICATION DATA DECLARATIONS

In conventional C/C++ programs, data declarations are sometimes made specific to particular procedures or subprocedures. Other times, they are declared as global to the entire application. And, in DOS programming, application-specific data is often declared within the main() procedure. In Windows programming, however, a different approach is required, and the application's data—to be accessible—must be declared global and, specifically, outside of the scope of WinMain().

WINDOWS TERMINOLOGY AND PROGRAMMING CONVENTIONS

Programming a Windows application involves a number of differences from conventional C/C++ programming. Of these differences some, such as the PASCAL declarations, are required by the Windows environment, while others, such as Hungarian notation, are optional but also semi-official, and a few are simply a matter of personal taste.

The declaration of export procedures as

```
long FAR PASCAL ProcName( ... )
```

falls into the first category and is required by the Windows environment, as is the use of the PASCAL declaration in WinMain().

In brief, the PASCAL keyword simply instructs the compiler/linker that all parameters will follow Pascal conventions rather than C/C++ conventions because this is how Windows passes messages and parameters. For local procedures, however, parameters are passed following C/C++ conventions, and no special provisions are required.

For exported procedures, the use of the FAR declaration should be fairly obvious. It simply provides a far address rather than the default near address for the procedure. Conventional C/C++ programs use purely local procedures and functions by default and do not—except in unusual circumstances—require far addresses. On the other hand, exported procedures are not necessarily local to the Windows segment that will be calling them and, therefore, require far addresses.

HUNGARIAN NOTATION

Hungarian notation falls into the second category mentioned above: optional but demi-officially sanctioned. But, because Hungarian notation is useful, it will be followed in most of the examples in this book. In essence, Hungarian notation is a shorthand form consisting of one or more lower-case letters prefacing variable names and is used to identify variable types within their nomenclature. This form of identification is credited to Microsoft programmer Charles Simonyi and follows the format shown in Table 1.1.

Table 1.1: Hungarian Notation

Prefix	Data type
b	BOOL or Boolean integer
by	byte or unsigned char
c	char
cx, cy	short int used as x or y lengths
dw	DWORD—double word or unsigned long
fn	function
h	handle
i	integer
l	LONG
n	short or integer
s	string
sz	ASCIIZ (null-terminated) string
w	WORD (unsigned int)
x, y	short int used as x or y coordinates

NOTE: Charles Simonyi proposes a slightly different series of definitions from those shown preceding (*Byte*, August 1991, "The Hungarian Revolution"). At the time that article appeared, however, Hungarian notation had been in use for some time and had appeared in several variations—including variations used by Simonyi, Petzold, and others. Therefore, the preceding are simply the variations which I personally use. They should not be considered as constituting either standard or nonstandard usage.

CONSTANT TYPES AND IDENTIFIERS

Windows uses a variety of predefined constants as messages, flag values and operational parameters. These constants—defined in Windows.H—are always full uppercase. In most cases they include a two- or three-letter prefix set off by an underscore and identify the general category of the constant or message as shown in Table 1.2.

Table 1.2: Message Prefix Identifiers

Prefix	Category	Example
CS_	class style	CS_HREDRAW
CW_	create window	CW_USERDEFAULT
DT_	draw text	DT_VCENTER
IDC_	cursor id	IDC_ARROW
IDI_	icon id	IDI_APPLICATION
WM_	window message	WM_PAINT
WS_	window style	WS_OVERLAPPEDWINDOW

WINDOWS DATA TYPES

In addition to the conventional data types defined in C/C++, several new data type definitions are provided in Windows.H. A selection of new types that are used extensively is shown in Table 1.3.

Table 1.3: Windows Data Types

Data Type	Size/Meaning
DWORD	double word, 32-bit unsigned long integer
FAR	same as far
LONG	32-bit signed long integer
LPSTR	long (far) pointer to character string
PASCAL	same as pascal
WORD	16-bit unsigned integer

WINDOWS STRUCTURES

A number of data structures are defined in Windows.H. Five of these that are used extensively are identified in Table 1.4.

Table 1.4: Windows Structures

Type	Structure Purpose
MSG	message structure
PAINTSTRUCT	paint structure
POINT	point structure (mouse position)
RECT	rectangle structure
WNDCLASS	window class structure

These structures will be discussed further when appropriate but are all used regularly.

HANDLE IDENTIFIERS

In Windows, handles are 16-bit indexes to a table entry identifying program elements. Several common handle types appear in Table 1.5.

Table 1.5: Handle Type Identifiers

Handle ID	Handle Type
HANDLE	generic handle
HBRUSH	paintbrush handle
HDC	device-context handle
HPALETTE	logical (color) palette handle
HPEN	drawing-pen handle
HWND	window handle

Detailed definitions for each of these data types, structures, and handles appear in the *Microsoft Windows Programmer's Reference* or in Borland's *Windows API Reference Guide,* Volume 2.

COMPILING AND LINKING WINDOWS PROJECTS

In most respects, compiling and linking is the same for a Windows application as for any other application. There are, however, a few differences that must be observed.

One of the principal differences found with Windows applications lies in the use of resource files. Resource files are compiled units containing application resources that are not and cannot be supplied within the program source code. These include dialog boxes, menus, bitmaps, icons, custom cursors, keyboard accelerators, and even custom fonts. For these resources to be available for use by the application, however, they must be linked to the finished .EXE program.

NOTE: Resource types, files, and scripts will be discussed further in Chapter 3 and Appendix A contains a comparison of several resource editors.

A second difference is the use of .DEF module definition files, which were discussed previously.

Because of these differences, the conventional practice of simply compiling the .C source code to produce an .EXE executable program is no longer sufficient for the task. Instead, several sources are required during the linking process. As an absolute minimum, these are the .C source code and the .DEF module-definition file but, in virtually all cases, this will also include either a .RES resource file or an .RC resource script.

Now, using the command-line compiler version (BCC) and a .MAK file to handle compiling and linking, there would be no particular problem involved in linking multiple sources—assuming, of course, that you prefer using the command-line compiler over the convenience of an integrated development environment.

This is precisely the reason why the TCW compiler offers a new option: the Project option. Project files serve two main purposes. The first (see Figure 1.2) is to list multiple source files that are required during linking to produce the desired executable file. In the example shown, only three files are required: the .C source code, the .RES resource file (containing an optional application icon), and the .DEF module-definition file. In other circumstances, however, the project file could also specify multiple source code files (which could be all in .C/.CPP or a mixture of .C/.CPP and .ASM files) or could be a series of .OBJ object modules from previous compilations or from library sources.

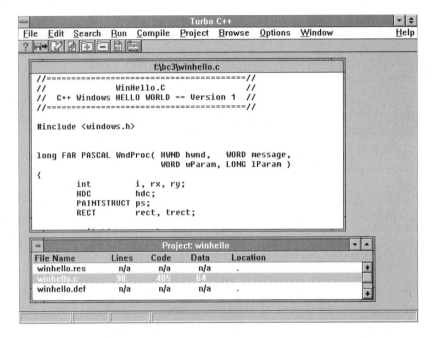

Figure 1.2: Compiling as a project

After a project is created, selecting Compile/Build All causes all project elements to be compiled—if necessary—and to be linked into the .EXE program. But the project files serve a second important purpose. In addition to file specifications, projects also permit selection of a number of application, compiler, linker, and library options, which can be unique for each project and are saved in the .PRJ file.

In addition to the .PRJ file, the saved project contains a second file: the .DSK (desktop) file. While the desktop file does not include information essential to creating the project, it does include such auxiliary information as context information for each file in the project, history lists for input boxes, desktop window layouts, a clipboard and contents, and any watch expressions and breakpoints that have been set in any of the source files.

Most, though not all, of the options provided are relevant to both TCW for Windows applications and BC for DOS applications. For greater detail, instructions for using project files are covered in the Borland C++ 3.0 users guide and are also available through on-line help.

SUMMARY

In Chapter 1, the basics of creating and compiling a simple Windows application, WinHello.C, have been covered, together with an introduction to some of the special terminology, abbreviations, and type definitions that will be encountered in later material.

At the same time, the example program, WinHello, contains material that will not be explained until later in this book, though the complete source code—with the exception of the .DEF and .RES files—appears following.

Next, in Chapter 2, application child processes will be demonstrated together with samples using dialog boxes and stock icons.

PROGRAM LISTING OF WINHELLO.C

```
//===========================//
//          WinHello.C          //
//===========================//

#include <windows.h>

long FAR PASCAL WndProc( HWND hwnd,   WORD message,
                         WORD wParam, LONG lParam )
{
   int          i, rx, ry;
   HDC          hdc;
   PAINTSTRUCT  ps;
   RECT         rect, trect;

   switch( message )
   {
      case WM_PAINT:
         hdc = BeginPaint( hwnd, &ps );
         GetClientRect( hwnd, &rect );
         rx = ( rect.right - rect.left ) / 11;
         ry = ( rect.bottom - rect.top ) / 10;
         trect.left = trect.top = 0;
         trect.right = 2 * rx;
         trect.bottom = ry;
         for( i=0; i<8; i++ )
         {
            DrawText( hdc, "Hello, World!", -1,
                      &trect,
                      DT_SINGLELINE | DT_CENTER |
                      DT_VCENTER );
```

```
                    trect.left += rx;
                    trect.right += rx;
                    trect.top += ry;
                    trect.bottom += ry;
                }
            trect.left -= rx;
            trect.right += rx;
            trect.top += ry;
            trect.bottom += ry;
            SetTextColor( hdc, 0x000000FF );
            DrawText( hdc, "... is there an echo in here?",
                        1, &trect,
                        DT_SINGLELINE | DT_CENTER |
                        DT_VCENTER );
            EndPaint( hwnd, &ps );
            return( 0 );
        case WM_DESTROY:
            PostQuitMessage( 0 );
            return( 0 );
    }
    return( DefWindowProc( hwnd,   message,
                            wParam, lParam ) );
}

int PASCAL WinMain( HANDLE hInstance,
                    HANDLE hPrevInstance,
                    LPSTR  lpszCmdParam,
                    int    nCmdShow )
{
    static char szAppName[] = "WinHello";
    HWND        hwnd;
    MSG         msg;
    WNDCLASS    wc;

    if( ! hPrevInstance )
    {
        wc.style         = CS_HREDRAW | CS_VREDRAW;
        wc.lpfnWndProc   = WndProc;
        wc.cbClsExtra    = 0;
        wc.cbWndExtra    = 0;
        wc.hInstance     = hInstance;
        wc.hIcon         = LoadIcon( hInstance, szAppName );
        wc.hCursor       = LoadCursor( NULL, IDC_ARROW );
        wc.hbrBackground = GetStockObject( WHITE_BRUSH );
        wc.lpszMenuName  = NULL;
        wc.lpszClassName = szAppName;
```

```
        RegisterClass( &wc );
    }
    hwnd = CreateWindow(
            szAppName,              // window class name
            "Greetings!",           // window caption
            WS_OVERLAPPEDWINDOW,    // window style
            CW_USEDEFAULT,          // initial X position
            CW_USEDEFAULT,          // initial Y position
            CW_USEDEFAULT,          // initial X size
            CW_USEDEFAULT,          // initial Y size
            NULL,                   // parent window handle
            NULL,                   // window menu handle
            hInstance,              // program instance handle
            NULL  );                // creation parameters
    ShowWindow( hwnd, nCmdShow );
    UpdateWindow( hwnd );
    while( GetMessage( &msg, NULL, 0, 0 ) )
    {
        TranslateMessage( &msg );
        DispatchMessage( &msg );
    }
    return msg.wParam;
}
```

Windows Messages and Child Processes

Chapter

2

In Chapter 1, the WinHello program provided a simple example illustrating the basics of Windows programming. The basics of creating a Windows program were shown. This included using a module definition file and registering and creating a simple child process that was called indirectly by Windows instead of directly by the application. Even though the WinHello sample was extremely simple, there were still a number of items that were not explained in any detail.

In this chapter, several child processes will be used but, instead of simply writing a display, the child processes will create a series of simple dialog boxes while the main program provides elementary responses to the messages generated by the dialog box selections. At the same time, the dialog boxes will use both icon images and graphics buttons as displays.

Figure 2.1 shows the menu and four of the five dialog boxes used by the Dialog1 program. The fifth dialog box, which responds to the menu's Exit Demo option (not shown), is created directly by Windows and the BCW compiler. But, for the four dialog boxes illustrated, the menu and each of the dialog elements, together with the icons used, is created using Borland's Resource Workshop.

The principal purpose behind the present sample, however, is not creating the dialog resources but showing how child processes can assume control of the application (and of Windows itself) and how graphic control elements—in this case, control buttons—function within the Windows environment.

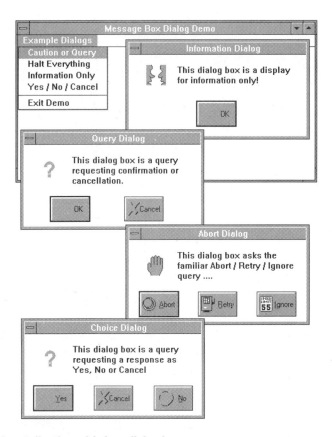

Figure 2.1: An application with four dialog boxes

The complete program listings for Dialog1.C, Dialog1.H, and Dialog1.DEF appear at the end of this chapter as well as on the source disk accompanying this volume. In addition, the source disk includes the complete Dialog1.RES resource file providing the dialog boxes, application menu, and icons shown in Figure 2.1.

You should also be aware that the application demonstrated requires Borland's BCW or BC compiler and the BWCC.LIB library. Other compilers will require some modifications to the source code and/or resource definitions.

BITMAPPED DISPLAYS AND CONTROLS

In the dialog boxes illustrated, three icons have been used to accent the purposes of each dialog box. These are standard icons created as a part of the application resource file and inserted within the individual dialog boxes as icon controls. (See Chapter 3 for further details on creating icons and other bitmaps.)

While a bitmapped image of any size could have been used for a similar purpose, each of these icons has been assigned a return value of −1, is not selectable, and does not respond to mouse clicks.

The iconized buttons are selectable and each button returns the message value assigned to it when the dialog box was created (in the Resource Workshop). These are not conventional control buttons, however, because the standard controls provided by Windows lack the bitmapped embellishments shown here. Instead, these buttons are a feature of the BCW compiler and the BWCC library (in the \LIB directory).

> **CAUTION!** Access to these features does require two special provisions in creating the program: the #include <bwcc.h> statement in the Dialog1.C source code and, in the application project, inclusion of the BWCC.LIB file. Omitting either or both of these provisions will not cause a compile/link error and, while the BCW compiler is loaded, the application will execute normally. But, if the BCW compiler is not loaded, the compiled application will not be able to find the BWCC.DLL (Dynamic Link Library) required to provide these features.

Of course, at the same time, before the application can execute on another system, the BWCC.DLL library must be available there also—i.e., this or any other .DLLs must be distributed with the applications.

CONTROLS AND CONTROL BUTTONS

The Dialog1 program demonstrates one type of Windows control: the control button. But, by this time, if you have used the Resource Workshop (or any of a variety of other Windows programs), you should have encountered several other types of controls including—but not limited to—check boxes, radio buttons, and scroll bars. Many of these controls will be used in later samples but, in all cases, the interactions between the control elements and the applications are similar.

In the sample shown in this chapter, each of the control buttons, when selected by clicking with the mouse, posts a message to the parent application—for example, the exported InfoProc, QueryProc, AbortProc, or ChoiceProc procedures—where response handling is provided. (Creating dialog box resources is discussed in Chapter 3.)

In this application, the dialog boxes are generated in response to command messages that are initiated by users' selections from the pull-down menu. These menu response messages are generated by Windows rather than as provisions within the application, but subsequently they are handled by the exported WndProc procedure as shown in the sample below:

```
case WM_COMMAND:
   switch( wParam )
```

```
{
    case IDM_INFO:
        lpProc = MakeProcInstance( InfoProc,
                                        hInst );
        DialogBox( hInst, "Dialog_1",
                    hwnd, lpProc );
        FreeProcInstance( lpProc );
        return( TRUE );
    case IDM_QUERY:
        lpProc = MakeProcInstance( QueryProc,
                                        hInst );
        DialogBox( hInst, "Dialog_2",
                    hwnd, lpProc );
        FreeProcInstance( lpProc );
        return( TRUE );
    case IDM_ABORT:
        lpProc = MakeProcInstance( AbortProc,
                                        hInst );
        DialogBox( hInst, "Dialog_4",
                    hwnd, lpProc );
        FreeProcInstance( lpProc );
        return( TRUE );
    case IDM_CHOICE:
        lpProc = MakeProcInstance( ChoiceProc,
                                        hInst );
        DialogBox( hInst, "Dialog_3",
                    hwnd, lpProc );
        FreeProcInstance( lpProc );
        return( TRUE );
    case IDM_QUIT:
        if( MessageBox( hwnd,
                "Exit application?", "Exit?",
                MB_ICONQUESTION | MB_YESNOCANCEL |
                MB_DEFBUTTON2 ) == IDYES )
        PostQuitMessage( 0 );
        return( 1 );
}
```

In the sample code shown, notice that three tasks are required, beginning with a call to the MakeProcInstance to register the exported dialog box handling procedure, followed by a call to the DialogBox procedure to actually create (display) the desired dialog box. After returning from the message dialog box, a final procedure call to FreeProcInstance removes the dialog box subprogram from memory.

In practice, these dialog boxes—with the exception of the IDM_QUIT case— would probably be called under other circumstances, commonly because of circumstances arising from the application's operation or because of choices executed within the application. And these dialog boxes would not necessarily be called by the WndProc procedure but could be called from anywhere within the application including, frequently, from another dialog box.

The QueryProc procedure following shows a sample response handling.

```
BOOL FAR PASCAL QueryProc( HWND hDlg,    WORD msg,
                           WORD wParam, LONG lParam )
{
   switch( msg )
   {
      case WM_INITDIALOG:  return( TRUE );
      case WM_COMMAND:
         switch( wParam )
         {
            case IDOK:
            case IDCANCEL: EndDialog( hDlg, TRUE );
                           return( TRUE );
                  default: return( TRUE );
      }    }
   return( FALSE );
}
```

Since these samples provide only simple message dialog boxes, the WM_INITDIALOG message requires nothing except acknowledgment. In other situations, such as a filelist selection or a choice of flag settings, a more elaborate initialization, as well as more elaborate responses to returned messages, would be required.

For purposes of demonstration, however, the responses provided are minimal, with each *WM_COMMAND: switch(wParam)...case* statement handling all expected messages with the single response consisting of calling the EndDialog procedure. Of course, in an actual application, even for these samples, a separate response would be desired for each case, though most cases would still terminate the dialog box with a call to the EndDialog procedure.

While running this example, you should also note that each of these dialog boxes preempts all other activity within the current application, preventing any other windows belonging to this application from responding to the mouse until the present dialog box has terminated.

The DIALOG1 program also provides an example of a stock dialog message box in response to the menu's Exit Demo selection (IDM_QUIT):

```
      case IDM_QUIT:
         if( MessageBox( hwnd,
              "Exit application?", "Exit?",
```

```
                    MB_ICONQUESTION | MB_YESNOCANCEL |
                    MB_DEFBUTTON2 ) == IDYES )
              PostQuitMessage( 0 );
              return( 1 );
         }
```

Because this message box is generated by Windows, no exported procedure is required. Instead, the second and third calling parameters specify the message and caption to be displayed while the fourth parameter specifies inclusion of the question mark icon (MB_ICONQUESTION) and three buttons (MB_YESNOCANCEL), setting the second button (NO) as the default.

In response, the generated message dialog box can return three messages—IDYES, IDNO, IDCANCEL—while the IDYES message triggers the PostQuit-Message to terminate the application. Compare this message box with the custom ChoiceProc message box that returns the same three choices but uses a different display format and different handling.

SUMMARY

While messages are only one form of dialog box, this sample does show the basic handling required for a dialog window, and similar dialog boxes will be used extensively in many applications.

Keep in mind that dialog boxes can be generated as required and then discarded when finished—therefore occupying memory only temporarily.

In Chapter 3, this review of introductory Windows programming concludes by covering design considerations for application resources and looking at resource editors. Part 2 proceeds to the principal topic: Windows graphics programming.

PROGRAM LISTING OF DIALOG1.C

```
//===========================//
//          Dialog1.C        //
//   Simple Windows Dialogs  //
//===========================//

#include <windows.h>
#include <bwcc.h>
#include "dialog1.h"

HANDLE  hInst;                  // global instance handle

BOOL FAR PASCAL InfoProc( HWND hDlg,   WORD msg,
                          WORD wParam, LONG lParam )
```

```
{
   switch( msg )
   {
      case WM_INITDIALOG:  return( TRUE );
      case WM_COMMAND:
         switch( wParam )
         {
            case IDOK: EndDialog( hDlg, TRUE );
                          return( TRUE );
               default: return( TRUE );
      }      }
   return( FALSE );
}

BOOL FAR PASCAL QueryProc( HWND hDlg,   WORD msg,
                           WORD wParam, LONG lParam )
{
   switch( msg )
   {
      case WM_INITDIALOG:  return( TRUE );
      case WM_COMMAND:
         switch( wParam )
         {
            case IDOK:
            case IDCANCEL: EndDialog( hDlg, TRUE );
                           return( TRUE );
                  default: return( TRUE );
      }      }
   return( FALSE );
}

BOOL FAR PASCAL AbortProc( HWND hDlg,   WORD msg,
                           WORD wParam, LONG lParam )
{
   switch( msg )
   {
      case WM_INITDIALOG:  return( TRUE );
      case WM_COMMAND:
         switch( wParam )
         {
            case IDABORT:
            case IDRETRY:
            case IDCANCEL: EndDialog( hDlg, TRUE );
                           return( TRUE );
                  default: return( TRUE );
      }      }
```

```
      return( FALSE );
}

BOOL FAR PASCAL ChoiceProc( HWND hDlg,    WORD msg,
                                WORD wParam, LONG lParam )
{
   switch( msg )
   {
      case WM_INITDIALOG:  return( TRUE );
      case WM_COMMAND:
         switch( wParam )
         {
            case IDYES:
            case IDNO:
            case IDCANCEL: EndDialog( hDlg, TRUE );
                           return( TRUE );
                  default: return( TRUE );
      }     }
   return( FALSE );
}

long FAR PASCAL WndProc( HWND hwnd,    WORD message,
                             WORD wParam, LONG lParam )
{
   FARPROC    lpProc;

   switch( message )
   {
      case WM_COMMAND:
         switch( wParam )
         {
            case IDM_INFO:
               lpProc = MakeProcInstance( InfoProc,
                                               hInst );
               DialogBox( hInst, "Dialog_1",
                          hwnd,  lpProc );
               FreeProcInstance( lpProc );
               return( TRUE );
            case IDM_QUERY:
               lpProc = MakeProcInstance( QueryProc,
                                               hInst );
               DialogBox( hInst, "Dialog_2",
                          hwnd,  lpProc );
               FreeProcInstance( lpProc );
               return( TRUE );
            case IDM_ABORT:
```

```
                lpProc = MakeProcInstance( AbortProc,
                                           hInst );
                DialogBox( hInst, "Dialog_4",
                           hwnd,  lpProc );
                FreeProcInstance( lpProc );
                return( TRUE );
            case IDM_CHOICE:
                lpProc = MakeProcInstance( ChoiceProc,
                                           hInst );
                DialogBox( hInst, "Dialog_3",
                           hwnd,  lpProc );
                FreeProcInstance( lpProc );
                return( TRUE );
            case IDM_QUIT:
                if( MessageBox( hwnd,
                    "Exit application?", "Exit?",
                    MB_ICONQUESTION | MB_YESNOCANCEL |
                    MB_DEFBUTTON2 ) == IDYES )
                PostQuitMessage( 0 );
                return( 1 );
            }
        case WM_DESTROY:
            PostQuitMessage( 0 );
            return( 0 );
    }
    return( DefWindowProc( hwnd,   message,
                           wParam, lParam ) );
}


#pragma argsused

int PASCAL WinMain( HANDLE hInstance,
                    HANDLE hPrevInstance,
                    LPSTR  lpszCmdParam, int nCmdShow )
{
    static char szAppName[] = "DIALOG1";
    HWND        hwnd;
    MSG         msg;
    WNDCLASS    wc;

    if( ! hPrevInstance )
    {
        wc.hInstance      = hInstance;
        wc.lpfnWndProc    = WndProc;
        wc.cbClsExtra     = 0;
        wc.cbWndExtra     = 0;
```

```
      wc.lpszClassName = szAppName;
      wc.hIcon         = LoadIcon( hInstance, szAppName );
      wc.lpszMenuName  = (LPSTR) szAppName;
      wc.hCursor       = LoadCursor( NULL, IDC_ARROW );
      wc.hbrBackground = GetStockObject( WHITE_BRUSH );
      wc.style         = CS_HREDRAW | CS_VREDRAW;
      RegisterClass( &wc );
   }
   hInst = hInstance;      // assign global instance handle
   hwnd = CreateWindow( szAppName,
                "Message Box Dialog Demo",
                WS_OVERLAPPEDWINDOW,
                CW_USEDEFAULT, CW_USEDEFAULT,
                CW_USEDEFAULT, CW_USEDEFAULT,
                NULL, NULL, hInstance, NULL  );
   ShowWindow(   hwnd, nCmdShow );
   UpdateWindow( hwnd );
   while( GetMessage( &msg, NULL, 0, 0 ) )
   {
      TranslateMessage( &msg );
      DispatchMessage(  &msg );
   }
   return( msg.wParam );
}


//===============//
// Dialog1.h    //
//===============//
#define  IDM_QUERY    101
#define  IDM_ABORT    102
#define  IDM_INFO     103
#define  IDM_CHOICE   104
#define  IDM_QUIT     106


;=====================================;
;  Dialog1.DEF module definiton file  ;
;=====================================;


NAME          DIALOG1
DESCRIPTION   "Windows Dialog Demo"
EXETYPE       WINDOWS
STUB          "WINSTUB.EXE"
CODE          PRELOAD MOVEABLE DISCARDABLE
DATA          PRELOAD MOVEABLE MULTIPLE
HEAPSIZE      1024
STACKSIZE     8192
```

```
EXPORTS         WndProc
                InfoProc
                QueryProc
                AbortProc
                ChoiceProc
```

Windows Application Resources

DEFINING APPLICATION RESOURCES

SUMMARY

I n Chapter 2, two types of application resource—icons and dialogs—
were introduced within the Dialog1 sample. Thus far, however, nothing has been said about how to create application resources, and in all
honesty, application resources are far too extensive a topic to be covered in a
single chapter.

But, at the same time, a review of Windows programming can hardly afford
to simply skip over the topic. Therefore, this chapter will briefly discuss application resources and resource editors with primary emphasis on designing menus,
dialog boxes and icon resources—the three most commonly used resources.
Since resources generally require header files, these will also be covered. The
chapter concludes with references to sources for additional explanation.

For the present, the resource editor used will be the Resource Workshop distributed with Borland's Turbo C/C++ for Windows. However, you may also
wish to refer to Appendix A, where several resource editors and other Windows utilities will be reviewed.

DEFINING APPLICATION RESOURCES

Although application resources are defined and created outside of the programming process, resource creation is not entirely independent of application program development.

Granted, in some instances, such as icon creation, the connection between developing the individual resources and developing the program is tenuous at best.
In other circumstances, such as dialog box or menu creation, the connection is

both immediate and directly relevant, if only because the dialog box or menu must fit together with the program's requirements and, in turn, the program must respond to the messages returned by the resource.

ICONS AND OTHER BITMAPS

The most immediate resource type, of course, is the icon, since every application is expected to have at least one icon as an identifying symbol. In essence, icons are specialized bitmaps with fixed dimensions: either 32 by 32 pixels or 32 by 16 pixels with color resolutions ranging from monochrome to 16 colors on EGA/VGA displays to 256 colors on SVGA displays. Low-resolution icons (32 by 16 pixels) were originally established as a provision for low-resolution monitors (CGA and some EGA). In like fashion, monochrome palettes (black and white) were devised for use with Hercules monitors, but these still have some value for use with portables and laptops using LCD and plasma screens.

For all practical purposes, however, icons are best designed using the 16-color palette. Although the 256-color palette does offer a wider range of shades, a 32 by 32 pixel image offers little scope for subtle variations in chromatic toné, and remember, the primary purpose of an icon is to be readily identifiable.

Figure 3.1 shows a representative selection of icons which were taken from Borland's Screenery 1 Icon Pak.

Figure 3.1: Selected icon samples

The icons shown are displayed half and half against white and neutral-gray backgrounds. Normally, a horizontally divided background would not be expected, but here it serves to demonstrate the appearance of several icons against various backdrops.

Special colors for icons   Icons also have one provision that is not available for conventional bitmaps: the transparent and inverted-color selections. Pixels that are painted transparent are just that: transparent, allowing the background pixel to show through. Likewise, the color of inverted pixels also depends on the background image (for example, the wallpaper image or other underlying screen). For inverted pixels, however, the background color is XOR'd with white (FFFFFFh) to produce an inversion of the existing image.

Inverted pixels can provide contrast or accents against almost any background (except, obviously, neutral gray). This effect is used with varying efficiency but shouldn't be relied on too heavily because inverted figures tend to disappear or become confused against non-uniform backgrounds such as wallpaper bitmaps.

More appropriately, transparent pixels can be used to create icon shapes in place of the default square blocks. As an example, the conference, game, and tool icons (fourth, fifth and sixth from the right in Figure 3.1) are at least partially transparent and, therefore, do not appear as solid blocks as do the three left-most icons.

Cursor bitmaps   Cursors, like icons, are a special type of bitmap and are restricted both in color and size. For cursors (mouse pointers), color is restricted to black and white and the two special colors: transparent and inverted. Size is always 32 by 32 pixels.

Unlike with icons, transparent and inverted are the primary paint colors for use with cursors. When a new cursor is created, the initial image field will always be transparent.

While both black and white can be used to create the cursor image, neither color will show up well against a matching background. Using inverted as the primary drawing color should make the cursor appear cleanly against any background.

Figure 3.2 shows eight sample cursors titled, from left to right: CHECK, GRASPING, GUNSIGHT, HALT, POINTING, R_ARROW, SHOOT, and WAND. In each case, an active sample of the cursor appears overlying the cursor editor image. The results vary in visibility, primarily because of the limits of gray-scale reproduction; this will provide some indication of how well a cursor will appear against a busy background.

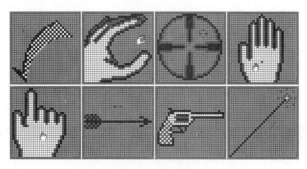

Figure 3.2: Sample cursor images

Perhaps the three hand images offer the best appearance because they are created as heavy black outlines with white fill and because the black outline is traced with an inner, inverted outline. In this fashion, the primary outline is thickened when the cursor appears against a light background. Alternately, against a dark background, the inverted outline is visually added to the inner shape.

At the same time, R_ARROW and WAND are difficult to see here even though both appear very cleanly against less cluttered backgrounds. Both could be improved by adding outlines using inverted pixels.

The CHECK cursor can be excellent against a solid white background where it appears as gray, but it is lost against a mixed background. Last, the SHOOT cursor is simply too busy to appear well except against a solid, light color.

Conventional bitmaps   Bitmaps as application resources are bitmaps with no special restrictions on their size or color. As such, this type of bitmap can be created with any .BMP-compatible editor including the Paintbrush program distributed with Windows and the Resource Workshop program.

> **NOTE:** Anytime 256-color bitmaps are used in 16-color environments, Windows will dither and/or translate colors to the closest possible match. For monochrome systems, shades of gray will be attempted—if they are supported. Although both conversions will result in loss of detail or, depending on the importance of the exact colors, distortion of the image presented, this does permit flexibility and relieve the need for separate bitmaps to match each environment.

MENUS

Following icons, menus are probably the next most common type of application resource. Figure 2.1 (Chapter 2) shows a typical menu bar with a single pull-down menu.

Except for the header file required by the application compiler, the Resource Workshop provides everything necessary to create application menus. There are, however, a few items that assist in creating menus.

  ▸ The ampersand (&) is used in menu item entries to denote the underscored hotkey, which can be used to select the menu item. Remember, provisions for implementing the hotkey indicated must be provided in the accelerator resource. As an example, a menu entry written as E&xit would be displayed as Exit, indicating the x as the hotkey for selecting this option.

▶ A tab character can be included to cause everything following the tab to be right-justified. This is commonly used to show function key assignments. It is used only on pull-down menus, never on menu bar entries.

▶ A single help item can be set flush right on the menu bar using the *New help popup* item type in the menu editor.

▶ The horizontal separator can be used to break long pull-down menus into subcategories, and the vertical break separators are used to create multiple columns.

▶ Any item on a pull-down menu may be used to call a further pull-down menu.

▶ If a menu becomes too complicated, then it is probably time to reorganize and move items to one or more dialog boxes. Menus should be kept as simple as practical and be used only for important, entry-level selections.

DIALOG BOXES

Dialog boxes are an important element in Windows programming, both for presenting information and for offering choices and selections.

In Chapter 2, a simple program used a series of message dialog boxes with button responses. That example was about as simple as a dialog box can be. More complex examples are readily available within any of a variety of Windows applications, including both the TCW compiler and the Resource Workshop.

In general, dialog box tasks can be grouped in three categories: message, flag select and list selections.

▶ Message dialog boxes, as demonstrated in Chapter 2, simply provide a message or brief information requiring a minimal response.

▶ Flag select dialog boxes offer groups of check box and/or radio button selections. These are referred to as flag selections because they are toggled (on/off) and are used only to set two-state values. Common examples can be found in the dialog boxes called from the Options menu in the TCW compiler.

▶ List selection dialogs are, perhaps, the most complicated of the three types, if only because, compared with other dialog boxes, they require more elaborate provisions within the application to supply the information for display. A good example of a list selection dialog box is found in TCW's file selection dialog box.

Obviously, these three types can be used in any variety of combinations as needed to suit specific tasks. Just as menus should be kept simple, overly complex dialog boxes should probably be split into two or more simpler boxes.

RESOURCE SCRIPTS AND RESOURCE COMPILERS

While interactive resource compilers, such as the Resource Workshop, permit the direct creation of all types of resources, there is also a second method that predates the availability of resource compilers: *resource scripts.*

Resource scripts are ASCII text files—similar to macro scripts or to program source codes—that contain instructions for the creation of an individual application resource. These are subsequently compiled as binary resources by utilities such as the Resource Workshop or Microsoft's SDK, and then linked to the application code for execution.

Following is a resource script producing the menu used by the Dialog1 application in Chapter 2:

```
DIALOG1 MENU
BEGIN
   POPUP "Example Dialogs"
   BEGIN
      MENUITEM "Caution or Query",   101
      MENUITEM "Halt Everything",    102
      MENUITEM "Information Only",    103
      MENUITEM "Yes / No / Cancel",  104
      MENUITEM SEPARATOR
      MENUITEM "Exit Demo",          106
   END
END
```

But while any resource element—even including icons, cursors and bitmaps—can be created as a resource script, this is considerably less convenient than using the interactive resource editors. Obviously, for any of the bit-mapped resources, the resource scripts would be rather cumbersome in size as well as very difficult to create or edit. And in all honesty, the preceding sample was created by a resource editor from an already compiled resource.

Application resources, whether created as scripts or directly using interactive resource compilers, do require one additional element before use: linking together with the application. Before the link step can be accomplished, the application compiler needs access to the ID codes assigned to the individual resource components. For example, before the menu used in the Dialog1 example could be linked with the compiled program, the compiler/linker required the message codes be returned by the menu items.

Because this information is not directly available from the compiled resources (the .RES file), header files (.H) are used to define the message/ID values that the application compiler will require.

CREATING HEADER FILES FOR RESOURCES

Unfortunately, Borland's Resource Workshop does not, at present, have the facilities to open a header file except while working with text resources (.RC resource scripts). Instead, while creating resources using the Workshop, the Windows Clipboard or any editor program can be used to create a .H header file.

Fortunately, the header files required are not complex. They consist simply of a series of #DEFINE statements as shown in the following listing:

```
//============================//
//          dialog1.h         //
//============================//
#define  IDM_QUERY    101
#define  IDM_ABORT    102
#define  IDM_INFO     103
#define  IDM_CHOICE   104
#define  IDM_QUIT     106
```

REMEMBER: Header files must be flat ASCII and cannot contain any typesetting or formatting instructions.

The example just shown is quite simple and consists of the header file for the DIALOG1 program demonstrated in Chapter 2. In other examples, however, the IDs defined may have duplicate values. This is because while elements with a resource must have unique values, elements in separate resources—within the same application—may have duplicate values.

The header file caption (the lines identified as comments by the leading double slashes) is optional.

FURTHER RESOURCE WORKSHOP FACILITIES

Although several of the Resource Workshop editors have been discussed, one of the primary functions of the Resource Workshop has not been discussed for the simple reason that it is transparent to the user. This is the Resource Workshop facility that compiles (and decompiles) resources into a binary format (the .RES file) for direct inclusion within the .EXE code.

At the same time, using the Resource Workshop's decompiler capability, existing resources within compiled .EXE programs can be extracted for editing, for replacement, or—either after saving as individual resources or through the Clipboard—for inclusion in the resource files of other applications.

In like fashion, the Resource Workshop can compile .RC resource scripts into .RES binary resources or convert binary resources into resource scripts.

Finally, to invoke the binary resources during your compile/link process, all that is required is to include the .RES resource file in your compiler project (the .PRJ file created using Borland's IDE) together with the .C source code and .DEF definition files. Once this is done, linking the compiled resources becomes automatic. Of course, if you are one of those individuals who, masochistically, prefer .RC resource scripts, these can also be included in the project list, and again, the resource compiler will be invoked automatically.

Summary

The preceding three chapters have offered a brief review of Windows application programming, but they are not intended to provide complete instructions for beginning programmers—only a refresher for those with some experience in this field.

For further information, either as a beginning Windows programmer or simply for additional refresher material, there are a variety of titles on C++ and Windows programming available. Two titles I recommend are:

- ▸ *Borland C++ 3.0 Programming* by Ben Ezzell, Addison-Wesley Publishing Company.

- ▸ *Programming Windows* by Charles Petzold, Microsoft Press.

Both of these titles—if you will pardon my own prejudices—offer excellent introductory through advanced Windows programming instructions together with a variety of examples and utilities.

2

The Windows
Graphics Device Interface

GRAPHICS SYSTEMS

IDENTIFYING SYSTEM GRAPHICS
CAPABILITIES

COLORS AND COLOR PALETTES

Graphics Systems

CHARACTERISTICS OF GRAPHICS DEVICES

WINDOWS 3.1 GRAPHICS (MAPPING) MODES

THE DEVICE CONTEXT AS A VIRTUAL
  SCREEN

SUMMARY

PROGRAM LISTING OF WINMODES.C

PROGRAM LISTING OF WINMODES.DEF

PROGRAM LISTING OF WINMODES.H

PROGRAM LISTING OF LIFE.C

PROGRAM LISTING OF LIFE.DEF

PROGRAM LISTING OF LIFE.H

W hile presenting a brief review of Windows programming practices, the sample applications have made use of the Windows Graphics Device Interface (commonly referred to as the GDI). So far there has not, however, been any explanation of what the GDI is or why and how it operates.

In conventional programming—that is, under DOS—graphics operations and graphics applications must either be restricted to supported graphics hardware or include internal provisions to adapt to whatever graphics hardware is available on the executing system. Granted, DOS programming enhancements, such as the Borland Graphics Interface (BGI), have eliminated many of the difficulties inherent in adaptation to different graphics environments, but even this has still left a major portion of graphics programming tasks to the programmer.

Under Windows, the Graphics Device Interface follows a different approach, providing an environmental shell that translates between the application's graphics requirements and the graphics capabilities of the system where the application executes. Thus, Windows applications may move from monochrome graphics to EGA to SVGA with little or no adaptation required by the application. And, at the same time, the Windows GDI extends beyond supporting the video environment to include support for the hard-copy output devices as well, a feature that few other graphics interfaces incorporate.

Thus, under Windows, applications operate within a single virtual environment—independent of the actual system hardware—while Windows, in turn, maps the application's virtual display to the actual physical display. In this fashion, a display that executes in 256 colors on SVGA is mapped to 16 dithered colors for standard EGA/VGA and to shades of gray on a monochrome system.

Of course, there are limits to Windows support and there are existing devices, such as 3-D displays and color-dispersion printers, that are limited in application and not yet supported by Windows drivers. Still, as newer video and hard-copy devices appear, developers are quickly providing their own drivers and interface enhancements adding to Windows's capabilities. Significantly, these enhancements do not require revisions by the application programmer—only by the hardware manufacturers.

Despite Windows's capabilities for providing a uniform virtual graphic environment, the actual display and hard-copy characteristics are, obviously, dependent on the physical hardware devices. And, also obvious, before Windows can translate from a virtual environment to a physical environment, information about the physical equipment is essential. Once Windows has obtained information about the physical environment, this data is also available to the application, if required.

Before examining the types of information available and how they are accessed, a brief review of hardware types and capabilities is in order.

CHARACTERISTICS OF GRAPHICS DEVICES

With the exception of pen-based plotters (and a few more esoteric devices), all graphics devices are inherently *pointillistic*—that is, each uses a pixel- or dot-based display. Granted, like all CRT displays, video monitors use raster scanning (and LaserJet printers use a similar mechanism) but the data provided by the computer for display is always bitmapped, irrespective of the mechanisms of the actual physical devices. Therefore, the physical display—the actual video monitor—is of secondary importance because it is the graphics video card that determines video resolution.

There are, of course, LCD displays (both monochrome and color) that are actually digital devices, but these still depend on some equivalent of the graphics video card. The card is still more important than the physical screen.

IN THE BEGINNING

Years past, when microcomputers were relatively new, IBM introduced the CGA (Color Graphics Adapter) video adapter. This initial video adapter supported graphics (up to 640 by 200 pixels) but both its resolution and color were limited. Still, since prior "display" devices had been limited to text-only CRTs or, in many cases, to line printers, even these primitive graphic displays were loudly hailed as a serious advance—at least until programmers discovered just how limited CGA displays really were.

And quickly enough, newer video cards were introduced: first, the EGA (Enhanced Graphics Adapter) with 640-by-350 pixel resolution, and then the VGA (Variable Graphics Adapter) with 640 by 480 pixels and the 8514/A with 1,024 by 768 pixels. Of these, the EGA cards are still found but are not common on new machines, while the 8514/A proved limited in popularity, largely because of its price and restricted compatibility.

Today, the VGA—or, increasingly, the SVGA (Super VGA)—has become the new popular standard. VGA/SVGA cards exist in a variety of configurations and capacities. Table 4.1 shows representative characteristics for the four principal video types. The information shown is excerpted from the DC (Device Context) program discussed later in this chapter. The exact data reported for individual video cards/monitors may vary depending on equipment, configuration, and mode settings.

Table 4.1: Typical Video Card Resolutions

GetDeviceCaps	Units	CGA	EGA	VGA	SVGA
HORSIZE	mm	240	240	240	280
VERTSIZE	mm	180	175	180	210
HORZREZ	pixels	640	640	640	1,024
VERTREZ	pixels	200	350	480	768
ASPECTX	---	5	38	36	14
ASPECTZ	---	12	48	36	14
aspect ratio	xy ratio	0.416	0.791	1.000	1.000
ASPECTXY	diagonal	13	61	51	19
LOGPIXELSX	pixels/inch	96	96	96	120
LOGPIXELSY	pixels/inch	48	72	96	120

GRAPHICS MONITORS VERSUS GRAPHICS VIDEO BOARDS

Graphics monitors are largely—though not entirely—independent of the graphics video boards used to drive them. Even very old video monitors may prove compatible with modern graphics boards and capable of displaying in high-resolution video modes.

As an example, a multisync monitor—originally purchased several years ago for use with an EGA video card—was subsequently used with a newer computer equipped with a VGA graphics card and, still later, with an SVGA video card. Although the monitor was originally designed to be driven as a 640 by 350 color monitor, the end configuration was still capable of 1,024-by-768,256-pixel color resolution. (Minor adjustments were required on the vertical sync for the highest resolution modes.)

The same is true of many older monitors, though some may require similar sync adjustments or may not be capable of matching the required synchronization speeds.

MEMORY AND VIDEO RESOLUTION

What is essential for higher-resolution displays is simply enough memory—not on the motherboard, but on the video card. A minimum of 4Mb of RAM on the motherboard is a good minimum for Windows operations, but this memory is not available for the video display.

Ideally, an SVGA graphics card should have 1Mb of video RAM to support a 1,024-by-768,256-pixel color video display, though many SVGA cards are equipped with a scant 512k of RAM. Others are sold with an essentially inadequate 256k but can be upgraded to the 512k minimum required for 640-by-480,256-pixel color video.

NOTE: The 1,024-by-768,256-pixel color resolution requires a full 1Mb of RAM.

In the future you can expect to see even higher-resolution graphics video boards—in particular, the new 24-bit color boards that provide (within visual limitations) true-color graphics. In addition to substantial memory and various graphics coprocessors, each true-color board will also supply its own appropriate Windows drivers—a consideration that might make the future a bit more rosy for graphics programmers.

GRAPHICS COPROCESSORS

Graphics coprocessors are 1992's newest high-tech buzzword, the hottest piece of vaporware on the market, and, at the same time, very definitely the wave of the future. But before looking at what a graphics coprocessor is and what it does, the first step is to understand how graphics work without a coprocessor.

In conventional graphics displays, to draw a circle on the screen, an application must calculate where each point required to display the circle is located. Granted, unless you're using assembly language, this is a relatively simple matter from a programming standpoint and generally requires a single call such as C++'s *circle* function, which is invoked with arguments specifying the center position and the radius. (Windows requires a slightly different function which is discussed later.) But even though the operation can be invoked quite easily, execution of the operation still requires extensive calculations and more than a little CPU time. Similar considerations apply to all graphics operations—even such a simple operation as drawing a line on the screen.

In like fashion, graphics text (which uses stroked fonts) requires more time to display than conventional (DOS) text that uses bitmapped characters.

But, even while graphics displays are intrinsically slower than character-based displays, for most practical purposes, the display speed remains adequate. However, "adequate" and "practical" are the operative terms here and like most programmers, you probably consider both as limitations rather than as acceptable standards. (Most programmers—like hotrodders—are notorious for demanding every pico-second of speed that can be coaxed from their systems, even when these fragmentary gains are effectively invisible to the users and can only be detected by sophisticated profiling tests.)

Still, in the final analysis, coaxing additional microseconds of speed out of the system is exactly where graphics coprocessors come into the picture and happily, the prices of the newer graphics boards are dropping rapidly to compete heavily with their less sophisticated predecessors. Therefore, while it would be silly to go hungry just to gain a small edge, for many of us the price difference is not a great consideration. A few dollars more for a 1Mb video card over a 256k video card is no great hardship and is well worth the investment.

Or, if you are really heavily into graphics and want the ultimate in display and performance—for example, for editing photos or artwork or for production-grade graphics designs—then by all means invest a few more extra dollars for any of the newest true-color graphics boards which, instead of supporting 256 color palettes, provide full 24-bit-per-pixel color definition for every pixel in a 1,024 by 768 image.

DRAWING WITH GRAPHICS COPROCESSORS

At present, there are no definitive standards for judging graphics coprocessors; the term itself is applied to a variety of devices that incorporate widely varying capabilities. In general, however, graphics coprocessors are specialized processor chips that are present on the video graphics board and that are designed to assume the computational responsibility for various drawing operations.

Thus, if an appropriate graphics coprocessor is present, instead of an application calculating the points necessary to draw a circle, the program would pass an instruction to the video board requesting a circle with a specified center location and radius (very much like the earlier reference to calling C++'s circle function). And, in response, the graphics coprocessor would use its own specialized hardware algorithms to calculate the necessary points. Hardware operations are intrinsically faster than software.

The operations supported by graphics coprocessors vary widely but are generally defined as belonging to five categories: raster, line, polygon, curve, and text operations. Further, within each category, the exact functions supported also vary greatly.

Using Windows, however, it is unnecessary for applications to know anything about which, if any, graphics coprocessor may be available on a specific system. On installation, Windows identifies the available hardware and is free to make use of most high-level hardware capabilities a system might provide.

Although it is not required for the application to directly identify video device capabilities (or hard-copy device capabilities), knowing what hardware support is available can still be useful. How to identify supported features will be discussed in Chapter 5. The more immediate topic is understanding the graphics modes that Windows uses.

WINDOWS 3.1 GRAPHICS (MAPPING) MODES

Earlier it was emphasized that, using Windows, the programmer is relieved of the task of making provisions within the application to identify the graphics hardware supplied by the system. But now comes an introduction to Windows graphics modes. So what's going on here?

The difference is quite simple: Instead of worrying about graphics modes which were set by varying hardware video cards, Windows's graphics modes are selected according to the application's requirements. And, most important, Windows's graphics modes are independent of the actual hardware! Thus, under Windows, the task is not identifying graphics modes but selecting the graphics mapping mode most appropriate to the task.

HARDWARE MAPPING MODES

While mapping modes may sound like something new and different, the truth of the matter is that mapping modes have been used since the earliest computer video systems began. Previously, however, only one or sometimes more mapping modes were available, and these were determined by the hardware (graphics card), not by the system.

To begin, the conventional DOS text display is the first and most familiar mapping mode, mapping a ROM-based character set (character pixel arrays) to the video graphics system. And, please note, this is true even on the very early systems where no true graphics mode was supported because, regardless of the system restrictions, the display itself was still graphical in nature.

Thus, in DOS text modes, the mapping mode is hardware-determined. To use a CGA system as an example, 8 by 9 character arrays are mapped to the 640 by 200 graphics video. At the same time, on most EGA systems, 8 by 14 character arrays are mapped to a 640 by 350 graphics video, and for most VGA systems, 8 by 19 character arrays are mapped to the 640 by 480 video. Alternately, for EGA systems using a 43-line text mode or VGA using a 50-line text mode, the graphics systems revert to mapping 8 by 9 characters—a change in both mapping modes and character sets.

Note that while SVGA video systems do support 1,024-by-768-pixel displays, this is only one of the supported modes rather than a restriction to a high-resolution display either in or out of Windows. Instead, SVGA video cards continue to support all earlier resolutions, including 800 by 600, 640 by 480, 640 by 320, 640 by 200, and 320 by 200 pixel displays. For Windows, a different resolution can be established by changing the video driver installed by the Windows SETUP program.

If you require frequent changes between video modes—for example, if you need 1,024 by 768 mode only occasionally and prefer to work in 640 by 480 normally—keep two copies of your SYSTEM.INI file, one for each mode, and use a .BAT file to switch them. This will provide a convenient mode for alteration.

If you are not sure about your video configuration, look inside the SYSTEM.INI file for a line beginning

```
[boot.description]
```

Immediately following, you should find a line like

```
display.drv=640x480 (256 color) for Ergo Super VGA
```

which tells Windows which mode to use when initializing the video graphics card.

Most SVGA cards require a driver supplied with the video card and should provide an installation program to install these drivers for Windows as well as for a number of other applications. If so, this installation utility should be used, but alternatively, if you are using a standard video card, the Windows SETUP program will also allow you to switch between a choice of video modes.

Remember, only one hardware device mode can be used at any time, even though different Windows applications may be using different Windows graphics modes simultaneously.

Of course, the actual graphics modes supported by each system are also hardware-dependent but, for EGA and VGA, mapping modes for the lower-resolution graphics are also supported.

Under Windows, however, the supported mapping modes are rather different and, most important, are independent of any restrictions set by the hardware.

WINDOWS MAPPING MODES

Windows supports eight mapping modes, each supplying a different unit of measure for screen (window) coordinate positions, as shown in Table 4.2.

Table 4.2: Windows Mapping Modes

Mapping Mode	Mode ID	Logical Units	Default Origin
MM_TEXT	1	pixels	upper left
MM_LOMETRIC	2	0.1mm	lower left
MM_HIMETRIC	3	0.01mm	lower left
MM_LOENGLISH	4	0.01 inch	lower left
MM_HIENGLISH	5	0.001 inch	lower left
MM_TWIPS	6	1/1,440 inch	lower left
MM_ISOTROPIC	7	variable (x=y)	variable
MM_ANISOTROPIC	8	variable (x<>y)	variable

The MM_TEXT mode (default) is essentially the equivalent of the DOS text-mapping mode. The difference is that where DOS operates in character positions, the MM_TEXT mode allows applications to work in terms of device pixels. As in DOS text mode, the screen (window) origin defaults to the upper-left corner with x and y coordinates increasing to the right and down—just as in conventional DOS or DOS graphics. And, in Windows, the MM_TEXT mode is used for essentially the same purpose as in DOS: for text displays for documents, tables, lists, or reports.

In other cases, however, the Windows mapping modes present an abrupt departure from the DOS standards because the default origins lie at the lower-left corner of the window with coordinate values increasing up and right (in essence, Cartesian coordinates). Alternately, in the MM_ISOTROPIC and MM_ANISOTROPIC modes, the point of origin may lie anywhere within or outside the active window but, again, the coordinate system remains Cartesian.

Also, in the English and metric modes, coordinate positions are defined in inches (in) or millimeters (mm) rather than in pixels—a particular convenience for any application, such as a drafting program, that needs to display graphics corresponding to real-world units. Granted, even in pixel modes such as MM_TEXT, conversions could be applied for the same purpose but, using any of the English or metric modes, the conversions from real units to the pixel display can be left to Windows without worrying about the device resolution.

The MM_TWIPS mode is another convenience mode but this one is designed for typesetting applications. TWIPS is a somewhat mangled acronym for "twentieths of a point"; a point is a printer's measure for type size and 72 points equal 1 inch. Thus the TWIPS unit is equal to 1/1,440th of an inch and a 10-point typeface can be drawn using a resolution of 200 logical units (TWIPS), regardless of whether the actual display is capable of a similar resolution (most are not). See Figure 4.1, following, for a comparison of mapping modes.

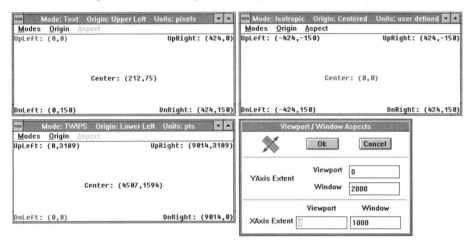

Figure 4.1: Text, TWIPs, and isotropic mappings with coordinates

Last, the MM_ISOTROPIC and MM_ANISOTROPIC mapping modes, instead of being designed for specific circumstances, provide both variable logical units and variable points of origin. Thus, to graph a sine display, the origin might be set at the center-left of the window, permitting points to be plotted vertically with both negative and positive values and only plotting points with positive value horizontally.

In the MM_ISOTROPIC mode, the x- and y-axis units are equal. This is useful when it is important to maintain the relative aspect of a figure. On the other hand, the MM_ANISOTROPIC mode permits setting different x- and y-axis scales that might be used, as an example, to plot a waveform in milliseconds along the x-axis and in volts along the y-axis. Thus, continuing the example, the time axis might be defined as 1,000 units (milliseconds = 1 second full range) while the vertical axis would be defined as ±5,000 units (millivolts = ±5 volts full range). In this fashion, a waveform could be plotted as voltage against time without converting either unit to correspond to the actual display resolution.

COMPARATIVE RESOLUTIONS

Describing mapping modes with resolutions much higher than the display resolutions is all very well but it brings up two questions: What is the purpose of having such high resolutions and how does the display show images mapped using these resolutions?

Taking the second question first—sorry if the answer sounds like a cop-out—the simple fact is that Windows maps image points from the high-resolution context (the device context or DC) to the actual display or printer resolution. The precise algorithm(s) used are irrelevant and vary depending on the type of image data (lines, screens, fonts, or bitmaps) used.

But returning to the first question, the purpose of high-resolution mapping modes, there isn't a single answer because there are a variety of reasons.

The first and principal reason for having high-resolution maps has already been referred to both in talking about TWIPS and in illustrating a possible use of the MM_ANISOTROPIC mode for displaying a waveform as voltage against time. By matching the device-context resolution to the data to be plotted or drawn, the need to perform conversions to match specific video, printer, or plotter capabilities is removed. Instead, data is plotted on a best-fit basis and then the result is mapped to the actual device with all necessary conversions executed by Windows.

The second main reason is that device resolutions vary tremendously and video device resolutions are low compared to the output resolutions of other device types. As an illustration, Table 4.3 compares typical resolutions for a number of video and hard-copy devices together with representative Windows mapping resolutions.

NOTE: Plotter resolutions vary widely. Values shown are representative for a pen-based plotter, while film (optical) plotters commonly achieve resolutions that are orders of magnitude higher.

SETTING MAPPING MODES

Figure 4.1 shows three of the eight mapping modes demonstrated by the WinModes.C program. Note, however, that the captions displayed were not written while the modes demonstrated were active. Instead, the selected mapping mode for the window is set first, then the present window coordinates are read with the mode active, and finally the active mapping mode is reset to MM_TEXT before the captions are written.

Table 4.3: Comparing Mapping and Device Resolutions

Physical Device	Logical Size	Units	Resolution in Inches	Resolution in Millimeters
EGA (H/V)	640/350	pixels	0.01480/0.01970	0.3750/0.5000
VGA (H/V)	640/480	pixels	0.12795	0.3250
MM_LOENGLISH	0.01	in	0.01000	0.2540
MM_LOMETRIC	0.1	mm	0.00394	0.1000
LaserJet	300	dpi	0.00333	0.0846
MM_HIENGLISH	0.0001	in	0.00100	0.0254
Plotter (1)	1,000	lpi	0.00100	0.0254
MM_TWIPS	1/20	in	0.00069	0.0176
Typesetter	2,400	dpi	0.00042	0.0106
MM_HIMETRIC	0.01	mm	0.00039	0.0100

Switching modes in this fashion does not erase the existing display but does permit employing whichever mode may be optimal for the specific purpose. Most important, of course, is that—unlike changing modes in DOS—a change in mapping modes does not change the display. It does, however, change the method and coordinate system in which subsequent displays are executed.

Ergo, while mapping modes can be switched as often as desired for the convenience of the application, each time the window is redrawn, the application must repeat the same cycle of mapping modes required for each drawing operation.

In its simplest form, setting a mapping mode requires only one instruction, SetMapMode, as shown:

```
case WM_PAINT:
    hdc = BeginPaint( hwnd, &ps );
    ...
    SetMapMode( hdc, nMode - IDM_TEXT + 1 );
    SetWindowOrg( hdc, 0, 0 );
```

Aside from the device context (hdc), SetMapMode requires only one argument, the mode ID number. The second instruction, SetWindowOrg, is called principally as a precaution, insuring that a known initial origin has been established. Later, a specific origin setting will be established according to the window size, mapping mode, and origin request.

With the exception of the MM_ISOTROPIC and MM_ANISOTROPIC modes, the window coordinate systems are fixed and, therefore, the window and viewport extents are predetermined. In the isotropic and anisotropic modes, however, the window coordinates are indeterminate until explicitly established using the SetWindowExt and SetViewportExt functions.

The SetWindowExt function defines the x- and y-extent (size) of the window (identified by the device context) in logical units with negative arguments inverting the scale directions. (Positive axis logical positions are mapped to negative axis device positions and vice versa.)

The SetViewportExt function also defines x- and y-axis mapping but, in this case, it defines how logical system coordinates are stretched or shrunk to fit device-context units. Again, negative arguments map positive values to negative values and vice versa.

```
switch( nMode )
{
    case IDM_ISOTROPIC:
        SetWindowExt( hdc, XWinAspect,
                            YWinAspect );
        if( XViewAspect && YViewAspect )
            SetViewportExt( hdc, XViewAspect,
                                 YViewAspect );
        else SetViewportExt( hdc, 1000, 1000 );
        break;
```

Remember, in isotropic mode, the x- and y-axis are always scaled equally, maintaining a constant aspect for figures and images (insuring that circles remain round and squares do not become rectangular). Because of this, the second argument in the call to SetViewportExt is ignored; but, of course, it must still be supplied. Also, in isotropic mode, SetWindowExt must always be called before calling SetViewportExt.

Alternatively, in anisotropic mode, separate x- and y-scalings can be assigned, creating quite different mapping appearances. Thus, in anisotropic mode, circles may become ellipses and squares may become ordinary rectangles. Of course, this elongation and shrinkage is always along the x- or y-axis and this is hardly an appropriate method for creating elliptical figures.

```
    case IDM_ANISOTROPIC:
        SetWindowExt( hdc, XWinAspect,
                            YWinAspect );
        if( XViewAspect && YViewAspect )
            SetViewportExt( hdc, XViewAspect,
                                 YViewAspect );
```

```
            else SetViewportExt( hdc, XWinAspect,
                                      YWinAspect );
            break;
      }
```

In addition to setting mapping modes, the SetWindowOrg function, which was called earlier to establish a "safe" 0,0 coordinate origin, can be called to set the origin anywhere within the current window. To do so, however, the first step—after setting the mapping mode and, if necessary, the viewport and window extents—is to get the current window's rectangle.

```
      GetClientRect( hwnd, &rect );
      DPtoLP( hdc, (LPPOINT) &rect, 2 );
```

But because the value returned by calling GetClientRect is given in device coordinates, the second step is to call the DPtoLP function to translate these coordinates into logical coordinates, or coordinates expressed in terms corresponding to the current map mode and using the window and viewport origins and extents.

With the conversion accomplished, the WinModes program offers three origin points: upper-left, centered or lower-left.

```
      switch( nOrigin )
      {
         case IDM_UPLEFT:
              SetWindowOrg( hdc, 0, 0 );
              break;
         case IDM_CENTER:
              SetWindowOrg( hdc,
                 - ( rect.left + rect.right ) / 2,
                 - ( rect.top + rect.bottom ) / 2 );
              break;
         case IDM_DNLEFT:
              SetWindowOrg( hdc, 0, -rect.bottom );
              break;
      }
      GetClientRect( hwnd, &rect );
      ...
      EndPaint( hwnd, &ps );
      return(0);
```

Last, after setting the origin point (in window coordinates) and again retrieving the window coordinates, the remaining task consists of first, restoring the original mapping mode (MM_TEXT) and, second, writing the coordinate information to the screen. (The necessary programming instruction for these last tasks have been omitted in the preceding fragments.)

THE DEVICE CONTEXT AS A VIRTUAL SCREEN

In DOS applications, graphics and text programs not only commonly write directly to the video screen, but also quite commonly bypass the BIOS screen routines while doing so. Under Windows, however, the situation is somewhat different.

In the first place, under Windows, the physical video screen is a shared resource, and applications must operate through the Windows API functions for all display actions—whether text or graphics. At the same time, any attempt to bypass the API functions is treated as a system violation, causing the offending application to be terminated.

Second, screen operations under Windows are not written to the physical display at all—not even when the API functions are used. Instead, applications requesting write operations—either text or graphics—result in the material being written to a virtual screen (that is, the Device Context or DC).

Last, after the application has written to the virtual screen, Windows copies—or maps—the virtual screen to the physical display. It shows as much or as little of the application's display as fits into the application's screen window—or, at least, that portion of the application's screen window that is not obscured by other applications' windows or is not physically positioned beyond the limits of the physical display.

A simple version of the program Life will be used to demonstrate mapping from a virtual screen to the physical screen and, at the same time, to further demonstrate the isotropic and anisotropic mapping modes.

THE LIFE PROGRAM

The Life program is a simple computer version of a much older game that was originally played with paper, pencil, and (mostly) patience. The rules are simple. Life is played in a world of rectilinear cells in which, initially, each cell may be alive (black) or dead (white).

In this sample, the grid world is closed; that is, the left side of the grid is treated as wrapping continuously to the right side, the top wrapping to the bottom, and vice versa. Topologically, this is analogous to a torus (or donut), but it is presented here as a 50 by 50 flag grid as shown in Figure 4.2.

For demonstration purposes, the initial conditions can be set either as a random selection of life points or, using the Launcher option, as an initial seed that eventually will launch two "flyers"—cyclic figures consisting of groups of five cells that "walk" or "fly" across the screen (see Figure 4.3). The illustration in Figure 4.2 was randomly seeded.

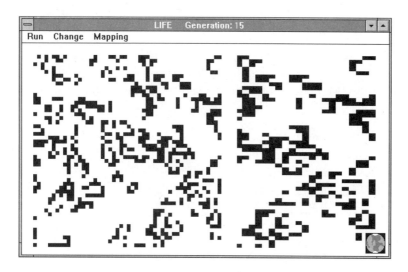

Figure 4.2: The Life program

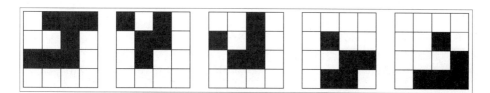

Figure 4.3: Five cyclic forms comprising a "flyer"

Once the initial conditions have been set, the state of each cell in subsequent generations is determined by its neighbors, according to three simple rules:

▶ If any live cell has fewer than two live neighbors (horizontally, vertically, or diagonally), that cell dies in the following generation.

▶ If any cell, alive or dead, has exactly three live neighbors, that cell will be alive or born in the next generation.

▶ If any live cell has more than three live neighbors, that cell dies from overcrowding in the next generation.

NOTE: In more elaborate versions of Life, initial conditions can also be drawn into the grid by using the mouse. The present version, however, is sufficient for demonstrating mapping using the isotropic and anisotropic modes—which is the real point of this demonstration.

MAPPING THE VIRTUAL SCREEN TO THE PHYSICAL DISPLAY

The Life demo sets up a virtual screen that is 55 by 55 units in size—regardless of the physical size of the application's window. This is accomplished in response to the WM_PAINT message, as shown in the following fragment:

```
case WM_PAINT:
    hdc = BeginPaint( hwnd, &ps );
    GetClientRect( hwnd, &rect );
    SetMapMode( hdc, MapMode );
    SetWindowOrg( hdc, 0, 0 );
    SetWindowExt( hdc, 110000 / rect.right,
                       110000 / rect.bottom );
    SetViewportExt( hdc, 2000, 2000 );
```

In this sample, the window extent has been scaled, both vertically and horizontally, as 110,000 units divided by the actual pixel size. Thus, assuming the window is to be 325 pixels horizontally, the horizontal scaling becomes 338 (338.4615...) units per pixel. And at the same time, the viewport is scaled as 2,000 units, yielding 55 units logical width (110,000/2,000) or 5.9 (5.90909...) pixels per logical unit. In this fashion, one unit in the viewport is mapped to ~6 pixels.

Because this mapping is approximate, however, 5 out of 6 units are mapped as 6 pixels while the sixth unit is mapped as 5 pixels width in the actual display—an irregularity that will be visible (but varying as the window size changes) in the demo program.

```
for( i=0; i<GRID; i++ )
    for( j=0; j<GRID; j++ )
        if( ThisGeneration[i][j] )
        {
            SetRect( &rect, i+3, j+3, i+4, j+4 );
            FillRect( hdc, &rect,
                GetStockObject( BLACK_BRUSH ) );
        }
EndPaint( hwnd, &ps );
return(0);
```

As an alternative, you might also like to try replacing the preceding SetRect and FillRect functions with a single SetPixel instruction, thus:

```
for( j=0; j<GRID; j++ )
    if( ThisGeneration[i][j] )
        SetPixel( hdc, i+3, j+3, 0L );
```

As you will observe by experimentation, using the SetPixel instruction produces a quite different result from the rectangle instructions. At the same time, note that the mapping modes are still in effect, controlling the spacing of the pixels even though only single pixels are drawn.

The conclusion is simple: The SetPixel instruction may not always be compatible with all mapping modes.

Summary

The complete program listings for both the WinModes.C and Life.C programs appear following as well as on the disk accompanying this volume. In addition to the WinModes.C and .DEF listings, a menu script is included for Win-Modes. The WinModes icon and dialog box appear in Figure 4.1, preceding.

In both cases—WinModes and Life—the principal purpose is to permit you to play with different mapping modes and origin points and to see how the window extent and point coordinates change with each. Although these examples may appear trivial, understanding Windows mapping modes is anything but trivial.

Mapping modes, however, are only one fashion in which Windows translates between a virtual and a physical environment. In Chapter 5, the hardware environment will be examined further, together with the functions and capabilities employed by Windows to take optimal advantage of the available hardware.

Program listing of WinModes.C

```
//========================//
//        WinModes.C      //
// Windows Mapping Modes  //
//========================//

#include <windows.h>
#include <bwcc.h>        // BCWW.LIB must be included in Project
#include <string.h>
#include "winmodes.h"

#define  RED    0x000000FF
#define  BLACK  0x00000000

HANDLE  hInst;
int     XViewAspect, YViewAspect, XWinAspect, YWinAspect;

#pragma argsused
```

```
// procedure for handling Aspect Dialog Box
BOOL FAR PASCAL AspectProc( HWND hdlg,    WORD msg,
                               WORD wParam, LONG lParam )
{
   char szAspect[10];

   switch( msg )
   {
      case WM_INITDIALOG:  // initializes the dialog
         sprintf( szAspect, "%d", XViewAspect );
         SendDlgItemMessage( hdlg, IDD_XVIEWASPECT,
                               EM_LIMITTEXT, 10, 0L );
          // limits user input to 10 character length
         SetDlgItemText( hdlg, IDD_XVIEWASPECT, szAspect );
          // sends initial value to dialog box
         sprintf( szAspect, "%d", YViewAspect );
         SendDlgItemMessage( hdlg, IDD_YVIEWASPECT,
                               EM_LIMITTEXT, 10, 0L );
         SetDlgItemText( hdlg, IDD_YVIEWASPECT, szAspect );
         sprintf( szAspect, "%d", XWinAspect );
         SendDlgItemMessage( hdlg, IDD_XWINASPECT,
                               EM_LIMITTEXT, 10, 0L );
         SetDlgItemText( hdlg, IDD_XWINASPECT, szAspect );
         sprintf( szAspect, "%d", YWinAspect );
         SendDlgItemMessage( hdlg, IDD_YWINASPECT,
                               EM_LIMITTEXT, 10, 0L );
         SetDlgItemText( hdlg, IDD_YWINASPECT, szAspect );
         return( TRUE );

      case WM_COMMAND:
         switch( wParam )
         {
            case IDOK:
               GetDlgItemText( hdlg, IDD_XVIEWASPECT,
                               szAspect, 10 );
               XViewAspect = atoi( szAspect );
               GetDlgItemText( hdlg, IDD_YVIEWASPECT,
                               szAspect, 10 );
               YViewAspect = atoi( szAspect );
               GetDlgItemText( hdlg, IDD_XWINASPECT,
                               szAspect, 10 );
               XWinAspect = atoi( szAspect );
               GetDlgItemText( hdlg, IDD_YWINASPECT,
                               szAspect, 10 );
               YWinAspect = atoi( szAspect );
               EndDialog( hdlg, TRUE );
```

```
                break;
            case IDCANCEL:
                EndDialog( hdlg, FALSE );
                break;
            default:  return( FALSE );
        }
     default: return( FALSE );
} }
     // main message processing procedure
long FAR PASCAL WndProc( HWND hwnd,   WORD msg,
                         WORD wParam, LONG lParam )
{
   static  int  nOrigin = IDM_UPLEFT, nMode = IDM_TEXT;
   static char *szMode[] =
              { "Text", "Low Metric", "High Metric",
                "Low English", "High English", "TWIPS",
                "Isotropic", "Anisotropic" },
              *szOrigin[]  =
              { "Upper Left", "Centered", "Lower Left" },
              *szUnits[] =
              { "pixels", "mm", "mm", "in", "in", "pts",
                "user defined", "user defined" };
   int        nBuff, xLeft, xRight, xCenter,
              yTop, yBottom, yCenter, OrgDC,
              cxChr, cyChr;
   char       szBuff[64];
   HDC        hdc, hdcInfo;
   HMENU      hMenu;
   DWORD      WinSize;
   RECT       rect;
   POINT      pt;
   PAINTSTRUCT ps;
   TEXTMETRIC tm;
   FARPROC    lpProc;

   switch( msg )
   {
     case WM_CREATE:
        sprintf( szBuff,
                "Mode: %s    Origin: %s    Units: %s",
                szMode[nMode-IDM_TEXT],
                szOrigin[nOrigin-IDM_UPLEFT],
                szUnits[nMode-IDM_TEXT] );
        SetWindowText( hwnd, szBuff );
         // display mode information in window header
        return(0);
```

```
case WM_COMMAND:
    hMenu = GetMenu( hwnd );
    CheckMenuItem( hMenu, nMode, MF_UNCHECKED );
    CheckMenuItem( hMenu, nOrigin,  MF_UNCHECKED );
    switch( wParam )
    {
//============ handle user choices from Aspect dialog
        case IDM_ASPECT:
            lpProc = MakeProcInstance( AspectProc,
                                       hInst );
                // create AspectProc in memory
            DialogBox( hInst, "WINASPECT",
                    hwnd, lpProc );
                // operate AspectProc and return
            FreeProcInstance( lpProc );
                // remove AspectProc, free memory
            return( TRUE );
//============ handle user choices from Mode menu
        case IDM_TEXT:
            EnableMenuItem( hMenu, IDM_ASPECT,
                            MF_GRAYED );
                // gray-out (disable) Aspect menu item
            DrawMenuBar( hwnd );   // redraw menu bar
            nMode = wParam;
            nOrigin  = IDM_UPLEFT;
            break;
        case IDM_TWIPS:
        case IDM_LOMETRIC:    case IDM_HIMETRIC:
        case IDM_LOENGLISH:   case IDM_HIENGLISH:
            EnableMenuItem( hMenu, IDM_ASPECT,
                            MF_GRAYED );
            DrawMenuBar( hwnd );
            nMode = wParam;
            nOrigin  = IDM_DNLEFT;
            break;
        case IDM_ISOTROPIC:
        case IDM_ANISOTROPIC:
            EnableMenuItem( hMenu, IDM_ASPECT,
                            MF_ENABLED );
                // enable Aspect menu choice
            DrawMenuBar( hwnd );
                // redraw menu bar
            nMode = wParam;
            nOrigin  = IDM_CENTER;
            break;
```

```
//============ handle user choices from Origin menu
        case IDM_UPLEFT:   nOrigin = IDM_UPLEFT;
                           break;
        case IDM_CENTER:   nOrigin = IDM_CENTER;
                           break;
        case IDM_DNLEFT:   nOrigin = IDM_DNLEFT;
                           break;
        }
//============ after any Command , redraw the Window
        InvalidateRect( hwnd, NULL, TRUE );
            // invokes WM_PAINT message
        CheckMenuItem( hMenu, nMode, MF_CHECKED );
        CheckMenuItem( hMenu, nOrigin,  MF_CHECKED );
        sprintf( szBuff,
                "Mode: %s     Origin: %s     Units: %s",
                szMode[nMode-IDM_TEXT],
                szOrigin[nOrigin-IDM_UPLEFT],
                szUnits[nMode-IDM_TEXT] );
        SetWindowText( hwnd, szBuff );
            // rewrite window header with new values
        return(0);
    case WM_DEVMODECHANGE:
        InvalidateRect( hwnd, NULL, TRUE );
        return(0);
    case WM_PAINT:
        hdc = BeginPaint( hwnd, &ps );
            // repaint window, starting in default mode
        SelectObject( hdc,
            GetStockObject( SYSTEM_FIXED_FONT ) );
        GetTextMetrics( hdc, &tm );
        cxChr = tm.tmAveCharWidth;
        cyChr = tm.tmHeight + tm.tmExternalLeading;
            // get text metrics for later use
        OrgDC = SaveDC( hdc );
            // save the default (MM_TEXT) mode
        SetMapMode( hdc, nMode - IDM_TEXT + 1 );
            // set selected map mode
        SetWindowOrg( hdc, 0, 0 );
            // initialize window origin at 0,0
        switch( nMode )
        {
            // set window and viewport extent if required
            // by the selected mapping mode
            case IDM_ISOTROPIC:
                SetWindowExt( hdc, XWinAspect,
                                   YWinAspect );
```

```
            if( XViewAspect && YViewAspect )
                SetViewportExt( hdc, XViewAspect,
                                     YViewAspect );
            else SetViewportExt( hdc, 1000, 1000 );
            break;
        case IDM_ANISOTROPIC:
            SetWindowExt( hdc, XWinAspect,
                               YWinAspect );
            if( XViewAspect && YViewAspect )
                SetViewportExt( hdc, XViewAspect,
                                     YViewAspect );
            else SetViewportExt( hdc, XWinAspect,
                                      YWinAspect );

            break;
    }
    GetClientRect( hwnd, &rect );
    DPtoLP( hdc, (LPPOINT) &rect, 2 );
    switch( nOrigin )
    {
        // set window origin per earlier selection
        case IDM_UPLEFT:
            SetWindowOrg( hdc, 0, 0 );
            break;
        case IDM_CENTER:
            SetWindowOrg( hdc,
                - ( rect.left + rect.right ) / 2,
                - ( rect.top + rect.bottom ) / 2 );
            break;
        case IDM_DNLEFT:
            SetWindowOrg( hdc, 0, -rect.bottom );
            break;
    }
    GetClientRect( hwnd, &rect );
        // get the coordinates for this mapping mode
    DPtoLP( hdc, (LPPOINT) &rect, 2 );
        // convert to window relative coordinates
    xLeft   = rect.left;
    xRight  = rect.right;
    yTop    = rect.top;
    yBottom = rect.bottom;
        // save window relative coordinates for mode
    xCenter = ( xRight + xLeft ) / 2;
    yCenter = ( yTop + yBottom ) / 2;
        // calculate center point relative to window
    RestoreDC( hdc, OrgDC );
        // restore default (MM_TEXT) mode
```

```
        GetClientRect( hwnd, &rect );
            // get text-mode coordinates
        DPtoLP( hdc, (LPPOINT) &rect, 2 );
            // convert to window-relative coordinates and
            // print coordinates at corners and center
        if( nOrigin == IDM_UPLEFT )
            SetTextColor( hdc, RED );
        nBuff = sprintf( szBuff, "UpLeft: (%d,%d)",
                            xLeft, yTop);
        TextOut( hdc, rect.left, rect.top,
                szBuff, nBuff );
        SetTextColor( hdc, BLACK );
        if( nOrigin == IDM_CENTER )
            SetTextColor( hdc, RED );
        nBuff = sprintf( szBuff, "Center: (%d,%d)",
                            xCenter, yCenter );
        TextOut( hdc,
                (rect.right-rect.left-nBuff*cxChr) / 2,
                (rect.bottom-rect.top) / 2,
                szBuff, nBuff );
        SetTextColor( hdc, BLACK );
        if( nOrigin == IDM_DNLEFT )
            SetTextColor( hdc, RED );
        nBuff = sprintf( szBuff, "DnLeft: (%d,%d)",
                            xLeft, yBottom );
        TextOut( hdc, rect.left, rect.bottom-cyChr,
                szBuff, nBuff );
        SetTextColor( hdc, BLACK );
        nBuff = sprintf( szBuff, "UpRight: (%d,%d)",
                            xRight, yTop);
        TextOut( hdc, rect.right-(nBuff*cxChr),
                rect.top, szBuff, nBuff );
        nBuff = sprintf( szBuff, "DnRight: (%d,%d)",
                            xRight, yBottom );
        TextOut( hdc, rect.right-(nBuff*cxChr),
                rect.bottom-cyChr, szBuff, nBuff );
        EndPaint( hwnd, &ps );
        return(0);

    case WM_DESTROY:
        PostQuitMessage(0);
        return(0);
    }
    return( DefWindowProc( hwnd, msg, wParam, lParam ) );
}
```

```
#pragma argsused
//============= stock WinMain procedure
int PASCAL WinMain( HANDLE hInstance,
                    HANDLE hPrevInstance,
                    LPSTR  lpszCmdParam, int nCmdShow )
{
   static char szAppName[] = "WINMODES";
   HWND         hwnd;
   MSG          msg;
   WNDCLASS     wc;

   XViewAspect = YViewAspect = 0;
   XWinAspect = 1000;
   YWinAspect = 2000;
   if( ! hPrevInstance )
   {
      wc.hInstance      = hInstance;
      wc.lpfnWndProc    = WndProc;
      wc.cbClsExtra     = 0;
      wc.cbWndExtra     = 0;
      wc.lpszClassName  = szAppName;
      wc.hIcon          = LoadIcon( hInstance, szAppName };
      wc.lpszMenuName   = (LPSTR) szAppName;
      wc.hCursor        = LoadCursor( NULL, IDC_ARROW );
      wc.hbrBackground  = GetStockObject( WHITE_BRUSH );
      wc.style          = CS_HREDRAW | CS_VREDRAW;
      RegisterClass( &wc );
   }
   hInst = hInstance;
   BWCCGetVersion();
   hwnd = CreateWindow( szAppName,
                        "Windows Mapping Modes",
                        WS_OVERLAPPEDWINDOW,
                        CW_USEDEFAULT, CW_USEDEFAULT,
                        CW_USEDEFAULT, CW_USEDEFAULT,
                        NULL, NULL, hInstance, NULL  );
   ShowWindow(   hwnd, nCmdShow );
   UpdateWindow( hwnd );
   while( GetMessage( &msg, NULL, 0, 0 ) )
   {
      TranslateMessage( &msg );
      DispatchMessage(  &msg );
   }
   return( msg.wParam );
}
```

PROGRAM LISTING OF WinModes.Def

```
;==============================
;   WINMODES.DEF
;==============================

NAME            MODES
DESCRIPTION     "WINDOWS MODES"
EXETYPE         WINDOWS
STUB            "WINSTUB.EXE"
CODE            PRELOAD MOVEABLE DISCARDABLE
DATA            PRELOAD MOVEABLE MULTIPLE
HEAPSIZE        1024
STACKSIZE       8192
EXPORTS         WndProc
                AspectProc
```

PROGRAM LISTING OF WinModes.H

```
//===============//
//   WINMODES.H   //
//===============//

#define  IDM_TEXT         201
#define  IDM_LOMETRIC     202
#define  IDM_HIMETRIC     203
#define  IDM_LOENGLISH    204
#define  IDM_HIENGLISH    205
#define  IDM_TWIPS        206
#define  IDM_ISOTROPIC    207
#define  IDM_ANISOTROPIC  208

#define  IDM_UPLEFT       301
#define  IDM_CENTER       302
#define  IDM_DNLEFT       303

#define  IDM_ASPECT       401

#define  IDD_XVIEWASPECT  501
#define  IDD_YVIEWASPECT  502
#define  IDD_XWINASPECT   503
#define  IDD_YWINASPECT   504

//=========================================//
//  Menu script for WinModes Resource File  //
//=========================================//
```

```
WINMODES MENU
BEGIN
     POPUP "&Modes"
     BEGIN
// Note: the values and order shown for the menu IDs
//       have been selected to correlate with values
//       needed as parameters for calls to SetMapMode()
         MENUITEM "&Text",         201, CHECKED
         MENUITEM "&LoMetric",     202
         MENUITEM "L&oEnglish",    204
         MENUITEM "&Isometric",    207
         MENUITEM "T&wips",        206, MENUBREAK
         MENUITEM "&HiMetric",     203
         MENUITEM "Hi&English",    205
         MENUITEM "&Anisometric",  208
     END
     POPUP "&Origin"
     BEGIN
         MENUITEM "&Upper Left",   301, CHECKED
         MENUITEM "&Center",       302
         MENUITEM "&Lower Left",   303
     END
     MENUITEM "&Aspect", 401, GRAYED
END
```

Program listing of Life.C

```
//=================//
//     Life.C      //
//=================//

#include <windows.h>
#include <string.h>
#include <stdlib.h>
#include "life.h"

#define  GRID      50
#define  RDX       random(GRID)
#define  ID_TIMER  1

HANDLE  hInst;

#pragma argsused

long FAR PASCAL WndProc( HWND hwnd,   WORD msg,
                         WORD wParam, LONG lParam )
```

```c
{
   static   int              ThisGeneration[GRID][GRID],
                             LastGeneration[GRID][GRID],
                             MapMode;
   static unsigned int       nGenerations = 0, Population;
// static variables are required to retain values set
// between calls to non-local Windows API functions
   int                       Neighbors, i, j, k, l, x, y;
   char                      szBuff[64];
   HDC                       hdc, hdcInfo;
   HMENU                     hMenu;
   RECT                      rect;
   PAINTSTRUCT               ps;
   FARPROC                   lpProc;

   switch( msg )
   {
      case WM_CREATE:
         MapMode = MM_ANISOTROPIC;
         PostMessage( hwnd, WM_COMMAND,
                      IDM_GRIDCLEAR, 0L );
         sprintf( szBuff, "LIFE      Generation: %d",
                  nGenerations );
         SetWindowText( hwnd, szBuff );
         return(0);

      case WM_COMMAND:
         switch( wParam )
         {
            case IDM_TIMESTOP:
               KillTimer( hwnd, ID_TIMER );
               return(0);
            case IDM_TIMESTART:
               SetTimer( hwnd, ID_TIMER, 500, NULL );
               return(0);
            case IDM_GRIDCLEAR:
               for( i=0; i<GRID; i++ )
                  for( j=0; j<GRID; j++ )
                     LastGeneration[i][j] =
                     ThisGeneration[i][j] = FALSE;
               PostMessage( hwnd, WM_COMMAND,
                            IDM_TIMESTOP, 0L );
               InvalidateRect( hwnd, NULL, TRUE );
               return(0);
            case IDM_RANDOM:
               randomize();
```

```
                    for( i=0; i<1000; i++ )
                        ThisGeneration[RDX][RDX] = TRUE;
                    PostMessage( hwnd, WM_COMMAND,
                                 IDM_TIMESTART, 0L );
                    InvalidateRect( hwnd, NULL, TRUE );
                    return(0);
                case IDM_LAUNCH:
                    randomize();
                    x = random(45)+1;
                    y = random(45)+1;
                    ThisGeneration[x+2][y+1] =
                    ThisGeneration[x+3][y+1] =
                    ThisGeneration[x+4][y+1] =
                    ThisGeneration[x+3][y+2] =
                    ThisGeneration[x+1][y+3] =
                    ThisGeneration[x+2][y+3] =
                    ThisGeneration[x+3][y+3] = TRUE;
                    PostMessage( hwnd, WM_COMMAND,
                                 IDM_TIMESTART, 0L );
                    InvalidateRect( hwnd, NULL, TRUE );
                    return(0);
                case IDM_ISOTROPIC:
                    MapMode  = MM_ISOTROPIC;
                    InvalidateRect( hwnd, NULL, TRUE );
                    return(0);
                case IDM_ANISOTROPIC:
                    MapMode = MM_ANISOTROPIC;
                    InvalidateRect( hwnd, NULL, TRUE );
                    return(0);
            }
            return(0);

        case WM_PAINT:
            hdc = BeginPaint( hwnd, &ps );
            GetClientRect( hwnd, &rect );
            SetMapMode( hdc, MapMode );
            SetWindowOrg( hdc, 0, 0 );
            SetWindowExt( hdc, 110000 / rect.right,
                               110000 / rect.bottom );
            SetViewportExt( hdc, 2000, 2000 );
            for( i=0; i<GRID; i++ )
                for( j=0; j<GRID; j++ )
                    if( ThisGeneration[i][j] )
                    {
//=================== for demo only ================//
//              SetPixel( hdc, i+3, j+3, 0L );    //
```

```
//=====================================================//
                SetRect( &rect, i+3, j+3, i+4, j+4 );
                FillRect( hdc, &rect,
                    GetStockObject( BLACK_BRUSH ) );
             }
        EndPaint( hwnd, &ps );
        return(0);

    case WM_TIMER:
        Population = 0;
        for( i=0; i<GRID; i++ )
            for( j=0; j<GRID; j++ )
            {
                LastGeneration[i][j] =
                    ThisGeneration[i][j];
                if( ThisGeneration[i][j] ) Population++;
            }
        if( !Population )
        {
            PostMessage( hwnd, WM_COMMAND,
                        IDM_TIMESTOP, 0L );
            return(0);
        }
        for( i=0; i<GRID; i++ )
            for( j=0; j<GRID; j++ )
            {
                if( LastGeneration[i][j] ) Neighbors = -1;
                                    else Neighbors =  0;
                for( k=-1; k<=1; k++ )
                {
                    x = i + k;
                    if( x <     0 ) x += GRID;
                    if( x >= GRID ) x -= GRID;
                    for( l=-1; l<=1; l++ )
                    {
                        y = j + l;
                        if( y <     0 ) y += GRID;
                        if( y >= GRID ) y -= GRID;
                        if( LastGeneration[x][y] )
                            Neighbors++;
                }  }
                switch( Neighbors )
                {
                    case 2:
                        ThisGeneration[i][j] =
                            LastGeneration[i][j];       break;
```

```
                        case 3:
                            ThisGeneration[i][j] = TRUE;  break;
                        default:
                            ThisGeneration[i][j] = FALSE;
                }   }
            sprintf( szBuff, "LIFE    Generation: %d",
                        nGenerations++ );
            SetWindowText( hwnd, szBuff );
            InvalidateRect( hwnd, NULL, TRUE );
            return(Ø);

        case WM_DESTROY:
            KillTimer( hwnd, ID_TIMER );
            PostQuitMessage(Ø);
            return(Ø);
    }
    return( DefWindowProc( hwnd, msg, wParam, lParam ) );
}


#pragma argsused

int PASCAL WinMain( HANDLE hInstance,
                    HANDLE hPrevInstance,
                    LPSTR  lpszCmdParam, int nCmdShow )
{
    static char szAppName[] = "LIFE";
    HWND        hwnd;
    MSG         msg;
    WNDCLASS    wc;

    if( ! hPrevInstance )
    {
        wc.hInstance      = hInstance;
        wc.lpfnWndProc    = WndProc;
        wc.cbClsExtra     = Ø;
        wc.cbWndExtra     = Ø;
        wc.lpszClassName  = szAppName;
        wc.hIcon          = LoadIcon( hInstance, szAppName );
        wc.lpszMenuName   = (LPSTR) szAppName;
        wc.hCursor        = LoadCursor( NULL, IDC_ARROW );
        wc.hbrBackground  = GetStockObject( WHITE_BRUSH );
        wc.style          = CS_HREDRAW | CS_VREDRAW;
        RegisterClass( &wc );
    }
    hInst = hInstance;
    hwnd = CreateWindow( szAppName, "LIFE",
```

```
                         WS_OVERLAPPEDWINDOW,
                         CW_USEDEFAULT, CW_USEDEFAULT,
                         CW_USEDEFAULT, CW_USEDEFAULT,
                         NULL, NULL, hInstance, NULL  );
    ShowWindow(   hwnd, nCmdShow );
    UpdateWindow( hwnd );
    while( GetMessage( &msg, NULL, 0, 0 ) )
    {
        TranslateMessage( &msg );
        DispatchMessage(  &msg );
    }
    return( msg.wParam );
}
```

PROGRAM LISTING OF LIFE.DEF

```
;===============================
;  LIFE.DEF
;===============================

NAME           LIFE
DESCRIPTION    "LIFE_1 DEMO"
EXETYPE        WINDOWS
STUB           "WINSTUB.EXE"
CODE           PRELOAD MOVEABLE DISCARDABLE
DATA           PRELOAD MOVEABLE MULTIPLE
HEAPSIZE       1024
STACKSIZE      8192
EXPORTS        WndProc
```

PROGRAM LISTING OF LIFE.H

```
//===========//
//  LIFE.H   //
//===========//

#define  IDM_TIMESTOP    101
#define  IDM_TIMESTART   102
#define  IDM_GRIDCLEAR   103
#define  IDM_RANDOM      104
#define  IDM_LAUNCH      105
#define  IDM_ISOTROPIC   106
#define  IDM_ANISOTROPIC 107


//==================//
```

```
//  LIFE Menu Script  //
//====================//
LIFE MENU
BEGIN
     POPUP "Run"
     BEGIN
          MENUITEM "Stop",         101
          MENUITEM "Start",        102
     END
     POPUP "Change"
     BEGIN
          MENUITEM "Clear all",    103
          MENUITEM "Random",       104
          MENUITEM "Launcher",     105
     END
     POPUP "Mapping"
     BEGIN
          MENUITEM "Isotropic",    106
          MENUITEM "Anisotropic",  107
     END
END
```

Identifying System Graphics Capabilities

C hapter 4 discussed Windows graphics mapping modes and, very briefly, mentioned graphics coprocessors and graphics device capabilities. For most purposes, as a programmer you can ignore the specifics of the available hardware capabilities and the presence or absence of video coprocessors, simply treating Windows as a uniform graphics environment without worrying about what special features a specific system may or may not support.

Still, most is not the same as all. There may be applications and/or circumstances in which it will be useful or even essential to know if the executing hardware can support specific desired features—which, obviously, is the principal topic of the current chapter.

While the reasons for requiring such information are sufficiently strange and varied to preclude any possibility of a complete listing, a few possible reasons for desiring this type of information include

- ▶ Information on supported palettes (colors)
- ▶ Sizing information for fonts (which fonts might be suitable for display and in what sizes)
- ▶ Available printer fonts
- ▶ Printer dot resolutions (necessary for optimizing bitmapped images)
- ▶ The presence or absence of special hardware

Still, if the reasons are many and varied, the possibilities are likewise.

IDENTIFYING VIDEO DEVICE (SYSTEM) CAPABILITIES

When Windows is installed (or when a new device is installed using Setup), the device drivers used for both video and printer devices provide information to Windows about special device capabilities. And, since Windows has this information, this data is also available to any applications that explicitly request access.

In most cases, and particularly in this volume, this information can simply be ignored, allowing Windows to treat the hardware in whatever manner is most appropriate. In this chapter, however, the DC (device-capacity) program will explicitly query and display device capabilities, demonstrating how other applications might execute similar queries.

What is not demonstrated, however, is how applications might respond to supported capabilities or their absence—an omission based on the fact that both circumstances and responses are too varied to attempt to predict or advise.

DEVICE PALETTE (COLOR) CAPACITIES

In general, when we speak of device palette capabilities, the first thought that comes to mind (or, probably, the only thought) is of video display capabilities. And in most cases, this is accurate simply because very few hard-copy devices support palettes of more than two colors (that is, black and white). But, while this chapter will follow this same normally unstated convention in speaking of device palettes, please be aware that the devices in question are not, any longer, explicitly limited to video devices. There are increasing numbers of printers, plotters, and other hard-copy devices that do support varying degrees of color capability.

Now, having stated this caveat, it is time to return to discussing video devices.

As a general rule, video palettes will be reported, by the DC program, as two elements: bits per pixel (BITSPIXEL) and color planes (PLANES). In most cases, one of these two elements will be reported as 1 and only the remaining element will be relevant in determining the device's supported color range. There is, however, a third element reported as Device Colors (NUMCOLORS) that, to some degree, saves calculations.

As an example, Figure 5.1 shows the device capabilities reported for an SVGA video that includes a Trident graphics coprocessor.

But, to show how the reported results vary according to equipment capabilities, compare the EGA/VGA device report with the SVGA device report in Table 5.1.

In Table 5.1 you've probably noticed a couple of discrepancies—such as the fact that, for SVGA, the palette size is calculated as 256 colors while the reported palette size is only 20. So, what gives?

```
┌──────────────────────────── Video Display ──────────────────────▼─▲┐
│ Device  Capabilities  Graphics                                Help│
│       ==data type==   ==value==units==              ==constant ID==│
│   Physical sizes                                                   │
│              Width:     240  mm                     HORZSIZE       │
│             Height:     180  mm                     VERTSIZE       │
│              Width:     640  pixels                 HORZRES        │
│             Height:     480  pixel/raster lines     VERTRES        │
│     Pixels per inch:     96  horz                   LOGPIXELSX     │
│     Pixels per inch:     96  vert                   LOGPIXELSY     │
│   Horizonal aspect:      36  pixel size             ASPECTX        │
│    Vertical aspect:      36  pixel size             ASPECTY        │
│        Pixel aspect:     51  pixel diagonal         ASPECTXY       │
│   Color characteristics                                            │
│               Color:      8  bits/pixel             BITSPIXEL      │
│        Color planes:      1                         PLANES         │
│       Device colors:     20                         NUMCOLORS      │
│     Palette entries:    256                         SIZEPALETTE    │
│    Reserved entries:     20                         NUMRESERVED    │
│    Color resolution:     18                         COLORRES       │
│   Device features                                                  │
│      Device brushes:     -1                         NUMBRUSHES     │
│        Device pens:     100                         NUMPENS        │
│     Device markers:       0                         NUMMARKERS     │
│       Device fonts:       0                         NUMFONTS       │
│    Device structure:     35  size                   PDEVICESIZE    │
│       Clipping flag:      1  boolean                CLIPCAPS       │
└────────────────────────────────────────────────────────────────────┘
```

Figure 5.1: A device capability report

The actual facts are quite simple: The reported palette size is the number of palette entries that are predefined, not the number of possible (calculated) palette entries. Thus, for an SVGA system, the actual palette size is 256 color entries even though 236 of these are not predefined, but must be defined by the application, or the user.

The moral, of course, is that the information reported by Windows about the system capabilities is useful but must also be tempered with knowledge of how these capabilities are derived and reported.

Table 5.1: Comparing Device Color Capabilities

Device Type	Color Planes	Bits/Pixel	Calculated Palette Size	Reported Palette Size	Possible Colors
EGA/VGA	4	1	16	16	256
SVGA	1	8	256	20	16,777,216
Printer	1	1	2	2	2
Plotter	1	1	2	8	n/a

Incidentally, you may also be wondering where the count of possible colors (right column) is determined. The fact is that this last piece of information is not inherent in the reported device capabilities. The details of color ranges will be deferred for coverage in Chapter 6. The raw data reported, however, is essentially correct.

THE GETDEVICECAPS FUNCTION

The DC program uses a single function, GetDeviceCaps, to retrieve any of a list of integer values describing specific device capabilities. In many cases, the information returned is a specific value, such as the supported vertical or horizontal pixel size, but, in other cases, the value returned may be a flag value where individual bits identify the presence or absence of specific capabilities.

GetDeviceCaps is called with two parameters. The first is a device-context handle (hDC) that identifies the actual device, such as a video display or a printer. The second is an integer argument specifying the information requested.

NOTE: A complete list of the information request values and their corresponding mnemonic identifiers can be found in Borland's *Windows API Reference Guide*, Volume 1.

In brief, these information requests fall into the following seven categories:

Version and device types Beginning at the beginning, the DRIVERVERSION and TECHNOLOGY index arguments request the device driver version number and device type.

Driver version numbers are reported as a word value in hexadecimal format. For example, a version number reported as 0x0103 would indicate version 1, revision 3.

Seven device types are defined as vector plotter, raster display (CRT), raster printer (laserjet), raster camera, character stream, metafile, or display file. Normally, of course, the video device would always be a raster display but, depending on equipment and configuration, the reported hard-copy device (printer) could be a vector plotter, raster printer, or raster camera—or even a metafile or display file.

Size and resolution Device size and resolution cover a variety of elements ranging from physical size, pixel or dot resolutions, colors and palettes, and pixel or dot aspect ratios—in effect, all salient information about a device's reproduction capabilities.

Raster capabilities   Because most output devices are raster devices (yes, including laser printers), the RASTERCAPS request reports on general device capabilities, such as banding (device memory dependent), bitmap handling, fill operations, scaling, and device palettes.

Curve capabilities   Curve-capability flags report the capability of the output device to handle its own curve definitions. These may include circles, arcs, pie wedges, and ellipses, as well as special borders.

Line capabilities   Line-capability flags report on line style support and some interior fill operations.

Polygon capabilities   Polygon-capability flags report on device capacities for executing alternate and winding fill operations on polygon figures, as well as plain and styled borders and interiors.

Text capabilities   Text-capability flags report device capacities for character output, including stroked output, character rotation and scaling, and clipping precision, as well as italics, boldface, underlining, and strikeouts. Also reported are handling capacities for both raster and vector fonts.

You may also refer to the LOGFONT data structure for further details on font capabilities. Refer to Volume 2 of Borland's *Windows API Reference Guide*.

GRAPHICS COPROCESSORS

In most cases, the capabilities reported by the GetDeviceCaps function are provided—to greater or lesser degrees—by graphics coprocessor devices incorporated in the output devices themselves. In the case of the video display, this would be a coprocessor found on the video card.

Alternately, in the case of hard-copy devices, the presence or absence of graphics coprocessor support is partially dependent on the age of the device and partially on the sophistication (and expense) of the model. As an example, older laser printers, while still capable of excellent print quality, often predate the development of graphics coprocessors. Other devices such as inkjet printers, while much more modern, may not only lack coprocessors but may also lack sufficient memory for full-page graphics and, therefore, may require banding (downloading page images in bands) support to be provided by Windows.

OTHER VIDEO GRAPHICS SUPPORT

While the preceding covers all defined graphics support types, bitmap operations deserve some additional mention.

In the GetDeviceCaps function, bitmap operations are reported as flag capabilities under the heading of raster capabilities. These are also, however, probably the most important device capabilities available—at least, from a graphics operation standpoint.

Bitmaps inherently require more than a little handling to write to the screen or to move, superimpose, or to manipulate in any other fashion.

Characters, whether bitmapped or stroked, are commonly written to the screen as foreground images only and, therefore, generally leave the greater portion of the screen unaffected. A rough estimate suggests that 20 percent or less of the screen pixels are actually written during text operations. Because of this, character operations are inherently faster than bitmapped image operations which require writing all pixels within the image area.

To offset this speed discrepancy, sophisticated graphics coprocessors include special hardware functions that are devoted to fast bitmap transfers, handling bitmaps larger than 64k, and bitmap scaling operations. If any of these capabilities are supported, the end result is that most common graphics operations are executed at much higher speeds than with unsupported video equipment (or printers).

INFORMATION CONTEXT VERSUS DEVICE CONTEXT

In previous examples, when access to a device such as the video display was required, the *GetDC* function was used to return a handle (*hdc*) to the device context.

In this example, however, two device-context handles have been declared: *hdc* and *hdcInfo*. Since either handle could be used for either purpose, this is slightly redundant. Still, using two handles provides emphasis for the fact that two quite different device contexts will be used: a conventional hardware device context and an information device context (see the program excerpt in the next section).

The difference between these two device contexts is simple. Unlike the conventional device context, which is used for output, the information context provided by CreateIC provides access to information but does not provide any output capabilities. At the same time, however, the information context requires less overhead, and if all that is needed is information, the information context is quite sufficient.

THE DC (DEVICE CONTEXT) DEMO PROGRAM

The DC program (see Figure 5.1 preceding and 5.2 following) reads the device capabilities information from Windows, displaying the data for either your video or hard-copy device as a series of six menu-selected screens. A brief help screen is also supplied as a dialog box. Figure 5.2 shows both the menu structures and the help dialog box (together with a sample icon) while the source code and resource scripts appear at the end of this chapter.

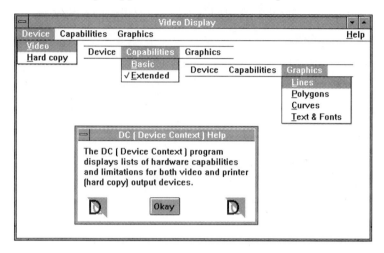

Figure 5.2: DC's menus and dialog display

Before returning to graphics screens and a beginning sample employing graphics processing, however, a few notes on the DC program may help clarify the use of the GetDeviceCaps function.

A large part of the DC program consists of static data definitions that in turn consist of the index values used to call GetDeviceCaps together with string labels organized in a series of subroutines for the several major categories of information. Essentially, each of these should be self-explanatory.

In the exported WndProc procedure, however, there is one piece of code deserving a degree of special explanation. In response to the WM_PAINT message, the *switch(nCurDev)* case statement is used to switch between the video display and the hard-copy device context (for example, the printer), thus:

```
case WM_PAINT:
    ...
    switch( nCurDev )
    {
        case IDM_VIDEO:
            hdcInfo = CreateIC( "DISPLAY", NULL,
                                NULL, NULL );
            SetWindowText( hwnd, "Video Display" );
            break;
```

The first case, IDM_VIDEO, is relatively simple. The *hdcInfo* context handle receives the information device context created by the CreateIC function. Because the video is a stock device, the string "DISPLAY" and three null parameters are sufficient to identify the desired hardware and, subsequently, the *hdcInfo* handle will be used to query the device capabilities.

The final instruction, SetWindowText, simply resets the window caption to show the selected context.

In the second case, IDM_HC, a slightly more complex approach is required because the hard-copy or printer device is not a stock item (and more than one output device may be defined). In this case, the response begins by querying Windows for a device name using the GetProfileString function.

GetProfileString is called with two specification strings naming the entry in the WIN.INI file to be returned: "WINDOWS", which names the application, and "Device", which identifies the key name for the installed (default) printer. The third field is left blank but could be used to specify a default value to be returned if the search failed.

> **NOTE:** The actual entry in WIN.INI consists of a single line containing the device name, the device driver, and the output port, delimited by commas.

```
case IDM_HC:
    GetProfileString( "WINDOWS", "Device", "",
                         szPrn, sizeof( szPrn ) );
    if( ( szDevice = strtok( szPrn, "," ) ) &&
        ( szDriver = strtok( NULL,  "," ) ) &&
        ( szOutPut = strtok( NULL,  "," ) ) )
        hdcInfo = CreateIC( szDriver, szDevice,
                             szOutPut, NULL );
    else hdcInfo = NULL;
    SetWindowText( hwnd, szPrn );
}
```

On return, the response string (*szPrn*) is decoded to derive the device (*szDevice*), driver (*szDriver*) and output (*szOutPut*) labels. Subsequently, these three labels are used to create an information context or, if any of these three fields are not found, to set the information context to null.

Overall, this is fairly simple but other queries—for example, determining if special equipment is present and, if so, in what configuration—might legitimately be made by applications that require the presence of custom or unusual devices. For example, a drafting program might wish to respond quite differently when outputting to a plotter (a vector device) than when it is outputting to a laser printer (a raster device).

SUMMARY

As mentioned, most applications will have little or no need for access to details about equipment capabilities and may easily and safely leave this to Windows. There will be instances, however, when an application might well improve performance by being aware of device capabilities and by changing performance accordingly.

Of course, you may be curious about what, if any, special hardware support is present in your system. For this purpose, the DC program, whose listing follows, is quite informative.

And, aside from either, as Alexander Pope advises:

> A little learning is a dang'rous thing;
> Drink deep or taste not the Pierian spring:
> There shallow draughts intoxicate the brain,
> And drinking largely sobers us again.

(Pope, An Essay on Criticism)

PROGRAM LISTING OF DC.C

```
//============================//
//            DC.C            //
//  Windows Device Capacity   //
//============================//

#include <windows.h>
#include <string.h>
#include "dc.h"

#define RED    0x000000FF
#define BLUE   0x00FF0000
#define BLACK  0x00000000

typedef struct {   int   nMask;
                   char *szMask;
                   char *szDescript;  }  BITSTRUCT;
HANDLE  hInst;
int     cxChr, cyChr;

void BasicCap( HDC hdc, HDC hDcInfo )
{
   char  szBuff[80];
   int   i, nLine, ValidFlag;
   static struct { int   nDisplay;
```

```
                   int   nIndex;
                   char *szConstant;
                   char *szDescript;
                   char *szNotes;  } info[] =
//=======================================//
// flag constant  constant text       //
//     item label          unit(s)     //
//=======================================//
   { Ø, Ø, "", "Physical sizes", "",
      1, HORZSIZE,    "HORZSIZE",
         "Width",            "mm",
      1, VERTSIZE,    "VERTSIZE",
         "Height",           "mm",
      1, HORZRES,     "HORZRES",
         "Width",            "pixels",
      1, VERTRES,     "VERTRES",
         "Height",           "pixel/raster lines",
      1, LOGPIXELSX, "LOGPIXELSX",
         "Pixels per inch", "horz",
      1, LOGPIXELSY, "LOGPIXELSY",
         "Pixels per inch", "vert",
      1, ASPECTX,     "ASPECTX",
         "Horizonal aspect", "pixel size",
      1, ASPECTY,     "ASPECTY",
         "Vertical aspect", "pixel size",
      1, ASPECTXY,    "ASPECTXY",
         "Pixel aspect",    "pixel diagonal",

      Ø, Ø, "", "Color characteristics", "",
      1, BITSPIXEL,  "BITSPIXEL",
         "Color",            "bits/pixel",
      1, PLANES,      "PLANES",
         "Color planes",     "",
      1, NUMCOLORS,  "NUMCOLORS",
         "Device colors",    "",
      1, SIZEPALETTE, "SIZEPALETTE",
         "Palette entries", "",      // note 1
      1, NUMRESERVED, "NUMRESERVED",
         "Reserved entries", "",     // note 1
      1, COLORRES,    "COLORRES",
         "Color resolution", "",     // note 1

      Ø, Ø, "", "Device features", "",
      1, NUMBRUSHES, "NUMBRUSHES",
         "Device brushes",   "",
      1, NUMPENS,     "NUMPENS",
```

```
        "Device pens",         "",
    1, NUMMARKERS,  "NUMMARKERS",
        "Device markers",      "",
    1, NUMFONTS,     "NUMFONTS",
        "Device fonts",        "",
    1, PDEVICESIZE, "PDEVICESIZE",
        "Device structure", "size",
    1, CLIPCAPS,     "CLIPCAPS",
        "Clipping flag",     "boolean"
};


//=======================================================//
//   Note 1: These three indexes are valid only if   //
//   the RC_PALETTE bit in the RASTERCAPS index is    //
//   set and only available if the Windows driver     //
//   version is 3.0 or higher.                        //
//=======================================================//

SetTextColor( hdc, RED );
TextOut( hdc, cxChr, 0, szBuff,
         sprintf( szBuff, "%37s%28s",
             "==data type==  ==value==units==",
             "==constant ID==" ) );
ValidFlag = ( GetDeviceCaps( hDcInfo, RASTERCAPS )
              & RC_PALETTE );
for( i=0; i<sizeof(info)/sizeof(info[0]); i++ )
{
    SetTextColor( hdc, BLACK );
    if( ! info[i].nDisplay )
    {
        SetTextColor( hdc, BLUE );
        TextOut( hdc, cxChr*2, cyChr*(i+1), szBuff,
                 sprintf( szBuff, "%s",
                          info[i].szDescript ) );
    }
    else
    switch( info[i].nIndex )
    {
      case SIZEPALETTE:
      case NUMRESERVED:
      case COLORRES:
        TextOut( hdc, cxChr, cyChr*(i+1), szBuff,
            sprintf( szBuff,
                    "%17s:      n/a  %-20s  %s",
                    info[i].szDescript, "",
                    info[i].szConstant ) );
```

```
                    if( ! ValidFlag ) break;
            default:
                TextOut( hdc, cxChr, cyChr*(i+1), szBuff,
                        sprintf( szBuff,
                            "%17s:      %5d  %-20s  %s",
                            info[i].szDescript,
                            GetDeviceCaps( hDcInfo,
                                        info[i].nIndex ),
                            info[i].szNotes,
                            info[i].szConstant ) );
} } }

void ExtendCap( HDC hdc, HDC hDcInfo )
{
    char  szBuff[80];
    int   i, j = GetDeviceCaps( hDcInfo, DRIVERVERSION );
    static BITSTRUCT raster[] =
    {
        RC_BANDING,      "RC_BANDING",
            "Requires banding support",
        RC_BITBLT,       "RC_BITBLT",
            "bitmap transfer",
        RC_BITMAP64,     "RC_BITMAP64",
            "bitmaps larger than 64K",
        RC_DI_BITMAP,    "RC_DI_BITMAP",
            "SetDIBits and GetDIBits",
        RC_DIBTODEV,     "RC_DIBTODEV",
            "SetDIBitsToDevice",
        RC_FLOODFILL,    "RC_FLOODFILL",
            "floodfill",
        RC_GDI20_OUTPUT, "RC_GDI20_OUTPUT",
            "Windows 2.0 features",
        RC_PALETTE,      "RC_PALETTE",
            "Palette-based device",
        RC_SCALING,      "RC_SCALING",
            "scaling",
        RC_BIGFONT,      "RC_BIGFONT",
            "fonts larger than 64K",
        RC_STRETCHBLT,   "RC_STRETCHBLT",
            "StretchBlt",
        RC_STRETCHDIB,   "RC_STRETCHDIB",
            "StretchDIBits"
    };
    static char *szTech[] =
    { "Vector plotter   (DT_PLOTTER)",
      "Raster display   (DT_RASDISPLAY)",
```

```
          "Raster printer    (DT_RASPRINTER)",
          "Raster camera     (DT_RASCAMERA)",
          "Character stream (DT_CHARSTREAM)",
          "Metafile          (DT_METAFILE)",
          "Display file      (DT_DISPFILE)"  };

     TextOut( hdc, cxChr, 0, szBuff,
              sprintf( szBuff, "Driver Version: %2d.%02d",
                         HIBYTE(j), LOBYTE(j) ) );
     TextOut( hdc, cxChr, cyChr, szBuff,
              sprintf( szBuff, "    Technology: %s",
                   szTech[ GetDeviceCaps( hDcInfo,
                                       TECHNOLOGY ) ] ) );
     TextOut( hdc, cxChr, cyChr*2, szBuff,
              sprintf( szBuff,
                 "Raster capabilities (RASTERCAPS)" ) );
     SetTextColor( hdc, RED );
     TextOut( hdc, cxChr, cyChr*4, szBuff,
              sprintf( szBuff, "%17s%39s",
                         "data type", "constant ID" ) );
     SetTextColor( hdc, BLACK );
     for( i=0; i<sizeof(raster)/sizeof(raster[0]); i++ )
        switch( raster[i].nMask )
        {
           case RC_BANDING:
           case RC_PALETTE:
              TextOut( hdc, cxChr*5, cyChr*(i+5), szBuff,
                 sprintf( szBuff, "[%c] %-34s    %s",
                    GetDeviceCaps( hDcInfo, RASTERCAPS ) &
                              raster[i].nMask ? 'X' : ' ',
                              raster[i].szDescript,
                              raster[i].szMask ) );
              break;
           default:
              TextOut( hdc, cxChr*5, cyChr*(i+5), szBuff,
                 sprintf( szBuff,
                         "[%c] Supports %-25s    %s",
                    GetDeviceCaps( hDcInfo, RASTERCAPS ) &
                              raster[i].nMask ? 'X' : ' ',
                              raster[i].szDescript,
                              raster[i].szMask ) );
     }     }


void LineCap( HDC hdc, HDC hDcInfo )
{
    static char szBuff[80];
```

```
int    i;
static BITSTRUCT lines[] =
{ LC_POLYLINE,     "LC_POLYLINE",
      "polylines",
    LC_MARKER,       "LC_MARKER",
       "markers",
    LC_POLYMARKER,   "LC_POLYMARKER",
       "polymarkers",
    LC_WIDE,         "LC_WIDE",
       "wide lines",
    LC_STYLED,       "LC_STYLED",
       "styled lines",
    LC_WIDESTYLED,   "LC_WIDESTYLED",
       "wide and styled lines",
    LC_INTERIORS,    "LC_INTERIORS",
       "interiors:"   };

TextOut( hdc, cxChr, 0, szBuff,
    sprintf( szBuff, "Line Capabilities (LINECAPS)" ) );
SetTextColor( hdc, RED );
TextOut( hdc, cxChr, cyChr*2, szBuff,
    sprintf( szBuff, "%20s%29s",
             "graphics feature", "constant ID" ) );
SetTextColor( hdc, BLACK );
for( i=0; i<sizeof(lines)/sizeof(lines[0]); i++ )
    TextOut( hdc, cxChr, cyChr*(i+3), szBuff,
        sprintf( szBuff, "[%c] Supports %-22s   %s",
                 GetDeviceCaps( hDcInfo, LINECAPS ) &
                        lines[i].nMask ? 'X' : ' ',
                        lines[i].szDescript,
                        lines[i].szMask ) );
}

void PolyCap( HDC hdc, HDC hDcInfo )
{
    static char szBuff[80];
    int    i;
    static BITSTRUCT poly[] =
    { PC_POLYGON,      "PC_POLYGON",
         "alternate fill polygon",
        PC_RECTANGLE,   "PC_RECTANGLE",
           "rectangle",
        PC_TRAPEZOID,   "PC_TRAPEZOID",
           "winding number fill polygon",
        PC_SCANLINE,    "PC_SCANLINE",
           "scan lines",
```

```
        PC_WIDE,           "PC_WIDE",
          "wide borders",
        PC_STYLED,         "PC_STYLED",
          "styled borders",
        PC_WIDESTYLED,     "PC_WIDESTYLED",
          "wide and styled polygons",
        PC_INTERIORS,      "PC_INTERIORS",
          "interiors"                       };

    TextOut( hdc, cxChr, 0, szBuff,
        sprintf( szBuff,
          "Polygonal capabilities (POLYGONALCAPS)" ) );
    SetTextColor( hdc, RED );
    TextOut( hdc, cxChr, cyChr*2, szBuff,
        sprintf( szBuff, "%20s%34s",
                "graphics feature", "constant ID" ) );
    SetTextColor( hdc, BLACK );
    for( i=0; i<sizeof(poly)/sizeof(poly[0]); i++ )
        TextOut( hdc, cxChr, cyChr*(i+3), szBuff,
            sprintf( szBuff, "[%c] Supports %-27s  %s",
                GetDeviceCaps( hDcInfo, POLYGONALCAPS ) &
                            poly[i].nMask ? 'X' : ' ',
                            poly[i].szDescript,
                            poly[i].szMask ) );
}

void CurveCap( HDC hdc, HDC hDcInfo )
{
    static char szBuff[80];
    int    i;
    static BITSTRUCT curves[] =
    { CC_CIRCLES,       "CC_CIRCLES",
        "circles",
      CC_PIE,           "CC_PIE",
        "pie wedges",
      CC_CHORD,         "CC_CHORD",
        "chord arcs",
      CC_ELLIPSES,      "CC_ELLIPSES",
        "ellipses",
      CC_WIDE,          "CC_WIDE",
        "wide borders",
      CC_STYLED,        "CC_STYLED",
        "styled borders",
      CC_WIDESTYLED,    "CC_WIDESTYLED",
        "wide and styled borders",
      CC_INTERIORS,     "CC_INTERIORS",
```

```
                  "interiors"   };

        TextOut( hdc, cxChr, 0, szBuff,
           sprintf( szBuff,
                    "Curve capabilities (CURVECAPS)" ) );
        SetTextColor( hdc, RED );
        TextOut( hdc, cxChr, cyChr*2, szBuff,
           sprintf( szBuff, "%20s%30s",
                    "graphics feature", "constant ID" ) );
        SetTextColor( hdc, BLACK );
        for( i=0; i<sizeof(curves)/sizeof(curves[0]); i++ )
           TextOut( hdc, cxChr, cyChr*(i+3), szBuff,
              sprintf( szBuff, "[%c] Supports %-23s   %s",
                       GetDeviceCaps( hDcInfo, CURVECAPS ) &
                               curves[i].nMask ? 'X' : ' ',
                               curves[i].szDescript,
                               curves[i].szMask ) );
    }

    void TextCap( HDC hdc, HDC hDcInfo )
    {
        static char szBuff[80];
        int    i;
        static BITSTRUCT text[] =
        {  TC_OP_CHARACTER, "TC_OP_CHARACTER",
              "Character output precision",
           TC_OP_STROKE,    "TC_OP_STROKE",
              "Stroke output precision",
           TC_CP_STROKE,    "TC_CP_STROKE",
              "Stroke clip precision",
           TC_CR_90,        "TC_CR_90",
              "90-degree char rotation",
           TC_CR_ANY,       "TC_CR_ANY",
              "Any character rotation",
           TC_SF_X_YINDEP,  "TC_SF_X_YINDEP",
              "Independent x / y scaling",
           TC_SA_DOUBLE,    "TC_SA_DOUBLE",
              "Doubled character scaling",
           TC_SA_INTEGER,   "TC_SA_INTEGER",
              "Integer multiple scaling",
           TC_SA_CONTIN,    "TC_SA_CONTIN",
              "Any multiples for exact scaling",
           TC_EA_DOUBLE,    "TC_EA_DOUBLE",
              "Double-weight characters",
           TC_IA_ABLE,      "TC_IA_ABLE",
              "Italics",
```

```
        TC_UA_ABLE,        "TC_UA_ABLE",
          "Underlining",
        TC_SO_ABLE,        "TC_SO_ABLE",
          "Strikeouts",
        TC_RA_ABLE,        "TC_RA_ABLE",
          "Raster fonts",
        TC_VA_ABLE,        "TC_VA_ABLE",
          "Vector fonts"          };

   TextOut( hdc, cxChr, 0, szBuff,
      sprintf( szBuff,
              "Text capabilities (TEXTCAPS)" ) );
   SetTextColor( hdc, RED );
   TextOut( hdc, cxChr, cyChr*2, szBuff,
          sprintf( szBuff, "%13s%36s",
                  "data type", "constant ID" ) );
   SetTextColor( hdc, BLACK );
   for( i=0; i<sizeof(text)/sizeof(text[0]); i++ )
      TextOut( hdc, cxChr, cyChr*(i+3), szBuff,
         sprintf( szBuff, "[%c] %-31s   %s",
                  GetDeviceCaps( hDcInfo, TEXTCAPS ) &
                          text[i].nMask ? 'X' : ' ',
                          text[i].szDescript,
                          text[i].szMask ) );
}


#pragma argsused

BOOL FAR PASCAL HelpProc( HWND hDlg,   WORD msg,
                          WORD wParam, LONG lParam )
{
   switch( msg )
   {
      case WM_INITDIALOG:  return( TRUE );
      case WM_COMMAND:
         switch( wParam )
          {
             case IDOK: EndDialog( hDlg, TRUE );
                        return( TRUE );
              default: return( TRUE );
      }       }
   return( FALSE );
}


long FAR PASCAL WndProc( HWND hwnd,   WORD msg,
                         WORD wParam, LONG lParam )
```

```
        {
           static  int  nCurDev = IDM_VIDEO,
                        nCurInfo = IDM_BASIC;
           char         szPrn[64];
           char         *szDevice, *szDriver, *szOutPut;
           HDC          hdc, hdcInfo;
           HMENU        hMenu;
           POINT        pt;
           PAINTSTRUCT  ps;
           TEXTMETRIC   tm;
           FARPROC      lpProc;
           int          iReturn;

           switch( msg )
           {
              case WM_CREATE:
                 hdc = GetDC( hwnd );
                 SelectObject( hdc,
                    GetStockObject( SYSTEM_FIXED_FONT ) );
                 GetTextMetrics( hdc, &tm );
                 cxChr = tm.tmAveCharWidth;
                 cyChr = tm.tmHeight + tm.tmExternalLeading;
                 ReleaseDC( hwnd, hdc );
                 return(0);

              case WM_COMMAND:
                 hMenu = GetMenu( hwnd );
                 switch( wParam )
                 {
                    case IDM_VIDEO:   case IDM_HC:
                       CheckMenuItem( hMenu, nCurDev,
                                      MF_UNCHECKED );
                       nCurDev = wParam;
                       CheckMenuItem( hMenu, nCurDev,
                                      MF_CHECKED );
                       InvalidateRect( hwnd, NULL, TRUE );
                       return(0);
                    case IDM_BASIC:   case IDM_EXTENDED:
                    case IDM_LINE:    case IDM_POLYGON:
                    case IDM_CURVE:   case IDM_TEXT:
                       CheckMenuItem( hMenu, nCurInfo,
                                      MF_UNCHECKED );
                       nCurInfo = wParam;
                       CheckMenuItem( hMenu, nCurInfo,
                                      MF_CHECKED );
                       InvalidateRect( hwnd, NULL, TRUE );
```

```
        return(0);
    case IDM_ABOUT:
        lpProc = MakeProcInstance( HelpProc,
                                   hInst );
        DialogBox( hInst, "DC", hwnd, lpProc );
        FreeProcInstance( lpProc );
        return(0);
    }  break;

case WM_DEVMODECHANGE:
    InvalidateRect( hwnd, NULL, TRUE );
    return(0);

case WM_PAINT:
    hdc = BeginPaint( hwnd, &ps );
    SelectObject( hdc,
        GetStockObject( SYSTEM_FIXED_FONT ) );
    switch( nCurDev )
    {
        case IDM_VIDEO:
            hdcInfo = CreateIC( "DISPLAY", NULL,
                                NULL, NULL );
            SetWindowText( hwnd, "Video Display" );
            break;
        case IDM_HC:
            GetProfileString( "WINDOWS", "Device", "",
                              szPrn, sizeof(szPrn) );
            if( ( szDevice = strtok( szPrn, "," ) ) &&
                ( szDriver = strtok( NULL,  "," ) ) &&
                ( szOutPut = strtok( NULL,  "," ) ) )
                hdcInfo = CreateIC( szDriver, szDevice,
                                    szOutPut, NULL );
            else hdcInfo = NULL;
            SetWindowText( hwnd, szPrn );
    }
    if( hdcInfo )
    {
        switch( nCurInfo )
        {
            case IDM_BASIC:
                BasicCap( hdc, hdcInfo ); break;
            case IDM_EXTENDED:
                ExtendCap( hdc, hdcInfo ); break;
            case IDM_LINE:
                LineCap( hdc, hdcInfo ); break;
            case IDM_POLYGON:
```

```
                            PolyCap(   hdc, hdcInfo ); break;
                    case IDM_CURVE:
                        CurveCap(  hdc, hdcInfo ); break;
                    case IDM_TEXT:
                        TextCap(   hdc, hdcInfo ); break;
                }
                DeleteDC( hdcInfo );
            }
            EndPaint( hwnd, &ps );
            return(0);

        case WM_DESTROY:
            PostQuitMessage(0);
            return(0);
    }
    return( DefWindowProc( hwnd, msg, wParam, lParam ) );
}

#pragma argsused

int PASCAL WinMain( HANDLE hInstance,
                    HANDLE hPrevInstance,
                    LPSTR  lpszCmdParam,
                    int    nCmdShow )
{
    static char szAppName[] = "DC";
    HWND        hwnd;
    MSG         msg;
    WNDCLASS    wc;

    if( hPrevInstance ) return( FALSE );
    wc.hInstance       = hInstance;
    wc.lpfnWndProc     = WndProc;
    wc.cbClsExtra      = 0;
    wc.cbWndExtra      = 0;
    wc.lpszClassName   = szAppName;
    wc.hIcon           = LoadIcon( hInstance, szAppName );
    wc.lpszMenuName    = (LPSTR) szAppName;
    wc.hCursor         = LoadCursor( NULL, IDC_ARROW );
    wc.hbrBackground   = GetStockObject( WHITE_BRUSH );
    wc.style           = CS_HREDRAW | CS_VREDRAW;
    RegisterClass( &wc );
    hInst = hInstance;
    hwnd = CreateWindow( szAppName,
                         "System Device Capabilites",
                         WS_OVERLAPPEDWINDOW,
```

```
                     CW_USEDEFAULT, CW_USEDEFAULT,
                     CW_USEDEFAULT, CW_USEDEFAULT,
                     NULL, NULL, hInstance, NULL  );
   ShowWindow(   hwnd, nCmdShow );
   UpdateWindow( hwnd );
   while( GetMessage( &msg, NULL, 0, 0 ) )
   {
      TranslateMessage( &msg );
      DispatchMessage(  &msg );
   }
   return( msg.wParam );
}


;==============================
;  DC.DEF ( Device Context )
;==============================

NAME           DC

DESCRIPTION    "DEVICE CONTEXT CAPABILITIES"
EXETYPE        WINDOWS
STUB           "WINSTUB.EXE"
CODE           PRELOAD MOVEABLE DISCARDABLE
DATA           PRELOAD MOVEABLE MULTIPLE
HEAPSIZE       1024
STACKSIZE      8192
EXPORTS        WndProc
               HelpProc


//=================================//
//  DC.H ( DEVICE CONTEXT PROGRAM  //
//=================================//
#define  IDM_VIDEO     101
#define  IDM_HC        102
#define  IDM_BASIC     103
#define  IDM_EXTENDED  104
#define  IDM_LINE      105
#define  IDM_POLYGON   106
#define  IDM_CURVE     107
#define  IDM_TEXT      108
#define  IDM_ABOUT     999
```

Colors and Color Palettes

WINDOWS PALETTES

DEFINING COLORS

GRAY-SCALING COLOR CONVERSIONS

SUMMARY

PROGRAM LISTING OF COLOR1.C

PROGRAM LISTING OF COLOR2.C

PROGRAM LISTING OF COLOR3.C

Not long past, a color monitor referred to an amber or green video display—both were popularly credited with reducing eye-strain—while multicolor monitors were the hallmarks of hobbyists with deep pockets. Of course, at the same time, these early color systems were more useful for playing Pong or Pac-Man than for any real applications, and even hobbyists regarded four-color palettes and 320-by-200 pixel displays with more than a little dissatisfaction.

Today, in contrast, even LCD displays are appearing in full glorious color, while amber and green monitors have become almost as common as hen's teeth, and monochrome graphics monitors are virtually an endangered species.

The reasons for these changes and contrasts are threefold.

First and principal is that the cost of memory has been falling continuously as monolithic ICs have been fabricated in higher and higher densities at lower and lower costs. And memory—video RAM—is the single most important requirement for a color display. Remember, even when monochrome monitors were standard, color TVs were equally standard, notwithstanding that the video resolutions of the two systems were and are quite different.

Thus, while the earliest graphics video cards provided video RAM (VRAM) on the order of 32k to 64k—enough for simple displays with limited color—modern video cards, such as SVGA (Super-VGA) cards, provide 512k to 1,024k of RAM, sufficient to support 1,024-by-768 pixel, or 256-color, displays.

The falling cost of video memory, however, is only part of the story. The second reason is psychological rather than material. Quite bluntly, except for special circumstances such as typesetting or drafting applications, we prefer color to black and white (or black and amber, or black and green) and, in the absence of monetary disincentives, the move to full-color systems has hardly surprised anyone.

But the third reason is perhaps the most significant, and certainly so in the present context: the heavy support in the form of applications that use color to provide information in forms more readily recognizable than mere black-and-white imagery.

Although DOS applications have always had the option of using color, color has never (with a few exceptions) been integral to DOS applications. With Windows, however, color has not only become an integral part of the operating system's display but also has become, if not essential, certainly an expected part of any application. As an example, even such a relatively simple application as the editor that is presently being used to write this chapter displays the text as black on white; but at the same instant, the toolbar incorporates at least three shades of gray in addition to black and white. Granted, the only real color is the light-blue title bar supplied by Windows, but the principle remains: The display is not monochrome and, therefore, is easier to read and, as a bare minimum, more impressive.

In part, the use of color—or shades of gray, when more appropriate—simply presents a display with a greater appearance of depth and detail than a similar monochrome display. And, although first impressions are hardly an appropriate basis for judging an application's design and usefulness, first impressions are still important if for no other reason than initial appearances may well determine what consideration a prospective customer gives to your application and how much effort he or she expends in discovering the real strengths of your design. First impressions do count, and even simple applications can benefit, in the commercial sense, from making a good impression.

Of course, there's also a flip side to this same coin. Excessively elaborate graphics or absurdly garish color choices may have precisely the opposite of the desired effect—a bad first impression or general confusion while operating an application. Thus, restraint is also appropriate.

Still, this is not a lecture on the aestethics of design, however relevant the topic might be. Instead, the present topic is how colors can be used. How you use colors remains up to you.

WINDOWS PALETTES

In Chapter 5, device palettes—specifically video palettes—were mentioned briefly, and as you may recall, the EGA/VGA device type was identified as having a 16-color palette and the SVGA device type reported a palette with 20 defined colors out of 256 possible palette entries (see Table 5.1).

In the first instance, the EGA/VGA device type, the available colors are limited to 16 colors, being defined by four color planes which have one bit per pixel. The four color planes used by the EGA/VGA driver consist of red, green, blue, and intensity, with the intensity plane (or bit) shifting between green and light green, blue and light blue, and so forth. Thus the 16 colors in the stock palette are determined solely by the available combinations of three colors and intensity. (White consists of RGB and I, light gray is produced by combining RGB, and dark gray is set by the intensity bit alone—that is, very low levels of RGB.)

For a VGA system, however, despite a simplistic definition inherited from EGA hardware limitations, there are actually six color planes: red consisting of both a high- and a low-intensity red (R and r), a high and a low green (G and g), and a high and a low blue (B and b). Thus the VGA video card actually supports 64 (2^6) individual colors even though the Windows-supported palette uses only 16 of these.

Even with 16-color-palette limitations imposed, many Windows applications will include additional color choices by dithering existing colors. The practice and limitations of color dithering will be explained presently.

For SGVA systems, however, the color definition shifts from four color planes and one bit per pixel to one color plane and eight bits per pixel, yielding a palette with 256 entries (of which 20 hold predefined hues).

Most SVGA video cards support color gradations defined by eight-bits per color (RGB), giving each pure color a total of 256 levels (from black to full intensity) and a total of 16,77,216 possible colors (combining the possible RGB levels). Remember, however, that only 256 of these possible 16 million colors can be defined in the device palette.

But, while SVGA video cards are capable of near-photographic-quality video, still newer devices are now appearing on the market with the generic name "true-color" video cards. These newer video devices are characterized by VRAM ranging from 2Mb to 6Mb—in theory, a bit more than 2Mb of RAM is required to display a 1,024-by-768 pixel screen using 24 bits per pixel—as well as sophisticated graphics coprocessors such as the Tseng ET-4000 or, in more advanced versions, the TI 34020 graphics coprocessors.

Ideally, true-color video boards provide enough memory to hold 24 bits per pixel of color information—again, eight bits each of red, green, and blue—but instead of being limited to a palette consisting of a selection of 256 of the possible colors, each pixel in the image has its own independent color definition. Thus, the full range of 16 million colors can be displayed even though a 1,024-by-768 pixel screen provides only enough pixels to show ~ 5 percent of the total possible hues.

In fact, however, many very sophisticated true-color video systems, such as the TARGA+ cards, provide 16-bit-per-pixel color which, to the human eye (even to those possessing superior color vision), is indistinguishable from 24- or 32-bit-per-pixel images. And, when you consider that a 512-by-400 pixel image, at 16 bits per pixel, requires 400k of storage, an indistinguishable 24- or 32-bit image definitely becomes overkill.

For the present, however, these true-color video cards are not in common use (although most will support the more conventionally used SVGA video modes) and should figure in your programming considerations only in unusual and specialized circumstances. Still, there's certainly no harm in being aware of the future...particularly when it's hovering on the horizon...in full, living color.

DEFINING COLORS

Previously, using DOS, the video color palette has been defined in a relatively restrictive fashion. Originally, for CGA systems, colors were defined using the RGBI flag system, which provided a total of 16 colors (2^4) by controlling the red, green, and blue color guns together with a single intensity control. In this fashion, white was defined as iRGB, blue as i..B, and so on.

Table 6.1 shows a complete list of color values for CGA, EGA/VGA, and Windows equivalents.

With the introduction of EGA/VGA video boards, the CGA standard palette of 16 colors expanded to 64 (2^6) colors, exchanging the single intensity bit to three separate intensity bits, one each for the red, green, and blue guns. The resulting RrGgBb color palette is, again, illustrated in Table 6.1. And you may notice that the standard EGA/VGA color palette jumps abruptly in value between Light Gray and Dark Gray and leaves most of the 64 possible colors undefined.

Windows, however, provides a distinct departure from previous color-definition schemes by defining colors as long integer values (four bytes) in the format 0x00BBGGRR. In this format, the least significant byte (eight bits) holds the value for red, the second byte green, the third byte blue while the fourth and most significant byte remains zero.

> **NOTE.** The most significant byte is used, in other circumstances, as a flag value indicating the type of color reference, as will be explained presently—see "Palette Index COLORREF Values" and "Palette-relative COLORREF Values," following.

Table 6.1: System Color Definitions

Color Names	CGA Colors		EGA/VGA Colors		Windows Equivalents
	binary	iRGB	binary	rgbRGB	0x..BBGGRR
Black	0000	....	000000	......	0x00000000
Dark Blue	0001	...B	000001	.....B	0x00770000
Dark Green	0010	..G.	000010	....G.	0x00007700
Dark Cyan	0011	..GB	000011	....GB	0x00777700
Dark Red	0100	.R..	000100	...R..	0x00000077
Dark Magenta	0101	.R.B	000101	...R.B	0x00770077
Brown	0110	.RG.	010100	.g.R..	0x00007777
Light Gray	0111	.RGB	000111	...RGB	0x00808080
Dark Gray	1000	i...	111000	rgb...	0x003F3F3F
Light Blue	1001	i..B	111001	rgb..B	0x00FF0000
Light Green	1010	i.G.	111010	rgb.G.	0x0000FF00
Light Cyan	1011	i.GB	111011	rgb.GB	0x00FFFF00
Light Red	1100	iR..	111100	rgbR..	0x000000FF
Light Magenta	1101	iR.B	111101	rgbR.B	0x00FF00FF
Yellow	1110	iRG.	111110	rgbRG.	0x0000FFFF
White	1111	iRGB	111111	rgbRGB	0x00FFFFFF

In this fashion, the individual primaries (red, green, and blue) have possible ranges of 0..255 while individual colors are specified as 24-bit values, yielding a total of 16,777,216 possible hues.

However, because most video boards—the newest 24-bit video boards excepted—cannot support individual pixel color specifications, these 24-bit values are written to a color palette while the pixels in the image map itself consist of references to the palette values.

Thus, while an SVGA video card can support 24-bit color specifications, it can only do so as a palette containing 256 entries. At the same time, a conventional EGA or VGA video card only supports a 16-color palette selected from 64 possible colors.

Windows, however, at least partially circumvents these color limitations, first by providing a uniform (device-independent) method of defining colors, and second by mapping Windows-defined colors to the actual device-supported palettes. In a moment, we'll look at some of the methods used by Windows to handle such adaptations (see Palette Capabilities/Limitations/Dithering).

STOCK PALETTES

In DOS, we normally assume the presence of a stock palette consisting of the 16 standard colors originally supported by the EGA video standard or of their counterparts on VGA/SVGA systems (see Table 6.1).

Under Windows, there's also a stock palette defined, but instead of 16 colors derived from the EGA RGBI capabilities, Windows defines a stock palette consisting of 20 static colors (the default palette). Of course, in many cases, such as the case of Windows applications operating on an EGA or VGA system, only 16 of these 20 colors actually correspond to displayable colors; the remaining four can only be displayed by dithering. (Dithering is demonstrated on EGA/VGA systems by the Color1 demo and on all systems by the Color2 demo.)

Alternately, on SVGA systems, since the hardware supports a device palette of 256 colors, the 20 default colors appear as individual hues without adjustments.

In either case, whether you have EGA/VGA or SVGA capabilities, the Color1.C program (whose complete listing appears both at the end of this chapter and on the accompanying disk) demonstrates the stock palette's 20 colors as shown in Figure 6.1. The following is a key to the colors in the figure:

Black (0)	Dark Red (1)	Dark Green (2)	Gold (3)	Dark Blue (4)
Violet (5)	Dark Cyan (6)	Light Gray (7)	Pale Green (8)	Pale Blue (9)
Off-white (10)	Medium Gray (11)	Dark Gray (12)	Red (13)	Green (14)
Yellow (15)	Blue (16)	Magenta (17)	Light Cyan (18)	White (19)

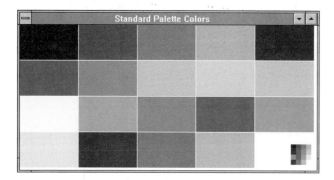

Figure 6.1: Windows stock palette colors (see key above)

Technically, the 20 standard colors belonging to the system palette are inviolable and cannot be altered by an application even when an application defines its own color values for these palette entries. Because color priority is given to the foreground application, however, and the application's palette takes priority over the standard palette, background displays may be remapped, appearing in whatever application colors provide the closest match to the standard colors—even when this results in a distinct change in appearance.

In some cases the color difference may be quite striking, such as when a 256-color bitmap is used as wallpaper and an application has defined its own 256-color palette. The ShowPCX demo program (in Chapter 8) will provide a striking example of this effect because, as ShowPCX is loading an image from the file (having already defined a new palette), the background image will be displayed using the application's palette. But, after the new image is displayed, the background colors should return to their original palette colors. Similar effects can be observed using a painting program such as ZSoft's PhotoFinish when multiple images are loaded or while switching between images when a few moments are required to switch between two or more quite different palettes.

THE COLOR1 PROGRAM

The Color1 program was created to demonstrate the Windows stock color palette as shown in Figure 6.1. Since the illustration is in black and white (well, halftone anyway), you'll have to rely on the actual program to show you the available colors.

Except for an optional icon, Color1.C has no menu, dialog boxes, or other resources. It is executed entirely within the exported WndProc procedure with a minimum of operations. Still, there are a few points of interest worth discussing, beginning with the GetSystemPaletteEntries function.

The GetSystemPaletteEntries function is used here, not to store the system palette colors, but to retrieve the system colors for display. But, before retrieving a palette, a means of storing this information is needed, and this is provided by the *HPALETTE hPal* variable.

```
long FAR PASCAL WndProc(...)
{
    HBRUSH        hBrush;
    HPEN          hPen;
    HDC           hdc;
    HPALETTE      hPal;
    PAINTSTRUCT   ps;
    static int    i, j, xSize, ySize;

    switch( msg )
    {
        case WM_SIZE: ...
        case WM_PAINT:
            hdc = BeginPaint( hwnd, &ps );
            GetSystemPaletteEntries( hdc, 0, 20, hPal );
```

A second requirement, before retrieving palette entries, is to have a handle to the device context—a provision that is accomplished by calling the Begin-Paint function. And, in addition to the device context, a range of palette entries is also required, in this case, beginning with 0 (the first palette entry) and extending through 20 entries (0..19).

After retrieving the palette colors, a simple double loop is provided to display these colors as a series of 20 rectangles using the CreatePen and Create-SolidBrush functions.

```
for( j=0; j<ySteps; j++ )
    for( i=0; i<xSteps; i++ )
    {
        hPen = SelectObject( hdc,
                    CreatePen( PS_SOLID, 1,
                            PalIndex ) );
        hBrush = SelectObject( hdc,
                    CreateSolidBrush( PalIndex ) );
```

Absolute RGB COLORREF values   Both CreatePen and CreateSolidBrush are called with a color reference parameter which conventionally, as in the WinMain() procedure, for example, is an RGB long integer following the form 0x00BBGGRR. Thus, for a white brush, the color value would be specified as 0x00FFFFFF or, for black, as 0x00000000.

In all cases, the most significant byte is zero while the red, green, and blue values are each specified by byte (eight-bit) values as previously described.

Palette index COLORREF values   In the Color1 example, instead of using absolute RGB values, a second COLORREF format is used in which the color parameter is a palette index. For palette index entries, the COLORREF value takes the form 0x0100iiii with the two low-order bytes (a 16-bit integer) providing an index to a logical palette—in this case, the palette retrieved using the GetSystemPaletteEntries function.

In the preceding fragment, this palette index is provided by a macro, PalIndex, which is defined as:

```
#define  PalIndex    0x01000000 + i + ( j * 5 )
```

Palette-relative RGB COLORREF values   Windows 3.x also supports a third format for specifying COLORREF values: the palette-relative RGB value. For this format, the high-order byte value is 2 and the COLORREF value has the format 0x02rrggbb. This format is used for output devices that support logical palettes, allowing Windows to match a palette-relative RGB value to the nearest actual color supported by the output device.

Alternatively, if the output device doesn't support a logical palette, Windows treats the palette-relative value as if it were an absolute RGB value; instead of palette mapping, Windows attempts to handle the RGB value directly.

PALETTE CAPABILITIES/LIMITATIONS/DITHERING

While individual palette colors can be assigned any of the 16 million possible hues, this does not guarantee that the physical display device is capable of displaying such a wide range of colors. As explained previously, this limitation is imposed by the graphics video card's limits much more than by the video monitor's. Most monitors are capable of near-infinite color resolution. Of course, a second limiting factor is also present: The human eye, even with excellent color vision, can only distinguish a fraction of the possible and supported hues.

Limitations imposed by the graphics hardware, however, can be circumvented through a process known as "dithering."

I'll use the Sunday comics and comic books as an introduction to the dithering process, even though the precise techniques are not the same. In the comic papers and in colored ads, a fairly wide range of colors are produced by combining three or four primary colors to create what the eye perceives as many gradations of color.

While the computer (or TV) screen creates colors by combining red, green, and blue light with a black background, printed materials use a white background and combine light-absorbing inks consisting of cyan, magenta, yellow, and black (CMYK). In this fashion, a strong brown, for example, is produced by placing dots of black or magenta and cyan over a near-solid yellow background, while a softer brown would consist of a halftone of yellow with fewer blacks. Similarly, pinks or certain fleshtones combine yellow and magenta dots with the white showing through while dark colors use greater or lesser degrees of black.

On the computer screen, the same principle applies, except that we are using lights in primary colors rather than their complements as inks. Figure 6.2 illustrates this principle by showing several dithered color patterns produced by the Color2 demo on an SVGA graphics system. Of course, in the samples shown, instead of being limited to three primary colors, the dithered patterns shown have a total of 20 main colors on SVGA (16 on EGA/VGA) to compose these patterns.

Figure 6.2: Sample dithered color patterns

In the illustrated dithered patterns, Windows was deliberately limited to using the default color palette (20 pure colors) even though the SVGA system could have defined and displayed any of the generated colors directly. Obviously doing so would have circumvented the purpose of this demo, which was to demonstrate both color specifications and to display dithering.

Although dither patterns are an artifact provided by Windows and do not require or demand your attention, there are several points that you should note:

▶ Dithered colors are always an 8-by-8 pattern, spreading the simulated color over a minimum area of 64 pixels. At the same time, dithering cannot be used for lines, which are always drawn using a primary hue supported by the display device.

▶ Even though 20 (or more) individual hues are available, dithered colors are composed of four individual shades. (These are not the same four shades in all cases.)

▶ While dithered colors will fill irregular outlines, individual pixels in the fill may combine (visually) with outlines or borders, creating some apparent irregularity.

Of course, dithering is not limited to color systems but is also applied to monochrome and gray-scaled displays, as will be discussed presently.

CREATING CUSTOM COLORS

The Color2 demo program (whose complete listing appears at the end of this chapter and on the program disk) shows how Windows translates color specifications into dithered color patterns. Figure 6.3 shows a simple program using three scroll bars to define the color components of an RGB specification with the resulting color displayed as a dithered background.

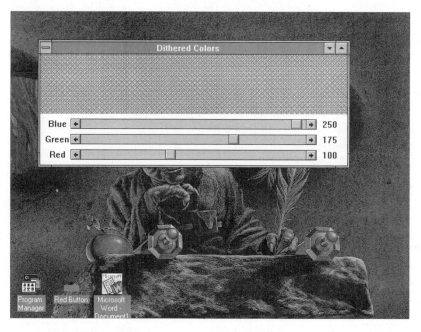

Figure 6.3: Custom RGB colors

The Color2 program uses three scroll bars to adjust the red, green, and blue components, then uses the resulting values as an RGB color to set the background brush, thus painting the window background with the selected color. Because the selected color has not been made a palette entry, however, Windows uses existing palette colors, dithering the window background to approximate the selected hue.

In many cases, dithered colors are perfectly acceptable and, chances are, if you are using an EGA/VGA display, the colored background of the window title bar of any application appears as a dithered color. Alternatively, on an SVGA system, this same hue will appear as palette entry No. 7 in the standard palette (as shown by the Color1 demo program), with no dithering required. But, the point is simple: The effect is the same in either case and produces no practical difference in the overall appearance of the application window.

In other cases, however, precise color control can be a very important element—or often the only important element. When this is the case, dithered colors just aren't in the running. It's either precise color control or nothing!

CHANGING PALETTE COLORS

When exact colors are required, the solution, of course, is to reset one or more palette entries to produce the desired hues. Although this sounds simple enough, in practice there are a few requirements and limitations.

The primary limitation is physical. Windows, no matter how sophisticated, cannot change the physical characteristics of the system video card. If the physical device only supports a palette of 16 colors, then only 16 custom colors can be displayed and all remaining palette entries will be mapped to the 16 supported physical colors. In like fashion, for an SVGA system, a physical palette limitation of 256 colors is imposed by the system hardware.

Of course, if you are using one of the new true-color video cards which, instead of palettes, support 24 bits of color information per pixel, then all of this becomes a moot point and you're perfectly free to write any information desired to the screen.

This particular freedom, however, applies to very few of us and, for all practical purposes, can be ignored. Either an application works with the hardware generally available and uses color palettes or the application works only with specialized hardware and lets you ignore palette requirements entirely.

Therefore, since most of our applications are bound by hardware limitations, the Color3 demo program combines elements of both the Color1 and Color2 demos to show handling for custom palette colors.

Palette color settings   In the Color1 demo, the standard palette was displayed as an array of color rectangles while in the Color2 demo, three scroll bars were used to select color settings for a single colored area that was displayed by dithering colors from the standard palette. In the Color3 demo, illustrated in

Figure 6.4, a new palette is created by using custom color settings that can be adjusted individually by using the same control set illustrated in Color2.

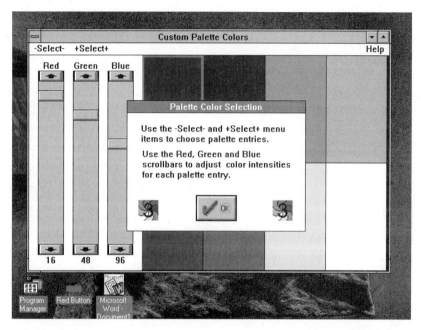

Figure 6.4: Custom palette colors

For demonstration purposes, the custom palette used will be limited to eight entries—a range that is supported by all video graphics cards and, at the same time, is large enough to compare several color rectangles while still small enough to present a clean display.

Three scroll bars control the red, green, and blue color specifications as well as showing the present levels. The *-Select-* and *+Select+* menu items step through the eight palette entries while the active selection is indicated by a gray outline. (The indicator outline is more readily distinguished on a color screen than in the black-and-white illustration.)

The first step in creating a custom palette requires a few declarations, such as

```
long FAR PASCAL WndProc( ... )
{
   static LPLOGPALETTE  lPal;
   ...
   HPALETTE    NewPal,  OldPal;
   HBRUSH      NewBrush, OldBrush;
```

```
HPEN          NewPen,   OldPen;
...
```

The *lPal* variable is a static pointer to a logical palette structure; the remaining variables provide handles (pointers) to two palettes, two brushes, and two pens, which will be used presently. Also defined but not shown is an array of color values that are used to initialize the color palette and to track changes in the color palette settings.

The logical palette structure (LOGPALETTE) referenced by *lPal* is defined in Windows.H as:

```
typedef struct
{
   WORD          palVersion;    // Win version (0x0300)
   WORD          palNumEntries; // size of array
   PALETTEENTRY  palPalEntry[]; // array of colors
} LOGPALETTE;
```

Nominally, the version number is 0x0300 (version 3.0) even if you are using Windows 3.1. The *palPalEntry* field specifies an array of PALETTEENTRY data structures defining the actual color entries. The PALETTEENTRY structure is defined as:

```
typedef struct
{
   BYTE  peRed;
   BYTE  peGreen;
   BYTE  peBlue;
   BYTE  peFlags;
} PALETTEENTRY;
```

The three color bytes accept values in the range 0..255 while the *peFlags* field accepts three flag values specifying how the palette entry will be used. Flag values are defined in Borland's *Windows API Reference Guide, Volume II*.

Much of the processing in Color3 should be familiar from earlier examples both in the present and preceding chapters. The principal elements relevant here are found in the WndProc procedure's message-handling provisions.

The initial provision is found in the response to the WM_CREATE message where memory allocation is made for the *lPal* palette structure and two initial values are assigned: the palette version and the number of entries in the palette.

```
switch( msg )
{
   case WM_CREATE:   // initialize the logical palette
      lPal = (LPLOGPALETTE)
         farmalloc( sizeof(LOGPALETTE) +
```

```
                sizeof(PALETTEENTRY) * 8 );
    1Pal->palVersion = 0x300;
    1Pal->palNumEntries = 8;
    return(0);
```

Next, in response to the WM_COMMAND message, the IDM_PLUS
(+*Select*+) and IDM_MINUS (-*Select*-) instructions step through the palette
entries but also update the positions of the three scroll bars and the text displays for each to correspond to the current palette settings.

```
case WM_COMMAND:
    switch( wParam )
    {
        case IDM_PLUS:
            nPal++;
            if( nPal >= 8 ) nPal = 0;
            ...
        case IDM_MINUS:
            nPal--;
            if( nPal < 0 ) nPal = 7;
            for( i=0; i<3; i++ )
            {
                SetScrollPos( hwndScrl[i], SB_CTL,
                            CVal[i][nPal], TRUE );
                SetWindowText( hwndVal[i],
                    itoa( CVal[i][nPal], szBuff, 10 ) );
            }
            InvalidateRect( hwnd, 0L, TRUE );
            break;
        case IDM_HELP: ...
    }
    return(0);
```

The scroll bars used for controls in both the Color2 and Color3 demos are
the Windows analog of a vernier or potentiometer control and should be familiar from many Windows applications. Most often, of course, scroll bars are
used to scroll a display window as, for example, in a text editor or a painting
program. The scroll bar feature, however, can be used in any context where a
variable control is needed.

Handling for the three scroll bars is found in three separate locations: in the
WinMain procedure where the scroll bars are created, and in two of the message responses in the WndProc procedure.

The first provision, at the same time the three scroll bars are created, is to assign a range to each scroll bar, consisting of minimum and maximum values.
In each of the scroll bars used, the range assigned is 0..255, corresponding to

the range of the RGB color values. Initial values (thumbpad positions) are also assigned at this time.

Next, in the response to the WM_SIZE message, the scroll bars are positioned and sized within the application window—a relatively simple procedure. Last, in the response to the WM_HSCROLL message, the position of each scroll bar's thumbpad is adjusted according to where the scroll bar was clicked or where the thumbpad was dragged.

The *CVal* variable consists of a three-by-eight array of byte values containing the RGB color values for the eight palette entries used.

The last provision in the WM_COMMAND handler—responding to the Help menu option—simply calls the dialog box shown in Figure 6.4.

The real work of displaying the palette occurs in response to the WM_PAINT message and begins, as usual, with a BeginPaint instruction. But, before painting anything, a loop is used to read the present values from the *CVal* array into the palette entries indicated by *lPal*.

```
case WM_PAINT:
    hdc = BeginPaint( hwnd, &ps );
    for( i=0; i<8; i++ )
    {
        lPal->palPalEntry[i].peRed   = CVal[0][i];
        lPal->palPalEntry[i].peGreen = CVal[1][i];
        lPal->palPalEntry[i].peBlue  = CVal[2][i];
        lPal->palPalEntry[i].peFlags = PC_RESERVED;
    }
    NewPal = CreatePalette( lPal );
    SelectPalette( hdc, NewPal, FALSE );
    RealizePalette( hdc );
```

After initializing the palette values (in memory), the CreatePalette function creates a new logical palette before the SelectPalette function is called to make *NewPal* the current palette. Optionally, SelectPalette returns a handle to the old (default) palette.

Last, RealizePalette is called to activate the newly selected palette—that is, to make this the current drawing palette within the present device-context handle (hdc).

At this point, the device-context handle is ready for drawing by using the new palette. The next segment of code consists of provisions for drawing the eight rectangles composing the palette display.

```
for( i=0; i<8; i++ )
{
    j = i % 4;   k = (int) i / 4;
```

```
    if( i == nPal )   // highlight selected color
        NewPen = CreatePen( PS_SOLID, 5,
                            0x007F7F7F );
    else       // Default is same color as palette.
        NewPen = CreatePen( PS_SOLID, 1,
                            PALETTEINDEX(i) );
    OldPen = SelectObject( hdc, NewPen );
    NewBrush =
        CreateSolidBrush( PALETTEINDEX(i) );
    OldBrush = SelectObject( hdc, NewBrush );
    Rectangle( hdc,
               xOffset + j * xSize,
               k * ySize,
               xOffset + ( j + 1 ) * xSize - 1,
               ( k + 1 ) * ySize - 1 );
```

Notice, within the loop, that a parallel to the CreatePalette/SelectPalette provisions is made for both the pen and the brush used to draw the rectangles. Handles to the original (default) pen and brush have been saved as the OldPen and OldBrush handles.

Default palette restoration   Within the current loop, the pen and brush will be changed a total of eight times, and in like fashion, the original pen and brush will be restored and the new pen and brush deleted, thus:

```
        SelectObject( hdc, OldBrush );
        DeleteObject( NewBrush );
        SelectObject( hdc, OldPen );
        DeleteObject( NewPen );
    }
    EndPaint( hwnd, &ps );
    DeleteObject( NewPal );
    return(0);
```

When the loop is finished, the same provisions are made for restoring the original palette and deleting the new palette structure.

Each of these provisions is every bit as important as creating a palette, pen, and brush in the first place because Windows can support only a limited number of handles to logical devices. If these handles are not released when not in use—and the originals restored—not only can the current application fail suddenly, but you can also leave Windows itself in a very hazardous state. (If you wish to experiment, simply comment out the restore provisions... but save your work first.)

Last, the new palette is deleted before the WM_PAINT message response is finished. But, at the same time, the memory allocated for the palette structure and the pointer *lPal* are not released; these remain available for further use and will be needed the next time the window is updated. All that has been lost is a temporary palette, a temporary pen, and a temporary brush while the originals have been restored, leaving the Windows system in the proper condition for other applications or for other actions by the present application.

Remember, restoring the original condition is not just good manners, it's essential.

There is also one more element of cleanup required, though this last is only necessary when the application exits and is handled in response to the WM_DESTROY message.

```
case WM_DESTROY:
    farfree( lPal );
    PostQuitMessage(0);
    return(0);
}
```

The WM_DESTROY message is an application's opportunity for final cleanup before exiting. In previous samples, it has responded simply by posting a quit message to notify any child processes of an impending exit (a standard default provision even if there are no child processes). In this case, however, this is the appropriate point in time to release the memory allocated for the palette structure as shown above—before notifying WinMain's message loop to exit.

All special brushes and pens and the logical palette have already been taken care of within the paint procedure, and this completes cleanup for the application.

GRAY-SCALING COLOR CONVERSIONS

In general, Windows already handles most gray-scale conversions, for color programs executing on monochrome video systems, without intervention or provision by the programmer.

Alternatively, on many plasma and LCD screens, even though the display is technically monochrome, the video system accepts color input information, variously translating the color data into 16, 32, or 64 gray scales—again without intervention or provision by the programmer.

At the same time, in either of these cases, not only is the process of converting colors to gray scale handled without the programmer's participation, but the programmer also is effectively forbidden to intervene in the process—aside, of course, from offering palette choices that produce the optimum in contrast and readability.

Circumstances still remain where programmers must supply their own gray-scale conversions. How they do so, however, depends entirely on the circumstances, the equipment, and the desired results. There are no hard and fast rules and there are no absolutes.

Following are a few options and provisions which can be used to produce gray-scale conversions. Of course, while these methods are directed principally toward hard-copy output devices (to printers, either dot-matrix, laserjet, or inkjet), the same techniques can also be applied to monitors.

GRAY-SCALE PALETTES

One popular method of treating gray-scale conversion is to create a palette of grays suitable for mapping the original color palette. As an example, assume a palette of 16 colors (as per EGA/VGA) which range from white to black. The obvious gray-scale palette for correspondence would be a 4-by-4 pixel (or dot) pattern as shown in Figure 6.5, following.

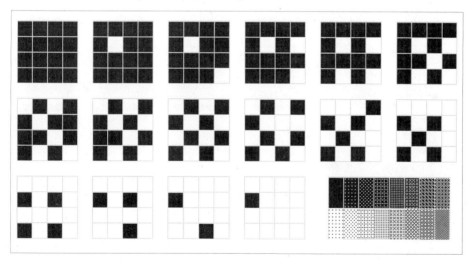

Figure 6.5: A 16-bit gray scale

As shown, the 16-bit patterns range from solid black to one-sixteenth black. (Reduced views of the same patterns appear at the lower right.) As an alternative, one of the intermittent patterns could be dropped to adjust the scale range from solid black to solid white.

Previously, however, as you should recall, dithered colors used an 8-by-8 pixel pattern, and applying similar patterns in black and white would offer a possible scale of 64 grays, either providing a wider range of grays or providing a finer texture for hard-copy output.

> **WARNING!** Adjacent elements in a 64-level gray-scale palette can be very difficult to distinguish. Select carefully.

TRUE-COLOR GRAY SCALES

The gray-scale patterns suggested form a uniform range which is about the best that can be accomplished with only 16 elements. Moving up to a 64-bit pattern, however, at least opens the possibility of matching the gray-scale density to the intensity (or darkness) of the color being mapped.

To do so, the first step is to understand a few basic principles of color perception. The human eye does not perceive all colors equally—not in terms of absolute intensity. Instead, of the three primary colors, red, green, and blue, the eye perceives green almost twice as strongly as red. In turn, the eye's blue response is approximately one-third the response to red. A gray-scale formula reflecting the perception curve of the human eye is approximated as: Red * 0.30 + Green * 0.59 + Blue * 0.11.

Thus, since Windows uses RGB values in the range 0..255, the gray equivalent matching a 24-bit-color specification becomes:

$$W = \frac{(R^* 0.30)}{(255)} + \frac{(G^* 0.59)}{(255)} + \frac{(B^* 0.11)}{(255)}$$

If R, G, and B are all at maximum—255—then the result is white on the screen while the formula shown yields a value of 100.0 percent white, 0.0 percent black.

$$W = \frac{(192^* 0.30)}{255} + \frac{(128^* 0.59)}{255} + \frac{(64^* 0.11)}{255} = \ldots$$

As a more relevant example, applying this formula to the palette entry shown in Figure 6.4 (a light brown was shown as the active palette entry 0), the equivalent proportions of white to black can be calculated thus:

$$\ldots = 0.226 + 0.296 + 0.0276 = 54.96 \text{ percent White}$$

Since the gray scale is being calculated for a percentage of black, 45.04 percent of the gray bit pattern should be black. Thus, assuming an 8-by-8-bit pattern, the optimum gray would be 29 parts black (ink) versus 35 parts white (paper).

Again referring to Figure 6.4, on screen, the light brown field is surrounded by a gray outline with an intensity level equivalent to 50 percent white, which is gray-scaled—again on the 64-bit pattern—as 32 parts black to 32 parts white. And, as you may observe, this does not provide a strong contrast, as a gray scale, to the light brown which it surrounds.

Still, this process provides an optimum match between shades of gray and color intensities, while a similar process is used in newspaper halftones and other black-and-white reproduction methods.

GRAY SCALES AND PLAIDS

There is one hazard inherent in using gray scales on black-and-white output devices: *plaiding*, which occurs when the gray-scale pattern is not matched to the device resolution. Figure 6.6 shows an example of plaiding, not on the printer, but deliberately produced on the screen—which goes to show that video devices are no more immune than printers.

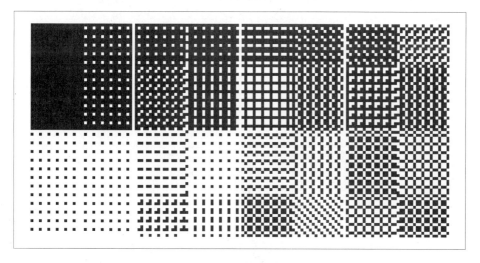

Figure 6.6: Plaiding in gray scales

The illustration shown in Figure 6.6 is an excerpt from Figure 6.5, enlarged to show the mismatch between the image's dot pattern and the screen resolution. As a simple rule of thumb, to prevent plaiding, the pixel dimension of the image, after conversion to gray scale, should always be an even multiple of the dot resolution of the reproduction size.

As an example, assume a 200-by-150-pixel bitmap is converted to a 16-shade gray scale. After conversion, the result is 800 by 600 pixels. Now, to reproduce this image on a laser printer with a resolution of 300 dpi, without plaiding, the minimum size would be 2.6666 inches wide by 2 inches high for a printed image size of 800 by 600 dots. Or, for a larger image, an image 8 inches wide by 6 inches high would also fit with the image scaled to 2,400 by 1,800 dots.

Alternatively, if the image used a 64-shade gray scale, the smallest acceptable image would be 5.333 inches by 4 inches.

Of course, how you employ gray-scaling is up to you and your requirements. Moreover, if you are content with Windows's conversion capabilities, you will probably have little need for this facility. Still, if you need it, you now have the basics for color to gray scale conversion.

Summary

Colors and color handling, under Windows, are a distinct departure from color procedures used under DOS. In part, this results in some additional complexity for the programmer but, overall, provides greater flexibility by virtue of the fact that the application programmer no longer has to make separate provisions for various hardware capabilities. Rather, the programmer is free to devote his or her time to the application's principal objectives instead of trying to provide for a myriad of display systems.

Between color palettes, custom colors, and gray-scale conversions, the basic tools for Windows graphics are fairly complete. Therefore, in Chapter 7, the topic will move from features of the Windows API functions to applying these functions—first, to capturing and restoring screen images and then, in later chapters, to more advanced techniques for manipulating images and image information.

Program listing of Color1.C

```
//====================//
//      Color1.C      //
//  Standard Colors   //
//====================//

#include <windows.h>
#include <stdlib.h>

#define  PalIndex     0x01000000 + i + ( j * 5 )
    // PalIndex returns a value in the range 0..19 in the
    // low byte while the high byte indicates this is a
    // palette index value ...
#define  xSteps       5
```

```
#define  ySteps       4

long FAR PASCAL WndProc( HWND hwnd,    WORD msg,
                         WORD wParam, LONG lParam )
{
   HBRUSH        hBrush;
   HPEN          hPen;
   HDC           hdc;
   PAINTSTRUCT   ps;
   static int    i, j, xSize, ySize;

   switch( msg )
   {
      case WM_SIZE:
            // rescale display when window size changes
         xSize = ( LOWORD( lParam ) ) / xSteps;
         ySize = ( HIWORD( lParam ) ) / ySteps;
         return(0);

      case WM_PAINT:
            // display first twenty system palette entries
         hdc = BeginPaint( hwnd, &ps );
         for( j=0; j<ySteps; j++ )
            for( i=0; i<xSteps; i++ )
            {
               hPen = SelectObject( hdc,
                        CreatePen( PS_SOLID, 1,
                                   PalIndex ) );
               hBrush = SelectObject( hdc,
                          CreateSolidBrush( PalIndex ) );
               Rectangle( hdc,
                          i * xSize,
                          j * ySize,
                          ( i + 1 ) * xSize - 1,
                          ( j + 1 ) * ySize - 1 );
               DeleteObject( hPen );
               DeleteObject( hBrush );
                  // delete graphics objects after use
            }
         EndPaint( hwnd, &ps );
         return(0);

      case WM_DESTROY:
         PostQuitMessage(0);
         return(0);
   }
```

```
      return( DefWindowProc( hwnd, msg, wParam, lParam ) );
}

#pragma argsused
                              // stock WinMain procedure
int PASCAL WinMain( HANDLE hInst, HANDLE hPrevInst,
               LPSTR  lpCmd, int    nCmdShow )
{
   static char szAppName[] = "COLOR1";
   HWND       hwnd;
   MSG        msg;
   int        i;
   WNDCLASS   wc;

   if( ! hPrevInst )
   {
      wc.hInstance     = hInst;
      wc.lpfnWndProc   = WndProc;
      wc.cbClsExtra    = 0;
      wc.cbWndExtra    = 0;
      wc.lpszClassName = szAppName;
      wc.hIcon         = LoadIcon( hInst, szAppName );
      wc.lpszMenuName  = (LPSTR) szAppName;
      wc.hCursor       = LoadCursor( NULL, IDC_ARROW );
      wc.hbrBackground = GetStockObject( WHITE_BRUSH );
      wc.style         = CS_HREDRAW | CS_VREDRAW;
      RegisterClass( &wc );
   }
   hwnd = CreateWindow( szAppName,
            "Standard Palette Colors",
            WS_OVERLAPPEDWINDOW | WS_CLIPCHILDREN,
            CW_USEDEFAULT, CW_USEDEFAULT,
            CW_USEDEFAULT, CW_USEDEFAULT,
            NULL, NULL, hInst, NULL  );
   ShowWindow(   hwnd, nCmdShow );
   UpdateWindow( hwnd );
   while( GetMessage( &msg, NULL, 0, 0 ) )
   {
      TranslateMessage( &msg );
      DispatchMessage(  &msg );
   }
   return( msg.wParam );
}


;===============================
;  COLOR1.DEF
;===============================
```

```
NAME          COLOR1

DESCRIPTION   "Standard Color Palette"
EXETYPE       WINDOWS
STUB          "WINSTUB.EXE"
CODE          PRELOAD MOVEABLE DISCARDABLE
DATA          PRELOAD MOVEABLE MULTIPLE
HEAPSIZE      1024
STACKSIZE     8192
EXPORTS       WndProc
```

PROGRAM LISTING OF COLOR2.C

```
//================//
//   Color2.C     //
// Custom Colors  //
//================//

#include <windows.h>
#include <stdlib.h>

#define  CHILD_STYLE    WS_CHILD | WS_VISIBLE
#define  MIN( i )       min( 255, i + 1 )
#define  MAX( i )       max(   0, i - 1 )

HWND      hwndScrl[3], hwndTag[3], hwndVal[3], hwndRect;
int       nFocus, CVal[3] = { 100, 175, 250 };
char      szBuff[10];

long FAR PASCAL WndProc( HWND hwnd,    WORD msg,
                         WORD wParam, LONG lParam )
{
   HDC           hdc;
   int           i, cxWnd, cyWnd, cyChr, cxChr, OrgY;
   TEXTMETRIC    tm;

   switch( msg )
   {
     case WM_SIZE:
             // rescale display when window size changes
         cxWnd = LOWORD( lParam );
         cyWnd = HIWORD( lParam );
         hdc = GetDC( hwnd );
         GetTextMetrics( hdc, &tm );
         cyChr = tm.tmHeight;
```

```
cxChr = tm.tmAveCharWidth;
ReleaseDC( hwnd, hdc );
   // resize the main display
MoveWindow( hwndRect,              // window handle
            0,                     // x origin
            cyWnd - 5 * cyChr,     // y origin
            cxChr,                 // width
            cyWnd,                 // height
            TRUE );                // repaint flag
for( i=0; i<=2; i++ )
{
   OrgY = cyWnd - ( (i +1) * 1.5 * cyChr );
      // for each of the scrollbars ...
      // ... reposition and resize scrollbar ...
   MoveWindow(
      hwndScrl[i],              // scrollbar handle
      7 * cxChr,                // x origin
      OrgY,                     // y origin
      cxWnd - ( 14 * cyChr ),   // width
      ScyChr,                   // height
      TRUE );                   // repaint flag
      // ... reposition label ...
   MoveWindow(   hwndTag[i],
      cxChr,
      OrgY,
      cxChr * 6,
      cyChr,
      TRUE );
      // ... and reposition number value
   MoveWindow(   hwndVal[i],
      cxWnd - 7 * cxChr
      OrgY,
      cxChr * 6,
      cyChr,
      TRUE );
}
SetFocus( hwnd );
return(0);

case WM_HSCROLL:        // handle scrollbar settings
                        // and reset display color
   i = GetWindowWord( HIWORD( lParam ), GWW_ID );
   switch( wParam )
   {
      case SB_PAGEDOWN:
         CVal[i] += 15;           // no break!
```

```
          case SB_LINEDOWN:
              CVal[i]  = MIN( CVal[i] );    break;
          case SB_PAGEUP:
              CVal[i] -= 15;            // no break!
          case SB_LINEUP:
              CVal[i]  = MAX( CVal[i] );    break;
          case SB_TOP:
              CVal[i]  =   Ø;               break;
          case SB_BOTTOM:
              CVal[i]  = 255;              break;
          case SB_THUMBPOSITION:
          case SB_THUMBTRACK:
              CVal[i] = LOWORD( lParam );   break;
          default:                          break;
      }
      SetScrollPos( hwndScrl[i], SB_CTL,
                    CVal[i], TRUE );
      SetWindowText( hwndVal[i],
                     itoa( CVal[i], szBuff, 1Ø ) );
      DeleteObject( GetClassWord( hwnd,
                      GCW_HBRBACKGROUND ) );
          // delete background brush
      SetClassWord( hwnd, GCW_HBRBACKGROUND,
          CreateSolidBrush(
             RGB( CVal[Ø], CVal[1], CVal[2] ) ) );
             // create a new brush using the
             // new RGB color value settings
      InvalidateRect( hwnd, ØL, TRUE );
             // repaint window with new brush
      return(Ø);

   case WM_DESTROY:
      DeleteObject( GetClassWord( hwnd,
                    GCW_HBRBACKGROUND ) );
          // delete the background brush
      PostQuitMessage(Ø);
      return(Ø);
   }
   return( DefWindowProc( hwnd, msg, wParam, lParam ) );
      // Since only stock objects are used in this demo,
      // WM_PAINT messages can be handled by the default
}     // Windows procedures; no special handling required.

#pragma argsused

int PASCAL WinMain( HANDLE hInst, HANDLE hPrevInst,
```

```
              LPSTR    lpCmd, int    nCmdShow )
   {
      static char szAppName[] = "COLOR2";
      static char *szColorLabel[] =
                    { "Red", "Green", "Blue"  };
      HWND       hwnd;
      MSG        msg;
      int        i;
      WNDCLASS   wc;

      if( ! hPrevInst )
      {
         wc.hInstance    = hInst;
         wc.lpfnWndProc  = WndProc;
         wc.cbClsExtra   = 0;
         wc.cbWndExtra   = 0;
         wc.lpszClassName = szAppName;
         wc.hIcon        = LoadIcon( hInst, szAppName );
         wc.lpszMenuName = (LPSTR) szAppName;
         wc.hCursor      = LoadCursor( 0L, IDC_ARROW );
         wc.hbrBackground =
              CreateSolidBrush(
                 RGB( CVal[0], CVal[1], CVal[2] ) );
         wc.style         = CS_HREDRAW | CS_VREDRAW;
         RegisterClass( &wc );
      }
      hwnd = CreateWindow( szAppName, "Dithered Colors",
               WS_OVERLAPPEDWINDOW | WS_CLIPCHILDREN,
               CW_USEDEFAULT, CW_USEDEFAULT,
               500, 200,
               0L, 0L, hInst, 0L  );
      hwndRect = CreateWindow( "static", 0L,
                  CHILD_STYLE | SS_WHITERECT,
                  0, 0, 0, 0, hwnd, 10, hInst, 0L );
      lpfnKeybdProc =
         MakeProcInstance( (FARPROC) KeybdProc, hInst );
      for( i=0; i<=2; i++ )
      {
          // create a series of child windows to handle the
          // scrollbars, titles, and values displayed
         hwndScrl[i] =
            CreateWindow( "scrollbar", 0L,
               CHILD_STYLE | WS_TABSTOP | SBS_HORZ,
               0, 0, 0, 0, hwnd, i,   hInst, 0L );
         hwndTag[i]  =
            CreateWindow( "static",   szColorLabel[i],
```

```
                CHILD_STYLE | SS_CENTER,
                0, 0, 0, 0, hwnd, i+4, hInst, 0L );
        hwndVal[i]  =
            CreateWindow( "static",
                itoa( CVal[i], szBuff, 10 ),
                CHILD_STYLE | SS_CENTER,
                0, 0, 0, 0, hwnd, i+7, hInst, 0L );
            // No positions or sizes are assigned when these
            // child windows are created -- instead, these
            // are set in WndProc in response to the WM_SIZE
            // message.
        lpScrlFnc[i] =
            (FARPROC) GetWindowLong( hwndScrl[i],
                                    GWL_WNDPROC );
            // assign a default handler for each scrollbar
        SetWindowLong( hwndScrl[i], GWL_WNDPROC,
                        (LONG) lpfnKeybdProc );
        SetScrollRange( hwndScrl[i], SB_CTL,
                        0, 255, FALSE );
        SetScrollPos(   hwndScrl[i], SB_CTL,
                        CVal[i], FALSE );
    }
    ShowWindow(   hwnd, nCmdShow );
    UpdateWindow( hwnd );
    while( GetMessage( &msg, 0L, 0, 0 ) )
    {
        TranslateMessage( &msg );
        DispatchMessage(  &msg );
    }
    return( msg.wParam );
}


;============================
;  COLOR2.DEF
;============================

NAME            COLOR2

DESCRIPTION     "Custom Colors"
EXETYPE         WINDOWS
STUB            "WINSTUB.EXE"
CODE            PRELOAD MOVEABLE DISCARDABLE
DATA            PRELOAD MOVEABLE MULTIPLE
HEAPSIZE        1024
STACKSIZE       8192
EXPORTS         WndProc
```

Program listing of Color3.C

```
//==================//
//     Color3.C     //
//  Windows Colors  //
//==================//

#include <alloc.h>
#include <windows.h>
#include <stdlib.h>
#include <bwcc.h>
#include "color3.h"

#define  PalIndex      0x01000000 + i + ( j * 5 )
#define  xSteps        4
#define  ySteps        2
#define  CHILD_STYLE   WS_CHILD | WS_VISIBLE
#define  MIN( i )      min( 255, i + 1 )
#define  MAX( i )      max(   0, i - 1 )

FARPROC  lpScrlFnc[3];
HWND     hwndScrl[3], hwndTag[3], hwndVal[3], hwndRect;
HANDLE   hInst;
char     szBuff[10];
static int  nFocus, nPal = 0, CVal[3][8]  =
        { 0x00, 0x00, 0x00, 0x00, 0xFF, 0xFF, 0xFF, 0xFF,
          0x00, 0x00, 0xFF, 0xFF, 0x00, 0x00, 0xFF, 0xFF,
          0x00, 0xFF, 0x00, 0xFF, 0x00, 0xFF, 0x00, 0xFF };
   // create an array RGB color values with initial values

long FAR PASCAL KeybdProc( HWND hwnd,    WORD msg,
                           WORD wParam, LONG lParam )
{
   int i = GetWindowWord( hwnd, GWW_ID );
   switch( msg )
   {
      case WM_KEYDOWN:
         if( wParam == VK_TAB )
         {
            if( GetKeyState( VK_SHIFT ) ) i--;
                                    else i++;
            if( i < 0 ) i = 2;
            else
            if( i > 2 ) i = 0;
            SetFocus( hwndScrl[ i % 3 ] );
         } break;
```

```
        case WM_SETFOCUS:  nFocus = i;  break;
    }
    return( CallWindowProc( lpScrlFnc[i], hwnd, msg,
                            wParam, lParam ) );
}

#pragma argsused

BOOL FAR PASCAL HelpProc( HWND hDlg,   WORD msg,
                          WORD wParam, LONG lParam )
{
    switch( msg )
    {
        case WM_INITDIALOG:  return( TRUE );
        case WM_COMMAND:
            switch( wParam )
            {
                case IDOK: EndDialog( hDlg, TRUE );
                           return( TRUE );
                default: return( TRUE );
    }    }
    return( FALSE );
}


long FAR PASCAL WndProc( HWND hwnd,   WORD msg,
                         WORD wParam, LONG lParam )
{
    static LPLOGPALETTE  lPal;
    static int           i, j, k,  xSize, ySize, xOffset,
                         cxWnd, cyWnd, cyChr, cxChr;
    FARPROC        lpProc;
    HPALETTE       NewPal;
    HBRUSH         NewBrush, OldBrush;
    HPEN           NewPen,  OldPen;
    HDC            hdc;
    PAINTSTRUCT    ps;
    TEXTMETRIC     tm;

    switch( msg )
    {
        case WM_CREATE:    // initialize the logical palette
            lPal = (LPLOGPALETTE)
                farmalloc( sizeof(LOGPALETTE) +
                           sizeof(PALETTEENTRY) * 8 );
            lPal->palVersion = 0x300;
            lPal->palNumEntries = 8;
```

```
            return(0);

        case WM_COMMAND:    // handle menu bar selections
            switch( wParam )
            {
              case IDM_PLUS:
                nPal++;
                if( nPal >= 8 ) nPal = 0;
                for( i=0; i<3; i++ )
                {
                    SetScrollPos( hwndScrl[i], SB_CTL,
                                    CVal[i][nPal], TRUE );
                    SetWindowText( hwndVal[i],
                                    itoa( CVal[i][nPal],
                                        szBuff, 10 ) );
                }
                InvalidateRect( hwnd, 0L, TRUE );
                break;
              case IDM_MINUS:
                nPal--;
                if( nPal < 0 ) nPal = 7;
                for( i=0; i<3; i++ )
                {
                    SetScrollPos( hwndScrl[i], SB_CTL,
                                    CVal[i][nPal], TRUE );
                    SetWindowText( hwndVal[i],
                                    itoa( CVal[i][nPal],
                                        szBuff, 10 ) );
                }
                InvalidateRect( hwnd, 0L, TRUE );
                break;
              case IDM_HELP:
                lpProc =
                    MakeProcInstance( HelpProc, hInst );
                DialogBox( hInst, "COLOR3", hwnd, lpProc );
                FreeProcInstance( lpProc );
                InvalidateRect( hwnd, 0L, TRUE );
                break;
            }
            return(0);

        case WM_PAINT:
            hdc = BeginPaint( hwnd, &ps );
            for( i=0; i<8; i++ )
            {
                lPal->palPalEntry[i].peRed   = CVal[0][i];
```

```
      lPal->palPalEntry[i].peGreen = CVal[1][i];
      lPal->palPalEntry[i].peBlue  = CVal[2][i];
      lPal->palPalEntry[i].peFlags = PC_RESERVED;
   }
   NewPal = CreatePalette( lPal );
   SelectPalette( hdc, NewPal, FALSE );
   RealizePalette( hdc );
   for( i=0; i<8; i++ )
   {
      j = i % 4;
      k = (int) i / 4;
      if( i == nPal )
         NewPen = CreatePen( PS_SOLID, 5,
                             0x007F7F7F );
      else
         NewPen = CreatePen( PS_SOLID, 1,
                             PALETTEINDEX(i) );
      OldPen = SelectObject( hdc, NewPen );

      NewBrush = CreateSolidBrush(PALETTEINDEX(i));
      OldBrush = SelectObject( hdc, NewBrush );

      Rectangle( hdc,
                 xOffset + j * xSize,
                 k * ySize,
                 xOffset + ( j + 1 ) * xSize - 1,
                 ( k + 1 ) * ySize - 1 );
      SelectObject( hdc, OldBrush );
      DeleteObject( NewBrush );
      SelectObject( hdc, OldPen );
      DeleteObject( NewPen );
   }
   EndPaint( hwnd, &ps );
   DeleteObject( NewPal );
   return(0);

case WM_SIZE:
   cxWnd = LOWORD( lParam );
   cyWnd = HIWORD( lParam );

   hdc = GetDC( hwnd );
   GetTextMetrics( hdc, &tm );
   cyChr = tm.tmHeight;
   cxChr = tm.tmAveCharWidth;
   ReleaseDC( hwnd, hdc );
   xOffset = cxChr * 26;
```

```
        xSize = ( cxWnd - xOffset ) / xSteps;
        ySize =  cyWnd / ySteps;
        MoveWindow( hwndRect, 0, 0,
                    cxChr * 26, cyWnd, TRUE );
        for( i=0; i<=2; i++ )
        {
            MoveWindow( hwndTag[i],
                        cxChr * ( ( i * 8 ) + 2 ),
                        cyChr * 0.5,
                        cxChr * 6,
                        cyChr,
                        TRUE );
            MoveWindow( hwndVal[i],
                        cxChr * ( ( i * 8 ) + 2 ),
                        cyWnd - ( cyChr * 1.5 ),
                        cxChr * 6,
                        cyChr,
                        TRUE );
            MoveWindow( hwndScrl[i],
                        cxChr * ( ( i * 8 ) + 2 ),
                        cyChr * 1.5,
                        cxChr * 6,
                        cyWnd - ( 3 * cyChr ),
                        TRUE );
        }
        SetFocus( hwnd );
        return(0);

    case WM_VSCROLL:
        i = GetWindowWord( HIWORD( lParam ), GWW_ID );
        switch( wParam )
        {
            case SB_PAGEDOWN:
                CVal[i][nPal] += 15;      // no break!
            case SB_LINEDOWN:
                CVal[i][nPal]  = MIN( CVal[i][nPal] );
                                          break;
            case SB_PAGEUP:
                CVal[i][nPal] -= 15;      // no break!
            case SB_LINEUP:
                CVal[i][nPal]  = MAX( CVal[i][nPal] );
                                          break;
            case SB_TOP:
                CVal[i][nPal]  =  0;      break;
            case SB_BOTTOM:
```

```
                CVal[i][nPal]  = 255;            break;
            case SB_THUMBPOSITION:
            case SB_THUMBTRACK:
                CVal[i][nPal] = LOWORD( lParam );
                                                break;
        }
        SetScrollPos( hwndScrl[i], SB_CTL,
                    CVal[i][nPal], TRUE );
        SetWindowText( hwndVal[i],
                    itoa( CVal[i][nPal],
                    szBuff, 10 ) );
        InvalidateRect( hwnd, 0L, TRUE );
        return(0);

    case WM_DESTROY:
        farfree( lPal );
        PostQuitMessage(0);
        return(0);
    }
    return( DefWindowProc( hwnd, msg, wParam, lParam ) );
}

#pragma argsused

int PASCAL WinMain( HANDLE hInstance, HANDLE hPrevInst,
                    LPSTR  lpCmd,      int    nCmdShow )
{
    static char szAppName[] = "COLOR3";
    static char *szColorLabel[] =
                    { "Red", "Green", "Blue" };
    FARPROC     lpfnKeybdProc;
    HWND        hwnd;
    MSG         msg;
    int         i;
    WNDCLASS    wc;

    if( ! hPrevInst )
    {
        wc.hInstance      = hInstance;
        wc.lpfnWndProc    = WndProc;
        wc.cbClsExtra     = 0;
        wc.cbWndExtra     = 0;
        wc.lpszClassName  = szAppName;
        wc.hIcon          = LoadIcon( hInst, szAppName );
        wc.lpszMenuName   = (LPSTR) szAppName;
        wc.hCursor        = LoadCursor( 0L, IDC_ARROW );
```

```
        wc.hbrBackground = CreateSolidBrush( WHITE_BRUSH );
        wc.style         = CS_HREDRAW | CS_VREDRAW;
        RegisterClass( &wc );
    }
    hInst = hInstance;
    hwnd = CreateWindow( szAppName,
                "Custom Palette Colors",
                WS_OVERLAPPEDWINDOW | WS_CLIPCHILDREN,
                CW_USEDEFAULT, CW_USEDEFAULT,
                CW_USEDEFAULT, CW_USEDEFAULT,
                ØL, ØL, hInst, ØL  );

    hwndRect = CreateWindow( "static", ØL,
                            CHILD_STYLE | SS_WHITERECT,
                            Ø, Ø, Ø, Ø,
                            hwnd, 10, hInst, ØL );
    lpfnKeybdProc = MakeProcInstance( (FARPROC) KeybdProc,
                                    hInstance );
    for( i=Ø; i<=2; i++ )
    {
        hwndScrl[i] =
            CreateWindow( "scrollbar", ØL,
                CHILD_STYLE | WS_TABSTOP | SBS_VERT,
                Ø, Ø, Ø, Ø, hwnd, i,   hInstance, ØL );
        hwndTag[i]  =
            CreateWindow( "static",    szColorLabel[i],
                CHILD_STYLE | SS_CENTER,
                Ø, Ø, Ø, Ø, hwnd, i+4, hInstance, ØL );
        hwndVal[i]  =
            CreateWindow( "static",
                itoa( CVal[i][nPal], szBuff, 10 ),
                CHILD_STYLE | SS_CENTER,
                Ø, Ø, Ø, Ø, hwnd, i+7, hInstance, ØL );
        lpScrlFnc[i] =
            (FARPROC) GetWindowLong( hwndScrl[i],
                                    GWL_WNDPROC );
        SetWindowLong( hwndScrl[i], GWL_WNDPROC,
                    (LONG) lpfnKeybdProc );
        SetScrollRange( hwndScrl[i], SB_CTL,
                    Ø, 255, FALSE );
        SetScrollPos(   hwndScrl[i], SB_CTL,
                    CVal[i][nPal], FALSE );
    }
    ShowWindow(   hwnd, nCmdShow );
    UpdateWindow( hwnd );
    while( GetMessage( &msg, ØL, Ø, Ø ) )
```

```
    {
        TranslateMessage( &msg );
        DispatchMessage(  &msg );
    }
    return( msg.wParam );
}

//================
//  Color3.H
//================

#define IDM_PLUS  201
#define IDM_MINUS 202
#define IDM_HELP  203


;==============================
;  COLOR3.DEF
;==============================

NAME          COLOR3

DESCRIPTION   "Custom Colors"
EXETYPE       WINDOWS
STUB          "WINSTUB.EXE"
CODE          PRELOAD MOVEABLE DISCARDABLE
DATA          PRELOAD MOVEABLE MULTIPLE
HEAPSIZE      1024
STACKSIZE     8192
EXPORTS       WndProc
              KeybdProc
              HelpProc
```

Part 3

Beyond the GDI

GRAPHICS UTILITIES

ALTERNATIVE IMAGE FORMATS

IMAGE ENHANCEMENT

PRINTING GRAPHICS

CURSORS, BITMAPS, AND SIMPLE IMAGE
  ANIMATIONS

INTERACTIVE IMAGES

BITMAPS IN BUSINESS APPLICATIONS

GRAPHIC SIMULATIONS

SUPER VGA (SVGA) GRAPHICS FOR
  MS-DOS AND WINDOWS

Graphics Utilities

Before computers acquired video terminals—yes, there was such a time, though most of us have happily forgotten those days— computer graphics were pretty simple. They generally consisted of ingenious printed graphs using the standard characters supported by hard-copy devices. Granted, there were also some rather expensive devices known as plotters which, while slow, were somewhat less limited than most printers, but most hard-copy devices were simply glorified typewriters or, for some, converted teletype printers.

As dot-matrix printers appeared, there was a small but determined stampede attempting to extend the internal character sets, first in the form of the extended ASCII (graphics) characters and then in the form of direct control over the printer heads to produce graphics dot images.

Later, even after video monitors became common, graphics remained fairly restricted. Even sophisticated applications relied on elaborate use of the extended ASCII character set—with or without reverse video—to present semi-graphic title screens. This restriction was not due to any lack of expertise by the developers, of course, but simply because programmers could not count on the end user's equipment to support elaborate graphic displays.

At the same time, for those who had equipment capable of graphic displays, a variety of formats were developed for saving, storing, and displaying graphics images. While Windows has its own "native" .BMP (or bitmap) format, a number of popular formats predated Windows, including ZSoft's Paintbrush's .PCX, CompuServe's GIF (Graphics Information Format) and, for more demanding circumstances, Truevision Inc.'s TARGA or TGA formats.

These formats have one factor in common: Each is designed for a specific image type or system. Truevision's TGA images, for example, are designed for video-camera images, generally incorporating 16-, 24- or 32-bit color per pixel. In contrast, ZSoft's .PCX, CompuServe's GIF, and Windows's native .BMP formats are palette-based, encoding images by first including palette information in the image file and then referencing the individual pixels as palette colors.

On the other hand, the TIFF format—discussed in Chapter 8, and one of the few successful standards ever developed by committee—incorporates a variety of methods for describing images and, depending on the implementation, may provide several different means of data compression.

This is not to say or imply that other graphics formats lack image compression. Virtually all systems include at least one method for compacting data to save space—a topic which will be discussed later in this chapter. Instead, the real contrast found in the TIFF format is simply that it provides a collection of formats and of compression methods such that different methods and formats can be used as demanded by circumstance. Remember, however, that these are provisions only of the TIFF specification. No actual implementation of the TIFF image software includes all possible formats or compression schemes.

Capturing and displaying screen images

Under Windows, where all displays are graphical in nature, a graphics screen-capture utility can be a basic tool for tranferring graphic information between applications or simply saving images for further use. At the same time, while capturing a screen under DOS can be a relatively involved procedure, the equivalent process under Windows is greatly expedited and simplified by features inherent within Windows.

Principal among these is the Windows Clipboard feature, a facility that provides both storage and information transfer between Windows applications. Although the Clipboard handles several types of information, each with a separate format, only the graphics image or bitmap format is relevant at this time.

The use of the Clipboard both to store a bitmap and to display a bitmap held by the Clipboard is demonstrated by the Capture1 program as shown—doubly—in Figure 7.1.

Figure 7.1 is not a trick but an actual screen display in which both Capture1 and Capture2—appearing later in this chapter—were loaded, then Capture1 was used to capture a portion of the screen, copying the captured area to the

Clipboard in bitmap format. Both programs were needed, of course, because the active copy—the copy executing the screen capture—removes itself from the screen (by reducing itself to an icon) during the capture process.

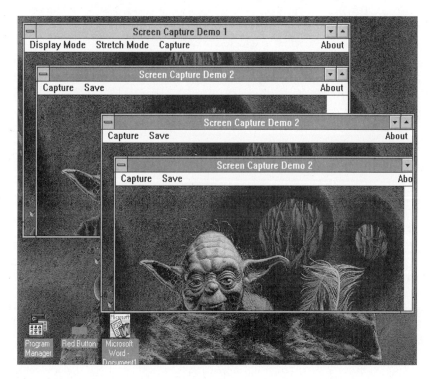

Figure 7.1: Self-referential screen captures

When the process is finished, however, the capturing copy of the application is restored to its previous size and, at this time, displays the captured area. But, when the second copy of the application becomes active, this copy will also display the same Clipboard contents as the first. Alternatively, if a different utility were used to capture a bitmap to the Clipboard, both utilities would display this image—or any other image which had been loaded into the Clipboard.

Other types of information loaded to the Clipboard—data, metafiles, or other non-bitmap formats—are ignored entirely. The Capture1 utility only stores and retrieves information that is in bitmap format.

CAPTURING AND WRITING BITMAP INFORMATION

Screen capture is based on rectangular coordinates that define the area to be copied to the Clipboard and to the Capture1 program display. To accomplish this task, three main provisions are made within the program: a means of selecting starting and ending coordinates; a method of indicating the selected area; and a provision to copy the selected area to the Clipboard.

In operation, the first provision involves one of two triggers: selecting the Capture menu item or clicking the left mouse button to initialize the capture mode. The following excerpt shows the initial response to the WM_COMMAND message IDM_CAPTURE:

```
case WM_COMMAND:
   switch( wParam )
   {
      ...
      case IDM_CAPTURE:
         ptStart.x = ptStart.y = ptFinish.x =
         ptFinish.y = 0;
         PostMessage( hwnd, WM_LBUTTONDOWN, 0L, 0L );
         break;
```

The response to the Capture menu command is quite simple. First, the *ptStart* and *ptFinish* coordinates are initialized as zero, then a WM_LBUTTONDOWN message is posted to the application message queue, simulating the left mouse button.

```
case WM_LBUTTONDOWN:
   if( ! fStart )
   {
      fStart = TRUE;
      SetCapture( hwnd );
      SetCursor( LoadCursor( NULL, IDC_CROSS ) );
      CloseWindow( hwnd );
      InvertBlock( hwnd, ptStart, ptFinish );
         // invert selected area on screen
   }
   else ...
```

In response to the WM_LBUTTONDOWN, the first step, calling SetCapture, ensures that the present window captures all subsequent mouse input, even after the CloseWindow call reduces the Capture1 window to an icon. In this fashion, the application is able to take control of the mouse even when the mouse is outside of the application's window—such as when the window is reduced to an icon.

The final provision, InvertBlock, calls a local subprocedure which inverts the colors of the selected screen area—even though the present area selected is, initially, less than one pixel on the screen.

If capture has already been initialized, for example, through WM_COMMAND / IDM_CAPTURE, when the left mouse button is physically pressed, an alternative provision creates a new starting point from the coordinate information contained in the lParam parameter.

```
else
if( ! fFinish )
{
    fFinish = TRUE;
    ptStart = MAKEPOINT( lParam );
}
return(0);
```

After capture initialization, each time a WM_MOUSEMOVE message is received, indicating that the mouse position has changed, a second coordinate pair is recorded and the area selected is shown by inverting the existing image.

```
case WM_MOUSEMOVE:
    if( fStart )
        SetCursor( LoadCursor( NULL, IDC_CROSS ) );
    if( fFinish )
    {
        InvertBlock( hwnd, ptStart, ptFinish );
            // restore previous inverted area on screen
        ptFinish = MAKEPOINT( lParam );
        ptFinish.x -= ptStart.x;
        ptFinish.y -= ptStart.y;
            // set new area limits
        InvertBlock( hwnd, ptStart, ptFinish );
            // invert new selected area
    }
    return(0);
```

Notice that two calls are made to the InvertBlock subroutine; first before the new coordinates are registered and, second, using the new coordinates. The InvertBlock routine was initially called when capture was initialized and the first call in this response restores the prior inversion. Then, after a new endpoint is registered, a new screen inversion is executed, showing the current area selection.

Last, when the WM_LBUTTONUP message is received indicating that the left mouse button has been released, the InvertBlock routine is called a final time, restoring the screen inversion before the actual capture is executed. After restoring the screen, the cursor is changed to IDC_WAIT (the hourglass cursor) and the cursor capture is released (ReleaseCapture).

```
case WM_LBUTTONUP:
    if( ! fFinish ) break;
    InvertBlock( hwnd, ptStart, ptFinish );
        // restore invert screen area (final)
    fStart = fFinish = FALSE;
    SetCursor( LoadCursor( NULL, IDC_WAIT ) );
    ReleaseCapture();
    if( ptFinish.x == 0 || ptFinish.y == 0 ) break;
```

At this time, if the area selected is empty, that is, the offset coordinates in *pt-Finish* are zero, the capture process is aborted.

But if not—if there is a valid area to capture—the capture process begins by first creating a compatible device context, and second by creating a compatible bitmap using the size shown by the offset specifications in *ptFinish*.

Please note that the compatible bitmap created here is not a display bitmap. Instead, *hdcMem* is a memory device-context handle that can contain a copy of the display image and where the image data can be manipulated without affecting the actual display.

```
hdc = GetDC( hwnd );
hdcMem = CreateCompatibleDC( hdc );
hBitmap = CreateCompatibleBitmap(
    hdc, abs( ptFinish.x ), abs( ptFinish.y ) );
```

If the call to CreateCompatibleBitmap is successful, *hBitmap* will be non-NULL and the capture process can proceed by calling SelectObject to select the bitmap, *hBitmap*, into the logical context, *hdcMem*. However, it is the subsequent StretchBlt instruction which actually transfers the image from the screen to the memory device-context handle.

```
if( hBitmap )
{
    SelectObject( hdcMem, hBitmap );
    StretchBlt( hdcMem, 0, 0, abs( ptFinish.x ),
                              abs( ptFinish.y ),
            hdc, ptStart.x,  ptStart.y,
                 ptFinish.x, ptFinish.y,
            SRCCOPY );
```

While both BitBlt and StretchBlt provide a means of copying information between display contexts—*hdc* and *hdcMem* in this example—StretchBlt optionally provides the capability of stretching (or shrinking) the image to fit the available display space. The BitBlt function simply executes an exact copy.

The memory device-context handle (*hdcMem*), however, is not our actual destination for this bitmap. Instead, *hdcMem* is used as an environment where the original, captured image can be stretched or shrunk to fit the application's display context. Instead, to give the bitmap a more permanent storage location and to make it accessible to other applications, OpenClipboard opens the Clipboard for examination while the next instruction, EmptyClipboard, gives the current application ownership—temporarily—of the Clipboard while dumping the present Clipboard contents, if any.

```
OpenClipboard( hwnd );
EmptyClipboard();
SetClipboardData( CF_BITMAP, hBitmap );
CloseClipboard();
...
}
```

Next, SetClipboardData is called to transfer new material, the bitmap image, to the Clipboard, specifying the data type with the CF_BITMAP argument. And, last, the Clipboard is closed, releasing ownership of the Clipboard.

NOTE. The preceding sequence is a fairly stock example of Clipboard use, beginning with Open... and ending with Close... commands. Between the Open... and Close... commands, a variety of different actions can be executed, but remember, control of the Clipboard is always temporary and should always be relinquished as soon as possible. See "Painting from the Clipboard," following, for a second example of Clipboard access.

After the bitmap is copied to the Clipboard, a bit of cleanup remains. This consists of deleting the temporary memory image, releasing the device context, and last, restoring the application window by calling OpenIcon.

```
DeleteDC( hdcMem );
ReleaseDC( hwnd, hdc );
OpenIcon( hwnd );
return(0);
```

PAINTING FROM THE CLIPBOARD

The Capture1 program, in response to the WM_PAINT message, displays any bitmap image contained by the Clipboard, regardless of the source of the image. Again, the first step (after initializing the customary display context) is to open the Clipboard, but this time, the EmptyClipboard function is not called and the application does not assume ownership, only access.

```
case WM_PAINT:
...
```

```
OpenClipboard( hwnd );
if( hBitmap = GetClipboardData( CF_BITMAP ) )
{
    SetCursor( LoadCursor( NULL, IDC_WAIT ) );
    hdcMem = CreateCompatibleDC( hdc );
    SelectObject( hdcMem, hBitmap );
    GetObject( hBitmap, sizeof( BITMAP ),
               (LPSTR) &bm );
```

Again, the *hBitmap* handle is used, but this time it is used to retrieve the bit-map from the Clipboard—assuming that there is one to retrieve. Alternately, if there is no bitmap image, the process is aborted.

Two methods of displaying a retrieved bitmap are used: either actual size or sized to fit (*fExpand*). In the first case, the BitBlt function is used to execute a direct copy to the window. In the second instance, one of three stretch modes can be selected before StretchBlt is called to copy the bitmap to fit the application window.

```
if( fExpand )
{
    SetStretchBltMode( hdc, iStrMode );
    StretchBlt( hdc, 0, 0, cxWnd, cyWnd,
                hdcMem, 0, 0,
                bm.bmWidth, bm.bmHeight,
                SRCCOPY );
}
else
    BitBlt( hdc, 0, 0, cxWnd, cyWnd,
            hdcMem, 0, 0, SRCCOPY );
    SetCursor( LoadCursor( NULL, IDC_ARROW ) );
    DeleteDC( hdcMem );
}
```

If you are using an SVGA system, a word of caution is in order here. SVGA modes (or, more specifically, 256-color palettes) may not perform well with the StretchBlt function, regardless of the stretch method chosen. The BitBlt function (exact size), however, will operate correctly, though the bitmap will be truncated if it exceeds the application window size.

Last, as before, the CloseClipboard function must be called before the paint operation concludes.

```
CloseClipboard();
EndPaint( hwnd, &ps );
return(0);
```

OTHER CLIPBOARD ACCESS

Once the Capture1 program has saved a screen image to the Clipboard, the bitmap image is immediately available to any other application, such as the Paintbrush program (PBRUSH.EXE) supplied with Windows. Because of this, one simple method of saving a bitmap is to use Paintbrush to retrieve the Clipboard contents and, subsequently, save the image as a .BMP file.

Remember, the Clipboard contents remain available even after the capturing application has closed—unless, of course, some other application has assumed ownership of the Clipboard and has erased the saved image in the meantime.

This is not, however, the only way to save an image to a file. Presently, the Capture2 program will demonstrate a second approach by writing a .BMP file directly.

THE BITMAP (.BMP) IMAGE FILE FORMAT

A bitmap image file consists of three parts:

- A file header (BITMAPFILEHEADER)
- An information header (BITMAPINFOHEADER), which includes color palette information
- The actual image information

Of these, the palette information and image data vary in structure depending on the type of color information and the encoding method (or lack thereof) used to store the image information.

In any case, the bitmap file begins with a file header defined by the BITMAPFILEHEADER data structure which contains information about the type, size, and layout of a device-independent bitmap (DIB) file. BITMAPFILEHEADER is defined in Windows.H as:

```
typedef struct tagBITMAPFILEHEADER
            {  WORD    bfType;
               DWORD   bfSize;
               WORD    bfReserved1;
               WORD    bfReserved2;
               DWORD   bfOffBits; } BITMAPFILEHEADER;
```

The contents of the BITMAPFILEHEADER fields are defined as shown in Table 7.1, while the following excerpt shows how these are set in the Capture2 program:

```
    // initialize bitmap file header structure //
  bmFH.bfType     = 0x424D;         // Type equals "BM"
```

```
bmFH.bfReserved1 = ØL;
bmFH.bfReserved2 = ØL;
bmFH.bfOffBits  = plSize +        // bitmap offset
                 sizeof( BITMAPINFO ) +
                 sizeof( BITMAPFILEHEADER );
bmFH.bfSize      = ImgSize +       // file size (DWORD)
                 bmFH.bfOffBits;
fwrite( &bmFH, sizeof( bmFH ), 1, Bf );
                                  // write file header
```

Table 7.1: BITMAPFILEHEADER Data Fields

Field	Description
bfType	specifies file type, must be "BM"
bfSize	specifies size of file in DWORDs
bfReserved1	reserved, must be zero
bfReserved2	reserved, must be zero
bfOffBits	offset in bytes from BITMAPFILEHEADER to the start of the actual bitmap in the file

Within the DIB file, the BITMAPFILEHEADER structure is followed immediately by either a BITMAPINFO or BITMAPCOREINFO data structure. In the Capture2 example, the BITMAPINFO structure defines the dimensions and color information for a DIB. BITMAPINFO is defined in Windows.H as follows and as described in Table 7.2:

```
typedef struct tagBITMAPINFO
                { BITMAPINFOHEADER  bmiHeader;
                  RGBQUAD           bmiColors[1];
                } BITMAPINFO;
```

The RGBQUAD structure will be detailed later in this chapter.

Table 7.2: BITMAPINFO Data Fields

Field	Description
bmiHeader	BITMAPINFOHEADER containing information about the dimensions and color format of a DIB
bmiColors	an array of RGBQUAD data structures defining the colors in the bitmap

The BITMAPINFOHEADER structure provides information about the size and organization of the bitmap image data and is defined in Windows.H as:

```
typedef struct tagBITMAPINFOHEADER
            {  DWORD   biSize;
               DWORD   biWidth;
               DWORD   biHeight;
               WORD    biPlanes;
               WORD    biBitCount
               DWORD   biCompression;
               DWORD   biSizeImage;
               DWORD   biXPelsPerMeter;
               DWORD   biYPelsPerMeter;
               DWORD   biClrUsed;
               DWORD   biClrImportant;
            }  BITMAPINFOHEADER;
```

Table 7.3 describes the BITMAPINFOHEADER data fields and, where applicable, the values permitted in various fields.

Table 7.3: BITMAPINFOHEADER Data Fields

Field	Description
biSize	number of bytes required by the BITMAPINFOHEADER structure
biWidth	width of the bitmap in pixels
biHeight	height of the bitmap in pixels
biPlanes	color planes for target device—must be 1
biBitCount	bits per pixel—must be 1, 4, 8, or 24 (see Table 7.4)
biCompression	type of compression for a compressed bitmap (see Table 7.5)
biSizeImage	image size in bytes
biXPelsPerMeter	horizontal resolution in pixels per meter of the optimum target device. Applications may use this value to select a bitmap from a resource group which best matches the characteristics of the current device.
biYPelsPerMeter	vertical resolution in pixels per meter of the desired target device
biClrUsed	number of color indexes in the color table used by the bitmap (see Table 7.6)
biClrImportant	number of color indexes considered important for displaying bitmap—if 0, all are important

The *biBitCount* field of the BITMAPINFOHEADER structure determines the number of bits defining each pixel as well as the maximum number of colors in the bitmap. This *biBitCount* field may be set to any of the values shown in Table 7.4.

Table 7.4: Bitmap Bit Count Values

Value	Description
1	Monochrome bitmap—*bmiColors* field must contain two entries while each bit in the bitmap array represents one pixel. If the bit is clear (0) the first color entry is used; if set (1), the second color entry is used.
4	Bitmap has 16 colors maximum; *bmiColors* field contains a maximum of 16 entries with each pixel in the bitmap represented by a four-bit index into the color table.
8	Bitmap has 256 colors maximum; *bmiColors* field contains a maximum of 256 entries. Each byte in the array represents a single pixel as a palette index.
24	Bitmap has 2^{24} colors maximum—*bmiColors* field is NULL and each three bytes in the bitmap array represents the relative pixel intensities of red, green, and blue.

Three compression formats are currently defined with the format identified in the *biCompression* field of the BITMAPINFOHEADER. (See Table 7.5)

NOTE: Run-length encoding is discussed further under the heading "Bitmap Compression Formats," following.

Table 7.5: Compression Formats

Type	Description
BI_RGB	Bitmap is not compressed.
BI_RLE8	Run-length encoded format for bitmaps with eight bits per pixel—two-byte format consisting of a count byte followed by a color-index byte.
BI_RLE4	Run-length encoded format for bitmaps with four bits per pixel—two-byte format consisting of a count byte followed by two word-length color indexes.

The *biClrUsed* field specifies the number of color indexes in the color table which are actually used by the bitmap. If the *biClrUsed* field is set to 0, the bitmap uses the maximum number of colors corresponding to the value of the *biBitCount* field. (See Table 7.6.)

Table 7.6: *biClrUsed* Values

Value	Description	
0	Bitmap uses the maximum number of colors specified by the *biBitCount* field.	
Non-zero	If *biBitCount* < 24, *biClrUsed* specifies actual number of colors accessed by device driver or graphics engine.	If *biBitCount* = 24, *biClrUsed* specifies size of reference table used to optimize Windows color palettes.

Colors in the *bmiColors* table should appear in order of importance. By identifying the order of importance—putting the highest-frequency colors first—if a bitmapped image is displayed on a device with a lower color resolution, the most important colors are placed in the system palette. Subsequently, lower-frequency colors are mapped to the high-frequency colors in the palette.

In the Capture2 demo, implementation of the BITMAPINFOHEADER structure is accomplished as follows:

```
if( LnWidth % sizeof( DWORD ) )
    LnPad = sizeof(DWORD) - ( LnWidth % sizeof(DWORD) );
                // scan line width must be DWORD multiple
ImgSize = (DWORD)( (DWORD)( LnWidth + LnPad ) *
                   (DWORD) Height );   // image size
plSize = CRes * sizeof( RGBQUAD );      // palette size
//=== initialize bitmap file header structure ============
bmFH.bfType      = 0x4D42;              // Type is "BF"
bmFH.bfReserved1 = 0L;
bmFH.bfReserved2 = 0L;
bmFH.bfOffBits   = plSize +            // bitmap offset
                   sizeof( BITMAPINFO ) +
                   sizeof( BITMAPFILEHEADER );
bmFH.bfSize      = ImgSize +           // file size
                   bmFH.bfOffBits;
fwrite( &bmFH, sizeof( bmFH ), 1, Bf );
                                // write file header
// the bitmap file header is initialized at this point
```

```
// as shown in a previous example
//=== initialize bitmap info header structure ============
   bmIH.biSize = (DWORD) sizeof( BITMAPINFOHEADER );
   bmIH.biWidth       = Width;
   bmIH.biHeight      = Height;
   bmIH.biPlanes      = 1;
// NOTE: bmIH.biBitCount has already been set.
   bmIH.biCompression  = BI_RGB;
   bmIH.biSizeImage    = 0L;
   bmIH.biXPelsPerMeter = 0L;
   bmIH.biYPelsPerMeter = 0L;
   bmIH.biClrUsed      = 0L;
   bmIH.biClrImportant = 0L;
   fwrite( &bmIH, sizeof( bmIH ), 1, Bf );
                                    // write info header
```

BITMAP COMPRESSION FORMATS

Compression is used with most image formats to reduce both memory and disk storage requirements. In Windows, two formats are supported for bitmap compression, one each for four and eight bits per pixel.

Eight-bit-per-pixel bitmaps   For eight-bit-per-pixel bitmaps, the BI_RLE8 format is used. It incorporates two modes: Absolute and Encoded. Note that both modes may occur anywhere within an individual bitmap.

Beginning with the Encoded mode, WORD values are used. The first byte of each WORD value specifies some number of consecutive values (01h..FFh) to be drawn using the color index indicated by the second byte.

As an exception, the first byte value can be set to zero, initiating an escape sequence denoting an end of line, an end of bitmap, or a delta with the second byte indicating the escape sequence. (See Table 7.7.)

Table 7.7: Compression Escape Sequences

Value	Definition
0	end of line
1	end of bitmap
2	delta—the two bytes following the escape sequence contain horizontal and vertical offsets (relative) to the next pixel position

Absolute mode is indicated by a WORD value with the first byte set to zero while the second byte is set to a value in the range 03h..FFh. The second byte represents the number of bytes which follow, each containing the color index of a single pixel.

When the second byte is set to 2 or less, the escape has the same meaning as in Encoded mode. In Absolute mode, each run must be aligned on a word boundary (scan lines are NULL-padded if necessary).

Following is an example of hexadecimal values from an eight-bit compressed bitmap together with the corresponding decompressed sequences:

```
03 04 05 06 00 03 45 56 67 00 02 78 00 02 05 01 02 78
00 00 09 1E 00 01
```

Compressed Bytes	Decompressed Results/Pixel Values
03 04	04 04 04
05 06	06 06 06 06 06
00 03 45 56 67 00	45 56 67
02 78	78 78
00 02 05 01	move 5 pixels right, 1 pixel down
02 78	78 78
00 00	end of line
09 1E	1E 1E 1E 1E 1E 1E 1E 1E 1E
00 01	end of RLE bitmap

Four-bit-per-pixel bitmaps   For four-bit-per-pixel bitmaps, the BI_RLE4 format is used. Like BI_RLE8, it incorporates two modes: Absolute and Encoded. Again, both modes may occur anywhere within an individual bitmap.

Beginning with the Encoded mode, WORD values are used. The first byte of each WORD value specifies some number of consecutive values (01h..FFh) to be drawn using the two-color index contained in the second byte. Since the second byte contains two-color indexes—one in the high-order nibble, one in the low-order nibble—the pixel sequence is drawn by alternating the two values indicated. That is, the first pixel uses the first color index; the second pixel uses the second color index; the third pixel uses the first color index, and so on, terminating when the indicated number of pixels has been drawn.

As an exception, the first byte value can be set to zero, initiating an escape sequence denoting an end of line, an end of bitmap, or a delta with the second byte indicating the escape sequence, as shown for the BI_RLE8 encoding format (preceding).

In Absolute mode, the first byte contains zero while the second byte specifies the number of color indexes (nibbles) following. Subsequent bytes contain pairs of color indexes in the high- and low-order nibbles, with one color index for each pixel. In Absolute mode, each sequence must be aligned on a WORD boundary (values are NULL-padded as necessary).

Following is an example of hexadecimal values from a four-bit compressed bitmap, together with the corresponding decompressed sequences. (Single-digit values represent color indexes for single pixels.)

```
06 40 05 06 00 06 45 56 67 00 08 77 00 02 05 01 04 78
00 00 09 1E 00 01
```

Compressed Bytes	Decompressed Results/Pixel Values
06 04	4 0 4 0 4 0
05 06	0 6 0 6 0
00 06 45 56 67 00	4 5 5 6 6 7
04 77	7 7 7 7 7 7 7 7
00 02 05 01	move 5 pixels right, 1 pixel down
04 78	7 8 7 8
00 00	end of line
09 1E	1 E 1 E 1 E 1 E 1
00 01	end of RLE bitmap

WRITING A BITMAP FILE

Thus far, only the header information has been written to the bitmap file, while both palette and image information remain. The Capture2 demo program is set for two types of bitmap, those with 16- or 256-color palettes. For monochrome or 24-bit-per-pixel bitmaps, additional provisions would be necessary as described previously.

Retrieving and converting palette colors   The following excerpt shows the handling for retrieving the palette color information and begins by allocating and locking sufficient memory space to contain the palette information:

```
hPal = GlobalAlloc( GHND, sizeof(LOGPALETTE) +
                  ( ( CRes - 1 ) *
                     sizeof(PALETTEENTRY) ) );
```

```
                        // allocate memory for palette
lp = (LPLOGPALETTE) GlobalLock( hPal );
                        // lock the memory allocated
lp->palNumEntries = CRes;
lp->palVersion    = 0x0300;
                        // fill in size and version (3.0)
GetSystemPaletteEntries( hdc, 0, CRes,
                    lp->palPalEntry );
                        // and get the palette information
```

After space is allocated for the palette information, the palette size is initialized (CRes) and the version number is set before calling GetSystemPalette-Entries to retrieve the palette color information.

Once the palette information is retrieved, however, before this data can be stored as a part of the bitmap image, the PALETTEENTRY RGB order must be converted to the RGBQUAD format used by bitmap images.

The PALETTEENTRY structure—as previously introduced—is defined in Windows.H as:

```
typedef struct {
    BYTE    peRed;
    BYTE    peGreen;
    BYTE    peBlue;
} PALETTEENTRY;
```

In contrast, the RGBQUAD structure used by bitmap images is the same size—four bytes—but uses an entirely different ordering for the colors. RGBQUAD is also defined in Windows.H as:

```
typedef struct tagRGBQUAD {
    BYTE    rgbBlue;
    BYTE    rgbGreen;
    BYTE    rgbRed;
    BYTE    rgbReserved;
} RGBQUAD;
```

As you can see, the PALETTEENTRY structure uses a red, green, blue order while the RGBQUAD structure orders colors as blue, green, red—and might have better been titled: BGRQUAD.

Because of this difference in order, provisions are necessary to convert the RGB order of the retrieved palette information to the bitmap's BGR order. Since Windows doesn't supply a macro or function for such conversions, the preceding provisions to allocate and lock memory for the palette information are quite necessary before the palette RGB values can be retrieved as the local variables *RVal*, *GVal* and *BVal*:

```
for( i=0; i<CRes; i++ )
{
    RVal = lp->palPalEntry[i].peRed;
    GVal = lp->palPalEntry[i].peGreen;
    BVal = lp->palPalEntry[i].peBlue;
    fputc( BVal, Bf );          // write blue first,
    fputc( GVal, Bf );          // green second,
    fputc( RVal, Bf );          // rcd third,
    fputc( 0x00, Bf );          // and null last
}
```

Finally, after these three values are extracted, they can be written to the .BMP file in BGR order, completing each with a null byte (for the *rgbReserved* field).

After looping through the palette information and creating the bitmap palette, the last step is to unlock and free the memory allocated to hold the palette:

```
GlobalUnlock( hPal );    // don't forget to unlock
GlobalFree( hPal );      // and release the memory
```

But the task is not finished yet. Thus far, the bitmap file and info headers have been written, followed by the color palette. The image data, however, has not been written ... yet.

Saving a 16-color image   For a 16-color image—ignoring RLE encoding—the image is written with each pixel defined as a nibble of data. Thus, each byte written to the file incorporates the data for two pixels. In this instance, for simplicity, the GetPixel function is used to retrieve the pixel color data:

```
if( CRes == 16 )                    // for 16-color image
{                                   // write image bits
    for( i=Height-1; i>=0; i-- )
    {
        for( j=0; j<Width; j+=2 )
            fputc( ( GetPixel( hdc, j,   i ) << 4 ) +
                     GetPixel( hdc, j+1, i ), Bf );
        for( j=0; j<LnPad; j++ ) fputc( 0x00, Bf );
} }
```

There is a drawback in this approach: Because the application is reading the pixel data from the application's display of the captured image, what happens if the image is larger than Capture2's display area? The alternative—and preferred—handling is shown in the 256-color image handling, following.

Still, regardless of the source, after each scan line is written to the file, the length of the scan line is padded to a WORD boundary with nulls.

Also, remember that the origin point for a bitmapped image is always at the lower-left. Thus the scan lines are written from the bottom up, not from the top down.

256-color images   In the case of a 256-color image, the second handling method is used. It begins by using the CreateCompatibleDC function to create a memory device context that is compatible with the hardware device context while the CreateCompatibleBitmap function creates a bitmap—in memory only.

```
hdcMem = CreateCompatibleDC( hdc );
hBitmap = CreateCompatibleBitmap( hdc, Width, 1 );
if( hBitmap )
{
```

Because a large bitmap (in SVGA mode) requires quite a bit of memory, a simple trick is used. Instead of allocating enough memory for the entire bitmap, sufficient memory is allocated for just one scan line of the bitmap.

If *hBitmap* is returned null, memory allocation and/or bitmap creation has failed and the entire process fails.

Assuming that all proceeds as expected, however, the next step parallels the preceding handling for the palette information by allocating memory for the bitmap—remember, it's only one scan line high—and then locking the memory reserved.

```
hMem = GlobalAlloc( GHND, Width );
lpBits = GlobalLock( hMem );
SelectObject( hdcMem, hBitmap );
```

And, after the allocation and locking of memory, the bitmap (*hBitmap*) is selected into the memory device-context handle (*hdcMem*).

SelectObject is only set up for the memory device-context handle. It's the loop following that copies bitmap data from the saved image (in *hdc*) to *hdcMem*, proceeding one line at a time—again, beginning at the bottom of the image, not at the top.

```
for( i=Height-1; i>=0; i-- )
{
    BitBlt( hdcMem, 0, 0, Width, 1,
            hdc, 0, i, SRCCOPY );
    GetBitmapBits( hBitmap, Width, lpBits );
```

After calling BitBlt and GetBitmapBits to transfer the data to the memory device-context handle, an inner loop is used to copy the data from *lpBits* to the file—one byte at a time.

```
for( j=0; j<LnWidth; j++ )
    fputc( lpBits[j], Bf );
for( j=0; j<LnPad;   j++ )
    fputc( 0x00, Bf );
}
```

And, again, each scan line is NULL-padded to a WORD width.

Previously, in the 16-color handling, the suggestion was made to change the handling shown there to the handling shown here—a task which is quite easily accomplished. There are, however, other possibilities that you may wish to consider—such as incorporating RLE or other encoding at this point. Remember, encoding should not be carried beyond the end of any scan line.

Copying the image information completes the creation of the bitmap file. The process concludes by freeing the allocated memory and releasing the device-context handle before closing the file.

```
    GlobalUnlock( hMem );    // again, unlock memory
    GlobalFree( hMem );      // and release to heap
  }
  DeleteDC( hdcMem );        // delete memory context
  ReleaseDC( hwnd, hdc );    // release device context
}
fclose( Bf );                // and close the file ...
}
```

SUMMARY

Even though the .BMP format is the native image format of Windows, this is only one graphics image format and is hardly sufficient for every situation. Therefore, in Chapter 8, the current topic will continue with a look at several other popular and prominent image formats, including the .PCX, GIF, and TGA formats.

PROGRAM LISTING OF CAPTURE1.C

```
//=========================//
//          CAPTURE1.C       //
//  Screen Capture Program   //
//=========================//


#include <windows.h>
#include <stdlib.h>
#include <bwcc.h>        // include bwcc.lib in project file
#include "capture1.h"


HANDLE    hInst;


#pragma argsused

BOOL FAR PASCAL AboutProc( HWND hDlg,    WORD msg,
                           WORD wParam, LONG lParam )
{
   switch( msg )
   {
     case WM_INITDIALOG:  return( TRUE );
     case WM_COMMAND:
        switch( wParam )
        {
           case IDOK: EndDialog( hDlg, TRUE );
                    return( TRUE );
             default: return( TRUE );
   }     }
   return( FALSE );
}


void InvertBlock( HWND hwnd, POINT ptStart,
                            POINT ptFinish )
{                  // inverts colors of the selected region
   HDC  hdc;

   hdc = CreateDC( "DISPLAY", NULL, NULL, NULL );
   ClientToScreen( hwnd, &ptStart );
   PatBlt( hdc, ptStart.x,  ptStart.y,
               ptFinish.x, ptFinish.y, DSTINVERT );
   DeleteDC( hdc );
}


long FAR PASCAL WndProc( HWND hwnd,   WORD msg,
                         WORD wParam, LONG lParam )
```

```
{
    static  BOOL  fStart = FALSE, fFinish = FALSE,
                  fExpand = FALSE;
    static  POINT ptStart, ptFinish;
    static  int   cxWnd, cyWnd;
    BITMAP        bm;
    HBITMAP       hBitmap;
    HDC           hdc, hdcMem;
    FARPROC       lpProc;
    PAINTSTRUCT   ps;
    RECT          rect;

    switch( msg )
    {
        case WM_SIZE:
            cxWnd = LOWORD( lParam );
            cyWnd = HIWORD( lParam );
            return(0);

        case WM_COMMAND:            // handles menu commands
            switch( wParam )
            {
                case IDM_EXACT:    // bitmap not resized
                    fExpand = FALSE;
                    PostMessage( hwnd, WM_PAINT, 0L, 0L );
                    break;
                case IDM_RESIZE:   // bitmap resized to window
                    fExpand = TRUE;
                    PostMessage( hwnd, WM_PAINT, 0L, 0L );
                    break;
                case IDM_CAPTURE:  // initialize capture
                    ptStart.x = ptStart.y = ptFinish.x =
                    ptFinish.y = 0;
                    PostMessage( hwnd, WM_LBUTTONDOWN, 0L, 0L );
                    break;          // post message to start
                                    // capture process
                case IDM_ABOUT:
                    lpProc = MakeProcInstance( AboutProc,
                                               hInst );
                    DialogBox( hInst, "ABOUT", hwnd, lpProc );
                    FreeProcInstance( lpProc );
                    break;
            }
            return(0);

        case WM_LBUTTONDOWN:
```

```
      if( ! fStart )
      {     // left button begins capture process
         fStart = TRUE;
         SetCapture( hwnd );
         SetCursor( LoadCursor( NULL, IDC_CROSS ) );
         CloseWindow( hwnd );
         InvertBlock( hwnd, ptStart, ptFinish );
            // invert selected area on screen
      }
      else  // reset capture process
      if( ! fFinish )
      {
         fFinish = TRUE;
         ptStart = MAKEPOINT( lParam );
      }
      return(0);

   case WM_MOUSEMOVE:  // provides visual feedback
      if( fStart )      // as mouse moves
         SetCursor( LoadCursor( NULL, IDC_CROSS ) );
      if( fFinish )
      {
         InvertBlock( hwnd, ptStart, ptFinish );
            // restore previous inverted area on screen
         ptFinish = MAKEPOINT( lParam );
         ptFinish.x -= ptStart.x;
         ptFinish.y -= ptStart.y;
            // set new area limits
         InvertBlock( hwnd, ptStart, ptFinish );
            // invert new selected area
      }
      return(0);

   case WM_LBUTTONUP: // end capture, copy to clipboard
      if( ! fFinish ) break;
      InvertBlock( hwnd, ptStart, ptFinish );
         // restore invert screen area (final)
      fStart = fFinish = FALSE;
      SetCursor( LoadCursor( NULL, IDC_WAIT ) );
      ReleaseCapture();
      if( ptFinish.x == 0 || ptFinish.y == 0 ) break;
      hdc = GetDC( hwnd );
      hdcMem = CreateCompatibleDC( hdc );
      hBitmap = CreateCompatibleBitmap(
         hdc, abs( ptFinish.x ), abs( ptFinish.y ) );
      if( hBitmap )
```

```
        {
          SelectObject( hdcMem, hBitmap );
          StretchBlt( hdcMem, 0, 0, abs( ptFinish.x ),
                                     abs( ptFinish.y ),
                      hdc, ptStart.x,  ptStart.y,
                           ptFinish.x, ptFinish.y,
                           SRCCOPY );
          OpenClipboard( hwnd );
          EmptyClipboard();
          SetClipboardData( CF_BITMAP, hBitmap );
          CloseClipboard();
          InvalidateRect( hwnd, NULL, TRUE );
        }              // force repaint of main window
        DeleteDC( hdcMem );
        ReleaseDC( hwnd, hdc );
        OpenIcon( hwnd );
        return(0);

    case WM_PAINT:
        InvalidateRect( hwnd, NULL, TRUE );
        hdc = BeginPaint( hwnd, &ps );
        OpenClipboard( hwnd );
        if( hBitmap = GetClipboardData( CF_BITMAP ) )
        {          // if clipbd has bitmap, display same
          SetCursor( LoadCursor( NULL, IDC_WAIT ) );
          hdcMem = CreateCompatibleDC( hdc );
          SelectObject( hdcMem, hBitmap );
          GetObject( hBitmap, sizeof( BITMAP ),
                     (LPSTR) &bm );
          if( fExpand )
          {          // use StretchBlt to size to window
            SetStretchBltMode( hdc, COLORONCOLOR );
            StretchBlt( hdc, 0, 0, cxWnd, cyWnd,
                        hdcMem, 0, 0,
                        bm.bmWidth, bm.bmHeight,
                        SRCCOPY );
          }
          else    // use BitBlt to copy exactly
            BitBlt( hdc, 0, 0, cxWnd, cyWnd,
                    hdcMem, 0, 0, SRCCOPY );
          SetCursor( LoadCursor( NULL, IDC_ARROW ) );
          DeleteDC( hdcMem );
        }
        CloseClipboard();
        EndPaint( hwnd, &ps );
        return(0);
```

```
        case WM_DESTROY:
            PostQuitMessage(0);
            return(0);
    }
    return( DefWindowProc( hwnd, msg, wParam, lParam ) );
}

#pragma argsused

int PASCAL WinMain( HANDLE hInstance,
                    HANDLE hPrevInstance,
                    LPSTR  lpszCmdParam, int nCmdShow )
{
    static char szAppName[] = "CAPTURE1";
    HWND        hwnd;
    MSG         msg;
    WNDCLASS    wc;

    if( ! hPrevInstance )
    {
        wc.hInstance      = hInstance;
        wc.lpfnWndProc    = WndProc;
        wc.cbClsExtra     = 0;
        wc.cbWndExtra     = 0;
        wc.lpszClassName  = szAppName;
        wc.hIcon          = LoadIcon( hInstance, szAppName );
        wc.lpszMenuName   = (LPSTR) szAppName;
        wc.hCursor        = LoadCursor( NULL, IDC_ARROW );
        wc.hbrBackground  = GetStockObject( WHITE_BRUSH );
        wc.style          = CS_HREDRAW | CS_VREDRAW;
        RegisterClass( &wc );
    }
    hInst = hInstance;      // assign global instance handle
    hwnd = CreateWindow( szAppName, "Screen Capture Demo 1",
        WS_OVERLAPPEDWINDOW,
        CW_USEDEFAULT, CW_USEDEFAULT,
        CW_USEDEFAULT, CW_USEDEFAULT,
        NULL, NULL, hInstance, NULL  );
    ShowWindow(   hwnd, nCmdShow );
    UpdateWindow( hwnd );
    while( GetMessage( &msg, NULL, 0, 0 ) )
    {
        TranslateMessage( &msg );
        DispatchMessage(  &msg );
    }
    return( msg.wParam );
}
```

```
;===========================;
;  CAPTURE1.DEF             :
;  module definition file   :
;===========================;

NAME          CAPTURE1
DESCRIPTION   "Screen Capture Program"
EXETYPE       WINDOWS
STUB          "WINSTUB.EXE"
CODE          PRELOAD MOVEABLE DISCARDABLE
DATA          PRELOAD MOVEABLE MULTIPLE
HEAPSIZE      1024
STACKSIZE     8192
EXPORTS       WndProc
              AboutProc


//================//
//   Capture1.H   //
//================//
#define   IDM_EXACT     101
#define   IDM_RESIZE    102
#define   IDM_CAPTURE   103
#define   IDM_WHITE     104
#define   IDM_COLOR     105
#define   IDM_BLACK     106
#define   IDM_ABOUT     107


//=====================//
//   CAPTURE1 MENU      //
//=====================//
BEGIN
   POPUP "Display Mode"
   BEGIN
     MENUITEM "Original Size",  101
     MENUITEM "Size To Window", 102
   END
   POPUP "Stretch Mode"
   BEGIN
     MENUITEM "White_on_Black", 104
     MENUITEM "Color_on_Color", 105
     MENUITEM "Black_on_White", 106
   END
   MENUITEM "Capture", 103
   MENUITEM "About",   107, HELP
END
```

Program listing of Capture2.C

```
//=========================//
//          CAPTURE2.C     //
//  Screen Capture Program //
//=========================//

#include <windows.h>
#include <stdlib.h>
#include <string.h>
#include <stdio.h>
#include <dir.h>
#include <bwcc.h>          // include bwcc.lib in project file
#include "capture2.h"

static    char        szFName[64];
HANDLE                hInst;
BITMAPFILEHEADER      bmFH;
BITMAPINFOHEADER      bmIH;
BITMAPINFO            bmInfo;

int ErrorMsg( HWND hwnd, char *Error )
{
   MessageBox( hwnd, Error, "MB_ICONASTERISK",
              MB_ICONASTERISK | MB_OK );
   return(0);
}

int CaptureBitmap( HWND hwnd, int Width, int Height )
{
   HDC          hdc, hdcMem;
   HANDLE       hMem;
   HBITMAP      hBitmap;
   HPALETTE     hPal;
   LPLOGPALETTE lp;
   FILE         *Bf;
   LPSTR        lpBits;
   DWORD        ImgSize, plSize;
   BYTE         RVal, GVal, BVal;
   int          i, j, CRes, LnWidth, LnPad = 0;

   if( ( Bf = fopen( szFName, "wt" ) ) == NULL )
       return( ErrorMsg( hwnd, "Can't open file" ) );
//=== get the palette information =========================
   hdc = GetDC( hwnd );
   CRes = GetDeviceCaps( hdc, SIZEPALETTE );
```

```
   if( CRes == 16 )
   {
      bmIH.biBitCount = 4;              // 2^4 colors = 16
      LnWidth = Width / 2;
   }
   else
   {
      bmIH.biBitCount = 8;              // 2^8 colors = 256
      LnWidth = Width;
   }
   if( LnWidth % sizeof( DWORD ) )
      LnPad = sizeof(DWORD) - ( LnWidth % sizeof(DWORD) );
                 // scan line width must be DWORD multiple
   ImgSize = (DWORD)( (DWORD)( LnWidth + LnPad ) *
                    (DWORD) Height ); // image size
   plSize = CRes * sizeof( RGBQUAD );      // palette size
//=== initialize bitmap file header structure ============
   bmFH.bfType     = 0x4D42;             // Type is "BF"
   bmFH.bfReserved1 = 0L;
   bmFH.bfReserved2 = 0L;
   bmFH.bfOffBits   = plSize +          // bitmap offset
                    sizeof( BITMAPINFO ) +
                    sizeof( BITMAPFILEHEADER );
   bmFH.bfSize     = ImgSize +          // file size
                    bmFH.bfOffBits;
   fwrite( &bmFH, sizeof( bmFH ), 1, Bf );
                                        // write file header
//=== initialize bitmap info header structure ============
   bmIH.biSize = (DWORD) sizeof( BITMAPINFOHEADER );
   bmIH.biWidth        = Width;
   bmIH.biHeight       = Height;
   bmIH.biPlanes       = 1;
   bmIH.biCompression  = BI_RGB;
   bmIH.biSizeImage    = 0L;
   bmIH.biXPelsPerMeter = 0L;
   bmIH.biYPelsPerMeter = 0L;
   bmIH.biClrUsed      = 0L;
   bmIH.biClrImportant = 0L;
   fwrite( &bmIH, sizeof( bmIH ), 1, Bf );
                                        // write info header
//=== add the palette color information ==================
            // note: GHND = GMEM_FIXED | GMEM_ZEROINIT
   hPal = GlobalAlloc( GHND, sizeof(LOGPALETTE) +
                    ( CRes *
                      sizeof(PALETTEENTRY) ) );
                    // allocate memory for palette
```

```
        lp = (LPLOGPALETTE) GlobalLock( hPal );
                        // lock the memory allocated
        lp->palNumEntries = CRes;
        lp->palVersion    = 0x0300;
                        // fill in size and version (3.0)
        GetSystemPaletteEntries( hdc, 0, CRes,
                            lp->palPalEntry );
                        // and get the palette information
//========= Structure definitions ========================
//    Palette Entry          RGB Quad for Bitmap
//
//      typedef struct {       typedef struct tagRGBQUAD {
//          BYTE  peRed;           BYTE  rgbBlue;
//          BYTE  peGreen;         BYTE  rgbGreen;
//          BYTE  peBlue;          BYTE  rgbRed;
//          BYTE  peFlags;         BYTE  rgbReserved;
//      } PALETTEENTRY;       } RGBQUAD;
//
//========================================================
        // record each PALETTEENTRY as RGBQUAD format
        for( i=0; i<CRes; i++ )
        {
          RVal = lp->palPalEntry[i].peRed;
          GVal = lp->palPalEntry[i].peGreen;
          BVal = lp->palPalEntry[i].peBlue;
          fputc( BVal, Bf );            // put blue first,
          fputc( GVal, Bf );            // green second,
          fputc( RVal, Bf );            // red third,
          fputc( 0x00, Bf );            // and null last
        }
        GlobalUnlock( hPal );    // don't forget to unlock
        GlobalFree( hPal );      // and release the memory

//=== now store the actual image information =============
    if( CRes == 16 )                // for 16-color image
    {                               // write image bits
      for( i=Height-1; i>=0; i-- )
      {
        for( j=0; j<Width; j+=2 )
          fputc( ( GetPixel( hdc, j,   i ) << 4 ) +
                 GetPixel( hdc, j+1, i ), Bf );
        for( j=0; j<LnPad; j++ ) fputc( 0x00, Bf );
    } }
    else                            // for 256-color image
    {                               // create bitmap image
      hdcMem = CreateCompatibleDC( hdc );
```

```
        hBitmap = CreateCompatibleBitmap( hdc, Width, 1 );
        if( hBitmap )
        {
            hMem = GlobalAlloc( GHND, Width );
            lpBits = GlobalLock( hMem );
            SelectObject( hdcMem, hBitmap );
            for( i=Height-1; i>=0; i-- )
            {
                BitBlt( hdcMem, 0, 0, Width, 1,
                        hdc, 0, i, SRCCOPY );
                GetBitmapBits( hBitmap, Width, lpBits );
                for( j=0; j<LnWidth; j++ )
                    fputc( lpBits[j], Bf );
                for( j=0; j<LnPad;   j++ )
                    fputc( 0x00, Bf );
            }
            GlobalUnlock( hMem );    // again, unlock memory
            GlobalFree( hMem );      // and release to heap
        }
        DeleteDC( hdcMem );          // delete memory context
        ReleaseDC( hwnd, hdc );      // release device context
    }
    fclose( Bf );                    // and close the file ...
    return(0);
}

#pragma argsused

BOOL FAR PASCAL AboutProc( HWND hDlg,   WORD msg,
                           WORD wParam, LONG lParam )
{
    switch( msg )
    {
        case WM_INITDIALOG:  return( TRUE );
        case WM_COMMAND:
            switch( wParam )
            {
                case IDOK: EndDialog( hDlg, TRUE );
                           return( TRUE );
                default: return( TRUE );
    }   }
    return( FALSE );
}


void InvertBlock( HWND hwnd,
                  POINT ptStart, POINT ptFinish )
{
```

```
    HDC   hdc;

    hdc = CreateDC( "DISPLAY", NULL, NULL, NULL );
    ClientToScreen( hwnd, &ptStart );
    PatBlt( hdc, ptStart.x,  ptStart.y,
                    ptFinish.x, ptFinish.y, DSTINVERT );
    DeleteDC( hdc );
}

BOOL FAR PASCAL FileNameDlgProc( HWND hDlg, WORD msg,
                                 WORD wParam, LONG lParam )
{
    switch( msg )
    {
        case WM_INITDIALOG:
            SendDlgItemMessage( hDlg, IDD_FNAME,
                                EM_LIMITTEXT, 80, NULL );
            SetDlgItemText( hDlg, IDD_FNAME, szFName );
            return( TRUE );
        case WM_COMMAND:
            switch( wParam )
            {
                case IDD_FNAME:
                    if( HIWORD( lParam ) == EN_CHANGE )
                        EnableWindow( GetDlgItem( hDlg, IDOK ),
                            (BOOL) SendMessage( LOWORD( lParam ),
                                WM_GETTEXTLENGTH, 0, 0L ) );
                    break;
                case IDOK:
                    GetDlgItemText( hDlg, IDD_FNAME,
                                    szFName, 80 );
                    EndDialog( hDlg, TRUE );
                    break;
                case IDCANCEL:
                    EndDialog( hDlg, FALSE );
                    break;
                default:  return( FALSE );
}
    return( FALSE );
}

int CallFileOpenDlg( HANDLE hInst, HWND hwnd )
{
    FARPROC   lpProc;
    int       iReturn;

    lpProc = MakeProcInstance( FileNameDlgProc, hInst );
```

```
    iReturn = DialogBox( hInst, "GETNAME", hwnd, lpProc );
    FreeProcInstance( lpProc );
    return( iReturn );
}

long FAR PASCAL WndProc( HWND hwnd,   WORD msg,
                         WORD wParam, LONG lParam )
{
    static  BOOL  fStart = FALSE, fFinish = FALSE;
    static  POINT ptStart, ptFinish;
    static  int   cxWnd, cyWnd;
    BITMAP        bm;
    HBITMAP       hBitmap;
    HDC           hdc, hdcMem;
    FARPROC       lpProc;
    PAINTSTRUCT   ps;

    switch( msg )
    {
       case WM_SIZE:
           cxWnd = LOWORD( lParam );
           cyWnd = HIWORD( lParam );
           return(0);

       case WM_COMMAND:
           switch( wParam )
           {
              case IDM_CAPTURE:
                 ptStart.x = ptStart.y =
                 ptFinish.x = ptFinish.y = 0;
                 PostMessage( hwnd, WM_LBUTTONDOWN,
                              0L, 0L );
                 break;

              case IDM_GETNAME:
                 if( CallFileOpenDlg( hInst, hwnd ) )
                    PostMessage( hwnd, WM_COMMAND,
                                 IDM_SAVE, NULL );
                 break;

              case IDM_SAVE:
                 SetCursor( LoadCursor( NULL, IDC_WAIT ) );
                 CaptureBitmap( hwnd,
                                ptFinish.x, ptFinish.y );
                 SetCursor( LoadCursor( NULL, IDC_ARROW ) );
                 break;
```

```
            case IDM_ABOUT:
                lpProc = MakeProcInstance( AboutProc,
                                           hInst );
                DialogBox( hInst, "ABOUT", hwnd, lpProc );
                FreeProcInstance( lpProc );
                break;
        }
        return(0);

    case WM_LBUTTONDOWN:
        if( ! fStart )
        {
            fStart = TRUE;
            SetCapture( hwnd );
            SetCursor( LoadCursor( NULL, IDC_CROSS ) );
            CloseWindow( hwnd );
            InvertBlock( hwnd, ptStart, ptFinish );
        }      // invert selected region
        else
        if( ! fFinish )
        {
            fFinish = TRUE;
            ptStart = MAKEPOINT( lParam );
        }
        return(0);

    case WM_MOUSEMOVE:
        if( fStart )
            SetCursor( LoadCursor( NULL, IDC_CROSS ) );
        if( fFinish )
        {
            InvertBlock( hwnd, ptStart, ptFinish );
                // restore currently inverted region
            ptFinish = MAKEPOINT( lParam );
            ptFinish.x -= ptStart.x;
            ptFinish.y -= ptStart.y;
            InvertBlock( hwnd, ptStart, ptFinish );
                // invert selected region
        }
        return(0);

    case WM_LBUTTONUP:
        if( ! fFinish ) break;
        InvertBlock( hwnd, ptStart, ptFinish );
            // restore inverted region before capture
        fStart = fFinish = FALSE;
        SetCursor( LoadCursor( NULL, IDC_WAIT ) );
```

```
            ReleaseCapture();
            if( ptFinish.x == Ø || ptFinish.y == Ø ) break;
            hdc = GetDC( hwnd );
            hdcMem = CreateCompatibleDC( hdc );
            hBitmap = CreateCompatibleBitmap( hdc,
                    abs( ptFinish.x ), abs( ptFinish.y ) );
            if( hBitmap )
            {
               SelectObject( hdcMem, hBitmap );
               StretchBlt( hdcMem, Ø, Ø, abs( ptFinish.x ),
                                          abs( ptFinish.y ),
                        hdc, ptStart.x,  ptStart.y,
                                ptFinish.x, ptFinish.y,
                        SRCCOPY );
               OpenClipboard( hwnd );
               EmptyClipboard();
               SetClipboardData( CF_BITMAP, hBitmap );
               CloseClipboard();
               InvalidateRect( hwnd, NULL, TRUE );
            }
            DeleteDC( hdcMem );
            ReleaseDC( hwnd, hdc );
            OpenIcon( hwnd );
            return(Ø);

        case WM_PAINT:
            hdc = BeginPaint( hwnd, &ps );
            OpenClipboard( hwnd );
            if( hBitmap = GetClipboardData( CF_BITMAP ) )
            {
               SetCursor( LoadCursor( NULL, IDC_WAIT ) );
               hdcMem = CreateCompatibleDC( hdc );
               SelectObject( hdcMem, hBitmap );
               GetObject( hBitmap, sizeof( BITMAP ),
                    (LPSTR) &bm );
               BitBlt( hdc, Ø, Ø, cxWnd, cyWnd,
                    hdcMem, Ø, Ø, SRCCOPY );
               SetCursor( LoadCursor( NULL, IDC_ARROW ) );
               DeleteDC( hdcMem );
            }
            CloseClipboard();
            EndPaint( hwnd, &ps );
            return(Ø);

        case WM_DESTROY:
            PostQuitMessage(Ø);
```

```
            return(0);
    }
    return( DefWindowProc( hwnd, msg, wParam, lParam ) );
}

#pragma argsused

int PASCAL WinMain( HANDLE hInstance,
                    HANDLE hPrevInstance,
                    LPSTR  lpszCmdParam, int nCmdShow )
{
    static char szAppName[] = "CAPTURE2";
    HWND        hwnd;
    MSG         msg;
    WNDCLASS    wc;

    if( ! hPrevInstance )
    {
        wc.hInstance      = hInstance;
        wc.lpfnWndProc    = WndProc;
        wc.cbClsExtra     = 0;
        wc.cbWndExtra     = 0;
        wc.lpszClassName  = szAppName;
        wc.hIcon          = LoadIcon( hInstance, szAppName );
        wc.lpszMenuName   = (LPSTR) szAppName;
        wc.hCursor        = LoadCursor( NULL, IDC_ARROW );
        wc.hbrBackground  = GetStockObject( WHITE_BRUSH );
        wc.style          = CS_HREDRAW | CS_VREDRAW;
        RegisterClass( &wc );
    }
    hInst = hInstance;       // assign global instance handle
    hwnd = CreateWindow( szAppName,
                         "Screen Capture Demo 2",
                         WS_OVERLAPPEDWINDOW,
                         CW_USEDEFAULT, CW_USEDEFAULT,
                         CW_USEDEFAULT, CW_USEDEFAULT,
                         NULL, NULL, hInstance, NULL  );
    ShowWindow(   hwnd, nCmdShow );
    UpdateWindow( hwnd );
    while( GetMessage( &msg, NULL, 0, 0 ) )
    {
        TranslateMessage( &msg );
        DispatchMessage(  &msg );
    }
    return( msg.wParam );
}
```

```
;=========================;
;  CAPTURE2.DEF           ;
;  module definition file ;
;=========================;

NAME           CAPTURE2
DESCRIPTION    "Screen Capture Program"
EXETYPE        WINDOWS
STUB           "WINSTUB.EXE"
CODE           PRELOAD MOVEABLE DISCARDABLE
DATA           PRELOAD MOVEABLE MULTIPLE
HEAPSIZE       1024
STACKSIZE      8192
EXPORTS        WndProc
               AboutProc
               FileNameDlgProc


//================//
//   Capture2.H   //
//================//

#define IDM_CAPTURE   101
#define IDM_GETNAME   102
#define IDM_ABOUT     103
#define IDM_SAVE      105
#define IDD_FNAME     104


//==================//
// CAPTURE2 MENU    //
//==================//
BEGIN
   MENUITEM "Capture", 101
   MENUITEM "Save",    102
   MENUITEM "About",   103, HELP
END
```

Alternative Image Formats

Paintbrush's .PCX format

CompuServe's graphics interchange format (GIF)

Tagged image file format (TIFF)

Truevision's TARGA (TGA) format

24-bit conversions

Optimizing image displays

Summary

Program listing of ViewPCX.C

lthough the .BMP image format is ideal for Windows applications, a number of other image formats are useful for both importing and exporting. While limitations of space and time preclude attempting to list all popular formats, three of the most important formats are described following.

Other important formats that are not covered here include the GEM/IMG format used by Ventura Publisher among others, the PIC, or MacPaint, format used by Apple Macintosh computers, PostScript (.EPS) image formats, and perhaps the most versatile of all, the TIFF or Tagged Image File Format (.TIF). See Appendix A for notes on sources for these and other image file formats.

PAINTBRUSH'S .PCX FORMAT

ZSoft's Paintbrush (.PCX) format has long provided the de facto standard for non-Windows (DOS) bitmapped images, and most graphics programs contain some provision for conversion from their native formats to .PCX formats. At the same time, the PBRUSH.EXE Paintbrush program distributed with Windows was written by ZSoft and includes .PCX/.BMP conversion.

As graphics devices have become increasingly sophisticated, however, the .PCX image format has kept pace. Instead of being a single format, it comprises a series of formats including eight-, 16- and 24-bit color formats, as well as true-gray formats and monochrome formats.

.PCX image files begin with a header defined as:

```
typedef struct tagPCXHEAD
{
    char  manufacturer;       // always  0xA0
    char  version;            // version number
    char  encoding;           // should be 1
    char  bits_per_pixel;     // color depth
    int   xmin, ymin;         // image origin
    int   xmax, ymax;         // image dimensions
    int   hres, vres;         // image resolution
    char  palette[48];        // color palette
    char  reserved;
    char  color_planes;       // color planes
    int   bytes_per_line;     // line buffer size
    int   palette_type;       // gray or color palette
    int   hscreensize;        // horizontal screen size
    int   vscreensize;        // vertical screen size
    char  filler[54];         // null filler
} PCXHEAD;
```

The *manufacturer* byte is simply a check identifying the file as a Paintbrush format image. It should always be 0x0A.

The *version* byte identifies the version of PC Paintbrush that created the image file. If the version number is 0, no palette information is contained. (This represents Paintbrush 2.5—the earliest incarnation.) A version ID of 1 is not used. A version ID of 2 indicates valid palette information, while an ID of 3 indicates either monochrome or the display's default palette. Version ID 4 identifies PC Paintbrush for Windows, while version ID 5 indicates Paintbrush version 3.0 or later, including 24-bit image files.

The *encoding* value should always be 1, indicating that .PCX's run-length encoding has been used. Note, however, that future versions may incorporate new encoding schemes indicated by other values.

The *bits_per_pixel* value reports the number of bits to represent a pixel (per Plane). Possible values are one, two, four, or eight.

The *xmin*, *ymin*, *xmax*, and *ymax* values define the dimensions of the image in pixels. Normally, the *xmin* and *ymin* values will be 0 but may contain an offset origin. Also, the sizes indicated by *xmax* and *ymax* are off by 1; the actual pixel count begins at 0, and the values indicated should be incremented by 1 to give the actual count. Thus, if an image has a width of 480 pixels, these would be numbered as 0..479 and the *xmax* value would appear as 479.

Width and depth should be calculated thus:

```
width = ( pcxHead.xmax - pcxHead.xmin ) + 1;
depth = ( pcxHead.ymax - pcxHead.ymin ) + 1;
```

The *hres* and *vres* values can be ignored entirely, since these provide the resolution of the device (or video mode) where the image was created.

The *palette* buffer contains the palette color information for images with 16 or fewer colors (3 bytes per color or 48 bytes in length). For larger palettes, such as 256-color palettes, the palette information is appended at the end of the image data. In either case, the palette structure used consists of a series of RGB triplets with 1 byte defining the red level for a palette entry, 1 byte defining green and 1 byte blue.

The *color_planes* value is 1 for monochrome, or 4 for EGA 16-bit color images.

The *bytes_per_line* value reports the number of bytes to allocate for a scanline plane. This value *must* be an even number, and cannot be calculated from *xmax – xmin*.

The *palette_type* field originates with the advent of VGA graphics systems with a value of 1 for gray-scale and a value of 2 for full color. This field is ignored in Paintbrush IV and Paintbrush IV+.

The *hscreensize* and *vscreensize* fields report the horizontal and vertical screen size (of the original system) in pixels. These fields were defined for Paintbrush IV and Paintbrush IV+; for all other versions, these should be null.

The *filler* field pads the file header out to 128 bytes and should be filled with nulls (0s).

DECODING MONOCHROME .PCX IMAGES

The first step, obviously, in reading a .PCX image is to read the header information and determine the image type. And, of course, if necessary, read the palette information. After this, however, handling depends on the image type.

For monochrome .PCX files, decoding is quite simple. First, if the two high bits of a byte are set (AND with C0h), then the six least-significant bits are written to the image. (So if a bit is set, the pixel is on; otherwise the pixel is off.)

Alternately, if the two high bits are empty, an index count is created by ANDing the byte with 3Fh and using this index count (0..63) to write the next byte *count* times.

Obviously, the .PCX encoding scheme is heavily weighted for use with images containing large continuous areas. This is not, however, particularly efficient for scanned images (but, then, scanners were quite uncommon when the .PCX format was created).

EGA/VGA 16-COLOR PALETTE INFORMATION

In standard RGB format (IBM EGA, IBM VGA) the palette color data is stored as 16 triplet with each triplet a 3-byte quantity of red, green, and blue values. Because these values can range from 0 to 255, interpretation may be necessary. For example, in an EGA system, for each palette entry there are four possible levels for each color value. Table 8.1 shows video levels corresponding to palette entry values.

Table 8.1: EGA/VGA Palette Levels

Value	Level
0..63	0
64..127	1
128..193	2
194..255	3

DECODING 16-COLOR .PCX IMAGES

.PCX image files may have two, four, eight or 16 colors before jumping directly to 256-color images. But for 16 or fewer colors, the handling remains essentially the same because the image is treated as four interleaved monochrome images.

Although this format may sound mysterious, the reason lies in the structure of EGA video cards, which were the intended environment for the 16-color images. On EGA cards, four 32k memory pages are treated as layers, nominally one each for red, green, blue, and intensity. (Admittedly, this is an over-simplification.)

The point is that the four bits selecting a palette color are written one to each plane—if you're working directly in machine language and accessing these planes directly.

But, in this circumstance, the question is how to decode the image, not the mechanics of an EGA card.

To decode a 16-color .PCX image, four scan lines are read and, initially, treated as monochrome masks. To create color (palette) information, the first bit from each scan line is combined after decoding by shifting the second scan line left one place, the third scan line left two places and the fourth scan line left three places to create a four-bit nibble. This sequence of nibbles creates a single scan line for the image and can be written to the screen (or converted to another format) as index values for the 16-color palette.

THE VIEWPCX DEMO PROGRAM

The ViewPCX program (the complete listing appears at the end of this chapter and on the accompanying disk) demonstrates reading a 256-color .PCX image. At the same time, ViewPCX also provides an example of a file look-up dialog box used to select a .PCX file (Figure 8.1). Note, however, that no provisions are included for changing the file extension, nor are any provisions made for displaying any .PCX files that are not 256-color images.

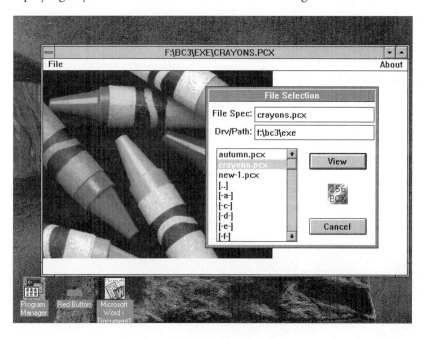

Figure 8.1: The ViewPCX demo with File Selection dialog box

Display provisions for black-and-white and 16-color palettes can easily be included here but are left as an exercise for the reader. For 24-bit-color images, slightly more elaborate provisions will be required—beginning, of course, with a 24-bit video board and an appropriate Windows driver. Remember, however, that no palette is included in 24-bit images; instead, each pixel contains its own color information.

VGA 256-COLOR PALETTE INFORMATION

Because 256-color palettes require three bytes per color or a total of 768 bytes to define the palette, the .PCX file header lacks sufficient space to contain the palette information. Instead, the palette information is appended to the end of the image file.

First, however, check the version number in the header; a value of 5 indicates the presence of a palette. Second, retrieve the palette information by using a seek to an offset from the end of the file as:

```
fseek( fp, -769L, SEEK_END );
```

At this point, the file should return a value of 0x0C, confirming the presence of 256-color palette information while the next 768 bytes contain the red, green, and blue triplets for 256-color palette entries. Because the VGA device expects palette RGB values in the range 0..63 rather than 0..255, the byte values read from the image file must be divided by four (or shifted right two places).

DECODING 256-COLOR .PCX IMAGES

After retrieving the image palette information, the application needs to return to the image data, a task easily accomplished as:

```
fseek( fp, 128L, SEEK_SET );
```

Because the .PCX header, regardless of the image type, is always 128 bytes in length, finding the beginning of the image data is easy. But, if finding the data is easy, decoding the data does require a few provisions.

A 256-color image always uses RLE (run-length encoding)—much the same as in other image formats. Thus, while reading the data, if the two high-bits are set—that is, the byte length is greater than 0Ch—then the byte read is a *count* byte specifying the repeat count for the byte following. As an example, the byte value FEh would indicate that the next byte read would be repeated 3Eh (FEh + C0h = 3Eh or 62) times.

Now, as you may realize, this also means that individual pixels with palette values in the range C0h..FFh (which make up 75 percent of the total palette) require two bytes rather than appearing as a single byte. Therefore, a run of pixels with the palette values DEh, DFh, DFh, EAh, E2h, E7h would be encoded as C1h, DEh, C2h, DFh, C1h, EAh, C1h, E2h, C1h, E7H—not precisely a savings. Overall, however, RLE encoding reduces file size rather than increasing it . . . unless, of course, you happen to be a pointillist.

There are, however, still a few tricks involved in decoding an RLE image, though these tricks are required more to circumvent a few idiosyncrasies in C/C++ than to handle the image encoding. As an example, the decoding provision used in ViewPCX begins by initializing two values, *i* and *j*, before initiating a loop for the scan lines.

```
i = j = 0;
```

```
while( j < depth )
{
    pcxIdx = fgetc(fp);
    if( ( pcxIdx & 0x00C0 ) == 0x00C0 )
    {
        count = pcxIdx & 0x003F;
        pcxIdx = fgetc(fp) & 0x00FF;
```

Granted, a conventional *for* loop could be used with the form *for(j=0; j<depth;)* and with *j* incremented elsewhere within the loop's controlled provisions, but this isn't the trick in question. Instead, the critical element involved here concerns the *fgetc* function.

Nominally, *fgetc* is used to return a *char* value, except that *fgetc* is defined as *int fgetc(FILE fp)*; and returns an integer rather than a *char* value. In most cases, this doesn't matter particularly because subsequent operations expect *char* values and impose automatic typecasting and truncation, as when *char* values become a part of a string.

In this case, however, the difference in the value type returned becomes critical. As an example of why, rewrite ViewPCX's source code as shown following:

```
pcxIdx = fgetc(fp);
if( pcxIdx & 0xC0 )
{
    count = pcxIdx & 0x3F;
    pcxIdx = fgetc(fp);
```

With the changes shown, two problems occur. First, the test i*f(pcxIdx & 0x0C)* will not necessarily detect only the desired high bits. Second and more important, the *count* values returned by *count = pcxIdx & 0x3F* will not fall in the range 0..63 (0h..3Fh). Instead, the count values found fall in the range 0h..FFFFh with a heavy weighting in the range FF00h..FFFFh.

Therefore, the solution is to mask the integer values returned by *fgetc* to the byte values actually needed.

Returning to the correct decoding provisions, as shown preceding, the *if* test branches and, assuming the two high-bits are set, the *count* value is extracted and a second byte is read to determine the palette index *(pcxIdx)* value to be repeated.

Next, a *for* loop is initiated to execute the repeat count—in this example, using the SetPixel function. Two considerations are included here. First, while *pcxHd.xmin* and *pcxHd.ymin* are usually zero, these two values may be used to provide x- and y-axis offsets and are included as part of the position parameters. This provision, however, may be included or omitted as desired.

The second consideration is more important: while the value *pcxIdx* is an index value to the palette array, the SetPixel function expects a COLORREF value, which is provided via the PALETTEINDEX macro.

```
for( k=0; k<count; k++ )
{
    SetPixel( hdc, pcxHd.xmin + i, pcxHd.ymin + j,
            PALETTEINDEX( pcxIdx ) );
    if( ++i >= pcxHd.bytes_per_line )
    {
        j++;
        i = 0;
        k = count;      // if the line's too long ...
} } }                   // just ignore any wraps
```

At this point, the outer loop, which was initiated as a *while* loop, is controlled by incrementing *j* anytime the end of the current scan line is reached. At the same time, *i* is reset to start the next scan line and, whether necessary or not, *k* is reset to terminate the repeat count loop. This last consideration is dictated by the simple fact that no repeat count should ever extend beyond the current scan line.

Of course, the case does remain when any pixels colored using the palette indexes 0h..3Fh occur only once and, therefore, appear as single byte values. Implementing this latter case, while relatively rare, is easily handled thus:

```
else
{
    SetPixel( hdc, pcxHd.xmin + i, pcxHd.ymin + j,
            PALETTEINDEX( pcxIdx ) );
    if( ++i >= pcxHd.bytes_per_line )
    {
        j++;
        i = 0;
} } }
```

24-BIT-PER-PIXEL .PCX FILES

24-bit images can only be displayed on a few true-color systems at the present time and will require both specialized hardware and vendor-supplied Windows drivers. These are, however, becoming increasingly common, so a brief sketch of 24-bit-color image handling is included here.

The first thing to remember is that 24-bit .PCX images do not contain any palette information. Instead these images provide full, 24-bit-color information for each pixel in the image. Twenty-four-bit .PCX images are identified as version ID 5 or above and store their data as eight bits per color plane in three planes. These are decoded in the same fashion as 16-color images except that byte values (eight-bits) are read as lines of red, green, and blue, in that order.

Therefore, to decode 24-bit .PCX images, three scan lines are read as red, green, and blue image lines and treated, after RLE-decoding, by combining the first byte of each scan line as an RGB-triplet pixel value, rather than as a palette value. The second pixel uses the second byte from each scan line, and so on. See "Truevision's TARGA (TGA) Format" later in this chapter for parallels and differences.

CompuServe's graphics interchange format (GIF)

Perhaps one of the most popular image formats in general use—and certainly the most popular in terms of images available on bulletin boards, disk libraries, and CD-ROMs—is the GIF image format.

The Graphics Interchange Format (GIF) was developed by CompuServe as a vehicle for graphics images that could be transferred between different computer systems. Although the GIF format is copyrighted by CompuServe, a blanket, nonexclusive, limited, royalty-free license has been granted to all developers, permitting free use of the GIF format in computer graphics applications.

Current standards and specifications for the GIF format (GIF89A) are readily available on CompuServe (GO GRAPHSUPPORT) as well as from a variety of other on-line services and many private BBSes. A wide variety of GIF display programs, format conversion programs, source-code examples, and GIF images are similarly available.

The GIF format has several features of interest, beginning with a very effective compression scheme utilizing variable-length LZW compression (named for its developers, Lempel, Ziv, and Welsh) . While relatively complex to encode or decode, LZW compression has an important advantage over the simpler RLE compression schemes used by .BMP and .PCX images: size. Images compressed using LZW are virtually always considerably smaller than corresponding images created using RLE compression.

LZW compression builds tables of patterns from the original, replacing repetitive patterns or pixel sequences with indexes to the table entries. LZW compression is also available in the public domain and is used in a variety of applications and forms, not just image compression.

Other features supported by the GIF format include provisions for multiple images within a single file, local color tables including as many as 256 colors, and interleaving scan lines (as used in .PCX formats). Last, the GIF format also has provisions for user-defined extensions.

GIF images are currently identified by two signatures, GIF87A and GIF89A, found in the first six bytes of the image and identifying, respectively, the original 1987 version and the 1989 revision.

Tagged image file format (TIFF)

The TIFF file format is perhaps the most complex of the popular formats. As with the GIF format, the TIFF file specification and format instructions are available on CompuServe (GO ALDUS) or by request from either Aldus or MicroSoft.

The TIFF image format is popular with typesetting and production graphics applications partially because this was one of the earlier formats capable of supporting high-resolution images and partially because the TIFF format provides several subformats optimized for different types of images.

The following five classes of TIFF image are supported:

▶ Class B TIFF files consist of black-and-white images coded as one bit per pixel. They provide three compression formats: none, CCITT Group 3, and PackBits.

▶ Class G TIFF files are used for gray-scale images consisting of four or eight bits per pixel (16 or 256 shades of gray). Class G files either are uncompressed or use LZW compression.

▶ Class P TIFF files support color palettes using one to eight bits per pixel. LZW compression may be used or files may be uncompressed.

▶ Class R TIFF files are used for 24-bit-per-pixel images and, optionally, may use LZW compression.

▶ Class F TIFF files are used for FAX images.

CAUTION: There are also a number of TIFF variations in use that do not follow any published standards. In general, these tend to consist of variant compression algorithms but may vary in other ways as well.

Typically, a TIFF encoder/decoder may run five to ten thousand lines of code. A variety of examples are available for a variety of systems, including UNIX and DOS.

Truevision's TARGA (TGA) format

The TARGA file format, originally developed by Truevision, Inc., is the predominant 24-bit image format used with frame-grabber boards. Truevision markets computer-camera-interface boards that are used extensively in machine imaging as well as for a variety of other applications. Using TARGA cards, or any of a number of competing brands, images are captured directly from video cameras, typically with an image size of 400 by 512 pixels and a pixel depth of 16, 24 or 32 bits.

Previously, a TARGA card or equivalent was required to display .TGA images, and a second, high-resolution monitor was commonly required for the display. Currently, however, a number of 24-bit video cards are appearing on the market, and more than a few of these can display .TGA images directly.

The three image formats supported—16, 24, or 32 bits-per-pixel—can all be considered true-color formats. And, speaking from personal experience in a color-critical application, differences between images using these three formats are quite indistinguishable to the human eye.

Pixels in the 24-bit image format consist of three eight-bit color values in RGB order. The 32-bit-per-pixel format also contains three eight-bit-color values but adds a fourth eight-bit field which is null and is simply ignored.

The third format, 16 bits per pixel, consists of three five-bit color values with the high bit treated as an intensity bit. If the high bit is set, the three five-bit-color values each correspond to the five most-significant-bits in 24-bit- or 32-bit-image color values. If the high bit is zero, the three five-bit values are shifted right 1 bit, decreasing color intensity.

TARGA image file specifications may be requested from:

Truevision, Inc.
7340 Shadeland Station
Indianapolis, IN 46256-3919
(317) 841-0332 (voice)
(317) 576-7700 (fax)

24-BIT CONVERSIONS

While 24-bit true-color cards are becoming popular, these are still less than common. For the present, SVGA (256-color) cards remain the high-resolution standard and are likely to continue so for at least the next few years. At the same time, the 24-bit video frame-capture systems are also popular but cannot be readily displayed on SVGA systems.

Still, there is a solution: converting 24-bit color images captured by video cameras to 256-color palette images that can be displayed on available systems.

Granted, converting a potential palette of 16 million colors (2^{24} = 16,777,216) to a palette with a mere 256 colors does sound like a considerable degradation in image quality, but it isn't really as bad as it might sound. While the potential palette size of a 24-bit image is over 16 million colors, the actual image (assuming 400 by 512 pixels) contains a total of only 204,800 pixels. Thus, assuming that every pixel has a different 24-bit color, the result is an 800-to-1 color reduction. Commonly, however, a typical image will contain a much smaller range of actual colors—perhaps as many as four- or five-hundred distinct shades but more often fewer. And, even when the variation in color is high, many shades that are technically different will still be relatively close in hue and can be represented by single palette entries.

Several methods exist for converting 24-bit images to 256-color-palette images. The simplest method, though not necessarily the best, is to begin by constructing a 256-color palette containing a range of hues that can be used for a variety of images. The drawback to this method is that the resulting palette does not match any image very well and the resulting displays have a rather cartoonlike quality about them.

A second and better method is to begin by constructing a histogram of the colors present in a specific image. This entails processing the entire image to construct a record of each individual color in the image and the frequency of occurrence of each color. After this is completed, a custom, frequency-ordered palette can be constructed from the highest frequency colors, with the remaining image pixels mapped to their nearest equivalents in the constructed palette. (Hint: Reserve two of the 256 palette entries: one each for pure white and pure black.)

Next, after constructing a palette of the high-frequency colors, the original pixel values are mapped as indexes to their corresponding palette entries or, if no matching palette entry exists, to the closest available palette entry. An example of this approach is demonstrated by the TGA2VGA application (see notes following). And, as a bonus, a frequency-ordered palette can help optimize some compression formats, such as .PCX RLE encoding.

A third approach is also possible and follows the same general pattern of creating a histogram of the actual colors, but instead of simply taking 256 (or 254) of the highest-frequency colors to create the palette, a distributed palette is created. In this format, after creating a binary tree of color frequencies, the color tree is scanned—first, for the total number of entries, and second, for the range of differences between colors.

The first consideration is simply the number of colors in the tree. Obviously, if the tree contains fewer than 256 entries, then all entries can be included in the palette and the image encoded as before. In like fashion, if the number of colors in the tree is—to select an arbitrary threshold—less than one and a half times the palette size, a distributed palette probably isn't necessary. On the other hand, if the total number of colors is greater than the threshold level, a distributed palette may well provide a better color spread than a frequency-ordered palette.

Two considerations should be used in selecting entries for a distributed palette: first, the uniqueness of the palette entry and second, the frequency of the color.

Taking the second item first, it should be fairly obvious that there's little benefit in devoting a limited resource (for instance, a palette entry) to a color that is used by very few pixels in the image. Precisely where this cutoff is established is arbitrary but, out of an image composed of 200,000 pixels, a frequency of 20 pixels is 0.01 percent of the total or 0.25 percent of the average, a low enough value to suggest that the color in question could be safely eliminated from further consideration.

The uniqueness of a palette entry is a different matter. This factor must be calculated carefully, taking all three of the color components (red, green, and blue) into consideration.

The obvious method of comparing two color values is simple: Sum the absolute differences of the red, green, and blue components, thus:

$$dC = abs(R_1 - R_2) + abs(G_1 - G_2) + abs(B_1 - B_2)$$

The objective, however, is to emphasize the differences between two colors and to find which colors in the image are closest to each other and, therefore, can be represented by a single palette entry. The color difference (dC) can thus be emphasized by using a nonlinear formula:

$$dC = (R_1 - R_2)^2 + (G_1 - G_2)^2 + (B_1 - B_2)^2$$

This second formula shifts the weighting to emphasize differences in a single color component over differences distributed throughout the three color components.

For example, assume three colors, C_1, C_2, and C_3, with RGB color values 1F2C3Bh, 1F2A3Bh, and 1E2D3Ah, respectively. Using the first formula, C_1 and C_2 would have a color difference of 2 (in the green component) while C_1 and C_3 have a color difference of 3 (1 each in the red, green and blue components).

The human eye's response to colors, however, is nonlinear. Remember the gray-scale formula in Chapter 6? This nonlinearity applies to intensity as well as to sensitivity to different hues; like the human ear, the eye operates with a roughly logarithmic response. Therefore, in theory, the differences in each color component should be scaled logarithmically as well as weighted according to the eye's visual color response.

For present purposes, however, a simpler (non-floating point) operation will yield satisfactory results. Using the second formula, C_1 and C_2 have a calculated color difference of 4 while C_1 and C_3 still yield a calculated difference of 3.

This latter weighting, while technically inaccurate, better approximates the response of the human eye and, therefore, better approximates the relative importance of color differences than does the linear formula.

If you are interested, the Color3 program presented in Chapter 6 can easily be used to experiment and compare color differences. Points to look for are:

▶ What is the minimum total difference in all color components that can be readily identified by the human eye?

▶ What is the minimum difference in any one field that can be readily identified?

▶ How do differences in each of the three component fields (red, green, and blue) compare?

▶ How do differences in intensity compare at different absolute intensities (that is, how do absolute differences appear in proportion to absolute intensities)?

NOTE. Ignoring extreme variations in color perception (commonly referred to as color blindness), color perception still varies widely between individuals and may also be affected by age, health, or the use of corrective lenses.

A sample program, TGA2VGA.CPP, is included on the program disk accompanying this volume to further demonstrate how 16-bit TARGA files can be converted to a raw VGA image format. TGA2VGA features object-oriented methods and a binary tree structure to create a histogram of color frequencies together with color-matching provisions to map low-frequency colors to selected palette entries. After conversion, the resulting image may be stored, with a minimum of effort, in any format desired.

While the TGA2VGA example is not a Windows application per se, the code provided can be incorporated in Windows applications or adapted to 24- or 32-bit image formats.

OPTIMIZING IMAGE DISPLAYS

While the ViewPCX demo program demonstrates how to display a .PCX image, the method used—drawing with individual pixels—is not the optimal choice for the Windows environment. In a DOS environment, without multi-tasking, the approach demonstrated functions without penalty even though, technically, it is less efficient than writing image blocks directly to the video RAM. But under Windows, where each SetPixel operation is followed by Windows taking a time slice to attend to the needs of other applications, the display operation simply becomes tediously slow.

Furthermore, the ViewPCX processes can be contrasted, in Chapter 9, with the Shades program, where Windows's native .BMP file format is used. In the Shades program, display speeds (among other characteristics) are considerably more satisfactory. Note, however, that this change is not inherent in the source file format but in the chosen display method.

More important, the display process demonstrated in Chapter 9—creating a memory bitmapped image directly within the display (device) context—can be applied to any source format, although this does involve minimal conversion. Overall, however, the end result of working in the format native to the Windows environment more than offsets any delays inherent in changing from the source format.

SUMMARY

While several of the more common image formats have been described in this chapter, there are a wide variety of other graphics image formats in use. Some are specific to particular applications and others are more widely recognized. Given the sheer variety of formats extant, however, it is impractical to cover all formats, even briefly.

Therefore, in this chapter, several of the more important—or more interesting—formats have been discussed, including ZSoft's .PCX, Truevision's TARGA (.TGA), CompuServe's Graphics Interchange Format (GIF) and Aldus's TIFF Tagged Image File Format (.TIF).

Of these, only one is actually demonstrated—the .PCX 256-color format handled by the ViewPCX program following. The program disk accompanying this volume includes one sample program, TGA2VGA, which demonstrates decoding TARGA camera images and converting 16-bit-pixel-depth images to a more limited 256-color palette.

Because no single conversion from a true-color format to a 256-color palette is suitable for all circumstances, several alternative conversions have been suggested, while still others can be devised to suit special requirements. The important item in any case is simply to understand how 16- or 24-bit-color information is stored and how such images can be mapped to the more restrictive circumstance of a 256-color palette. Of course, mapping these further (to a 16-color palette) can also be attempted but, in most cases, tends to be relatively futile.

In Chapter 9, existing-image display capabilities will be extended by using image-processing techniques, including filtering and edge-detection algorithms.

Program listing of ViewPCX.C

```
//========================//
//       VIEWPCX.C        //
// 256-Color .PCX Viewer  //
//========================//

#include <windows.h>
#include <stdlib.h>
#include <stdio.h>
#include <conio.h>
#include <dir.h>
#include <string.h>
#include <alloc.h>
#include <bwcc.h>                // include bwcc.lib in project
#include "viewpcx.h"
#include "pcxhead.i"             // PCX image header definition

#define  wFileAttr  0x4010       // file attribute flag

HANDLE   hInst;                  // application hInstance
HWND     hwnd;                   // hwnd of main window
char     szFileSpec[80],         // initial file spec
         szFileExt[5],           // default extension
         szFileName[80],         // file name
         szFilePath[80],         // file path
         szFName[80] = "";       // file to display
WORD     wStatus;                // status of search

#pragma argsused

BOOL FAR PASCAL About( HWND hDlg,    WORD msg,
                       WORD wParam, LONG lParam )
```

```
{
   switch( msg )
   {
      case WM_INITDIALOG: return( TRUE );
      case WM_COMMAND:
         switch( wParam )
         {
            case IDOK: EndDialog( hDlg, TRUE );
                       return( TRUE );
               default: return( TRUE );
      }     }
   return( FALSE );
}


//=========================================================//
// FileOpenDlgProc - get the name of a file to open        //
//=========================================================//

BOOL FAR PASCAL FileOpenDlgProc( HWND hDlg, WORD msg,
                                 WORD wParam, LONG lParam )
{
   static char   OrgPath[80];
   char          cLastChar;
   int           nLen;
   struct ffblk  fileinfo;

   switch (msg)
   {
      case WM_INITDIALOG:
         getcwd( OrgPath, sizeof(OrgPath) );
         SendDlgItemMessage( hDlg, IDD_FNAME,
                             EM_LIMITTEXT, 80, 0L );
            // fill list box with files matching file spec
         DlgDirList( hDlg, szFileSpec, IDD_FLIST,
                     IDD_FPATH, wFileAttr );
         SetDlgItemText( hDlg, IDD_FNAME, szFileSpec );
            // show init filespec
         return( TRUE );
      case WM_COMMAND:
         switch( wParam )
         {
            case IDD_FLIST:
               switch( HIWORD(lParam) )
               {
                  case LBN_SELCHANGE:
                     if( DlgDirSelect( hDlg, szFileName,
```

```
                            IDD_FLIST ) )
                strcat( szFileName, szFileSpec );
            SetDlgItemText( hDlg, IDD_FNAME,
                            szFileName );
            break;
        case LBN_DBLCLK:
            if( DlgDirSelect( hDlg, szFileName,
                              IDD_FLIST ) )
            {
                strcat( szFileName, szFileSpec );
                DlgDirList( hDlg, szFileName,
                            IDD_FLIST, IDD_FPATH,
                            wFileAttr );
                SetDlgItemText( hDlg, IDD_FNAME,
                                szFileSpec );
            }
            else
            {
                SetDlgItemText( hDlg, IDD_FNAME,
                                szFileName );
                SendMessage( hDlg, WM_COMMAND,
                             IDOK, ØL );
            } break;
        } break;
    case IDD_FNAME:
        if( HIWORD(lParam) == EN_CHANGE )
        {
            EnableWindow( GetDlgItem( hDlg, IDOK ),
                (BOOL) SendMessage( LOWORD(lParam),
                       WM_GETTEXTLENGTH, Ø, ØL ) );
        } break;
    case IDOK:
        GetDlgItemText( hDlg, IDD_FNAME,
                        szFileName, 80 );
        nLen = strlen( szFileName );
        cLastChar = *AnsiPrev( szFileName,
                               szFileName + nLen );
        if( cLastChar == '\\' || cLastChar == ':' )
            strcat( szFileName, szFileSpec );
        if( strchr( szFileName, '*' ) ||
            strchr( szFileName, '?' ) )
        {
            if( DlgDirList( hDlg, szFileName,
                            IDD_FLIST, IDD_FPATH,
                            wFileAttr ) )
            {
```

```
                    strcpy( szFileSpec, szFileName );
                    SetDlgItemText( hDlg, IDD_FNAME,
                                    szFileSpec );
                }
                else MessageBeep(Ø);
                break;
            }
            if( DlgDirList( hDlg, szFileName,
                            IDD_FLIST, IDD_FPATH,
                            wFileAttr ) )
            {
                strcpy( szFileSpec, szFileName );
                SetDlgItemText( hDlg, IDD_FNAME,
                                szFileSpec );
                break;
            }
            szFileName[nLen] = '\Ø';
            if( findfirst( szFileName, &fileinfo, Ø ) )
            {
                strcat( szFileName, szFileExt );
                if( findfirst( szFileName,
                               &fileinfo, Ø ) )
                {
                    MessageBeep(Ø);    // if not file
                    break;             // beep and break
            }  }
            GetDlgItemText( hDlg, IDD_FPATH,
                            szFilePath, 8Ø );
            strupr( szFilePath );
            if( szFilePath[ strlen( szFilePath )-1 ]
                != '\\' ) strcat( szFilePath, "\\" );
            strcpy( szFileName, fileinfo.ff_name );
            chdir( OrgPath );
            EndDialog( hDlg, TRUE );     // return TRUE
            break;
        case IDCANCEL:
            chdir( OrgPath );
            EndDialog( hDlg, FALSE );   // return FALSE
            break;
        default:  return( FALSE );
        }  break;
    default: return( FALSE );
    }
    return( TRUE );
}
```

```
//===========================================================//
// CallFileOpenDlg: invokes FileOpenDlgProc to get          //
//                  name of file to open                    //
// parameters: szFileSpecIn  - initial file path            //
//             szFileExtIn   - initial file extension        //
// (returned)  szFilePathOut - selected file path           //
// (returned)  szFileNameOut - selected file name           //
//     return: TRUE if file selected, FALSE if not          //
//===========================================================//

int CallFileOpenDlg( HANDLE hInst, HWND  hwnd,
                     char *szFileSpecIn,
                     char *szFileExtIn,
                     char *szFilePathOut,
                     char *szFileNameOut )
{
   FARPROC   lpProc;
   int       iReturn;

   strcpy( szFileSpec, szFileSpecIn);   // save file spec
   strcpy( szFileExt, szFileExtIn);
   lpProc = MakeProcInstance( FileOpenDlgProc, hInst );
   iReturn = DialogBox( hInst, "OPENFILE", hwnd, lpProc );
   FreeProcInstance( lpProc );
   strcpy( szFilePathOut, szFilePath ); // return filepath
   strcpy( szFileNameOut, szFileName ); // return filename
   return( iReturn );
}

int ErrorMsg( HWND hwnd, char *Message )
{
   MessageBox( hwnd, Message, "Error!",
               MB_ICONQUESTION | MB_OK );
   return(0);
}

BOOL PaintImage( HWND hwnd, HDC hdc, char *PCXFile )
{
   static  int   i, j, k, width, depth, count, pcxIdx;
   PCXHEAD       pcxHd;
   FILE          *fp;
   LPLOGPALETTE  lPal;
   HPALETTE      hPCXPal, hOldPal;
   char          pcxPal[768], szBuff[50];

   if( strlen( PCXFile ) == 0 ) return(0);
```

```c
if( ( fp = fopen( PCXFile, "rb" ) ) == NULL )
{
   sprintf( szBuff, "Unable to open %s!", PCXFile );
   ErrorMsg( hwnd, szBuff );
   return( FALSE );
}
if( ( fread( (char *) &pcxHd, 1, sizeof(PCXHEAD), fp )
       != sizeof(PCXHEAD) ) ||
     ( pcxHd.manufacturer != 0x0A ) )
{
   fclose( fp );
   ErrorMsg( hwnd, "Not a valid .PCX file" );
   return( FALSE );
}
if( ( pcxHd.version != 5 ) ||
         // wrong version number
     ( fseek( fp, -769L, SEEK_END ) ) ||
         // wrong format -- too small for palette
     ( fgetc( fp ) != 0x000C ) ||
         // no palette identifier found
     ( fread( pcxPal, 1, 768, fp ) != 768 ) )
{         // error reading 256 color palette
   fclose( fp );
   ErrorMsg( hwnd, "Not a 256 color image format" );
   return( TRUE );
}
//========= create palette ==========================
lPal = (LPLOGPALETTE)
   farmalloc( sizeof(LOGPALETTE) +
              sizeof(PALETTEENTRY) * 256 );
lPal->palVersion = 0x0300;
lPal->palNumEntries = 256;
for( i=j=0; i<256; ++i )
{
   lPal->palPalEntry[i].peRed   = pcxPal[j++];
   lPal->palPalEntry[i].peGreen = pcxPal[j++];
   lPal->palPalEntry[i].peBlue  = pcxPal[j++];
   lPal->palPalEntry[i].peFlags = PC_NOCOLLAPSE;
   //  use PC_NOCOLLAPSE instead of PC_RESERVED -- //
   //  PC_RESERVED maps to nearest existing color  //
   //  but no good matches exist for this purpose  //
}
hPCXPal = CreatePalette( lPal );
hOldPal = SelectPalette( hdc, hPCXPal, FALSE );
RealizePalette( hdc );          // palette is now active
```

```
width = ( pcxHd.xmax - pcxHd.xmin ) + 1;    // optional
depth = ( pcxHd.ymax - pcxHd.ymin ) + 1;    // necessary
//========= reset file pointer to image ================
fseek( fp, 128L, SEEK_SET );
i = j = 0;                    // initialize image coordinates
while( j < depth )
{
    pcxIdx = fgetc(fp);
        // serious problem here -- fgetc returns int, not
        // char -- ergo, all ops must use integer masks
        // to prevent serious overrun errors on loops and
        // to avoid invalid palette index entries
    if( ( pcxIdx & 0x00C0 ) == 0x00C0 )
    {
        count = pcxIdx & 0x003F;
        pcxIdx = fgetc(fp) & 0x00FF;
        for( k=0; k<count; k++ )
        {
            SetPixel( hdc, pcxHd.xmin + i, pcxHd.ymin + j,
                    PALETTEINDEX( pcxIdx ) );
            if( ++i >= pcxHd.bytes_per_line )
            {
                j++;
                i = 0;
                k = count;    // if the line's too long ...
    } } }                     // just ignore any wraps
    else
    {
        SetPixel( hdc, pcxHd.xmin + i, pcxHd.ymin + j,
                PALETTEINDEX( pcxIdx ) );
        if( ++i >= pcxHd.bytes_per_line )
        {
            j++;
            i = 0;
} } }
    //========= restore original palette ==================
    SelectPalette( hdc, hOldPal, FALSE );
    DeleteObject( hPCXPal );          // delete custom palette
    farfree( lPal );                  // free memory allocated
    fclose( fp );
    return( TRUE );
}


long FAR PASCAL WndProc( HWND hwnd,    WORD msg,
                         WORD wParam, LONG lParam )
{
```

```
static char szTmpFilePath[80;
static char szTmpFileExt[5];
static char szTmpFileSpec[80];
static char szTmpFileName[80];

FARPROC        lpProc;          // pointer to dialog box
char           szBuff[128];     // temp buffer
int            i;
HDC            hdc;
PAINTSTRUCT    ps;

switch( msg )
{
   case WM_CREATE:
      getcwd( szTmpFilePath, sizeof(szTmpFilePath) );
      strcat( szTmpFilePath, "\\" );
      strcpy( szTmpFileExt,  szFileExt );
      strcpy( szTmpFileName, "" );
      return(0);
   case WM_COMMAND:
      switch( wParam )
      {
         case IDM_ABOUT:
            lpProc = MakeProcInstance( About, hInst );
            DialogBox( hInst, "ABOUT", hwnd, lpProc );
            FreeProcInstance( lpProc );
            break;
         case IDM_OPEN:    // setup initial search path
            strcpy( szTmpFileSpec, szTmpFilePath );
            strcat( szTmpFileSpec, "*" );
            strcat( szTmpFileSpec, szFileExt );
            if( CallFileOpenDlg( hInst, hwnd,
                  szTmpFileSpec, szFileExt,
                  szTmpFilePath, szTmpFileName ) )
            {
               strcpy( szFName, szTmpFilePath );
               strcat( szFName, szTmpFileName );
               sprintf( szBuff, "%s", szFName );
               SetWindowText( hwnd, szBuff );
               InvalidateRect( hwnd, NULL, TRUE );
               UpdateWindow( hwnd );
            } break;
         case IDM_QUIT:
            PostMessage( hwnd, WM_CLOSE, 0, 0L );
            break;
         default: break;
```

```
                } break;
            case WM_PAINT:
                hdc = BeginPaint( hwnd, &ps );
                PaintImage( hwnd, hdc, szFName );
                EndPaint( hwnd, &ps );
                return(0);
            case WM_DESTROY:
                PostQuitMessage(0);
                return(0);
        }
        return( DefWindowProc( hwnd, msg, wParam, lParam ) );
}

#pragma argsused

int PASCAL WinMain( HANDLE hInstance,
                    HANDLE hPrevInstance,
                    LPSTR  lpszCmdParam, int nCmdShow )
{
    static char szAppName[] = "ViewPCX";
    HWND        hwnd;
    MSG         msg;
    WNDCLASS    wc;

    if( ! hPrevInstance )
    {
        wc.hInstance     = hInstance;
        wc.lpfnWndProc   = WndProc;
        wc.cbClsExtra    = 0;
        wc.cbWndExtra    = 0;
        wc.lpszClassName = szAppName;
        wc.hIcon         = LoadIcon( hInstance, szAppName );
        wc.lpszMenuName  = (LPSTR) szAppName;
        wc.hCursor       = LoadCursor( NULL, IDC_ARROW );
        wc.hbrBackground = GetStockObject( WHITE_BRUSH );
        wc.style         = CS_HREDRAW | CS_VREDRAW;
        RegisterClass( &wc );
    }
    else GetInstanceData( hPrevInstance,
                          (PSTR) szAppName, 10 );
    strcpy( szFileExt, ".PCX" );   // set default extension
    strcpy( szFileSpec, "*" );     // set default filespec
    hInst = hInstance;             // global instance handle
    hwnd = CreateWindow( szAppName, "256-Color PCX Viewer",
                         WS_OVERLAPPEDWINDOW,
                         CW_USEDEFAULT, CW_USEDEFAULT,
```

```
                        CW_USEDEFAULT, CW_USEDEFAULT,
                        NULL, NULL, hInstance, NULL  );
    ShowWindow(    hwnd, nCmdShow );
    UpdateWindow( hwnd );
    while( GetMessage( &msg, NULL, 0, 0 ) )
    {
        TranslateMessage( &msg );
        DispatchMessage(  &msg );
    }
    return( msg.wParam );
}

//======================
// VIEWPCX.H
//======================
#define  IDS_NAME      1
#define  IDD_FNAME     16
#define  IDD_FPATH     17
#define  IDD_FLIST     18
#define  IDM_QUIT      101
#define  IDM_ABOUT     102
#define  IDM_OPEN      103



;========================
;  VIEWPCX.DEF
;  module definition file
;========================

NAME          VIEWPCX

DESCRIPTION   "View 256-Color PCX Images"
EXETYPE       WINDOWS
STUB          "WINSTUB.EXE"
CODE          PRELOAD MOVEABLE DISCARDABLE
DATA          PRELOAD MOVEABLE MULTIPLE
HEAPSIZE      1024
STACKSIZE     8192
EXPORTS       WndProc
              About
              FileOpenDlgProc
```

Image
Enhancement

Chapter
9

An ancient and venerable aphorism holds that a picture is worth a thousand words—a bit of folk wisdom that is probably more of an understatement than anything else. In evolutionary terms, however, a picture is also, conservatively, a million times more ancient. Remember, words, beginning with the earliest spoken language, are a recent invention while sight, in its most primitive forms, dates back virtually to the earliest primeval protoplasmic globules.

This is not simply a digression into natural history. The point here is, first, that vision has a long and complex history of evolutionary development. And, second, although computers can display and store images, they are not very good at processing—that is, recognizing—even the simplest of patterns. As an example, while the human eye (backed by a sophisticated neural network) can pick out even a deliberately camouflaged shape from a mixed and mottled background, teaching a computer to recognize a black square against a white background is more than slightly difficult.

Please note that the emphasis is on *recognize*. If all an application has to do is locate a known shape, this can be relatively simple. Recognition is an entirely different matter—and a very sophisticated process.

Still, given the average level of patience demonstrated by computer programmers, it hardly seems practical to consider waiting several million years for computers to evolve image recognition naturally. Therefore, in this chapter, the topic is image enhancement, a subject that is not only integral to pattern recognition—both for computers and for humans—but also is used in image processing for aesthetic purposes.

In Chapters 7 and 8, a variety of image formats were discussed. For machine vision, the TARGA 24-bit-per-pixel format is certainly one of the most popular for the simple reason that this format provides a maximum of data for processing. And, following Sherlock Holmes's caution that "it is a prime mistake to theorize in the absence of data," obviously, the more data available initially, the more information can be derived from the data.

But, for our present purposes of demonstration, a wealth of information also means an excess of processing. Therefore, the demonstration program in this chapter, Shades.C, will use 256-color .BMP images, sacrificing a richness of data for a simplicity of processing. The techniques demonstrated, however, not only are applicable to higher-resolution images but also tend to function even better as the degree of differentiation within the data increases.

CONVERTING IMAGES TO MAPS

The first step in image processing—artistic purposes excepted—is to convert a raw image into a map or outline of the principal elements of the image. This process is commonly known as *edge detection*. In image processing, edge detection is simply a process of identifying abrupt gradients between adjacent pixels. For this purpose, a variety of processes are available including the Sobel, smoothed, Laplace, isotropic, and stochastic algorithms, all of which will be demonstrated presently and which are included in the Shades.C demo program.

Too often, however, what would be a relatively simple process under ideal circumstances, in reality is complicated by noise or garbage within the original data (image). When this happens, other algorithms, such as high- and low-pass filters, or an averaging algorithm can be used to reduce the noise within the data. Although all three processes are discussed, Shades.C demonstrates the averaging algorithm, leaving alternatives as an exercise for the reader.

SIMPLIFYING COMPLEX INFORMATION

Referring to "noise" within an image is not entirely accurate and has connotations that could be misleading. For accuracy, it would be preferable to refer to the data as overly complex and refer to the treatment process as simplification. Regardless of the terminology, however, the process is essentially the same: removing a portion of the information or, if not removing it, decreasing the weight accorded to some portion of the information.

Data averaging   Data averaging is precisely what its name would suggest: treating each data element or pixel by averaging its value with the value of the surrounding elements. As an example, consider the following array of values:

```
9 9 8 9 9 8 7 6                            8 8 8 8 7 7 6 6
9 8 9 9 8 1 6 6         1 1 1             8 8 8 8 7 7 5 6
9 9 9 8 7 6 6 6    X    1 0 1    =        8 8 8 7 6 5 5 6
9 9 8 7 6 7 6 7         1 1 1             8 8 7 7 6 6 6 6
9 8 7 6 6 6 6 6                            8 7 7 6 6 6 6 6
```

In the raw data set (left), most elements within the data consist of the values 8 and 9 while a single noise element appears with a value of 1. On the right, a copy of the data set has been cleaned using a simple averaging algorithm, with the noisy 1 replaced by a 7 while the remainder of the data is considerably more homogenous than originally.

The mask array is applied to each data element in the original set, and weighing each element as the average of its neighbors' values while ignoring the element's own value. Thus, the mask is applied to the noisy data element as:

```
9 8 7           1 1 1
8 1 6     X     1 0 1   =   57 / 8   =   7.125   =   7
7 6 6           1 1 1
```

And the resulting value, 7, fits very nicely into the original data set.

NOTE. This algorithm does not use matrix multiplication, only a simple mask operation. Mathematicians may enjoy applying matrix algebra via a similar algorithm; the results can be very interesting.

Okay, the example is simple and only values in the range 0..9 have been used, but the principle remains valid, and this same mask will be applied to more complex data in image processing in the Shades.C program.

Depending on circumstances, a number of different masks can be applied. Three examples are:

```
1 1 1          1 1 1          1 1 1
1 1 1          1 4 1          1 8 1
1 1 1          1 1 1          1 1 1
```

In each case, the divisors used would be 9, 12, and 16, respectively, and each has changed the relative weighting given to the central or target data element. In the prior example, the target element was ignored entirely, but in the latter examples, first, all elements including the target receive equal weighting; second, the target element receives one-third weighting against the neighbors' two-thirds; and, third, the target element receives equal weighting against the sum of its neighbors.

Furthermore, in each case the severity of averaging decreases. Remember, however, that averaging the data also reduces the amount of information contained in the data.

Later, this same data set will be used to illustrate other filter processes. For the present, refer back to the preceding example and notice that the original data set was only moderately homogenous. That is, the areas which were predominately nines, also held a few eights and, to the lower-right of the set, where values are predominately sixes, there are also a few scattered sevens.

Also, since your attention has been called to the distribution of values, you should have noticed a diagonal "edge" consisting of eights and sevens, and forming a transition between one field consisting predominantly of nines and one which is predominantly sixes. Later, other algorithms will be applied to this same data set to demonstrate edge detection.

But, for the moment, the subject is averaging or noise removal. What you should particularly notice is that the algorithm applied has removed the noisy element and, at the same time, left the remainder of the data essentially unchanged, though slightly smoother.

Granted, such a thoroughly "hands-off" selectivity is not a reliable expectation, but the general result is that the homogenous areas remain relatively unaffected while noisy elements are smoothed out—at least to a degree. This process is demonstrated by the Shades.C program.

Border restrictions   With the exception of the color inversion procedure, all of the transforms demonstrated have a small limitation: The border pixels of the image cannot be included in the convolution. The reason is obvious with a bit of thought because each pixel (or data element) convoluted requires, using a 3-by-3 array, a border on each side of one column and one row. For the stochastic transform (discussed later), which uses a 5-by-5 or 7-by-7 mask, the border area increases accordingly. Also, for the data sets used as examples for each of these processes, an appropriate border has been added (but not shown) to permit executing the transforms across the entire data set that is displayed.

Granted, this may sound like a minor restriction, but it is still an important one. Under Windows, attempts to access array elements which are not defined (because they lie outside of the data set) will result in a system memory violation. Under DOS, the immediate effects of such errors may be less readily apparent but can still be quite serious.

For this reason, the loop calling the transform procedure is always indexed—both vertically and horizontally—with a high and low offset to accommodate the border requirements.

The DoAveragingTrns procedure The DoAveragingTrns procedure is one of the simpler examples of filtering a data array and will serve to introduce the technique used to implement a variety of other filters. DoAveragingTrns is called from a procedure that is scanning one copy of an image and writing the resulting values to a second copy.

DoAveragingTrns is called with an index (DWORD) to a one-dimensional array of data (the image), returning a byte value which, in this case, is the new palette index value.

```
BYTE DoAveragingTrns( DWORD dwPos )
{
   int   TxFrm[3][3] =
         { 1,  1,  1,
           1,  0,  1,
           1,  1,  1 };
   BYTE  RVal,  GVal,  BVal,  m;
   int   RtVal, GtVal, BtVal, i, j;
   DWORD dwOfs;

   RtVal = GtVal = BtVal = 0;
   for( i=-1; i<2; i++ )
      for( j=-1; j<2; j++ )
```

Within DoAveragingTrns, a double loop steps through the mask array but, instead of the usual loop from 0..2, a loop from -1..1 is used because the elements for comparison bracket the target element, appearing before, after, above, and below.

Within the loop, a second process is needed to address the appropriate pixel elements. Thus, *dwOfs* is calculated as an offset from *dwPos*. The value *bmScanWidth* is calculated when the image is loaded and, instead of the image width, provides the scan width, which must be an even WORD multiple.

```
      {
         dwOfs = (DWORD)(dwPos+i+(j*bmScanWidth));
         m = (BYTE) lpMBits[dwOfs];
                     // get palette index for pixel
```

After determining the appropriate offset (*dwOfs*), *m* retrieves the palette index value from the identified pixel. The value contained in *m* is only a palette index and, therefore, three separate values are extracted from the palette itself as red, green, and blue color values, all of which are multiplied by the present mask value.

```
         RtVal += TxFrm[i+1][j+1] *
                     pGLP->palPalEntry[m].peRed;
         GtVal += TxFrm[i+1][j+1] *
                     pGLP->palPalEntry[m].peGreen;
```

```
BtVal += TxFrm[i+1][j+1] *
                    pGLP->palPalEntry[m].peBlue;
}
```

Obviously, if loop values from –1 to 1 are used, some correction is required to reference the mask array, shifting the values from –1..1 to 0..2.

After the loop completes, one further series of choices is required because provisions have been made to permit operations on only one, any two, or all three of the color planes. But, assuming the color plane is enabled, the total in _tVal_ is divided by eight before typecasting as a BYTE value.

```
if(UseColors[0]) RVal = (BYTE)( RtVal / 8 );
            else RVal = pGLP->palPalEntry[m].peRed;
if(UseColors[1]) GVal = (BYTE)( GtVal / 8 );
            else GVal = pGLP->palPalEntry[m].peGreen;
if(UseColors[2]) BVal = (BYTE)( BtVal / 8 );
            else BVal = pGLP->palPalEntry[m].peBlue;
return( GetNearestPaletteIndex( hGPal,
        RGB((BYTE)RVal,(BYTE)GVal,(BYTE)BVal)));
}
```

Last, the resulting red, green, and blue values are passed to the RGB macro and then to the GetNearestPaletteIndex function to return an appropriate palette index representing the resulting color (or, at least, the closest available match).

Low-pass filtering   A second filter process, known as *low-pass filtering* or *two-dimensional Gaussian weighting,* uses a filter matrix as shown below. In general, low-pass filters are used for noise smoothing and for interpolating missing or damaged data elements.

Although the actual Gaussian formula is somewhat more complex than the mask illustrated, this matrix does supply a good integer approximation of two-dimensional Gaussian weighting and, for computer processing purposes, is considerably faster than applying the real formula while proving every bit as effective.

Applying the low-pass mask to the data set illustrated previously produces the following results:

```
9 9 8 9 9 8 7 6                     8 8 8 8 8 7 6 6
9 8 9 9 8 1 6 6          1 2 1      8 8 8 8 7 5 5 6
9 9 9 8 7 6 6 6    X     2 4 2  =   8 8 8 7 6 5 5 6
9 9 8 7 6 7 6 7          1 2 1      8 8 7 7 6 6 6 6
9 8 7 6 6 6 6 6                     8 7 7 6 6 6 6 6
```

The results of the low-pass filter are quite similar to the results produced using the averaging filter. The primary difference between the two is simply that the noise elements are not quite as smoothed out as they were when using the averaging filter.

High-pass filtering   A third filter process, known as *high-pass filtering*, is essentially the reverse of the low-pass filter. High-pass filters are useful for enhancing contrast and for detecting edges. Of course, at the same time, high-pass filters also enhance any noise present within an image.

Following are the effects of applying a high-pass filter to the sample data set:

```
9 9 8 9 9 9 8 7 6                          1    4  -11   3   12   13    5   -6
9 8 9 9 9 8 1 6 6      -1 -2 -1             2  -11    5   7   13  -73    6   -1
9 9 9 8 7 6 6 6  X     -2 12 -2   =        1    3    7   1    4    4    3   -2
9 9 8 7 6 7 6 7        -1 -2 -1             1    6    1  -1   -8   11   -4   12
9 8 7 6 6 6 6 6                             6    1   -1  -6   -2   -2   -2   -2
```

In this case, the results no longer fit the range of the original data set. Of course, the results of the mask operation could be normalized as shown following:

```
1    4  -11   3   12   13    5   -6                8 8 7 8 9 9 9 8 7
2  -11    5   7   13  -73    6   -1                8 8 8 8 9 1 8 7
1    3    7   1    4    4    3   -2   (N₁) =       8 8 8 8 8 8 8 7
1    6    1  -1   -8   11   -4   12                8 8 8 7 7 8 7 9
6    1   -1  -6   -2   -2   -2   -2                8 8 7 7 7 7 7 7
```

Normalizing the data, while returning the data to the original range, has also destroyed most of the information gained from the high-pass filter. At the same time, it has fuzzed or blurred the original image.

More often, a high-pass filter would be used with a different criterion known as *range clipping*. Using range clipping, instead of normalizing all values to maintain a desired range, values rising above the maximum are simply truncated to the maximum, while values falling below the minimum range limit are returned as the minimum.

The effects of range clipping, however, tend to obscure details at both extremes of the range, and, therefore, are most useful when the contrasts within a data set (or an image) are relatively low and can be enhanced by this process without losing other important data.

Exercising a normalization of this type has a quite different effect as shown following:

```
1    4  -11   3   12   13    5   -6                1 4 0 3 9 9 5 0
2  -11    5   7   13  -73    6   -1                2 0 6 7 9 0 6 0
1    3    7   1    4    4    3   -2   (N₂)          1 3 7 1 4 4 3 0
1    6    1  -1   -8   11   -4   12                1 6 1 0 0 9 0 9
6    1   -1  -6   -2   -2   -2   -2                6 1 0 0 0 0 0 0
```

Employing range clipping does lose some information, in both the highs and the lows, but overall, it enhances the important contrasts—which, after all, is the entire objective.

Of course, a variety of high-pass filters can be applied to produce different degrees of contrast. The precise effect of variations in high-pass masks is left as an exercise for the reader but three matrix suggestions follow:

```
-1   -2   -1          -1   -3   -1          -2   -3   -2
-2   16   -2          -3   16   -3          -3   20   -3
-1   -2   -1          -1   -3   -1          -2   -3   -2
```

EDGE DETECTION ALGORITHMS

While high- and low-pass filters are useful, edge detection algorithms are always an important element of image processing and particularly so in machine vision applications. While it is possible to create a program to measure and identify clearly defined shapes, such ideal shapes are rarely, if ever, encountered in actual applications. Instead, commonly, even good image data generally consists of misaligned images obscured by shadows, highlights, and general noise.

And, in these circumstances, as well as others, edge detection algorithms become eminently important. While high-pass filters, as mentioned previously, do provide some edge detection, a variety of other functions are expressly designed to detect and identify sharp differentials in intensity and color which, visually, identify regional boundaries.

As an example, in Figure 9.1, at the left, a modernistic "painting" appears. The original image, titled simply MODERN.BMP is included on the program disk accompanying this volume together with a second, pastel version under the title MODERN2.BMP.

At the right of Figure 9.1, the same image is repeated after processing with an edge detection algorithm. Of course, the actual edge detection algorithm leaves the background black with the edges identified in color according to the degree of slope (color contrast). For purposes of reproduction—because large dark areas with relatively narrow light lines do not reproduce well in print—the Inverted option in the Shades program was used to reverse the image after edge detection.

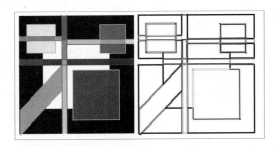

Figure 9.1: Edge detection with a color image

Which of the several edge detection algorithms was used is unimportant in this instance because all of the algorithms demonstrated work equally well with the cleanly defined original shown. In other circumstances, however, different edge detection algorithms vary in efficiency.

Unlike high-pass filters, all edge detection algorithms are highly directional, that is, a specific convolution matrix will detect slope or edges only in certain orientations. For this reason, edge detection algorithms commonly use four passes, rotating the matrix in 45 degree steps each time. (Or, more commonly, instead of rotating the matrix, a series of four mask rotations are defined and used in turn.)

Because each mask will return a positive or a negative value—depending on the direction of the slope encountered—the result of each mask convolution is used as an absolute value. When all four convolutions have been processed, the highest slope of the four detected is returned. Examples of this process are shown in the following section using a Sobel transform.

Sobel transforms   The Sobel transform (also called a convolution) is a relatively simple edge detection algorithm employing four 3-by-3 arrays as shown following:

```
-1 -2 -1      0 -1 -2      -1  0  1      -2 -1  0
 0  0  0      1  0 -1      -2  0  2      -1  0  1
 1  2  1      2  1  0      -1  0  1       0  1  2
```

The first matrix (left) detects edges oriented horizontally. The second detects edges slanting diagonally from upper-left to lower-right, the third detects vertical lines, and the fourth detects diagonals running from lower-left to upper-right. The matrix values (and sizes) used by other edge detection algorithms vary but follow essentially the same principle.

Beginning with the first matrix and applying convolution to the data set which has been used as an example previously, the result shows three data points which are identified as an edge element as shown following:

```
9 9 8 9 9 9 8 7 6                      0  2  0  1 10  7  1  4
9 8 9 9 9 8 1 6 6        -1  0  1      0  1  1  3 19  7  8  1
9 9 9 9 8 7 6 6 6   X    -2  0  2   =  0  1  4  7 12  4  5  0
9 9 8 7 6 7 6 7                        1  4  7  7  2  1  0  0
9 8 7 6 6 6 6 6         -1  0  1       4  7  7  4  0  0  0  0
```

Next, ignoring the result of the first test and applying the second matrix array, the Sobel convolution detects a very prominent edge running roughly diagonally from the lower-left toward the upper-right as shown below. Because this is not a "clean" line, the detected edge varies in width from one to three elements but, given the data set, is correct.

```
9 9 8 9 9 8 7 6                    Ø  1  Ø  1 18 16 1Ø  6
9 8 9 9 8 1 6 6      -2 -1  Ø       Ø  Ø  1  4 16 1Ø  Ø  2
9 9 9 8 7 6 6 6   X  -1  Ø  1  =    Ø  2  6 1Ø  8  1 12  1
9 9 8 7 6 7 6 7       Ø  Ø  2       2  6 1Ø 1Ø  5  2  Ø  Ø
9 8 7 6 6 6 6 6                     6 1Ø 1Ø  9  2  1  2  1
```

Still, this is only two passes and two further matrices remain to test the data set. Below is the result produced after all convolutions have been processed. The points shown in bold identify detected edges—or, at least points where the slope or difference between data elements and their neighbors is extreme.

```
Ø   2   Ø   1 18 19 13   6
Ø   2   1   4 16 1Ø  Ø   2
Ø   2   6 1Ø  8   1 12   2
2   6 1Ø 1Ø  5   2  Ø   Ø
6 1Ø 1Ø  6   2   1  2   1
```

Thus far, the Sobel transform has provided very good contrast and the detected edges should stand out well from the surrounding data. This contrast can be taken one step further by comparing the new data set with the original and applying three simple rules to create a third data set:

▸ First, if the data point after convolution is higher than the data point before convolution, the point is set to maximum.

▸ Second, if the data point remains the same or approximately the same—which can happen—a median value is assigned. What range is considered median can vary according to the application and the data set.

▸ Third, if the resulting data point is lower than the original, the value is set to a minimum.

Following is the result after maximizing contrasts.

```
Ø Ø Ø Ø 9 9 9 Ø
Ø Ø Ø Ø 9 9 Ø Ø
Ø Ø Ø 9 9 Ø 9 Ø
Ø Ø 9 9 Ø Ø Ø Ø
Ø 9 9 Ø Ø Ø Ø Ø
```

The maximizing process illustrated is optional and is not implemented in the Shades.C program but, if desired, can be added conveniently. Remember, however, that comparisons must be made not on the palette index values but on the actual color values. Furthermore, the red, green, and blue color values must be compared separately.

Smoothed transforms Smoothed transforms operate essentially the same as Sobel transforms except for the matrices used. For a smoothed (or Hough) transform, the four masks used are defined as:

```
-1  0  1      -1 -1  0      -1 -1 -1       0 -1 -1
-1  0  1      -1  0  1       0  0  0       1  0 -1
-1  0  1       0  1  1       1  1  1       1  1  0
```

Aside from the change in values, operations remain the same and the results are also similar.

Laplace transforms Laplace transforms present a distinct difference from the Sobel and smoothed transforms. Again, the Laplace transform uses a 3-by-3 array but the array is symmetrical and only one array is used, thus making the Laplace transform similar to the high-pass filters discussed earlier.

Although three separate Laplace transforms are provided, only one of these will be used as selected by the degree variable in Shades.C. The three transforms defined are:

```
 0 -1  0      -1 -1 -1       1 -2  1
-1  4 -1      -1  8 -1      -2  4 -2
 0 -1  0      -1 -1 -1       1 -2  1
```

Notice particularly that the sum of the elements in each mask is zero.

The Laplace transform (or Laplace operator) is also known as a zero-crossing operator and is useful with photographic (or video) images for outlining areas of constant intensity.

The Isotropic transform The isotropic transform parallels the Sobel and smoothed transforms in that it consists of four 3-by-3 masks but, instead of integer values, it ideally consists of real values defined as:

```
 -1   0   1     -√2  -1   0     -1  -√2  -1      0  -1 -√2
-√2   0  √2      -1   0   1      0   0    0      1   0  -1
 -1   0   1       0   1  √2      1  √2    1     √2   1   0
```

Because integer operations are faster than floating-point operations (and quite a few operations are required for this process), the transform matrices are defined as:

```
-100  0 100   -141 -100    0   -100 -141 -100     0 -100 -141
-141  0 141   -100    0  100      0    0    0    100    0 -100
-100  0 100      0  100  141    100  141  100    141  100    0
```

And, after these operators are used, the resulting values are simply divided by 100—in general, a much faster process than floating-point operations.

The Stochastic transform   As the isotropic transform, the stochastic transform uses floating-point operations and, again, can be approximated by changing from decimal values to integers in the matrix arrays. There is also a second difference: The stochastic transform uses a series of eight masks, each of which is 5-by-5 rather than 3-by-3.

Only one matrix array is illustrated, using the floating-point values, following:

```
0.802    0.836    0.000    -0.836    -0.802
0.845    0.897    0.000    -0.897    -0.845
0.870    1.000    0.000    -1.000    -0.870
0.845    0.897    0.000    -0.897    -0.845
0.802    0.836    0.000    -0.836    -0.802
```

The principal advantage of the stochastic transform lies in the size of the array, which makes it less susceptible to noise in the data than the other processes illustrated. Likewise, when necessary, even larger stochastic arrays may be used but, obviously, processing time increases proportionally.

A second advantage is that the values used for a stochastic transform can be optimized according to the signal-to-noise ratio in the data set. As an example, for a high signal-to-noise ratio, the preceding array might well be rewritten as:

```
0.267    0.364    0.000    -0.364    -0.267
0.373    0.562    0.000    -0.562    -0.373
0.463    1.000    0.000    -1.000    -0.463
0.373    0.562    0.000    -0.562    -0.373
0.267    0.364    0.000    -0.364    -0.267
```

Calculating values for matrix transforms   In each of the examples employing conformal transformations, whether for filtering or for edge detection, static arrays have been used. At the same time, floating-point values have been converted to integers to speed processing, with the resulting values restored to the original ranges.

Particularly in the case of the stochastic transform but also in the instance of the isotropic transform, instead of using static matrices, the size of the arrays used can be adjusted to suit the circumstances, with the necessary values derived by calculation. Also, in the case of the stochastic transform, values for the matrices can be optimized according to the noise levels within the image data or can even be varied according to the noise levels at different areas within an image.

References for further details on all of these transform methods are listed in Appendix A.

HARDWARE PROCESSING

While useful, software convolution methods are not—even using a fast 486—generally suitable for real-time applications. As you will observe when executing the Shades.C demo program, even for a small image, processing times run to several seconds (or longer on slower machines or 286 or 386 processors).

Thus, in real-time applications, instead of using software processing, the optimal choice lies in using a hardware image preprocessor or an image postprocessor.

In general, preprocessors operate inline with the image source —that is, a video camera—and provide real-time image processing, up to 30 frames per second, before the image reaches the capture equipment, whether the destination is a computer frame-grabber board or a recording device such as a videotape machine. As a general rule, preprocessors are a combination of dedicated graphics processors—frequently with several operating in tandem—and occasional hardware filters similar to those used in predigital days for audio and radio-frequency signal processing.

One drawback in such preprocessors is that, short of shutting off the preprocessor, the only image normally available is a black-and-white (or gray-scale) image; the original color image is lost. The principal reason for this restriction is that a single data set consisting of black-and-white intensity information in place of separate red, green, and blue color data requires two-thirds less processing. Of course, a second reason is that these devices are commonly designed for machine vision applications and, in these circumstances, color is generally less important than detecting edges and shapes.

The second approach to hardware image processing is found in post-processors where not only is time less critical—minutes, hours, or even days can be spent processing images after capture—but, given time, much more sophisticated processing can be used and color information can be preserved. Post-processors vary from simple, single-frame (single-image) processors used to enhance individual images to elaborate sequential image processors (such as the Video Toaster system from NewTek Inc. of Topeka, Kansas) which are used not only to enhance images but to edit, modify, or create entire video sequences.

Hardware processing, however, exists as a specialized area beyond the scope of this book and will not be discussed further. If your applications require this type of processing, consult your local computer dealers for sources of information and hardware suitable for your application.

OPTIMIZING IMAGE PROCESSING

While Windows is, in itself, a graphical environment, it is not necessarily the ideal environment for graphic image processing, if only because time-sharing—

inherent in any multitasking environment—increases the time necessary to complete what is already a laborious and computation-intensive task. For this reason, applications requiring intensive image processing may well fare better under DOS's single-tasking environment.

The presence of a numerical coprocessor is also an advantage as are both a better processor and a faster CPU.

Too often, however, the biggest drawback in processing images is simply that both DOS and Windows impose memory access limitations, resulting in a need to swap sections of an image in and out of extended memory, a process that often requires more time than the processing itself. (See also "Problems and Approaches" later in this chapter.) Thus, the ideal environment for image processing is one in which all memory is treated as flat memory and operations can be executed directly at any memory location within the available RAM.

At the time this book is being written, IBM's OS/2 version 2 has just been released and, overall, as an operating environment, is still subject to evaluation. Other questions aside, however, OS/2 does offer the distinct advantage of flat memory addressing. Alternately, Xenix provides a second choice for avoiding memory addressing restrictions.

Last, but probably most important, the greater the initial information in an image, the better the results after processing. Although 24-bit-per-pixel images are the optimal source images available, 256-color images have been used here simply because the former capability is not widely available.

IMPLEMENTING PROCESSING ALGORITHMS: THE SHADES.C PROGRAM

The Shades.C program is written to demonstrate a variety of convolution transforms. For simplicity, however, Shades.C also contains several limitations.

▶ First, only uncompressed, 256-color .BMP images are accepted. No provisions are included for reading other formats or other image types. Other formats can be added as desired.

▶ Second, the special code provisions required by large images (those with more than 64k of image data) are not implemented. For details on the reasons for this limitation and approaches to circumventing the problem, see "Problems and Approaches" later in this chapter.

▶ Third, two versions of the Sobel transform are included under the names DoSobelTrns and DoMaxSobelTrns. The latter version is provided to demonstrate how the effects of edge detection algorithms can be maximized, but this version of the algorithm is available only if the program is compiled using a *#define MAX_CONTRAST* statement. Similar enhancements can be added, if desired, to any of the other functions (with the exception, of course, of the color inversion provision).

Figure 9.2 shows four views—three after processing—of a face that only an iguana could love.

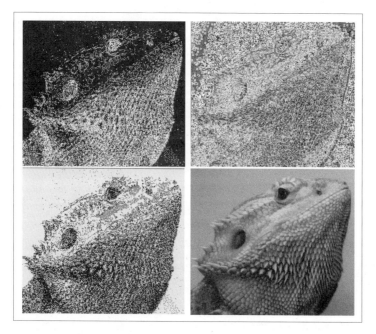

Figure 9.2: Four views of an iguana

At lower-right, the original image appears (as a gray-scale image) as clipped from an original 256-color bitmap supplied by ZSoft Corporation. On-screen, the color image exhibits near-photographic quality.

Immediately above the original, the image has been processed using the Sobel transform. Because of the image's complexity, so many edges appear in the post-process copy that the original is almost obscured. (In color, however, the post-process copy is much more interesting.)

At the left, both views have been subjected to contrast maximizing. The images are essentially the same except that the colors have been inverted to swap light for dark. In both cases, gray-scaling the print copy loses much of the original effect.

OPTIONS IN SHADES.C

The Shades demo offers two principal menu options. The first is Image, which calls a file-selection dialog box to choose and load a bitmap file.

The second, Transform, calls the dialog box shown in Figure 9.3, where two types of selection are provided. Under operation types, any of seven transform types can be selected, including pixel averaging, color inversion, isotropic, Laplace, smoothed, Sobel, and stochastic transforms.

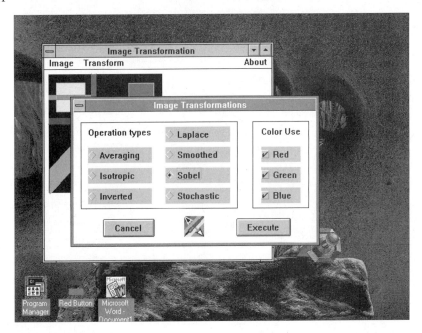

Figure 9.3: Image transform dialog box

At the right, the Color Use group shows three check boxes listing red, green, and blue, and permitting operations to be restricted to any one, two, or all three color planes. Note, however, that at least one of the three color planes must be selected.

Finally, two buttons—Cancel and Execute—complete the dialog box.

NOTE. This is not intended as a painting program, but only as a demonstration of image processing. No provisions have been included to save transformed images back to disk files. This option, however, may be added at the discretion of the programmer.

LOADING AND DISPLAYING BITMAP IMAGES

In prior chapters, several image formats have been discussed while one example has demonstrated painting a .PCX image directly to the screen. Windows's native image format, however, is the .BMP bitmap format and, by no particular coincidence, Windows has internal provisions for handling bitmap images that are smoother and superior, in a number of respects, to those for any other format.

Furthermore, any image format read should be displayed as a memory bitmap rather than painting the screen directly as was done previously with the .PCX image. When images are displayed as memory bitmaps, repainting the screen—as when the window is resized, moved, hidden, or revealed—becomes virtually automatic. At the very least, the conversion to memory bitmaps is considerably faster to display than any direct painting operation.

Reading bitmaps   The ReadBitmap procedure in Shades.C is called with a single parameter, a handle to the application window. In other circumstances, a similar procedure would also be called with a path or a file name but, in this case, these are available globally and are established by a file-list-selection dialog box similar to those demonstrated previously.

Also, because ReadBitmap may be called repeatedly and, if so, has stored global handles to bitmap and palette information, an initial provision is made to clean up any existing memory objects before loading a new bitmap from the disk and to reset (zero) global variables.

```
void ReadBitmap( HWND hwnd )
{
   ...
   if( lpMBits ) GlobalFree( (HANDLE) lpMBits );
   if( hGPal  ) GlobalFree( (HANDLE) hGPal );
   if( hGBM  ) GlobalFree( (HANDLE) hGBM );
   if( pGLP ) GlobalFree( (HANDLE) pGLP );
   bmWidth = bmHeight = bmImgSize = bmScanWidth = 0;
```

Because the directory path and the selected file name are stored separately (both are global variables), before opening the file, these two strings are concatenated.

```
   sprintf( szBuff, "%s%s", szFPath, szFName );
   hFile = _lopen( szBuff, OF_READ );;
   if( hFile == -1 )
   {
      sprintf( szBuff, "Can't open %s at %s",
                        szFName, szFPath );
      return( ErrorMsg( szBuff ) );
   }
```

Of course, if the file selected does not exist (unlikely unless the file-selection line has been edited directly) an error message is displayed reporting the problem before the process returns a FALSE result.

Even assuming that the file does exist, however, there are no assurances that the file is an acceptable image format—or even that the file is a bitmap image. Therefore, the next step is simply to perform a few checks, beginning by reading the file header and checking for the two-character key, "BF".

```
SetCursor( LoadCursor( NULL, IDC_WAIT ) );
_lread( hFile, (LPSTR) &bmFH,
        sizeof(BITMAPFILEHEADER) );
if( bmFH.bfType != 0x4D42 )   // if type isn't "BF" ...
    return( ErrorMsg( "Not a bitmap image" ) );
```

Having identified the file selected as a bitmapped image, the next step is to allocate and lock memory space for the bitmap information header before reading the data from the file. This is a more elaborate provision than the one used to read the file header, but at this point, the data read needs to be retained (and protected) at least long enough for a few tests and to extract a few facts.

```
pbmIH = (LPBITMAPINFOHEADER)
    GlobalLock( GlobalAlloc( GMEM_FIXED,
                            sizeof(BITMAPINFOHEADER) ) );
_lread( hFile, (LPSTR) pbmIH,
        sizeof(BITMAPINFOHEADER) );
if( (WORD) pbmIH->biBitCount != 8 ) // 2^8 colors = 256
    return( ErrorMsg( "Not a 256 color bitmap"));
if( (DWORD) pbmIH->biCompression != BI_RGB )
    return( ErrorMsg("Compressed images not accepted"));
PalSize = pbmIH->biClrUsed * sizeof(RGBQUAD);
GlobalUnlock( (HANDLE) pbmIH );
GlobalFree( (HANDLE) pbmIH );
```

After checking the bit count (to assure that this is a 256-color image), testing to see if the image is compressed, and retrieving the size of the color palette, the bitmap information header is no longer needed and can be released. Remember, memory should only be locked while access is required and should be released entirely when access is no longer needed.

NOTE. The memory allocation operations preceding use the global heap rather than the local heap—a consideration dictated primarily by the amount of bitmap space that may be required. When using the global heap, all well-behaved applications should observe a few brief rules:

▶ Memory must be locked while in use to prevent Windows from relocating data blocks during access.

▶ Whenever not actively being referenced, memory blocks should be unlocked and only relocked when access is required again.

▶ Last, as with any memory allocation, global memory blocks should be unlocked and freed as soon as the data is no longer needed.

Now that the size of the palette is known, the next step is to allocate memory for both the palette and the information header, and to set this new pointer back to the just-released information header data.

```
pbmInfo = (LPBITMAPINFO)
    GlobalLock( GlobalAlloc( GHND, PalSize +
                       sizeof(BITMAPINFOHEADER) ) );
pbmInfo->bmiHeader = *pbmIH;
```

Does this sound strange—releasing the memory and then reallocating it and locking it again? Perhaps this is a bit indirect, but now both the bitmap information header data and the paletted data are stored together in a single structure. And, remember, until the information header was read, the palette size wasn't known.

Before retrieving the palette data, there is another step that can be executed by using the information available: by saving the image size and color depth as a series of global variables, thus making these values readily accessible to other procedures within this application.

```
bmWidth     = (DWORD) pbmInfo->bmiHeader.biWidth;
bmHeight    = (DWORD) pbmInfo->bmiHeader.biHeight;
bmBitCount  = (WORD)  pbmInfo->bmiHeader.biBitCount;
bmImgSize   = (DWORD) pbmInfo->bmiHeader.biSizeImage;
bmScanWidth = (DWORD) bmWidth;
while( bmScanWidth % sizeof(WORD) ) bmScanWidth++;
if( pbmInfo->bmiHeader.biSizeImage == 0 )
{
    bmImgSize = bmScanWidth * bmHeight;
    pbmInfo->bmiHeader.biSizeImage = bmImgSize;
}
```

Two final provisions are made here. First, the image width (*bmWidth*) can be any value and can be odd or even. But each scan line in the image must end on a WORD boundary and must be reflected in the *bmScanWidth* value. Second, just in case the image size wasn't included in the image header data—because not all programs are well-behaved—a provision is included to calculate this essential piece of information.

Now, with these tasks completed, the palette information can be retrieved. But, before doing so, another test is necessary: checking to see that there is enough data to fill the palette structure.

```
if( _lread( hFile, (LPSTR) pbmInfo->bmiColors,
            PalSize ) != PalSize )
{
    GlobalFree( (HANDLE)
                GlobalHandle( HIWORD( pbmInfo ) ) );
    return( ErrorMsg( "Palette read error" ) );
}
```

Alternately, if the file size is wrong, then the error is reported and the process terminates, returning FALSE.

Assuming that the information was read correctly, memory is allocated for a logical palette structure, and the RGBQUAD values read from the .BMP file are converted to palette entry structures.

```
pRGB = pbmInfo->bmiColors;
    //====================================================//
    // check for short palette indicated by biClrUsed //
    //====================================================//
if( pbmInfo->bmiHeader.biClrUsed )
    CRes = pbmInfo->bmiHeader.biClrUsed;
if( pGLP != NULL ) GlobalFree( (HANDLE) pGLP );
pGLP = (LPLOGPALETTE)                // allocate and lock
    GlobalLock(                      // memory for palette
        GlobalAlloc( GHND, sizeof(LOGPALETTE) +
            ( ( CRes - 1 ) * sizeof(PALETTEENTRY) ) ) );
pGLP->palNumEntries = CRes;          // fill in size and
pGLP->palVersion    = 0x0300;        // version (3.0)
for( i=0; i<CRes; i++ )              // convert colors
{
    pGLP->palPalEntry[i].peRed   = pRGB[i].rgbRed;
    pGLP->palPalEntry[i].peGreen = pRGB[i].rgbGreen;
    pGLP->palPalEntry[i].peBlue  = pRGB[i].rgbBlue;
    pGLP->palPalEntry[i].peFlags = 0;
}
hNewPal = CreatePalette( pGLP );
GlobalUnlock( (HANDLE) pGLP );
```

Next, CreatePalette is called to create the palette from the color information. Last, the allocated memory is unlocked but not freed.

At this point, all of the information about the bitmap has been retrieved... except for the bitmap itself. Ergo, the next step is to allocate memory for the image data and then to initiate a loop to read blocks of memory until the entire image has been read.

```
hBM = GlobalAlloc( GHND, bmImgSize );
BytesLeft = ReadBytes = bmImgSize;
pBits = (BYTE huge *) GlobalLock( hBM );
while( BytesLeft > 0 )
{
    if( BytesLeft > 32767L ) GetBytes = 32768L;
                        else GetBytes = BytesLeft;
    if( (WORD) _lread( hFile, (LPSTR) pBits,
                    (WORD) GetBytes ) != GetBytes )
      if( ReadBytes <= 0 ) break; else return( FALSE );
    pBits += GetBytes;
    ReadBytes -= GetBytes;
    BytesLeft -= GetBytes;
}
_lclose( hFile );
```

Because the _lread_ function cannot read blocks larger than 64k, read operations are limited to 32k blocks with the *pBits* pointer—the location where the data will be stored—incremented after each read.

Also, if _lread_ returns fewer bytes than requested, odds are that a problem has occurred. Still, a check is not out of order and, if ReadBytes is zero, then the process finished normally. Otherwise, the process terminates.

But, as long as everything is proceeding normally, the bitmap file can be closed at this point. This does not mean that everything is finished—far from it. The next step is to make the new palette active by calling the SelectPalette and RealizePalette functions. At this point, if you're using any kind of wallpaper display, you'll probably see the background screen change colors as the new palette takes effect, normally a temporary effect.

```
hdc = GetDC( GetFocus() );
hOldPal = SelectPalette( hdc, hNewPal, FALSE );
RealizePalette( hdc );
```

After activating the palette, it's time to return to the bitmap itself, beginning by locking the previously allocated memory and then calling CreateDIBitmap (create device-independent bitmap) to write the bitmap into the device-context handle's memory.

```
lpBits = GlobalLock( hBM );
hBitmap = CreateDIBitmap( hdc,
    (LPBITMAPINFOHEADER) &pbmInfo->bmiHeader,
                CBM_INIT,
```

```
                             lpBits,
            (LPBITMAPINFO) pbmInfo,
                             DIB_RGB_COLORS );
    GlobalUnlock( hBM );
```

Once this is done, the memory (*hBM*) is unlocked again. But because this bitmap will be used for a few other purposes aside from the immediate display, global handles to both the bitmap and the palette are assigned. Of course, a provision also is included to abort—just in case the bitmap creation failed.

```
if( hBitmap != NULL )
{
    hGBM = hBitmap;                  // save global handle
    hGPal = hNewPal;                 // save global handle
} else ErrorMsg( "Bitmap failed" );
```

Next, there's a bit of cleanup remaining, beginning with restoring the original palette and releasing the device-context handle. There's still a handle to both the *pbmInfo* structure (which also must be unlocked) and the bitmap data itself; both need to be released. The only important elements—a global handle to the bitmapped image and palette—are already set and are not affected by the present actions.

```
    if( hOldPal ) SelectPalette( hdc, hOldPal, FALSE );
    ReleaseDC( GetFocus(), hdc );
    GlobalFree( (HANDLE)
                GlobalHandle( HIWORD( pbmInfo ) ) );
    GlobalFree( hBM );
    DeleteObject( hNewPal );
    SetCursor( LoadCursor( NULL, IDC_ARROW ) );
    InvalidateRect( hwnd, NULL, TRUE );
    return(0);
}
```

Finally, the new palette object can be deleted, the arrow cursor restored, and to ensure that the window is redrawing to display the bitmap, an InvalidateRect instruction is issued. This completes the task of reading and displaying the bitmap.

For other image formats, such as .PCX files, the ReadBitmap procedure can be modified to read the appropriate image format and to create a corresponding memory bitmap with similar handling.

Problems and approaches

Earlier mention was made of problems inherent in executing convolutions on larger bitmaps, that is, for bitmaps larger than 64k. This is a problem both under Windows and under MS-DOS for the same reasons—that array indexes are limited by segment boundaries, or more accurately, limited to values less than 64k. Ideally, *segment:offset* addresses would permit access to arrays of indefinite size, but that luxury is not permitted here.

Therefore, under either operating system, the solution to larger images lies in processing the images in blocks. Under Windows, this means copying sections smaller than 64k into a local array, operating on these, and then returning the result to the target bitmap image.

Under MS-DOS, the same process generally requires an XMS memory driver (see Appendix A for suggestions) and swapping image blocks in and out of extended memory. This is particularly a problem when working with 24-bit-per-pixel images, which can easily require 500k or 600k for both the original and the processed image.

In either system, however, please remember not to write the changed information back to the original source until all of the image has been transformed. The results of executing a transform using partially transformed results are, at best, undesirable.

Also, unfortunately, both processes are slower than direct memory addressing, but neither operating system offers a ready solution at the present time. Still, while there's room for drastic improvement in memory handling, there's also hope that future versions of both MS-DOS and Windows will abandon the restrictions and annoyances which were dictated by the simpler CPUs of an earlier age.

Summary

Although not every application requires image processing with smoothing or edge detection algorithms, these techniques are essential in some. Unfortunately, these algorithms are also slow and, at the present time, of limited efficiency. Ideally, at some point in time, someone will discover a tremendous image-enhancement algorithm that will be able to execute in real time, in software, with tremendous versatility and reliability equal to that in human optic processors (perhaps within a 100-GHz 80986 CPU).

Until such time, however, a selection of the best presently available algorithms has been discussed and are demonstrated in the Shades.C program whose listing follows.

Program listing of Shades.C

```
//==============================//
//          SHADES.C            //
//   Screen Capture Program     //
// compile using Compact model  //
//==============================//

#include <windows.h>
#include <stdlib.h>
#include <string.h>
#include <stdio.h>
#include <dir.h>
#include <bwcc.h>         // include bwcc.lib in project file
#include "shades.h"

#define  wFAttr   0x4010

enum  tagTransform
      { Averaging, Isotropic, Inverted, Laplace,
        Smoothed, Sobel, Stochastic  } iTransform;

static BOOL    UseColors[3];
static char    szFName[80], szFSpec[80] = "*.BMP",
               szCaption[20],
               szFPath[80], szFExt[5] = ".BMP";
static LPSTR   lpMBits;
static DWORD   bmWidth, bmHeight, bmImgSize, bmScanWidth;
static WORD    bmBitCount;
BYTE           degree = 0;  // default for Laplace trnsfrm
HANDLE         hInst;
HBITMAP        hGBM  = 0;
HPALETTE       hGPal = 0;
LPLOGPALETTE   pGLP  = 0;

int ErrorMsg( char *Error )
{
   MessageBox( GetFocus(), Error, "CAUTION!",
               MB_ICONASTERISK | MB_OK );
   return(0);
}

BYTE DoAveragingTrns( DWORD dwPos )
{
   int  TxFrm[3][3] =    // Averaging transformation
        { 1,  1,  1,
```

```
            1,  0,  1,
            1,  1,  1  };
   BYTE   RVal,  GVal,  BVal,  m;
   int    RtVal, GtVal, BtVal, i, j;
   DWORD  dwOfs;

   RtVal = GtVal = BtVal = 0;
   for( i=-1; i<2; i++ )
      for( j=-1; j<2; j++ )
      {
         dwOfs = (DWORD)(dwPos+i+(j*bmScanWidth));
         m = (BYTE) lpMBits[dwOfs];
                       // get palette index for pixel
         RtVal += TxFrm[i+1][j+1] *
                       pGLP->palPalEntry[m].peRed;
         GtVal += TxFrm[i+1][j+1] *
                       pGLP->palPalEntry[m].peGreen;
         BtVal += TxFrm[i+1][j+1] *
                       pGLP->palPalEntry[m].peBlue;
      }
   if(UseColors[0]) RVal = (BYTE)( RtVal / 8 );
            else RVal = pGLP->palPalEntry[m].peRed;
   if(UseColors[1]) GVal = (BYTE)( GtVal / 8 );
            else GVal = pGLP->palPalEntry[m].peGreen;
   if(UseColors[2]) BVal = (BYTE)( BtVal / 8 );
            else BVal = pGLP->palPalEntry[m].peBlue;
   return( GetNearestPaletteIndex( hGPal,
            RGB((BYTE)RVal,(BYTE)GVal,(BYTE)BVal)));
}


BYTE DoIsotropicTrns( DWORD dwPos )
{
   int  TxFrm[4][3][3] =     // Isotropic Transform
   { -100,    0,  100, -141, 0,  141, -100,    0, 100,
     -141, -100,    0, -100, 0,  100,    0,  100, 141,
     -100, -141, -100,    0, 0,    0,  100,  141, 100,
        0, -100, -141,  100, 0, -100,  141,  100,   0  };
   BYTE   m;
   WORD   RVal,  GVal,  BVal;
   int    RtVal, GtVal, BtVal, i, j, n;
   DWORD  dwOfs;

   RVal = GVal = BVal = 0;
   for( n=0; n<4; n++ )
   {
      RtVal = GtVal = BtVal = 0;
```

```
        for( i=-1; i<2; i++ )
          for( j=-1; j<2; j++ )
          {
              dwOfs = (DWORD)(dwPos+i+(j*bmScanWidth));
              m = (BYTE) lpMBits[dwOfs];
                      // get palette index for pixel
              RtVal += TxFrm[n][i+1][j+1] *
                          pGLP->palPalEntry[m].peRed;
              GtVal += TxFrm[n][i+1][j+1] *
                          pGLP->palPalEntry[m].peGreen;
              BtVal += TxFrm[n][i+1][j+1] *
                          pGLP->palPalEntry[m].peBlue;
          }
      if( abs(RtVal) > RVal ) RVal = abs( RtVal );
      if( abs(GtVal) > GVal ) GVal = abs( GtVal );
      if( abs(BtVal) > BVal ) BVal = abs( BtVal );
    }
    if( UseColors[0] ) RVal = (BYTE)( RVal / 100 );
                else RVal = pGLP->palPalEntry[m].peRed;
    if( UseColors[1] ) GVal = (BYTE)( GVal / 100 );
                else GVal = pGLP->palPalEntry[m].peGreen;
    if( UseColors[2] ) BVal = (BYTE)( BVal / 100 );
                else BVal = pGLP->palPalEntry[m].peBlue;
    return( GetNearestPaletteIndex( hGPal,
            RGB((BYTE)RVal,(BYTE)GVal,(BYTE)BVal)));
}


BYTE DoInvertedTrns( DWORD ofsPos )
{
    BYTE   m;
    int    RVal, GVal, BVal;

    m = (BYTE) lpMBits[ofsPos];
                // get palette index for pixel
    RVal = (BYTE) pGLP->palPalEntry[m].peRed;
    GVal = (BYTE) pGLP->palPalEntry[m].peGreen;
    BVal = (BYTE) pGLP->palPalEntry[m].peBlue;
    if( UseColors[0] ) RVal ^= 0xFF;
    if( UseColors[1] ) GVal ^= 0xFF;
    if( UseColors[2] ) BVal ^= 0xFF;
    return( GetNearestPaletteIndex(hGPal,
            RGB((BYTE)RVal,(BYTE)GVal,(BYTE)BVal)));
}


BYTE DoLaplaceTrns( DWORD dwPos, int n )
{
```

```
    int  TxFrm[3][3][3] =    // Laplace transformation
        {  0, -1,  0,   -1,  4, -1,   0, -1,  0,
          -1, -1, -1,   -1,  8, -1,  -1, -1, -1,
           1, -2,  1,   -2,  4, -2,   1, -2,  1  };
    BYTE   RVal, GVal, BVal, m;
    int    RtVal, GtVal, BtVal, i, j;
    DWORD  dwOfs;

    RVal = GVal = BVal = 0;
    RtVal = GtVal = BtVal = 0;
    for( i=-1; i<2; i++ )
        for( j=-1; j<2; j++ )
        {
            dwOfs = (DWORD)(dwPos+i+(j*bmScanWidth));
            m = (BYTE) lpMBits[dwOfs];
                    // get palette index for pixel
            RtVal += TxFrm[n][i+1][j+1] *
                        pGLP->palPalEntry[m].peRed;
            GtVal += TxFrm[n][i+1][j+1] *
                        pGLP->palPalEntry[m].peGreen;
            BtVal += TxFrm[n][i+1][j+1] *
                        pGLP->palPalEntry[m].peBlue;
        }
    if( abs(RtVal) > RVal ) RVal = abs( RtVal );
    if( abs(GtVal) > GVal ) GVal = abs( GtVal );
    if( abs(BtVal) > BVal ) BVal = abs( BtVal );
    if(!UseColors[0]) RVal = pGLP->palPalEntry[m].peRed;
    if(!UseColors[1]) GVal = pGLP->palPalEntry[m].peGreen;
    if(!UseColors[2]) BVal = pGLP->palPalEntry[m].peBlue;
    return( GetNearestPaletteIndex( hGPal,
            RGB((BYTE)RVal,(BYTE)GVal,(BYTE)BVal)));
}

BYTE DoSobelTrns( DWORD dwPos )
{
    int  TxFrm[4][3][3] =    // Sobel transformation
        { -1,  0,  1,   -2,  0,  2,   -1,  0,  1,
          -2, -1,  0,   -1,  0,  1,    0,  1,  2,
          -1, -2, -1,    0,  0,  0,    1,  2,  1,
           0, -1, -2,    1,  0, -1,    2,  1,  0  };
    BYTE   RVal, GVal, BVal, m;
    int    RtVal, GtVal, BtVal, i, j, n;
    DWORD  dwOfs;

    RVal = GVal = BVal = 0;
    for( n=0; n<4; n++ )
```

```
        {
            RtVal = GtVal = BtVal = 0;
            for( i=-1; i<2; i++ )
               for( j=-1; j<2; j++ )
               {
                   dwOfs = (DWORD)(dwPos+i+(j*bmScanWidth));
                   m = (BYTE) lpMBits[dwOfs];
                               // get palette index for pixel
                   RtVal += TxFrm[n][i+1][j+1] *
                                pGLP->palPalEntry[m].peRed;
                   GtVal += TxFrm[n][i+1][j+1] *
                                pGLP->palPalEntry[m].peGreen;
                   BtVal += TxFrm[n][i+1][j+1] *
                                pGLP->palPalEntry[m].peBlue;
               }
            if( abs(RtVal) > RVal ) RVal = abs( RtVal );
            if( abs(GtVal) > GVal ) GVal = abs( GtVal );
            if( abs(BtVal) > BVal ) BVal = abs( BtVal );
        }
        if(!UseColors[0]) RVal = pGLP->palPalEntry[m].peRed;
        if(!UseColors[1]) GVal = pGLP->palPalEntry[m].peGreen;
        if(!UseColors[2]) BVal = pGLP->palPalEntry[m].peBlue;
        return( GetNearestPaletteIndex( hGPal,
                  RGB((BYTE)RVal,(BYTE)GVal,(BYTE)BVal)));
}


BYTE DoSmoothedTrns( DWORD dwPos )
{
    int   TxFrm[4][3][3] =     // Smoothed transformation
          { -1,  0,  1,   -1,  0,  1,    -1,  0,  1,
            -1, -1,  0,   -1,  0,  1,     0,  1,  1,
            -1, -1, -1,    0,  0,  0,     1,  1,  1,
             0, -1, -1,    1,  0, -1,     1,  1,  0  };
    BYTE    RVal,  GVal,  BVal,  m;
    int     RtVal, GtVal, BtVal, i, j, n;
    DWORD   dwOfs;

    RVal = GVal = BVal = 0;
    for( n=0; n<4; n++ )
    {
        RtVal = GtVal = BtVal = 0;
        for( i=-1; i<2; i++ )
           for( j=-1; j<2; j++ )
           {
               dwOfs = (DWORD)(dwPos+i+(j*bmScanWidth));
               m = (BYTE) lpMBits[dwOfs];
```

```c
                         // get palette index for pixel
            RtVal += TxFrm[n][i+1][j+1] *
                          pGLP->palPalEntry[m].peRed;
            GtVal += TxFrm[n][i+1][j+1] *
                          pGLP->palPalEntry[m].peGreen;
            BtVal += TxFrm[n][i+1][j+1] *
                          pGLP->palPalEntry[m].peBlue;
        }
      if( abs(RtVal) > RVal ) RVal = abs( RtVal );
      if( abs(GtVal) > GVal ) GVal = abs( GtVal );
      if( abs(BtVal) > BVal ) BVal = abs( BtVal );
    }
  if(!UseColors[0]) RVal = pGLP->palPalEntry[m].peRed;
  if(!UseColors[1]) GVal = pGLP->palPalEntry[m].peGreen;
  if(!UseColors[2]) BVal = pGLP->palPalEntry[m].peBlue;
  return( GetNearestPaletteIndex( hGPal,
          RGB((BYTE)RVal,(BYTE)GVal,(BYTE)BVal)));
}


BYTE DoStochasticTrns( DWORD dwPos )
{
  int  TxFrm[8][5][5] =     // Stochastic transformation
  {  802,   836,     0,  -836,  -802,
     845,   897,     0,  -897,  -845,
     870,  1000,     0, -1000,  -870,
     845,   897,     0,  -897,  -845,
     802,   836,     0,  -836,  -802,      // Horz1

     870,   845,   802,   836,     0,
     845,  1000,   897,     0,  -836,
     802,   897,     0,  -897,  -802,
     836,     0,  -897, -1000,  -845,
       0,  -836,  -802,  -845,  -870,      // Diag1

     802,   845,   870,   845,   802,
     836,   897,  1000,   897,   836,
       0,     0,     0,     0,     0,
    -836,  -897, -1000,  -897,  -836,
    -802,  -845,  -870,  -845,  -802,      // Horz2

       0,   836,   802,   845,   870,
    -836,     0,   897,  1000,   845,
    -802,  -897,     0,   897,   802,
    -845, -1000,  -897,     0,   836,
    -870,  -845,  -802,  -836,     0,      // Diag2
```

```
   -802,   -836,      0,    836,    802,
   -845,   -897,      0,    897,    845,
   -870,  -1000,      0,   1000,    870,
   -845,   -897,      0,    897,    845,
   -802,   -836,      0,    836,    802,      // Horz3

   -870,   -845,   -802,   -836,      0,
   -845,  -1000,   -897,      0,    836,
   -802,   -897,      0,    897,    802,
   -836,      0,    897,   1000,    845,
      0,    836,    802,    845,    870,      // Diag3

   -802,   -845,   -870,   -845,   -802,
   -836,   -897,  -1000,   -897,   -836,
      0,      0,      0,      0,      0,
    836,    897,   1000,    897,    836,
    802,    845,    870,    845,    802,      // Horz4

      0,   -836,   -802,   -845,   -870,
    836,      0,   -897,  -1000,   -845,
    802,    897,      0,   -897,   -802,
    845,   1000,    897,      0,   -836,
    870,    845,    802,    836,      0  }; // Diag4

BYTE    RVal,  GVal,  BVal,  m;
int     RtVal, GtVal, BtVal,
        RsVal, GsVal, BsVal,  i, j, n;
DWORD   dwOfs;

RsVal = GsVal = BsVal = 0;
for( n=0; n<8; n++ )
{
   RtVal = GtVal = BtVal = 0;
   for( i=-2; i<3; i++ )
     for( j=-2; j<3; j++ )
       {
         dwOfs = (DWORD)(dwPos+i+(j*bmScanWidth));
         m = (BYTE) lpMBits[dwOfs];
           // get palette index for pixel
         RtVal += ( TxFrm[n][i+2][j+2] *
           pGLP->palPalEntry[m].peRed )   / 1000;
         GtVal += ( TxFrm[n][i+2][j+2] *
           pGLP->palPalEntry[m].peGreen ) / 1000;
         BtVal += ( TxFrm[n][i+2][j+2] *
           pGLP->palPalEntry[m].peBlue )  / 1000;
       }
```

```
      if( abs(RtVal) > RsVal ) RsVal = abs( RtVal );
      if( abs(GtVal) > GsVal ) GsVal = abs( GtVal );
      if( abs(BtVal) > BsVal ) BsVal = abs( BtVal );
   }
   if( UseColors[0] ) RVal = (BYTE) RsVal;
                 else RVal = pGLP->palPalEntry[m].peRed;
   if( UseColors[1] ) GVal = (BYTE) GsVal;
                 else GVal = pGLP->palPalEntry[m].peGreen;
   if( UseColors[2] ) BVal = (BYTE) BsVal;
                 else BVal = pGLP->palPalEntry[m].peBlue;
   return( GetNearestPaletteIndex( hGPal,
              RGB((BYTE)RVal,(BYTE)GVal,(BYTE)BVal)));
}


void TransformImage()
{
   LPSTR  lpLBits;
   DWORD  dwPos, dwTar, dwEnd;
   WORD   x, y;
   BYTE   m;

   SetCursor( LoadCursor( NULL, IDC_WAIT ) );
   GlobalLock( (HANDLE) pGLP );
   lpMBits = (LPSTR) GlobalLock(
                        GlobalAlloc( GHND, bmImgSize ) );
   GetBitmapBits( hGBM, bmImgSize, lpMBits );
   lpLBits = (LPSTR) GlobalLock(
                        GlobalAlloc( GHND, bmImgSize ) );
   GetBitmapBits( hGBM, bmImgSize, lpLBits );
   GlobalLock( hGPal );
   hGPal = CreatePalette( pGLP );
   if( bmImgSize > 0xFFFF )
   {
      ErrorMsg(
         "Warning, images larger than 65335 bytes\n"
         "require banding for proper processing" );  }
   switch( iTransform )
   {
      case Inverted:        m = 0;  break;
      case Averaging:  case Isotropic:
      case Laplace:    case Smoothed:
      case Sobel:           m = 1;  break;
      case Stochastic:      m = 2;  break;
   }
   for( y=m; y<bmHeight-m; y++ )
   for( x=m; x<bmWidth-m; x++ )
```

```
        {
            dwPos = (DWORD)( ( y * bmScanWidth ) + x );
            switch( iTransform )
            {
                case Averaging:
                    lpLBits[dwPos] = DoAveragingTrns( dwPos );
                    break;
                case Inverted:
                    lpLBits[dwPos] = DoInvertedTrns( dwPos );
                    break;
                case Isotropic:
                    lpLBits[dwPos] = DoIsotropicTrns( dwPos );
                    break;
                case Laplace:
                    lpLBits[dwPos] = DoLaplaceTrns( dwPos,
                                                     degree );
                    break;
                case Smoothed:
                    lpLBits[dwPos] = DoSmoothedTrns( dwPos );
                    break;
                case Sobel:
                    lpLBits[dwPos] = DoSobelTrns( dwPos );
                    break;
                case Stochastic:
                    lpLBits[dwPos] = DoStochasticTrns( dwPos );
                    break;
            }   }
        SetBitmapBits( hGBM, bmImgSize, lpLBits );
        GlobalFree( (HANDLE)
            GlobalHandle( HIWORD( lpLBits ) ) );
        GlobalFree( (HANDLE)
            GlobalHandle( HIWORD( lpMBits ) ) );
        GlobalFree( hGPal );
        GlobalUnlock( (HANDLE) pGLP );
        DeleteObject( hGPal );
        InvalidateRect( GetFocus(), NULL, TRUE );
        SetCursor( LoadCursor( NULL, IDC_ARROW ) );
}

int ReadBitmap( HWND hwnd )
{
    BITMAPFILEHEADER    bmFH;
    LPBITMAPINFOHEADER  pbmIH;
    LPBITMAPINFO        pbmInfo;
    RGBQUAD   FAR     * pRGB;
    BYTE      huge    * pBits;
```

```
    HDC                hdc;
    HANDLE             hBM;
    HBITMAP            hBitmap;
    HPALETTE           hOldPal, hNewPal;
    WORD               PalSize;
    int                hFile;
    char               szBuff[64];
    LPSTR              lpBits;
    int                i, j, CRes = 256;
    LONG               GetBytes, ReadBytes, BytesLeft;

//=== clean up any existing memory objects ===========
    if( lpMBits ) GlobalFree( (HANDLE) lpMBits );
    if( hGPal ) GlobalFree( (HANDLE) hGPal );
    if( hGBM ) GlobalFree( (HANDLE) hGBM );
    if( pGLP ) GlobalFree( (HANDLE) pGLP );
    bmWidth = bmHeight = bmImgSize = bmScanWidth = 0;
//=== open file ======================================
    sprintf( szBuff, "%s%s", szFPath, szFName );
    hFile = _lopen( szBuff, OF_READ );;
    if( hFile == -1 )
    {
        sprintf( szBuff, "Can't open %s at %s",
                        szFName, szFPath );
        return( ErrorMsg( szBuff ) );
    }
//=== read bitmap header =============================
    SetCursor( LoadCursor( NULL, IDC_WAIT ) );
    _lread( hFile, (LPSTR) &bmFH,
            sizeof(BITMAPFILEHEADER) );
    if( bmFH.bfType != 0x4D42 )   // if type isn't "BF" ...
        return( ErrorMsg( "Not a bitmap image" ) );
//=== read bitmap info header ========================
    pbmIH = (LPBITMAPINFOHEADER)
        GlobalLock( GlobalAlloc( GMEM_FIXED,
                                sizeof(BITMAPINFOHEADER) ) );
    _lread( hFile, (LPSTR) pbmIH,
            sizeof(BITMAPINFOHEADER) );
    if( (WORD) pbmIH->biBitCount != 8 ) // 2^8 colors = 256
        return( ErrorMsg( "Not a 256 color bitmap"));
    if( (DWORD) pbmIH->biCompression != BI_RGB )
        return( ErrorMsg("Compressed images not accepted"));
    PalSize = pbmIH->biClrUsed * sizeof(RGBQUAD);
    GlobalUnlock( (HANDLE) pbmIH );
    GlobalFree( (HANDLE) pbmIH );
//=== read palette info into bitmap info =============
```

```
    pbmInfo = (LPBITMAPINFO)
        GlobalLock( GlobalAlloc( GHND, PalSize +
                                    sizeof(BITMAPINFOHEADER) ) );
    pbmInfo->bmiHeader = *pbmIH;
//=== save size data for this image =====================
    bmWidth    = (DWORD) pbmInfo->bmiHeader.biWidth;
    bmHeight   = (DWORD) pbmInfo->bmiHeader.biHeight;
    bmBitCount = (WORD)  pbmInfo->bmiHeader.biBitCount;
    bmImgSize  = (DWORD) pbmInfo->bmiHeader.biSizeImage;
    bmScanWidth = (DWORD) bmWidth;
    while( bmScanWidth % sizeof(WORD) ) bmScanWidth++;
                            // must be an even WORD size !!!
//=== if image size not in header, calculate size ========
    if( pbmInfo->bmiHeader.biSizeImage == 0 )
    {
        bmImgSize = ( ( ( ( bmWidth * bmBitCount ) +
                            31 ) / 32 ) * 4 ) * bmHeight;
        pbmInfo->bmiHeader.biSizeImage = bmImgSize;
    }
//=== now read the palette information ===================
    if( _lread( hFile, (LPSTR) pbmInfo->bmiColors,
            PalSize ) != PalSize )
    {
        GlobalFree( (HANDLE)
                    GlobalHandle( HIWORD( pbmInfo ) ) );
        return( ErrorMsg( "Palette read error" ) );
    }
//=== allocate space for bitmap palette ==================
    pRGB = pbmInfo->bmiColors;
        //=================================================//
        // check for short palette indicated by biClrUsed //
        //=================================================//
    if( pbmInfo->bmiHeader.biClrUsed )
        CRes = pbmInfo->bmiHeader.biClrUsed;
    if( pGLP != NULL ) GlobalFree( (HANDLE) pGLP );
    pGLP = (LPLOGPALETTE)               // allocate and lock
        GlobalLock(                     // memory for palette
            GlobalAlloc( GHND, sizeof(LOGPALETTE) +
                ( ( CRes - 1 ) * sizeof(PALETTEENTRY) ) ) );
    pGLP->palNumEntries = CRes;         // fill in size and
    pGLP->palVersion    = 0x0300;       // version (3.0)
    for( i=0; i<CRes; i++ )             // convert colors
    {
        pGLP->palPalEntry[i].peRed   = pRGB[i].rgbRed;
        pGLP->palPalEntry[i].peGreen = pRGB[i].rgbGreen;
        pGLP->palPalEntry[i].peBlue  = pRGB[i].rgbBlue;
```

```
        pGLP->palPalEntry[i].peFlags = 0;
    }
    hNewPal = CreatePalette( pGLP );
    GlobalUnlock( (HANDLE) pGLP );
//=== now retrive actual image information ==============
    hBM = GlobalAlloc( GHND, bmImgSize );
    BytesLeft = ReadBytes = bmImgSize;
    pBits = (BYTE huge *) GlobalLock( hBM );
    while( BytesLeft > 0 )
    {
        if( BytesLeft > 32767L ) GetBytes = 32768L;
                        else GetBytes = BytesLeft;
            //==================================================//
            // limit block reads to 32k to avoid crossing //
            // segment boundary when calling _lread        //
            //==================================================//
        if( (WORD) _lread( hFile, (LPSTR) pBits,
                        (WORD) GetBytes ) != GetBytes )
            if( ReadBytes <= 0 ) break; else return( FALSE );
        pBits += GetBytes;
        ReadBytes -= GetBytes;
        BytesLeft -= GetBytes;
    }
    _lclose( hFile );
//=== make new palette active ============================
    hdc = GetDC( GetFocus() );
    hOldPal = SelectPalette( hdc, hNewPal, FALSE );
    RealizePalette( hdc );
//=== create DIB Bitmap ==================================
    lpBits = GlobalLock( hBM );
    hBitmap = CreateDIBitmap( hdc,
        (LPBITMAPINFOHEADER) &pbmInfo->bmiHeader,
                        CBM_INIT,
                        lpBits,
            (LPBITMAPINFO) pbmInfo,
                        DIB_RGB_COLORS );
    GlobalUnlock( hBM );
    if( hBitmap != NULL )
    {
        hGBM = hBitmap;              // save global handle
        hGPal = hNewPal;            // save global handle
    } else ErrorMsg( "Bitmap failed" );
//=== discard global memory object =======================
    if( hOldPal ) SelectPalette( hdc, hOldPal, FALSE );
    ReleaseDC( GetFocus(), hdc );
    GlobalFree( (HANDLE)
```

```
                    GlobalHandle( HIWORD( pbmInfo ) ) );
    GlobalFree( hBM );
    DeleteObject( hNewPal );
    SetCursor( LoadCursor( NULL, IDC_ARROW ) );
    InvalidateRect( hwnd, NULL, TRUE );
    return(0);
}


#pragma argsused

BOOL FAR PASCAL AboutProc( HWND hDlg,    WORD msg,
                                WORD wParam, LONG lParam )
{
    switch( msg )
    {
      case WM_INITDIALOG:  return( TRUE );
      case WM_COMMAND:
          switch( wParam )
          {
              case IDOK: EndDialog( hDlg, TRUE );
                         return( TRUE );
               default: return( TRUE );
      }    }
    return( FALSE );
}


#pragma argsused

int FAR PASCAL LaplaceDlgProc( HWND hDlg, WORD msg,
                                WORD wParam, LONG lParam )
{
    switch( msg )
    {
      case WM_INITDIALOG:          // initialize degree
          CheckRadioButton( hDlg, 1000, 1002,
                             1000 + degree );
          break;
      case WM_COMMAND:                // check degree selection
          switch( wParam )
          {
              case 1000:
              case 1001:
              case 1002: degree = wParam - 1000;   break;
              case IDOK: EndDialog( hDlg, TRUE );  break;
          }
        default: return( FALSE );
```

```
    }
    return(FALSE);
}

int CallLaplaceDlg( HANDLE hInst, HWND hwnd )
{
    FARPROC   lpProc;
    int       iReturn;

    lpProc = MakeProcInstance( LaplaceDlgProc, hInst );
    iReturn = DialogBox(hInst, "LAPLACE", hwnd, lpProc);
    FreeProcInstance( lpProc );
    return( iReturn );
}

#pragma argsused

int FAR PASCAL TransformDlgProc( HWND hDlg, WORD msg,
                                 WORD wParam, LONG lParam )
{
    int  i;

    switch( msg )
    {
      case WM_INITDIALOG:
        CheckRadioButton( hDlg,
                          IDD_AVERAGING,
                          IDD_STOCHASTIC,
                          IDD_AVERAGING + iTransform );
        for( i=IDD_RED; i<=IDD_BLUE; i++ )
            CheckDlgButton(hDlg, i, UseColors[i-IDD_RED]);
        break;
      case WM_COMMAND:
        switch( wParam )
        {
          case IDD_AVERAGING:    case IDD_SMOOTHED:
          case IDD_ISOTROPIC:    case IDD_SOBEL:
          case IDD_INVERTED:     case IDD_STOCHASTIC:
            iTransform = wParam - IDD_AVERAGING;
            break;
          case IDD_LAPLACE:
            iTransform = Laplace;
            CallLaplaceDlg( hInst, GetFocus() );
            break;          // option to change degree
          case IDD_RED:          case IDD_GREEN:
          case IDD_BLUE:
```

```
                    if(  UseColors[wParam-IDD_RED] )
                         UseColors[wParam-IDD_RED] = FALSE;
                    else UseColors[wParam-IDD_RED] = TRUE;
                    break;
                case IDD_EXECUTE:    case IDD_CANCEL:
                    if( !( UseColors[0] | UseColors[1] |
                          UseColors[2] ) )
                    {
                        ErrorMsg(
                          "One color plane must be selected" );
                        MessageBeep(0);
                        for( i=IDD_RED; i<=IDD_BLUE; i++ )
                        {
                            UseColors[i-IDD_RED] = TRUE;
                            CheckDlgButton( hDlg, i,
                              UseColors[i-IDD_RED] );
                        }
                        MessageBeep(0);
                    }
                    EndDialog( hDlg, (wParam == IDD_EXECUTE) );
                    break;
            }
        default: return( FALSE );
    }
    return(FALSE);
}


int CallTransformDlg( HANDLE hInst, HWND hwnd )
{
    FARPROC  lpProc;
    int      iReturn;

    lpProc = MakeProcInstance( TransformDlgProc, hInst );
    iReturn = DialogBox(hInst, "TRANSFORM", hwnd, lpProc);
    FreeProcInstance( lpProc );
    return( iReturn );
}


BOOL FAR PASCAL FileSelectDlgProc( HWND hDlg, WORD msg,
                             WORD wParam, LONG lParam )
{
    static char  OrgPath[64];
    struct ffblk fileinfo;
    char    cLastChar;
    int     nLen;
```

```
switch( msg )
{
    case WM_INITDIALOG:
        SetWindowText( hDlg, szCaption );
        getcwd( OrgPath, sizeof( OrgPath ) );
        SendDlgItemMessage( hDlg, IDD_FNAME,
                            EM_LIMITTEXT, 80, NULL );
        DlgDirList( hDlg, szFSpec, IDD_FLIST,
                    IDD_FPATH, wFAttr );
        SetDlgItemText( hDlg, IDD_FNAME, szFSpec );
        return( TRUE );

    case WM_COMMAND:
        switch( wParam )
        {
            case IDD_FLIST:
                switch( HIWORD( lParam ) )
                {
                    case LBN_SELCHANGE:
                        if( DlgDirSelect( hDlg, szFName,
                                          IDD_FLIST ) )
                            strcat( szFName, szFSpec );
                        SetDlgItemText( hDlg, IDD_FNAME,
                                        szFName );
                        break;
                    case LBN_DBLCLK:
                        if( DlgDirSelect( hDlg, szFName,
                                          IDD_FLIST ) )
                        {
                            strcat( szFName, szFSpec );
                            DlgDirList( hDlg, szFName,
                                IDD_FLIST, IDD_FPATH, wFAttr );
                            SetDlgItemText( hDlg, IDD_FNAME,
                                            szFSpec );
                        }
                        else
                        {
                            SetDlgItemText( hDlg, IDD_FNAME,
                                            szFName );
                            SendMessage( hDlg, WM_COMMAND,
                                         IDOK, 0L );
                        } break;
                } break;
            case IDD_FNAME:
                if( HIWORD( lParam ) == EN_CHANGE )
                    EnableWindow( GetDlgItem( hDlg, IDOK ),
```

```
                    (BOOL) SendMessage( LOWORD( lParam ),
                         WM_GETTEXTLENGTH, 0, 0L ) );
        break;
    case IDOK:
        GetDlgItemText( hDlg, IDD_FNAME,
                     szFName, 80 );
        nLen = strlen( szFName );
        cLastChar = *AnsiPrev( szFName,
                           szFName + nLen );
        if( cLastChar == '\\' || cLastChar == ':' )
            strcat( szFName, szFSpec );
        if( strchr( szFName, '*' ) ||
            strchr( szFName, '?' ) )
        {
            if( DlgDirList( hDlg, szFName,
                IDD_FLIST, IDD_FPATH, wFAttr ) )
            {
                strcpy( szFSpec, szFName );
                SetDlgItemText( hDlg, IDD_FNAME,
                             szFSpec );
            }
            else MessageBeep(0);
            break;
        }
        if( DlgDirList( hDlg, szFName,
                IDD_FLIST, IDD_FPATH, wFAttr ) )
        {
            strcpy( szFSpec, szFName );
            SetDlgItemText( hDlg, IDD_FNAME,
                         szFSpec );
            break;
        }
        szFName[nLen] = '\0';
        if( findfirst( szFName, &fileinfo, 0 ) )
        {
            strcat( szFName, szFExt );
            if( findfirst( szFName, &fileinfo, 0 ) )
            {
                MessageBeep(0);
                break;
        }   }
        GetDlgItemText( hDlg, IDD_FPATH,
                     szFPath, 80 );
        strupr( szFPath );
        if( szFPath[strlen(szFPath)-1] != '\\' )
            strcat( szFPath, "\\" );
```

```
                strcpy( szFName, fileinfo.ff_name );
                chdir( OrgPath );
                EndDialog( hDlg, TRUE );
                break;
            case IDCANCEL:
                chdir( OrgPath );
                EndDialog( hDlg, FALSE );
                break;
            default:  return( FALSE );
        } break;
    default: return( FALSE );
    }
    return( TRUE );
}


int CallFileLoadDlg( HANDLE hInst, HWND hwnd )
{
    FARPROC   lpProc;
    int       iReturn;

    strcpy( szCaption, "Load Image From:" );
    lpProc = MakeProcInstance( FileSelectDlgProc, hInst );
    iReturn = DialogBox(hInst, "SELECTFILE", hwnd, lpProc);
    FreeProcInstance( lpProc );
    return( iReturn );
}


long FAR PASCAL WndProc( HWND hwnd,   WORD msg,
                         WORD wParam, LONG lParam )
{
    HDC           hdc, hdcMem;
    FARPROC       lpProc;
    PAINTSTRUCT   ps;
    HBITMAP       hBMOld;
    HPALETTE      hPalOld;

    switch( msg )
    {
    case WM_COMMAND:
        switch( wParam )
        {
            case IDM_LOAD:
                if( CallFileLoadDlg( hInst, hwnd ) )
                    ReadBitmap( hwnd );
                break;
```

```
            case IDM_TRANSFORM:
                if( ! hGBM )
                {
                    ErrorMsg( "No bitmap selected" );
                    break;
                }
                if( CallTransformDlg( hInst, hwnd ) )
                    TransformImage();
                break;

            case IDM_ABOUT:
                lpProc = MakeProcInstance( AboutProc,
                                           hInst );
                DialogBox( hInst, "ABOUT", hwnd, lpProc );
                FreeProcInstance( lpProc );
                break;
        }
        return(0);

    case WM_PAINT:
        InvalidateRect( hwnd, NULL, TRUE );
        hdc = BeginPaint( hwnd, &ps );
        if( hGBM )
        {
            hdcMem = CreateCompatibleDC( hdc );
            hBMOld = SelectObject( hdcMem, hGBM );
            if( hGPal )
                hPalOld =
                    SelectPalette( hdc, hGPal, FALSE );
            BitBlt( hdc, 0, 0, bmWidth, bmHeight,
                    hdcMem, 0, 0, SRCCOPY );
            if( hGPal )
                SelectPalette( hdc, hPalOld, FALSE );
            SelectObject( hdcMem, hBMOld );
            DeleteDC( hdcMem );
        }
        EndPaint( hwnd, &ps );
        return(FALSE);
    case WM_DESTROY:
        if( pGLP != NULL ) GlobalFree( (HANDLE) pGLP );
        PostQuitMessage(0);
        return(0);
    }
    return( DefWindowProc( hwnd, msg, wParam, lParam ) );
}
```

```
#pragma argsused

int PASCAL WinMain( HANDLE hInstance,
                    HANDLE hPrevInstance,
                    LPSTR  lpszCmdParam, int nCmdShow )
{
    static char szAppName[] = "SHADES";
    int         i;
    HWND        hwnd;
    MSG         msg;
    WNDCLASS    wc;

    if( ! hPrevInstance )
    {
        wc.hInstance      = hInstance;
        wc.lpfnWndProc    = WndProc;
        wc.cbClsExtra     = 0;
        wc.cbWndExtra     = 0;
        wc.lpszClassName  = szAppName;
        wc.hIcon          = LoadIcon( hInstance, szAppName );
        wc.lpszMenuName   = (LPSTR) szAppName;
        wc.hCursor        = LoadCursor( NULL, IDC_ARROW );
        wc.hbrBackground  = GetStockObject( WHITE_BRUSH );
        wc.style          = CS_HREDRAW | CS_VREDRAW;
        RegisterClass( &wc );
    }
    hInst = hInstance;      // assign global instance handle
    iTransform = Sobel;     // set default transformation
    degree = 0;             // default for Laplace trnsfrm
    for( i=0; i<3; i++ ) UseColors[i] = TRUE;
    hwnd = CreateWindow( szAppName, "Image Transformation",
          WS_OVERLAPPEDWINDOW,
          CW_USEDEFAULT, CW_USEDEFAULT,
          CW_USEDEFAULT, CW_USEDEFAULT,
          NULL, NULL, hInstance, NULL  );
    ShowWindow(   hwnd, nCmdShow );
    UpdateWindow( hwnd );
    while( GetMessage( &msg, NULL, 0, 0 ) )
    {
        TranslateMessage( &msg );
        DispatchMessage(  &msg );
    }
    return( msg.wParam );
}


;===========================;
```

```
;  SHADES.DEF            ;
;  module definition file  ;
;===========================;

NAME          SHADES

DESCRIPTION   "Screen Capture Program"
EXETYPE       WINDOWS
STUB          "WINSTUB.EXE"
CODE          PRELOAD MOVEABLE DISCARDABLE
DATA          PRELOAD MOVEABLE MULTIPLE
HEAPSIZE      1024
STACKSIZE     8192
EXPORTS       WndProc
              AboutProc
              LaplaceDlgProc
              TransformDlgProc
              FileSelectDlgProc


//==============//
//   SHADES.H   //
//==============//

#define IDM_LOAD        101    // file operations
#define IDM_TRANSFORM   103    // transform dialog
#define IDM_ABOUT       104    // about dialog

#define IDD_RED         111    // colors
#define IDD_GREEN       112    // (checkboxes)
#define IDD_BLUE        113

#define IDD_AVERAGING   200    // process selection
#define IDD_ISOTROPIC   201    // (autoradio buttons)
#define IDD_INVERTED    202
#define IDD_LAPLACE     203
#define IDD_SMOOTHED    204
#define IDD_SOBEL       205
#define IDD_STOCHASTIC  206

#define IDD_FNAME       301    // filename dialog
#define IDD_FPATH       302
#define IDD_FLIST       303

#define IDD_EXECUTE     401    // execute transform
#define IDD_CANCEL      402    // cancel transform
```

Printing Graphics

I n many ways, Windows has greatly facilitated graphics image handling, with capabilities that range from providing hardware-independent graphics display environments to translating between different image formats. Just as support is provided for a wide variety of displays, support also is provided for a wide variety of printers, ranging from dot-matrix printers to all types of laser printers.

Furthermore, provisions even exist—using the BitBlt or StretchBlt functions—for copying images from a display context to a printer context . . . and, of course, from there to the printer itself. On the whole, Windows includes almost everything needed to provide hard-copy output of graphics images.

Unfortunately, however, almost is not everything and one fly remains in the ointment: the fact that, while most monitors are color, most printers are limited to black and white. And in this last respect, Windows does not offer any automatic solutions.

Still, if no automatic solution has been provided, a custom solution is not beyond the realm of the possible and practical, as will be shown momentarily. But before tackling the solution, the first step is to understand the problem and the available mechanisms.

PRINTER OPERATION

During installation, Windows offers an option to select one or more printers. In response, Windows copies the appropriate printer drivers to the Windows directory and lists these drivers in the WIN.INI file. A sample extract from WIN.INI appears following:

```
[windows]
...
device=HP LaserJet Series II,HPPCL,LPT1:
...

[devices]
HP LaserJet Series II=HPPCL,LPT1:

[HP LaserJet Series II,lPT1]
Paper Size=1
Number of Cartridges=1
Cartridge 1=17
Orientation=2
Brush=2

[PrinterPorts]
HP LaserJet Series II=HPPCL,LPT1:,15,45
```

For present purposes, the first portion of this listing is the most important. There, following the [*windows*] key string, WIN.INI identifies the HP LaserJet as the primary (and, in this case, only) printer (*device*). Further, this same entry identifies the printer driver, HPPCL, and the printer port, LPT1.

Other WIN.INI listings provide additional information, including the printer's default configuration, the cartridges installed (if any), additional information about the printer port(s), and information on supported fonts and type sizes (not shown in the preceding example). Most of this latter information was installed in WIN.INI not during Windows installation but, in this case, by Word for Windows during its own installation.

Thus, obviously, it would be inappropriate to count on all of this data being available—unless, of course, your own application makes similar provisions when it's initially installed.

Still, for the present purposes of graphics printing, the basic information about the printer type that Windows does ensure is available will be enough to allow us to ask for such additional data as may be required.

QUERYING THE PRINTER

In Chapter 5, a program titled DC (for Device Capacity) demonstrated how to query the system device drivers and how to obtain information about device capabilities and limitations. In DC's demonstration, all of the information available about a device—either display or printer—was shown.

To display all of these data elements, however, required a relatively long list of information requests. In other circumstances, instead of asking for everything available, a more moderate request will be made, restricting queries only to the appropriate or needed data.

In this chapter, a program titled GrayImg.C is used to demonstrate both printer access and the gray-scaling of images. A number of the features in GrayImg.C, such as selecting and displaying a .BMP image, should be familiar from earlier programs such as Shades and ViewPcx, but beyond these stock provisions, GrayImg introduces new mechanisms for handling printer input and output.

The first new provision is a function titled GetPrinterDC, which queries the Windows environment to determine two important elements: first, if a printer is available and, if so, whether the printer supports BitBlt operations.

The first portion of this task is accomplished by calling GetProfileString with parameters requesting a keyname (*device*) associated with an application header (*windows*). In other circumstances, the request might be made for data relevant to a particular rather than a generic application but, in the Windows context, printers are shared resources rather than application specific.

The third parameter (",,,") specifies a default string to be returned if the requested key is not found. In this instance, however, while a default string is specified, it is also a string which, if returned by default, will decode as NULLs.

The fourth parameter (*szPrn*) points to a buffer to receive the returned character string, and the fifth parameter (BUFF_SIZE) identifies the character count expected.

```
HDC NEAR GetPrinterDC( HWND hwnd )
{
   HDC      hdcPrn = NULL;
   char     szPrn[40];
   char     *szDevice, *szDriver, *szOutput;

   if( GetProfileString( "windows", "device", ",,,",
                           szPrn, BUFF_SIZE ) == 0 )
      return(
         ErrorMsg( "printer (device driver) not found" ));
   szDevice = strtok( szPrn, "," );
   szDriver = strtok( NULL, ", " );
   szOutput = strtok( NULL, ", " );
```

If the call to GetProfileString fails, then a simple error message is displayed before the procedure returns reporting a failure.

But, assuming success, the returned string is deciphered into three sub-strings that identify the device, the driver name, and the output port assignment. In the example cited, these would be reported as "HP LaserJet Series II", "HPPCL", and "LPT1:", respectively.

And, not entirely incidentally, notice that the first *strtok* call specifies only a comma delimiter while the second two calls specify both commas and spaces. Since the device name string often, as in this example, includes spaces, it would be inappropriate to use a space as a delimiter. For the device and output strings, however, spaces should be trimmed; if not removed, they would likely interfere with subsequent operations.

After deciphering the returned string, the next step is to create a device-context handle for the printer and to ensure that this step is successful.

```
hdcPrn = CreateDC( szDriver, szDevice, szOutput, ØL );
if( !hdcPrn )
    return( ErrorMsg( "Printer context failure" ) );
if( ! GetDeviceCaps( hdcPrn, RASTERCAPS ) & RC_BITBLT )
{   //                          check for BitBlt Support
    DeleteDC( hdcPrn );
    return(
        ErrorMsg( "No BitBlt support on printer" ) );
}
return( hdcPrn );
}
```

Once a printer device-context handle has been created, the single critical query required is to ensure that the printer supports BitBlt (BITBLockTransfer) operations. Again, if this feature is not supported, either by the physical device or by the device driver, the operations are aborted.

In either case, of course, before GetPrinterDC returns, the present printer device context (*hdcPrn*) should be deleted.

COLOR VERSUS BLACK-AND-WHITE PRINTERS

One assumption is included in the GetPrinterDC function: the assumption that the printer is, indeed, a monochrome device. And, since these are certainly the most common, this assumption is justifiable. However, color ink-jet printers, such as the HP Color Jet, are becoming popular, while an earlier generation of printers using colored ribbons has not yet faded from view.

As color printers become more common, and as they increase in diversity and capability, you may wish to include provisions to identify output devices that support color printing. To do so, check both the bits per pixel (BITSPIXEL) and the color planes (PLANES), or simply check the device colors (NUMCOLORS).

Before attempting to write color drivers for such devices, it would be worthwhile to begin with the assumption that the manufacturers have already provided their own Windows drivers and that the printer device can simply be treated in the same fashion as any other display or file context, allowing Windows to provide whatever color conversions are required.

Of course, if you want color-to-gray conversion on such a device, this may be a bit more difficult—or may simply be a matter of allowing the user to select the appropriate device mode, as discussed under "Controlling the Printer" later in this chapter.

Figure 10.1 shows an original 256-color bitmap at the left (gray-scaled for reproduction here) and the black-and-white image that would be produced by this preliminary version of the InitPrint procedure.

NOTE. Later revisions will provide gray-scale printing in place of the current black and white.

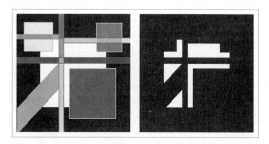

Figure 10.1: Printing color as black and white

Notice particularly that only the white areas in the original are reproduced as white, while all non-white areas (colors) have been mapped, by default, to black. At the same time, the gray-scale equivalent of this same image, using the algorithms demonstrated in GrayImg.C, appears quite similar to the left-hand image and is reproduced, from a printed copy, under "Mapping Color Images to Gray Patterns" later in this chapter.

COPYING FROM DISPLAY TO PRINTER CONTEXTS

Because the provisions included for selecting a .BMP file and for displaying the bitmapped image have been covered in previous chapters and have appeared in prior examples, the next step in this demonstration application begins by assuming that a bitmap is presently displayed by the GrayImg program.

> **NOTE.** For brevity, as with the prior Shades.C program, only 256-color bitmaps are supported by GrayImg.C. This limitation is for convenience only and is not a restriction, as the gray-scale-conversion function and printing methods demonstrated are equally applicable to both 16-color and 24-bit-per-pixel images. Monochrome bitmaps, of course, require no gray-scaling before printing.

Caveats aside, transferring a bitmapped image from a display context to a printer context does involve a slight degree of complexity and, unfortunately, is also an area where Windows might well have made better provisions. The principal problem is quite simple: that an image cannot be transferred directly from the display context to the printer context. Instead, an intermediate display context, *hdcMem* in the following example, is required. The bitmapped image is transferred first from the display context to the memory context and, only subsequently, from the memory context to the printer context.

Later, when gray-scale conversion is incorporated in the final InitPrint function, a fourth context will be used as an intermediary between the display and memory contexts. But, for the moment, three contexts will suffice to demonstrate the basic handling while the revisions required for the fourth are really quite simple.

The InitPrint function (either the black-and-white or gray-scale version) is called with two parameters: a handle for the application's window and a Boolean value selecting either 1-to-1 reproduction or a stretch-to-fit (to fill the printer page) option. Either option can be selected from the application menu to initiate printing.

Also, when finished, the InitPrint function returns an integer result which, nominally, is simply a true or false reporting of success or failure. As desired, of course, the returned value could be any value desired and could be used as an error report or simply be ignored entirely.

```
//=========================================================
// preliminary (non-gray-scale) version of InitPrint
//=========================================================
int FAR InitPrint( HWND hwnd, BOOL StretchMode )
{
   BITMAP   bm;
   HBITMAP  hLBM;
   HDC      hdc, hdcPrn, hdcMem, hdcBmp;
   FARPROC  lpCancelProc;       // cancel print procedure
   FARPROC  lpAbortProc;        // print error procedure
   RECT     rect;
```

```
char    szBuff[32];          // max size for job name
BOOL    bResult, bError;     // boolean flags
int     iPlanes, iBitPxl;
```

In addition to the standard device-context handle (*hdc*), three further device contexts are declared as *hdcPrn* (printer), *hdcMem* (memory), and *hdcBmp* (bitmap). Likewise, two far procedures are locally declared: *lpCancelProc* and *lpAbortProc*. Both of these will be discussed further presently.

One final declaration requires a brief explanation: the *szBuff* variable, which is declared with a size of 32 characters. Under Windows, instead of an application accessing the printer directly, all print operations are sent to the Print Manager, which is both a spooler and a printer task controller. Because the Print Manager, by design, assumes that it may be receiving tasks from multiple applications, it also expects to receive a job title along with each print job. While this task label may, nominally, be anything desired, there is a length limit of 32 characters imposed—hence the size of *szBuff*.

But, before sending anything at all—even a job title—to the printer, Init-Print begins with setup provisions. The first step is to ensure that a printer context is available (by calling the GetPrinterDC function introduced earlier).

```
if( ( hdcPrn = GetPrinterDC( hwnd ) ) == NULL )
    return( ErrorMsg( "No printer device context" ) );
GetObject( hGBM, sizeof(BITMAP), (LPSTR) &bm );
iBitPxl = GetDeviceCaps( hdcPrn, BITSPIXEL );
iPlanes = GetDeviceCaps( hdcPrn, PLANES );
hLBM = CreateBitmap( bm.bmWidth, bm.bmHeight,
                     iPlanes, iBitPxl, NULL );
if( !hLBM )
    return( ErrorMsg( "Bitmap creation error" ) );
```

After the printer context is retrieved and GetObject is called to retrieve the active bitmap (*hGBM*), GetDeviceCaps is called to retrieve the bits-per-pixel and color planes for the printer, though not, as suggested, to test for a color printer but simply to create a bitmap context (*hLBM*) that is compatible with the printer capabilities.

As already mentioned, however, copying directly from *hGBM* to *hLBM* is not permitted. Therefore, the next step is to create two device-context handles, one of which is compatible with the printer (*hdcMem*) and one of which is compatible with the present display and bitmap (*hdcBmp*), before releasing the original device-context handle (*hdc*).

```
if( hdc = GetDC( hwnd ) )
{
    hdcMem = CreateCompatibleDC( hdcPrn );
```

```
      hdcBmp = CreateCompatibleDC( hdc );
      ReleaseDC( hwnd, hdc );
   }
   if( !hdcMem || !hdcBmp )
   {
      if( hdcMem ) ReleaseDC( hwnd, hdcMem );
      if( hdcBmp ) ReleaseDC( hwnd, hdcBmp );
      return( ErrorMsg( "Memory allocation error" ) );
   }
   SelectObject( hdcMem, hLBM );
   SelectObject( hdcBmp, hGBM );
```

While relatively thorough error-trapping is provided in the InitPrint procedure, it is also (probably) a bit of overkill. Too much error-trapping, however, is always better than too little.

After creating the three contexts (*hdcBmp*, *hdcMem* and *hdcPrn*), InitPrint is ready to begin copying the bitmapped image, beginning by copying from the bitmap context to the memory-device context.

```
   if( BitBlt( hdcMem, 0, 0, bm.bmWidth, bm.bmHeight,
               hdcBmp, 0, 0, SRCCOPY ) )
   {
```

At this point, the BitBlt function is called with the SRCCOPY option. Any resizing desired, or other image conversions, will be left for the final transfer stage. Again, however, this operation is tested for possible errors and, if unsuccessful, InitPrint terminates, reporting a failure.

Before continuing with the print operation, InitPrint now introduces two new elements but begins by disabling the application window. This makes it impossible to close the window or to terminate the print process except in an orderly manner.

A word of caution on using the EnableWindow function: Anytime an application window is disabled—and particularly during development—ensure very carefully that EnableWindow is called a second time with a TRUE argument to re-enable the application window. If this is not done . . . well, quite simply, the only way to close the application will be to reboot or to close Windows.

```
   EnableWindow( hwnd, FALSE );
   bAbort = FALSE;
   lpCancelProc = MakeProcInstance( CancelProc, hInst);
   hCancelDlg = CreateDialog( hInst, "CANCEL",
                              hwnd, lpCancelProc );
   ShowWindow( hCancelDlg, SW_SHOW );
```

While disabling the application window should not be done lightly, the standard closure options need to be replaced with an alternative. In this case, the alternative is supplied by two provisions: by the cancellation dialog box, preceding, and indirectly, by the abort procedure, following.

The CancelProc dialog box, which is an exported procedure handled by Windows, not by the application, is shown in Figure 10.2.

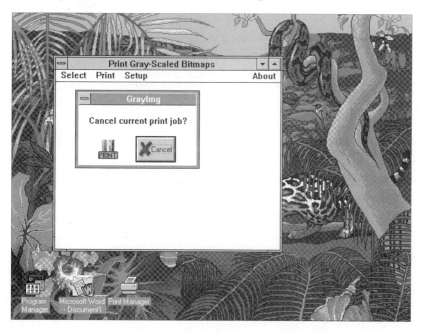

Figure 10.2: Printing cancellation dialog box for the GrayImg program

The print cancellation dialog box is displayed immediately and continues during the process of transferring the image from the intermediate memory-context handle (*hdcMem*) to the printer-context handle (*hdcPrn*). If the Cancel button is clicked at any time during this process, the *bAbort* flag is set, terminating the transfer process and, indirectly, clearing whatever portion of the image has already been sent to the Print Manager.

During this process, however, remember that the application window has been disabled and the normal options for closure are, temporarily, no longer present. Instead, the print cancellation dialog box provides the only way to break out of the present task, returning the application to its WinProc handler.

But the print cancellation dialog box is not the only way the process can be interrupted—just the only way the user can interrupt the process. As a guard against Print Manager errors, usually a lack of disk space, a second exported process, AbortProc, is established.

```
lpAbortProc = MakeProcInstance( AbortProc, hInst );
Escape( hdcPrn, SETABORTPROC, 0,
        (LPSTR) lpAbortProc, NULL );
```

By using the SETABORTPROC Escape, instead of simply failing on an error, the Print Manager calls an abort dialog box, which is defined not by the application but by the device driver. The abort procedure does not display a screen dialog box unless and until an error occurs during the image-transfer process. Instead, as you will observe in a moment, the abort procedure is called, repeatedly, during the image transfer to check for errors.

Further, since Windows is a multitasking environment, if an error occurs, the user does have the opportunity to leave the GrayImg program and, in the case of lack of disk space for temporary files, to call the File Manager to correct the situation before resuming. Alternately, the user may simply choose to abort the process. Like the print cancellation dialog box, the abort process handler sets the Boolean *bAbort* flag to terminate further processing within InitPrint's main loop.

NOTE. Due primarily to the difficulty in creating the conditions necessary for a problem to occur, the abort dialog box is not illustrated.

After establishing the cancellation and abort procedures, but before beginning the image transfer itself, a first step is to create a task name that can be passed to the Print Manager (as mentioned previously).

```
sprintf( szBuff, "%s - %s", szAppName, szFName );
if( ( Escape( hdcPrn, STARTDOC, sizeof(szBuff)-1,
              szBuff, NULL ) > 0 ) &&
    ( Escape( hdcPrn, NEXTBAND, 0, NULL,
              (LPSTR) &rect ) > 0 ) )
{
```

Finally, after creating a task name, two further Escape function calls are made. The first, STARTDOC, notifies the Print Manager that a new document is being initiated and passes the task name that identifies both the source application and the image name. Remember, this information is provided far more for the user than for the Print Manager. The second Escape function call, NEXTBAND, is used, nominally, to inform a device driver that an application has completed a band and to send the band to the Print Manager. At this point, NEXTBAND is being called as an initialization, setting the band rectangle (*rect*) to the device (printer) coordinates to receive the next band of data.

> **NOTE.** Banding is a process of passing only a part of an image or a page of text to the printer at a single time. It is particularly important when the destination device does not have enough memory to hold the entire image or text at one time. Ink-jet and dot-matrix printers, for example, rarely have sufficient memory to store a full-page image or, frequently, even a full page of text. Thus, using banding, the image or text is passed in smaller segments—normally a rectangular area the width of the page or image—that can be processed before further data is accepted.

While banding between the Print Manager and the actual device is handled automatically by the Print Manager, banding provisions also can be included for transfer between an application's device context and the Print Manager, improving operation when memory resources may be limited. When no provisions for banding are included in the application, banding operations may be supplied by Windows (through the device drivers) automatically.

The actual process of transferring an image from the memory context to the printer context takes place within a loop that executes until either the source band rectangle (*rect*) is empty or the Boolean flag *bAbort* is set TRUE (set by either the cancel or abort process).

```
while( ! IsRectEmpty( &rect ) && ! bAbort )
{
    (*lpAbortProc)( hdcPrn, Ø );
    DPtoLP( hdcPrn, (LPPOINT) &rect, 2 );
    (*lpAbortProc)( hdcPrn, Ø );
```

Having implemented band processing, the first step within the loop, after an initial check of the abort procedure, is to convert the coordinates in *rect* from device points to logical points. Remember, however, that the coordinates in *rect* were set by the printer context and, in this case, contain the entire printable page size.

Next, two options are provided in the GrayImg menu: the StretchBlt and BitBlt operations. The BitBlt operation copies the image one for one between contexts. Thus, each pixel in the display image becomes one dot or point in the printed copy. The drawback, of course, is that a 200-by-200-pixel image is, using a 300 dpi laser printer, only 2/3 of an inch square—not a very large image on paper.

```
if( !StretchMode )
{
    if( !BitBlt(
```

```
          hdcPrn, rect.left, rect.top,
                  rect.right - rect.left,
                  rect.bottom - rect.top,
          hdcMem, 0, 0, SRCCOPY ) )
          ErrorMsg( "Bitblt failed" );
  }
```

Alternately, the StretchBlt operation, in this application, stretches the area designated for the source image (the 0, 0 origin and *bm.bmWidth*, *bm.bmHeight* point pairs) to fit the destination area specified by *rect*.

```
      else
      {
          if( !StretchBlt(
              hdcPrn, rect.left, rect.top,
                      rect.right - rect.left,
                      rect.bottom - rect.top,
              hdcMem, 0, 0, bm.bmWidth, bm.bmHeight,
                      SRCCOPY ) )
              ErrorMsg( "StretchBlt failed" );
      }
```

If either case—BitBlt or StretchBlt—fails, an error message is displayed. However, no action is taken in response; instead, the error message is for information only.

Also note that BitBlt and StretchBlt errors do not produce abort errors and are not trapped by calls to the abort procedure. The exported abort procedure only responds to errors detected by the device driver.

Next, after calling one of the two transfer procedures, the abort procedure is checked for driver errors. Then, a NEXTBAND Escape call notifies the device driver that the band is completed and ready to be sent to the Print Manager. After this, the loop will continue, if necessary, until the entire image has been processed.

```
          (*lpAbortProc)( hdcPrn, 0 );
          if( Escape( hdcPrn, NEXTBAND, NULL,
                  NULL, (LPSTR) &rect ) < 0 )
          {
              bError = TRUE;
              break;
  }  }  }
  else bError = TRUE;
```

Once the processing loop terminates, two provisions are made: either terminate with an ABORTDOC Escape, which cancels any portion of the image that has already been sent, or terminate with an ENDDOC Escape to identify completion of the image.

```
if( !bError )
     Escape( hdcPrn, ABORTDOC, 0, NULL, NULL );
else Escape( hdcPrn, ENDDOC,   0, NULL, NULL );
if( !bAbort ) EnableWindow( hwnd, TRUE );
if( hCancelDlg ) DestroyWindow( hCancelDlg );
```

If the *bAbort* flag has been set, either the cancellation process or the abort process has already called EnableWindow to restore the application's normal response mechanisms. But if not, this task is still required, as is the Destroy-Window call, to remove the cancel dialog box display (if this hasn't already been done by the CancelDlg process).

Of course, there's always a bit of final cleanup to clear the two exported processes and the printer device context.

```
        FreeProcInstance( lpCancelProc );
        FreeProcInstance( lpAbortProc );
        DeleteDC( hdcPrn );
    }
    else bResult = ErrorMsg( "BitBlt failure to memory DC!" );
    if( hdcBmp ) DeleteDC( hdcBmp );
    if( hdcMem ) DeleteDC( hdcMem );
    DeleteObject( hLBM );
    return(bResult);
}
```

And, finally, the bitmap and memory-device contexts are deleted, as is the local bitmapped object, before the final result is returned to the calling process.

In some circumstances—such as copying a black-and-white image to a black-and-white printer or a color image to a color printer—the InitPrint procedure illustrated is all that would be required. For more common circumstances, however, additional provisions are required; first, to find gray (intensity) equivalents for image colors, and second, to print a gray equivalent of the image itself.

TRANSLATING COLORS TO GRAY INTENSITIES

The process of translating colors to grays has been discussed previously but merits a brief review before implementation is illustrated.

The first consideration is that, for the video display, colors are described by three digital values: red, green, and blue. Thus, using the RGBTriplet format, each of these color components has a value in the range 0..255 and the corresponding display ranges from black to full intensity. The result we see on the screen is a combination of the three primary colors with the relative intensities of each primary as well as the overall intensity determining the "color" or hue perceived.

But the human eye is not linear. It responds differently to each of the three primaries, with the strongest response (59 percent) being to green. Our second strongest response is to red (30 percent), and our response to blue is weakest at 11 percent.

Therefore, to translate red, green, and blue intensities into a gray scale, the absolute intensities of the three components must be weighted to match (or, more accurately, the relative darkness of each component will be weighted to produce the appropriate portion of black ink on the page).

CREATING A GRAY-SCALE

Before matching colors to gray equivalents, it will help to have a range of grays for the match. Thus, before writing the matching algorithm, the first step is to create a gray scale for the printer. For demonstration purposes, a simple 16-step (4x4) gray-scale will be used even though a 25-step (5x5), 36-step (6x6), 64-step (8x8), or even 256-step (16x16) gray-scale could be implemented.

> **NOTE.** The choice of a square gray-pattern is dictated by convenience but is not an absolute. Non-square grays, however, will require a quite different handling and mapping.

Figure 10.3 shows 16 4-by-4 matrixes ranging from full black to complete white. A DWORD hex value providing a binary description of each pattern appears below each matrix. Also, as you may note, one possible permutation of blacks and whites—eight of each distributed among the 16 squares—has been omitted.

The 16 patterns used were selected to provide as even a distribution as possible and, at the same time, to avoid as much as possible any undesired elements such as lines, herringbone patterns or other artifacts.

A LESS RIGOROUS GRAY-SCALE

While a predefined gray-scale is satisfactory for most uses, a less rigorous (and somewhat more versatile) gray-scale can be created by calculation instead. In its simplest form, each color pixel is, as in the GrayImg demonstration, mapped to a square grid in the printer context. However, instead of mapping the color pixel as a predefined pattern, each point in the square for the pixel is given a black or a white value in proportion to the calculated gray balance and the size of the square.

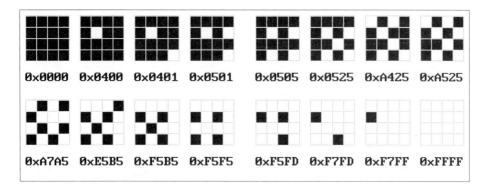

0x0000 0x0400 0x0401 0x0501   0x0505 0x0525 0xA425 0xA525

0xA7A5 0xE5B5 0xF5B5 0xF5F5   0xF5FD 0xF7FD 0xF7FF 0xFFFF

Figure 10.3: A gray-scale as a matrix series

Next, in place of a predetermined pattern, a pseudo-random generator (such as C's *random()* function) is used to assign the appropriate percentage of black and white pixels in an essentially random pattern.

In general, this approach works best with a relatively large matrix for each pixel (8x8 or larger) but does not require an exact match between the range of grays used and the size of the pattern matrix.

Of course, there are also a few disadvantages, such as a slight loss of edge definition, a need to keep the range of grays used relatively close to the matrix size, and some increase in mapping times because of increased complexity. But overall, the advantages can outweigh the disadvantages when wider ranges of grays are required.

Implementing this process is not illustrated by the GrayImg application and is left as an exercise for the reader.

MAPPING COLOR IMAGES TO GRAY PATTERNS

The process of mapping color images to gray patterns follows the process illustrated earlier for the InitPrint procedure. For this version however, as in the GrayImg program, a couple of additions are included.

First, several new variables are included in the declaration, starting with *lpGBits*, which is declared as a long pointer to a string and serves as a buffer for the gray-scaled image during conversion. At the same time, *hTBM* and *hdcTmp* are handles for a bitmap and device context for a new, intermediate transfer step during which the color image will be converted to a gray-scale image.

```
//=========================================================
// color (gray-scale) version of InitPrint
```

```
//===============================================================
int FAR InitPrint( HWND hwnd, BOOL StretchMode )
{
   ...
   LPSTR      lpGBits;
   HBITMAP    hLBM, hTBM;
   HDC        hdc, hdcPrn, hdcMem, hdcBmp, hdcTmp;
   ...
   int        iPlanes, iBitPxl, iGrayWd, iGrayHt;
   DWORD      Color, dwOfs;
   unsigned char  rVal, gVal, bVal;
   BYTE       Gray, Nibble;
   WORD       i, j, m, n, Mask;
   WORD       GrayPal[16] =          // gray scale masks
              { 0x0000, 0x0400, 0x0401, 0x0501,
                0x0505, 0x0525, 0xA425, 0xA5A5,
                0xA7A5, 0xE5B5, 0xF5B5, 0xF5F5,
                0xF5FD, 0xF7FD, 0xF7FF, 0xFFFF  };
```

The GrayPal (gray-palette) array, illustrated in Figure 10.3, is declared here as an array of DWORD. Later, however, the individual DWORD values will be treated as four nibbles (four-bit values).

After the current bitmap is retrieved, the *iGrayWd* and *iGrayHt* values are calculated.

```
   ...
   iGrayWd = 4 * bm.bmWidth;
   iGrayHt = 4 * bm.bmHeight;
   ...
   hLBM = CreateBitmap( iGrayWd, iGrayHt,
                        iPlanes, iBitPxl, NULL );
   hTBM = CreateBitmap( iGrayWd, 4,
                        iPlanes, iBitPxl, NULL );
```

In the earlier example, *hLBM* was defined with the width and height (*bm.-bmWidth* and *bm.bmHeight*) values derived from the original image. In this case, however, the intermediate bitmap desired is 16 times larger, providing space for a 4-by-4 gray pattern for each pixel in the original image.

At the same time, a temporary bitmap, *hTBM*, is defined with the same width, color planes (1) and bits per pixel (1) but with a vertical dimension of only four pixels, corresponding, after conversion to grays, to a single scan line in the original.

Further, both *hdcMem* and *hdcTmp* are created as device contexts compatible with the printer context.

```
hdcMem = CreateCompatibleDC( hdcPrn );
hdcTmp = CreateCompatibleDC( hdcPrn );
```

Everything thus far has been preparation. The real process of converting the color image to a gray-scaled equivalent begins by allocating and locking memory for the *lpGBits* array (string) with a size the same as the temporary bitmap *hTBM*.

```
lpGBits = GlobalLock(
              GlobalAlloc( GHND, iGrayWd * 2 ) );
for( i=0; i<bmHeight; i++ )
{
```

With memory allocated for a one–scan-line buffer, a loop is initiated to step through the original image, one scan line at a time. Next, within the primary loop, a second loop runs through the current scan line, using the GetPixel function to retrieve the RGB color value of each pixel.

```
for( j=0; j<bm.bmWidth; j++ )
{
    Color = GetPixel( hdc, j, i );
    rVal  = (unsigned char)(LOBYTE(HIWORD(Color)));
    gVal  = (unsigned char)(HIBYTE(LOWORD(Color)));
    bVal  = (unsigned char)(LOBYTE(LOWORD(Color)));
```

With the color value retrieved, the high byte of the high word is ignored while the remaining three bytes are separated as individual red, green, and blue values, each—for safety—explicitly cast as an *unsigned char* value.

Once individual color values for a pixel have been retrieved, a gray value can be calculated from the relative intensities.

```
Gray = (BYTE)( ( 0.30 / 16 * rVal ) +
               ( 0.59 / 16 * gVal ) +
               ( 0.11 / 16 * bVal ) );
```

While the individual color values are in the range 0..255, they will be mapped to a range of 16 gray levels, so a corrective range factor is applied as a divisor. However, rather than repetitively calculating the divisor as . . ./ (256/16) *. . ., the constant value 16 has been supplied. Of course, for other ranges of gray values, a different divisor would be required.

The present formula has been used because it is clear and easy to explain even though it is not, for practical purposes, the most efficient. Thus, for speed of execution, regardless of the range, the preceding formula could be re-written with three corrective factors (floating-point values) calculated outside of the processing loops as:

```
rAdj = 0.30 * ( gray_range / 256 );
gAdj = 0.59 * ( gray_range / 256 );
bAdj = 0.11 * ( gray_range / 256 );
```

Subsequently, within the processing loops, a much briefer calculation could be made as:

```
Gray = (BYTE)( ( rAdj * rVal ) +
               ( gAdj * gVal ) +
               ( bAdj * bVal ) );
```

Regardless of the calculation method used, the next step assigns Mask the appropriate pattern value from the GrayPal array before initiating another loop to copy nibble values from Mask into the *lpGBits* buffer.

```
Mask = GrayPal[Gray];
for( m=0; m<4; m++ )
{
    Nibble = (BYTE)( ( Mask >> (4*m) ) & 0x0F );
```

Within the four-step loop (since we're using a 4-by-4 pattern), Nibble is calculated by using a simple bit-shift and by masking the resulting byte value with 0x0F to effectively yield a nibble value, even though it is stored in a byte variable.

Next, an offset is calculated to find the appropriate position within the *lpGBits* buffer,

```
dwOfs = ( j / 2 ) + ( bm.bmWidth * m / 2 );
switch( j % 2 )
{
```

Because the *lpGBits* buffer is treated as an array of byte (or *unsigned char*), it can only be indexed as byte values or byte positions. The offset calculation takes this into account while the subsequent *switch* statement selects between odd and even values of *j* to decide if this nibble belongs high or low within the byte position.

While odd nibbles (odd values of *j*) become the high nibble within the targeted byte, there is no provision for directly writing nibble values into an array of byte nor is there any ready provision for treating arrays of byte as arrays of nibble and indexing them accordingly. Instead, what cannot conveniently be done directly, can be accomplished indirectly, thus:

```
case 0:                 // odd nibbles go left
    lpGBits[dwOfs] = (BYTE)
        ( ( lpGBits[dwOfs] & 0x0F ) |
          ( Nibble << 4 ) );  // shift left !
    break;
```

For odd index values, the original array value can be bit-wise AND'd with 0x0F (preserving the low nibble) and then bit-wise OR'd with the value in Nibble after this has been shifted left four bits (making it a high nibble, so to speak).

For even index values, the process is even simpler. The original byte values are AND'd with 0xF0 to preserve the high nibble and then OR'd with Nibble (without shifting).

```
case 1:                 // even nibbles go right
    lpGBits[dwOfs] = (BYTE)
        ( ( lpGBits[dwOfs] & 0xF0 ) |
            Nibble );           // no shift ...
    break;
}   }   }
```

The preceding process can be illustrated schematically beginning with a DWORD value N that is treated as four nibbles identified as N1, N2, N3, and N4.

```
...] [ K1 L1 ] [ M1 N1 ] [ O1 P1 ] [ Q1 R1 ] [...
...] [ K2 L2 ] [ M2 N2 ] [ O2 P2 ] [ Q2 R2 ] [...
...] [ K3 L3 ] [ M3 N3 ] [ O3 P3 ] [ Q3 R3 ] [...
...] [ K4 L4 ] [ M4 N4 ] [ O4 P4 ] [ Q4 R4 ] [...
```

In the diagram above, byte values are enclosed in brackets while the essentially linear array of *lpGBits* is folded to represent a two-dimensional array sized as *bm.bmWidth* x 2.

Outside of the two inner loops—that is, after each scan line has been processed—SetBitmapBits is called to write the gray-patterned bits in *lpGBits* into the temporary buffer before a call to BitBlt is used to copy this buffer into the memory-context handle (*hdcMem*).

```
SetBitmapBits( hTBM, iGrayWd*2, lpGBits );
BitBlt( hdcMem, 0, i*4, iGrayWd, 4,
        hdcTmp, 0, 0, SRCCOPY );
}
```

This concludes processing for one scan line of the original image. Of course, the initial, outer loop continues for subsequent scan lines until the entire image has been processed.

The remainder of the gray-scale version of InitPrint is essentially the same as the version discussed previously. The complete procedure (gray-scale version) appears in the GrayImg program listing at the end of this chapter, as well as on the accompanying program disk.

Overall, perhaps this may appear a rather roundabout fashion to map a color image to a gray-scaled equivalent. Still, this process does have several advantages, including the fact that there is no need for *far long* pointers to index bitmaps greater than 64k, that there is no need to convert palette color indexes into RGB values and that, on the whole, processing times are very fast.

Incidentally, as you may easily notice, the color-to-gray conversion itself tends to be considerably faster than the process of copying the gray image to the Print Manager.

Figure 10.4 shows an actual print using GrayImg to convert the 256-color original Modern.BMP to a gray-scaled hard copy. Output was executed on a 300 dpi laser printer.

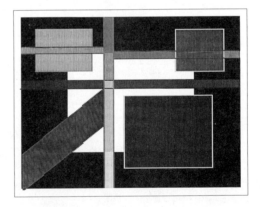

Figure 10.4: A true gray-scaled print

SIZING IMAGES TO AVOID PLAIDING

In both versions of the InitPrint process, the StretchBlt copy process used the *rect* coordinates derived from the printer context to size the bitmap to fill the entire page. However, for several reasons, this is not always an optimal choice. In actual applications—as opposed to a demo program—it is more likely first, that a specific size will be desired; and second, that vertical and horizontal proportions would have to be preserved (which was not done here). Third, but not necessarily least, it's also desirable to avoid plaiding in the printed image.

Happily, all of these conditions are also relatively easy to fulfill.

The first objective, a precise size, is simplicity itself. In the StretchBlt operation, replace the *rect* coordinates derived from the page size with the desired image size—remembering, of course, to convert from inches or millimeters or whatever unit into logical-device coordinates (pixels or printer dots). For this purpose, as you should recall, device resolution information is available using the GetDeviceCaps function.

The second objective, maintaining proportion, is equally easy and requires nothing more than—for maximal image size—comparing horizontal and vertical size ratios and then adjusting the greater ratio to maintain image proportions.

The third objective, avoiding plaiding, is perhaps the most difficult simply because this provision is not completely compatible with either of the first two even though, in execution, it is not exceedingly difficult.

In practice, the simplest solution is to size the image so that the dots in the output image are some multiple of the original pixel size (or, for gray-scales, some multiple of the gray-scaled pixel size). Thus, for a 200-by-200 pixel image converted into a 16-level gray-scale, the gray image is 800-by-800 pixels and could be printed as 800-by-800, 1,600-by-1,600 or 2,400-by-2,400 dots. (Assuming a 300 dpi laser printer, the largest, 2,400-dot image would be 8-inches wide.) For dot-matrix printers with lower resolutions, of course, the choices and possibilities are more restricted while typesetting printers and many of the newer laser printer designs offer more versatility.

The only real problem is found with devices that lack a 1-to-1 horizontal-to-vertical aspect ratio. As an example, some dot-matrix printers might provide a horizontal resolution of 96 dpi while their vertical resolution is 180 dpi, a ratio of 96-to-180 or 8-to-15—not an easy ratio to fit without distorting the image proportions. Fortunately, most laser and ink-jet printers do have 1-to-1 aspect ratios.

And there is one further consideration that can be applied: Many printers offer a choice of modes and resolutions.

CONTROLLING THE PRINTER

While querying printer capabilities are essential for the GrayImg application, a second provision has been included in the menu: a printer control feature.

Earlier, the GetPrinterDC procedure introduced a means of identifying the default printer and, incidentally, the appropriate library name. At that time, the only objective was to query the device capacity about specific features. But given the driver and the library name, there is a second objective that may also be quite useful: calling the driver's DEVICEMODE procedure.

Initially, the SetPrinterSettings procedure parallels the GetPrinterDC procedure.

```
void SetPrinterSettings( HWND hwnd )
{
    HANDLE    hDrvLib;
    FARPROC   lpDevModeProc;
    char      szPrn[40], szFDrv[13];
    char      *szDevice, *szDriver, *szOutput;

    if( GetProfileString( "windows", "device", ",,,",
    szPrn, BUFF_SIZE ) != 0 )
    {
        szDevice = strtok( szPrn, "," );
        szDriver = strtok( NULL, ", " );
        szOutput = strtok( NULL, ", " );
        strcpy( szFDrv, szDriver );
        strcat( szFDrv, ".DRV" );
        hDrvLib = LoadLibrary( szFDrv );
```

But after the printer and driver names are retrieved, the objective changes and the LoadLibrary function calls the driver library.

While the DEVICEMODE procedure contained in the driver library is not directly accessible, it is indirectly accessible by retrieving the process address as *lpDevModeProc* and then calling this process indirectly (by address), thus:

```
        if( hDrvLib >= 32 )
        {
            lpDevModeProc =
                GetProcAddress( hDrvLib, "DEVICEMODE" );
            if( lpDevModeProc )
            {
                (*lpDevModeProc)
                    ( (HWND)   hwnd,        // parent window
                      (HANDLE) hDrvLib,     // library name
                      (LPSTR)  szDevice,    // printer name
                      (LPSTR)  szOutput );  // port
            }
            else ErrorMsg( "Device Mode not available" );
            FreeLibrary( hDrvLib );
        }
```

Beyond calling the DEVICEMODE procedure the application requires nothing more. But for the user, a large bonus has been provided in the form of direct access—within the application—to the printer controls as shown in Figure 10.5.

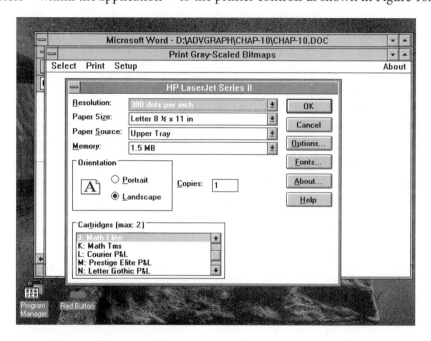

Figure 10.5: The printer control dialog

SUMMARY

Being able to print a graphic image is almost as important as creating the image in the first place—and in some cases, almost more important. The tools demonstrated in this chapter provide the basis for such facilities using both black-and-white and gray-scale color conversion.

   If and how these features are used depends entirely on the needs of your applications. Most likely, the features will require adaptation and/or provisions for specific controls that have not been provided here. Alternately, if you only require an occasional screen capture, you might prefer to combine the printer output procedures with one of the screen-capture processes demonstrated previously.

   However, the business graphics to be demonstrated in Chapter 11 are prime candidates for including a printer output provision. After all, given conventional business practices, even in the computer/video age there still seems to be little profit in generating elaborate graphics without also being able to generate printed copies (especially for those who are terminally computer phobic).

Incidentally, if you have or use color reproduction facilities, you might also consider adding provisions for printing color separations—that is, printing separate red, green, and blue images for use as color screens in conventional printing processes.

PROGRAM LISTING OF GRAYIMG.C

```
//==============================//
//            GrayImg.C         //
//  Gray-Scale Printer Support  //
//==============================//

#include <windows.h>
#include <string.h>
#include <stdlib.h>
#include <stdio.h>
#include <dir.h>
#include <bwcc.h>          // include bwcc.lib in project file
#include "grayimg.h"

#define  wFAttr      0x4010   // file attribute mask value
#define  BUFF_SIZE   0x0040   // device profile buffer size

static FARPROC lpAbortDlg;
static FARPROC lpAbortProc;

BOOL    bAbort = FALSE;
HWND    hAbortDlg, hCancelDlg;

static char    szFName[64], szFSpec[64] = "*.BMP",
               szCaption[] = "Print Gray-Scaled Bitmaps",
               szFPath[64], szFExt[5] = ".BMP",
               szAppName[]  = "GrayImg";
static LPSTR    lpMBits;
static DWORD    bmWidth, bmHeight, bmImgSize, bmScanWidth;
static WORD     bmBitCount;
HANDLE          hInst;
HBITMAP         hGBM  = NULL;
HPALETTE        hGPal = NULL;
LPLOGPALETTE    pGLP  = NULL;

int ErrorMsg( char *Error )
{
```

```
      MessageBox( GetFocus(), Error, "Warning",
                  MB_ICONASTERISK | MB_OK );
      return(0);
}


#pragma argsused

BOOL FAR PASCAL AboutProc( HWND hDlg,    WORD msg,
                           WORD wParam, LONG lParam )
{
   switch( msg )
   {
      case WM_INITDIALOG:  return( TRUE );
      case WM_COMMAND:
         switch( wParam )
         {
            case IDOK: EndDialog( hDlg, TRUE );
                       return( TRUE );
              default: return( TRUE );
      }     }
   return( FALSE );
}


#pragma argsused

int FAR PASCAL AbortDlg( HWND hwndDlg, WORD msg,
                         WORD wParam,  LONG lParam )
{
   switch( msg )
   {
      case WM_INITDIALOG:
         SetDlgItemText( hwndDlg, IDD_FNAME, szFName );
         SetFocus( GetDlgItem( hwndDlg, IDCANCEL ) );
         return( TRUE );

      case WM_COMMAND:
         switch( wParam )
         {
            case IDCANCEL:  bAbort = TRUE;  break;
            default:        bAbort = FALSE;
         }
         return( TRUE );
   }
   return( FALSE );
}
```

```
#pragma argsused

int FAR PASCAL CancelProc( HWND hDlg,    WORD msg,
                           WORD wParam, LONG lParam )
{
   switch( msg )
   {
      case WM_INITDIALOG:
         SetWindowText( hDlg, szAppName );
         SetDlgItemText( hDlg, IDD_FNAME,
            szFName[Ø] ? szFName : "untitled" );
         EnableMenuItem( GetSystemMenu( hDlg, FALSE ),
                         SC_CLOSE, MF_GRAYED );
         return( TRUE );
      case WM_COMMAND:
         bAbort = TRUE;
         EnableWindow( GetParent( hDlg ), TRUE );
         DestroyWindow( hDlg );
         hCancelDlg = NULL;
         return( TRUE );
      default:
         return( FALSE );
   }  }


#pragma argsused

int FAR PASCAL AbortProc( HDC hdcPrn, WORD nPrnStat )
{
   MSG   msg;

   while( ! bAbort &&
          PeekMessage( &msg, NULL, Ø, Ø, PM_REMOVE ) )
   {
      if( ! hCancelDlg ||
          ! IsDialogMessage( hCancelDlg, &msg ) )
      {
         TranslateMessage( &msg );
         DispatchMessage( &msg );
      }  }
   return( ! bAbort );
}


void SetPrinterSettings( HWND hwnd )
//=========================================================
//  call device driver procedure to set printer options
//=========================================================
```

```
{
    HANDLE    hDrvLib;
    FARPROC   lpDevModeProc;
    char      szPrn[40], szFDrv[13];
    char      *szDevice, *szDriver, *szOutput;

    if( GetProfileString( "windows", "device", ",,,",
                          szPrn, BUFF_SIZE ) != 0 )
    {
        szDevice = strtok( szPrn, "," );
        szDriver = strtok( NULL, ", " );
        szOutput = strtok( NULL, ", " );
//=== load device driver ================================
        strcpy( szFDrv, szDriver );
        strcat( szFDrv, ".DRV" );
        hDrvLib = LoadLibrary( szFDrv );
        if( hDrvLib >= 32 )
        {
//=== call Device Mode proc from driver ==================
            lpDevModeProc =
                GetProcAddress( hDrvLib, "DEVICEMODE" );
            if( lpDevModeProc )
            {
                (*lpDevModeProc)
                    ( (HWND)   hwnd,         // parent window
                      (HANDLE) hDrvLib,      // library name
                      (LPSTR)  szDevice,     // printer name
                      (LPSTR)  szOutput );   // port
            }
            else ErrorMsg( "Device Mode not available" );
            FreeLibrary( hDrvLib );
        }
        else ErrorMsg( "Error reading printer driver" );
    }
    else ErrorMsg( "printer (device driver) not found" );
}

#pragma argsused

HDC NEAR GetPrinterDC( HWND hwnd )
{
    HDC       hdcPrn = NULL;
    FARPROC   lpDevModeProc;
    char      szPrn[40];
    char      *szDevice, *szDriver, *szOutput;
```

```
    if( GetProfileString( "windows", "device", ",,,",
                            szPrn, BUFF_SIZE ) == 0 )
        return(
            ErrorMsg( "printer (device driver) not found" ));
    szDevice = strtok( szPrn, "," );
    szDriver = strtok( NULL, ", " );
    szOutput = strtok( NULL, ", " );
    hdcPrn = CreateDC( szDriver, szDevice, szOutput, 0L );
    if( !hdcPrn )
        return( ErrorMsg( "Printer context failure" ) );
    if( ! GetDeviceCaps( hdcPrn, RASTERCAPS ) & RC_BITBLT )
    {
        DeleteDC( hdcPrn );
        return(
            ErrorMsg( "No BitBlt support on printer" ) );
    }
    return( hdcPrn );
}

int FAR InitPrint( HWND hwnd, BOOL StretchMode )
{
    BITMAP    bm;
    LPSTR     lpGBits;
    HBITMAP   hLBM, hTBM;
    HDC       hdc, hdcPrn, hdcMem, hdcBmp, hdcTmp;
    FARPROC   lpCancelProc;        // cancel print procedure
    FARPROC   lpAbortProc;         // print error procedure
    RECT      rect;
    char      szBuff[32];          // max size for job name
    BOOL      bResult, bError;     // boolean flags
    int       iPlanes, iBitPxl, iGrayWd, iGrayHt;
    DWORD     Color, dwOfs;
    unsigned char  rVal, gVal, bVal;
    BYTE      Gray, Nibble;
    WORD      i, j, m, n, Mask;
    WORD      GrayPal[16] =        // gray scale masks
              { 0x0000, 0x0400, 0x0401, 0x0501,
                0x0505, 0x0525, 0xA425, 0xA5A5,
                0xA7A5, 0xE5B5, 0xF5B6, 0xF5F5,
                0xF5FD, 0xF7FD, 0xF7FF, 0xFFFF  };

    if( ( hdcPrn = GetPrinterDC( hwnd ) ) == NULL )
        return( ErrorMsg( "No printer device context" ) );
    GetObject( hGBM, sizeof(BITMAP), (LPSTR) &bm );
    iGrayWd = 4 * bm.bmWidth;
    iGrayHt = 4 * bm.bmHeight;
```

```
//=== create printer compatible bitmap ===================
    iBitPxl = GetDeviceCaps( hdcPrn, BITSPIXEL );
    iPlanes = GetDeviceCaps( hdcPrn, PLANES );
    hLBM = CreateBitmap( iGrayWd, iGrayHt,
                         iPlanes, iBitPxl, NULL );
    hTBM = CreateBitmap( iGrayWd, 4,
                         iPlanes, iBitPxl, NULL );
    if( !hLBM )
        return( ErrorMsg( "Bitmap creation error" ) );
//=== create compatible contexts =========================
    if( (hdc = GetDC( hwnd ) ) != NULL )
    {
        hdcMem = CreateCompatibleDC( hdcPrn );
        hdcTmp = CreateCompatibleDC( hdcPrn );
        hdcBmp = CreateCompatibleDC( hdc );
        ReleaseDC( hwnd, hdc );
    }
    if( !hdcMem || !hdcBmp || !hdcTmp )
    {
        if( hdcMem ) ReleaseDC( hwnd, hdcMem );
        if( hdcBmp ) ReleaseDC( hwnd, hdcBmp );
        if( hdcTmp ) ReleaseDC( hwnd, hdcTmp );
        return( ErrorMsg( "Memory allocation error" ) );
    }
    SelectObject( hdcMem, hLBM );
    SelectObject( hdcBmp, hGBM );
    SelectObject( hdcTmp, hTBM );
    SetCursor( LoadCursor( NULL, IDC_WAIT ) );
//=== convert image to grayscale =========================
    lpGBits = GlobalLock(
                GlobalAlloc( GHND, iGrayWd * 2 ) );
    for( i=0; i<bmHeight; i++ )
    {
        for( j=0; j<bm.bmWidth; j++ )
        {
            Color = GetPixel( hdc, j, i );
//=== separate color values from triplet =================
            rVal = (unsigned char)(LOBYTE(HIWORD(Color)));
            gVal = (unsigned char)(HIBYTE(LOWORD(Color)));
            bVal = (unsigned char)(LOBYTE(LOWORD(Color)));
//=== convert color to gray intensity ====================
            Gray = (BYTE)( ( 0.30 / 16 * rVal ) +
                           ( 0.59 / 16 * gVal ) +
                           ( 0.11 / 16 * bVal ) );
            Mask = GrayPal[Gray];
            for( m=0; m<4; m++ )
```

```
            {
                Nibble = (BYTE)( ( Mask >> (4*m) ) & ØxØF );
                dwOfs = ( j / 2 ) + ( bm.bmWidth * m / 2 );
                switch( j % 2 )
                {
                    case Ø:                 // odd nibbles go left
                        lpGBits[dwOfs] = (BYTE)
                            ( ( lpGBits[dwOfs] & ØxØF ) |
                              ( Nibble << 4 ) );  // shift left !
                        break;
                    case 1:                 // even nibbles go right
                        lpGBits[dwOfs] = (BYTE)
                            ( ( lpGBits[dwOfs] & ØxFØ ) |
                                Nibble );           // no shift ...
                        break;
            }   }   }
        SetBitmapBits( hTBM, iGrayWd*2, lpGBits );
        BitBlt( hdcMem, Ø, i*4, iGrayWd, 4,
                hdcTmp, Ø, Ø, SRCCOPY );
    }
    SetCursor( LoadCursor( NULL, IDC_ARROW ) );
//=== print the bitmap ===================================
    EnableWindow( hwnd, FALSE );
    bAbort = FALSE;
//=== display cancel dialog ==============================
    lpCancelProc = MakeProcInstance( CancelProc, hInst);
    hCancelDlg = CreateDialog( hInst, "CANCEL",
                                hwnd, lpCancelProc );
    ShowWindow( hCancelDlg, SW_SHOW );
//=== set up abort proc if needed ========================
    lpAbortProc = MakeProcInstance( AbortProc, hInst );
    Escape( hdcPrn, SETABORTPROC, Ø,
            (LPSTR) lpAbortProc, NULL );
//=== construct a job name for the spooler ===============
    sprintf( szBuff, "%s - %s", szAppName, szFName );
//=== set up print job ===================================
    if( ( Escape( hdcPrn, STARTDOC, sizeof(szBuff)-1,
                szBuff, NULL ) > Ø ) &&
        ( Escape( hdcPrn, NEXTBAND, Ø, NULL,
                (LPSTR) &rect ) > Ø ) )
    {
        while( ! IsRectEmpty( &rect ) && ! bAbort )
//=== if banding required by printer, loop repeats =======
        {
            (*lpAbortProc)( hdcPrn, Ø );
            DPtoLP( hdcPrn, (LPPOINT) &rect, 2 );
```

```
          (*lpAbortProc)( hdcPrn, 0 );
          if( !StretchMode )
          {
             if( !BitBlt( hdcPrn,
                          rect.left, rect.top,
                          rect.right - rect.left,
                          rect.bottom - rect.top,
                          hdcMem, 0, 0, SRCCOPY ) )
                ErrorMsg( "Bitblt failed" );
          }
          else
          {
             if( !StretchBlt( hdcPrn,
                              rect.left, rect.top,
                              rect.right - rect.left,
                              rect.bottom - rect.top,
                              hdcMem, 0, 0,
                              iGrayWd, iGrayHt,
                              SRCCOPY ) )
                ErrorMsg( "StretchBlt failed" );
          }
          (*lpAbortProc)( hdcPrn, 0 );
          if( Escape( hdcPrn, NEXTBAND, NULL,
                      NULL, (LPSTR) &rect ) < 0 )
          {
             bError = TRUE;
             break;
      }   }   }
   else bError = TRUE;
//=== image sent to print spooler, now clean up ==========
   if( !bError )
        Escape( hdcPrn, ABORTDOC, 0, NULL, NULL );
   else Escape( hdcPrn, ENDDOC,  0, NULL, NULL );
   if( !bAbort ) EnableWindow( hwnd, TRUE );
   if( hCancelDlg ) DestroyWindow( hCancelDlg );
   FreeProcInstance( lpCancelProc );
   FreeProcInstance( lpAbortProc );
   DeleteDC( hdcPrn );
   if( hdcBmp ) ReleaseDC( hwnd, hdcBmp );
   if( hdcMem ) ReleaseDC( hwnd, hdcMem );
   if( hdcTmp ) ReleaseDC( hwnd, hdcTmp );
   DeleteObject( hTBM );
   DeleteObject( hLBM );
   return(bResult);
}
```

```
int ReadBitmap( HWND hwnd )
{
   BITMAPFILEHEADER    bmFH;
   LPBITMAPINFOHEADER  pbmIH;
   LPBITMAPINFO        pbmInfo;
   RGBQUAD   FAR    * pRGB;
   BYTE     huge   * pBits;
   HDC                 hdc;
   HANDLE              hBM;
   HBITMAP             hBitmap;
   HPALETTE            hOldPal, hNewPal;
   WORD                PalSize;
   int                 hFile;
   char                szBuff[64];
   LPSTR               lpBits;
   int                 i, j, CRes = 256;
   LONG                GetBytes, ReadBytes, BytesLeft;

//=== clean up any existing memory objects ===============
   if( lpMBits ) GlobalFree( (HANDLE) lpMBits );
   if( hGBM ) GlobalFree( (HANDLE) hGBM );
   if( hGPal ) GlobalFree( (HANDLE) hGPal );
   if( pGLP ) GlobalFree( (HANDLE) pGLP );
   bmWidth = bmHeight = bmImgSize = bmScanWidth = 0;
//=== open file ==========================================
   sprintf( szBuff, "%s%s", szFPath, szFName );
   hFile = _lopen( szBuff, OF_READ );;
   if( hFile == -1 )
   {
      sprintf( szBuff, "Can't open %s at %s",
                       szFName, szFPath );
      return( ErrorMsg( szBuff ) );
   }
//=== read bitmap header =================================
   SetCursor( LoadCursor( NULL, IDC_WAIT ) );
   _lread( hFile, (LPSTR) &bmFH,
           sizeof(BITMAPFILEHEADER) );
   if( bmFH.bfType != 0x4D42 )   // if type isn't "BF" ...
      return( ErrorMsg( "Not a bitmap image" ) );
//=== read bitmap info header ============================
   pbmIH = (LPBITMAPINFOHEADER)
      GlobalLock(   GlobalAlloc( GMEM_FIXED,
                       sizeof(BITMAPINFOHEADER) ) );
   _lread( hFile, (LPSTR) pbmIH,
           sizeof(BITMAPINFOHEADER) );
   if( (WORD) pbmIH->biBitCount != 8 ) // 2^8 colors = 256
```

```
    {
        GlobalUnlock( (HANDLE) pbmIH );
        GLobalFree( (HANDLE) pbmIH );
        return( ErrorMsg("Not a 256-color bitmap"));
      if( (DWORD) pbmIH->biCompression != BI_RGB )
    {

        GlobalUnlock( (HANDLE) pbmIH );
        GLobalFree( (HANDLE) pbmIH );
        return( ErrorMsg("Compressed images not accepted"));
    }
      PalSize = pbmIH->biClrUsed * sizeof(RGBQUAD);
      GlobalUnlock( (HANDLE) pbmIH );
      GlobalFree( (HANDLE) pbmIH );
//=== read palette info into bitmap info ================
      pbmInfo = (LPBITMAPINFO)
          GlobalLock(   GlobalAlloc( GHND, PalSize +
                                  sizeof(BITMAPINFOHEADER) ) );
      pbmInfo->bmiHeader = *pbmIH;
//=== save size data for this image ====================
      bmWidth    = (DWORD) pbmInfo->bmiHeader.biWidth;
      bmHeight   = (DWORD) pbmInfo->bmiHeader.biHeight;
      bmBitCount = (WORD)  pbmInfo->bmiHeader.biBitCount;
      bmImgSize  = (DWORD) pbmInfo->bmiHeader.biSizeImage;
      bmScanWidth = (DWORD) bmWidth;
      while( bmScanWidth % sizeof(WORD) ) bmScanWidth++;
                          // must be an even WORD size !!!
//=== if image size not in header, calculate size ========
      if( pbmInfo->bmiHeader.biSizeImage == 0 )
      {
          bmImgSize = ( ( ( ( bmWidth * bmBitCount ) +
                          31 ) / 32 ) * 4 ) * bmHeight;
          pbmInfo->bmiHeader.biSizeImage = bmImgSize;
      }
//=== now read the palette information ==================
      if( _lread( hFile, (LPSTR) pbmInfo->bmiColors,
                  PalSize ) != PalSize )
      {
          GlobalFree( (HANDLE)
                      GlobalHandle( HIWORD( pbmInfo ) ) );
          return( ErrorMsg( "Palette read error" ) );
      }
//=== allocate space for bitmap palette ================
      pRGB = pbmInfo->bmiColors;
          //==================================================//
          // check for short palette indicated by biClrUsed //
          //==================================================//
```

```
    if( pbmInfo->bmiHeader.biClrUsed )
       CRes = pbmInfo->bmiHeader.biClrUsed;
    if( pGLP != NULL ) GlobalFree( (HANDLE) pGLP );
    pGLP = (LPLOGPALETTE)              // allocate and lock
       GlobalLock(                     // memory for palette
          GlobalAlloc( GHND, sizeof(LOGPALETTE) +
             ( ( CRes - 1 ) * sizeof(PALETTEENTRY) ) ) );
    pGLP->palNumEntries = CRes;        // fill in size and
    pGLP->palVersion    = 0x0300;      // version (3.0)
    for( i=0; i<CRes; i++ )            // convert colors
    {
       pGLP->palPalEntry[i].peRed   = pRGB[i].rgbRed;
       pGLP->palPalEntry[i].peGreen = pRGB[i].rgbGreen;
       pGLP->palPalEntry[i].peBlue  = pRGB[i].rgbBlue;
       pGLP->palPalEntry[i].peFlags = 0;
    }
    hNewPal = CreatePalette( pGLP );
    GlobalUnlock( (HANDLE) pGLP );
//=== now retrieve actual image information ===============
    hBM = GlobalAlloc( GHND, bmImgSize );
    BytesLeft = ReadBytes = bmImgSize;
    pBits = (BYTE huge *) GlobalLock( hBM );
    while( BytesLeft > 0 )
    {
       if( BytesLeft > 32767L ) GetBytes = 32768L;
                       else GetBytes = BytesLeft;
          //==============================================//
          // limit block reads to 32k to avoid crossing //
          // segment boundary when calling _lread       //
          //==============================================//
       if( (WORD) _lread( hFile, (LPSTR) pBits,
                    (WORD) GetBytes ) != GetBytes )
          if( ReadBytes <= 0 ) break; else return( FALSE );
       pBits += GetBytes;
       ReadBytes -= GetBytes;
       BytesLeft -= GetBytes;
    }
    _lclose( hFile );
//=== make new palette active ============================
    hdc = GetDC( GetFocus() );
    hOldPal = SelectPalette( hdc, hNewPal, FALSE );
    RealizePalette( hdc );
//=== create DIB Bitmap ==================================
    lpBits = GlobalLock( hBM );
    hBitmap = CreateDIBitmap( hdc,
       (LPBITMAPINFOHEADER) &pbmInfo->bmiHeader,
```

```
                              CBM_INIT,
                              lpBits,
                  (LPBITMAPINFO) pbmInfo,
                              DIB_RGB_COLORS );
   GlobalUnlock( hBM );
   if( hBitmap != NULL )
   {
      if( hGBM )                        // if old bitmap
         DeleteObject( hGBM );          //    delete same ...
      hGBM = hBitmap;                   // save global handle
      if( hGPal )                       // if old palette
         DeleteObject( hGPal );         //    delete same ...
      hGPal = hNewPal;                  // save global handle
   } else ErrorMsg( "Bitmap failed" );
//=== discard global memory object =======================
   if( hOldPal ) SelectPalette( hdc, hOldPal, FALSE );
   ReleaseDC( GetFocus(), hdc );
   GlobalFree( (HANDLE)
               GlobalHandle( HIWORD( pbmInfo ) ) );
   GlobalFree( hBM );
   DeleteObject( hNewPal );
   SetCursor( LoadCursor( NULL, IDC_ARROW ) );
   InvalidateRect( hwnd, NULL, TRUE );
   return(0);
}

BOOL FAR PASCAL FileSelectDlgProc( HWND hDlg, WORD msg,
                              WORD wParam, LONG lParam )
{
   static char  OrgPath[64];
   struct ffblk fileinfo;
   char    cLastChar;
   int     nLen;

   switch( msg )
   {
      case WM_INITDIALOG:
         SetWindowText( hDlg, szCaption );
         getcwd( OrgPath, sizeof( OrgPath ) );
         SendDlgItemMessage( hDlg, IDD_FNAME,
                             EM_LIMITTEXT, 80, NULL );
         DlgDirList( hDlg, szFSpec, IDD_FLIST,
                     IDD_FPATH, wFAttr );
         SetDlgItemText( hDlg, IDD_FNAME, szFSpec );
         return( TRUE );
```

```
            case WM_COMMAND:
               switch( wParam )
               {
                  case IDD_FLIST:
                     switch( HIWORD( lParam ) )
                     {
                        case LBN_SELCHANGE:
                           if( DlgDirSelect( hDlg, szFName,
                                             IDD_FLIST ) )
                              strcat( szFName, szFSpec );
                           Set.DlgItemText( hDlg, IDD_FNAME,
                                             szFName );
                           break;
                        case LBN_DBLCLK:
                           if( DlgDirSelect( hDlg, szFName,
                                             IDD_FLIST ) )
                           {
                              strcat( szFName, szFSpec );
                              DlgDirList( hDlg, szFName,
                                 IDD_FLIST, IDD_FPATH, wFAttr );
                              SetDlgItemText( hDlg, IDD_FNAME,
                                                szFSpec );
                           }
                           else
                           {
                              SetDlgItemText( hDlg, IDD_FNAME,
                                                szFName );
                              SendMessage( hDlg, WM_COMMAND,
                                             IDOK, ØL );
                           } break;
                     } break;
                  case IDD_FNAME:
                     if( HIWORD( lParam ) == EN_CHANGE )
                        EnableWindow( GetDlgItem( hDlg, IDOK ),
                        (BOOL) SendMessage( LOWORD( lParam ),
                              WM_GETTEXTLENGTH, Ø, ØL ) );
                     break;
                  case IDOK:
                     GetDlgItemText( hDlg, IDD_FNAME,
                                     szFName, 8Ø );
                     nLen = strlen( szFName );
                     cLastChar = *AnsiPrev( szFName,
                                            szFName + nLen );
                     if( cLastChar == '\\' || cLastChar == ':' )
                        strcat( szFName, szFSpec );
                     if( strchr( szFName, '*' ) ||
```

```
                  strchr( szFName, '?' ) )
          {
             if( DlgDirList( hDlg, szFName,
                  IDD_FLIST, IDD_FPATH, wFAttr ) )
             {
                strcpy( szFSpec, szFName );
                SetDlgItemText( hDlg, IDD_FNAME,
                             szFSpec );
             }
             else MessageBeep(0);
             break;
          }
          if( DlgDirList( hDlg, szFName,
                  IDD_FLIST, IDD_FPATH, wFAttr ) )
          {
             strcpy( szFSpec, szFName );
             SetDlgItemText( hDlg, IDD_FNAME,
                          szFSpec );
             break;
          }
          szFName[nLen] = '\0';
          if( findfirst( szFName, &fileinfo, 0 ) )
          {
             strcat( szFName, szFExt );
             if( findfirst( szFName, &fileinfo, 0 ) )
             {
                MessageBeep(0);
                break;
          }  }
          GetDlgItemText( hDlg, IDD_FPATH,
                       szFPath, 80 );
          strupr( szFPath );
          if( szFPath[strlen(szFPath)-1] != '\\' )
             strcat( szFPath, "\\" );
          strcpy( szFName, fileinfo.ff_name );
          chdir( OrgPath );
          EndDialog( hDlg, TRUE );
          break;
       case IDCANCEL:
          chdir( OrgPath );
          EndDialog( hDlg, FALSE );
          break;
       default:  return( FALSE );
    }  break;
  default: return( FALSE );
}
```

```
      return( TRUE );
}

int CallFileLoadDlg( HANDLE hInst, HWND hwnd )
{
   FARPROC   lpProc;
   int       iReturn;

   strcpy( szCaption, "Load Image From:" );
   lpProc = MakeProcInstance( FileSelectDlgProc, hInst );
   iReturn = DialogBox(hInst, "SELECTFILE", hwnd, lpProc);
   FreeProcInstance( lpProc );
   return( iReturn );
}

long FAR PASCAL WndProc( HWND hwnd,    WORD msg,
                          WORD wParam, LONG lParam )
{
   HMENU         hMenu;
   HDC           hdc, hdcMem;
   FARPROC       lpProc;
   PAINTSTRUCT   ps;
   HBITMAP       hBMOld;
   HPALETTE      hPalOld;

   switch( msg )
   {
      case WM_COMMAND:
         switch( wParam )
         {
            case IDM_LOAD:
               if( CallFileLoadDlg( hInst, hwnd ) )
                  ReadBitmap( hwnd );
               break;
            case IDM_BITBLT:
               if( hGBM ) InitPrint( hwnd, FALSE );
               else ErrorMsg( "Nothing to print!" );
               break;
            case IDM_STRETCH:
               if( hGBM ) InitPrint( hwnd, TRUE );
               else ErrorMsg( "Nothing to print!" );
               break;
            case IDM_SETPRINTER:
               SetPrinterSettings( hwnd );
               break;
            case IDM_ABOUT:
```

```
                   lpProc = MakeProcInstance( AboutProc,
                                              hInst );
                   DialogBox( hInst, "ABOUT", hwnd, lpProc );
                   FreeProcInstance( lpProc );
                   break;
            }
            return(0);

         case WM_PAINT:
            InvalidateRect( hwnd, NULL, TRUE );
            hdc = BeginPaint( hwnd, &ps );
            if( hGBM )
            {
               hdcMem = CreateCompatibleDC( hdc );
               hBMOld = SelectObject( hdcMem, hGBM );
               if( hGPal )
                  hPalOld =
                      SelectPalette( hdc, hGPal, FALSE );
               BitBlt( hdc, 0, 0, bmWidth, bmHeight,
                       hdcMem, 0, 0, SRCCOPY );
               if( hGPal )
                  SelectPalette( hdc, hPalOld, FALSE );
               SelectObject( hdcMem, hBMOld );
               DeleteDC( hdcMem );
            }
            EndPaint( hwnd, &ps );
            return(FALSE);

         case WM_DESTROY:
            if( pGLP != NULL ) GlobalFree( (HANDLE) pGLP );
            PostQuitMessage(0);
            return(0);
      }
   return( DefWindowProc( hwnd, msg, wParam, lParam ) );
}


#pragma argsused

int PASCAL WinMain( HANDLE hInstance,
                    HANDLE hPrevInstance,
                    LPSTR  lpszCmdParam,
                    int    nCmdShow )
{
   HWND      hwnd;
   MSG       msg;
   WNDCLASS  wc;
```

```
    int       i;

    if( ! hPrevInstance )
    {
        wc.hInstance      = hInstance;
        wc.lpfnWndProc    = WndProc;
        wc.cbClsExtra     = 0;
        wc.cbWndExtra     = 0;
        wc.lpszClassName  = szAppName;
        wc.hIcon          = LoadIcon( hInstance, szAppName );
        wc.lpszMenuName   = (LPSTR) szAppName;
        wc.hCursor        = LoadCursor( NULL, IDC_ARROW );
        wc.hbrBackground  = GetStockObject( WHITE_BRUSH );
        wc.style          = CS_HREDRAW | CS_VREDRAW;
        RegisterClass( &wc );
    }
    hInst = hInstance;
    hwnd = CreateWindow( szAppName, szCaption,
            WS_OVERLAPPEDWINDOW,
            CW_USEDEFAULT, CW_USEDEFAULT,
            CW_USEDEFAULT, CW_USEDEFAULT,
            NULL, NULL, hInstance, NULL  );
    ShowWindow(   hwnd, nCmdShow );
    UpdateWindow( hwnd );
    while( GetMessage( &msg, NULL, 0, 0 ) )
    {
        TranslateMessage( &msg );
        DispatchMessage(  &msg );
    }
    return( msg.wParam );
}



;==============;
;  Print.DEF  ;
;==============;


NAME          PRINT

DESCRIPTION   "Print Program"
EXETYPE       WINDOWS
STUB          "WINSTUB.EXE"
CODE          PRELOAD MOVEABLE DISCARDABLE
DATA          PRELOAD MOVEABLE MULTIPLE
HEAPSIZE      1024
STACKSIZE     8192
```

```
EXPORTS      WndProc
             AbortDlg
             AbortProc
             CancelProc


//===============//
//   PrintImg.H   //
//===============//

#define IDM_LOAD        101   // file operations
#define IDM_PRINT       102   // print image
#define IDM_SETPRINTER  103   // printer setup
#define IDM_ABOUT       104   // about dialog
#define IDM_BITBLT      105
#define IDM_STRETCH     106

#define IDD_FNAME       301   // filename dialog
#define IDD_FPATH       302
#define IDD_FLIST       303
```

Cursors, Bitmaps, and Simple Image Animations

T hus far, images have been displayed, enhanced, and printed, but little has been said of manipulating these images in other fashions. Therefore, in this chapter, under the guise of simple animated games, images will be used in an interactive fashion. The two games, Animate1 and Animate2, demonstrate cursor and bitmap interactions—in the first example, by using multiple cursor images for simple animation, and in the second, by replacing the restrictive cursor images with bitmaps. Note that this is not so much to demonstrate principles of animation as to introduce beginning techniques for using images in a nonstatic fashion.

Neither of these demo programs is offered as a polished example of animation. Both are crude and simplistic in design, limitations dictated both by a need to keep the demo programs brief and by the fact that creating an elaborate series of images is, at best, an extremely time-consuming process. (A third reason, of course, is a general lack of interest—on the author's part—in constructing video games.)

Lest ye despair, subsequent chapters will demonstrate a variety of other interactive image processes that, while not using animation directly, are more practical for general applications as well as simpler to design and implement. Of course, animation can be incorporated in any of these later examples as desired.

First, however, we'll return to the immediate topic: animating bitmap images.

PRINCIPLES OF ANIMATION

Computer animation, like other interactive imagery, rests on three principal requirements: timing mechanisms, images, and control mechanisms.

Timing mechanisms are generally used only by animated processes and may be ignored by other interactive graphics processes, which simply wait for user inputs before operating. Of course, many applications use both timed and command processes in various combinations.

Answering the second requirement, images can be provided by a variety of means.

- For very sophisticated images, graphics scanners can be used with photographs or artwork, and live images can be captured directly by video cameras.

- Perhaps most popular are images drawn on the computer using interactive programs such as the Windows Paint program, the Resource Workshop, or ZSoft's PhotoFinish.

- Images can be generated directly by the computer in response to either simple or sophisticated algorithms, depending on application requirements and on how much processing time can be devoted to the imagery.

Obviously, these processes can be combined in various fashions.

The third requirement, control mechanisms, is generally filled by the mouse or, in some cases, by the keyboard cursor keys, or simply by keyboard input. Of course, this ignores controls that are inherent within the application itself.

None of these three elements is entirely independent of the others. It is the interactions among these elements that constitute the presentation, which is the heart of this type of graphics application. At the same time, because it is the interactions that are most important, we'll begin by looking at timing mechanisms.

TIMING MECHANISMS

Most applications are written either to do nothing until receiving input—even if only from a user pressing the Enter key or clicking the mouse—or to do everything possible quickly. Animation, however, is generally based on sequencing a collection of images, with the sequencing timed to present a specific appearance. For this purpose, timer functions become integral to the application.

Under MS-DOS, or any other single-tasking environment, the usual approach to timing has consisted of using a simple delay function by which execution of the application was halted until a specified number of milliseconds had elapsed. Alternately, when time delays longer than a few seconds were required, an application might check the system clock and then loop until the desired interval had elapsed.

In a multitasking environment such as Windows, however, this approach is neither practical nor permitted. Under Windows, any application that deliberately sought to interrupt all execution for any interval—even a few milliseconds—would be quite correctly characterized as very badly written.

However, Windows offers an alternative in the form of timer processes. Timer processes establish a system timer that, at the requested interval posts a timer message to the requesting application. At least one example of this process is provided by Windows's Clock application, which, in either digital or analog form, is notified at intervals of one second, enabling it to update its display.

In general, establishing a timer function consists of three elements, beginning by calling the SetTimer function, thus:

```
WORD    ActiveTimer, ...
   ...
   ActiveTimer = SetTimer( hwnd, InitTimer,
                           FlipTime, NULL );
```

The SetTimer function is called with four parameters.

- The handle of the application window that owns the timer (*hwnd*).

- An integer identifying the timer or timer-event (InitTimer).

- A WORD value setting the clock interval (FlipTime) in milliseconds.

- A fourth parameter (NULL in this instance) that can be used to specify a long pointer (*lpTimerFunc*) to a procedure address to be notified when the timer event occurs. Because this parameter is specified as NULL, the WM_TIMER messages returned are sent to the application queue identified by the *hwnd* parameter.

The timer owner can be identified as NULL if the timer does not need to be associated with a specific window (that is, is to be shared with several windows or application instances).

The return value (ActiveTimer) is a WORD value identifying this specific timer process. It will be used later when calling the KillTimer function to terminate the timer event. As is customary, the return value is zero if the timer cannot be created. No error checking for such a circumstance, however, is included in either Animate1 or Animate2. But, because timers are a limited system (global) resource, applications should check the returned value to ensure that a time is available. For the same reason, timers should be killed when they are no longer needed.

Once a timer has been created, the timer process continues independent of the application, but at the requested intervals, it posts a WM_TIMER message with the *wParam* argument specifying the timer ID. The WM_TIMER message will be sent to the window procedure owning the timer (identified by the *hwnd* parameter), or to an exported procedure if the fourth parameter is non-NULL; or, if no owner or destination process is identified, the message will be sent to the main window procedure.

Handling for the WM_TIMER message can occur either in the application's WndProc procedure in the exported window-handling procedure of the window that owns the timer, or, if specified, in another exported timer procedure. In either situation, the message-processing switch-case statement should not simply respond to the timer event but should contain provisions to identify the specific timer issuing the event message as shown following:

```
switch( msg ) ...

    case WM_TIMER:
        switch( wParam )
        {
            case InitTimer: ...
            case StartTimer: ...
            case RunTimer: ...
        }
        break;
```

Both the Animate1 and Animate2 demos use a series of three timers, although only one timer is active at any point. Each of these timers has a different ID and controls a different process. Alternately, more than one timer might be active, each reporting events requiring different intervals.

Last, as mentioned previously, every event timer needs to be killed when not in use. When each timer was initiated, the WORD value returned by the SetTimer function was saved as *ActiveTimer* and is used subsequently when calling the KillTimer function.

```
KillTimer( hwnd, ActiveTimer );
ActiveTimer = NULL;
```

If the timer's owner was originally identified as NULL (that is, as not belonging to a specific window or instance) a NULL argument must also be used at this point. The second argument, however, must identify the timer's handle (as assigned by Windows rather than the timer's ID assigned by the application).

Obviously, if more than one timer is to be active at any point, multiple timer handles will also be required. Don't forget, however, that each timer will also need to be killed when finished.

IMAGES

The three timers employed by the Animate1 and Animate2 demos are used to control three different animation sequences. The first two timers, InitTimer and StartTimer, each control the presentation of a sequence of images appearing in Figure 11.1.

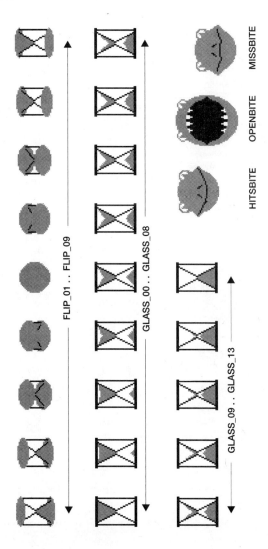

Figure 11.1: Images used in Animate2

Figure 11.1 shows three sets of bitmapped images, beginning at the top with a sequence of nine images which show an hourglass in the process of being flipped (turned over) and are presented under the control of the InitTimer at 5 millisecond intervals.

The second sequence of 14 images shows the sands running through the hourglass and are sequenced by the StartTimer clock with an interval of 100 milliseconds ($\frac{1}{10}$th second).

The third timer, RunTimer, is used for a different purpose: to control the rate at which the target balls drop. The final three images included in Figure 11.1 provide the game "cursor."

NOTE. The images used in the Animate1 demo are actually cursor images rather than bitmaps and are not shown but, except for the final three, are similar to the bitmaps illustrated.

Unfortunately, the images required for animation are perhaps the most time-consuming (and space-consuming) portion of the process. In the Animate2 application, the 26 images used consume nearly 9k and required an inordinate amount of time to construct. (They also required almost as much time to prepare as an illustration for this book.)

Note particularly that because the images used are contained in the application's .RES file and at link time are joined to the application code, no time is needed or wasted loading the images from external files. Loading the images from external files would greatly diminish performance.

CONTROL MECHANISMS

While images and image sequencing may be sufficient for cartoon programs where the application code (or the artist/programmer) handles all aspects of the process, in computer animation—or, at least, in computer games—another degree of control is necessary to respond to user input.

User input in computer games generally relies on either a mouse or a joystick. For Windows, however, since joysticks are not directly supported, the mouse event messages become the control mechanism of choice.

Thus far, the mouse has been used only by default, allowing Windows to supply the handling for buttons, scroll bars, and other stock objects. But while the default handling is sufficient for stock objects, for custom objects, applications must supply their own responses to the various mouse messages.

In the Animate1 demo, where different cursor shapes are used, the only mouse event that requires a response is the WM_LBUTTONDOWN message issued when the left mouse button is pressed. Windows provides complete mouse handling, including event messages for both two- and three-button mice that identify when buttons are being pressed, released, or double-clicked—as well as mouse movements.

For example, Windows issues three event messages for the left mouse button: WM_LBUTTONDBLCLK, WM_LBUTTONDOWN, and WM_LBUTTONUP. Each of these event messages is accompanied by the lParam value containing the x and y cursor coordinates with the x-coordinate in the low-order word and the y-coordinate in the high-order word. Note that the coordinates reported are relative to the window origin (upper-left corner), not to the screen coordinates.

Furthermore, the *wParam* word value accompanying each mouse-event message is a flag combination indicating the present condition both of the two- or three-button mice—the MK_LBUTTON, MK_MBUTTON, and MK_RBUTTON flags are set if the corresponding button(s) are pressed—and of the Control and Shift keys (MK_CONTROL and MK_SHIFT).

In addition, the WM_MOUSEMOVE message reports any mouse movement—unless, of course, the mouse has moved outside of the application window.

Other mouse messages are provided for events outside of the application window (when the application continues to capture the mouse-event focus, as in the Capture1 and Capture2 programs), for mouse events occurring in inactive child or parent windows, and for other non-client mouse events. These latter events, however, are not relevant to the present circumstance.

Both the Animate1 demo, which uses custom cursor shapes for animation, and the Animate2 program, which uses bitmapped images, respond to the WM_LBUTTONDOWN message by comparing the cursor (mouse) position to a target position to determine if a hit or a miss has occurred.

```
case WM_LBUTTONDOWN:
    ptCursor.x = LOWORD( lParam );
    ptCursor.y = HIWORD( lParam );
    if( ( abs(Balls[aBall].pt.x-ptCursor.x) < 6 ) &&
        ( abs(Balls[aBall].pt.y-ptCursor.y) < 6 ) )
    {
```

In the Animate2 demo, the stock cursor has been replaced with a bitmapped image tracking the cursor position. In this case, the WM_MOUSEMOVE message is monitored to erase the old bitmap, update the current position, and draw the new bitmapped image on the screen.

```
case WM_MOUSEMOVE:
    if( !bStatic )
    {
```

```
            DrawCursor( hwnd, ptReserve, WHITENESS );
            GetCursorPos( &ptCursor );
            ScreenToClient( hwnd, &ptCursor );
            DrawCursor( hwnd, ptCursor, SRCCOPY );
            ptReserve = ptCursor;
      }
    break;
```

The DrawCursor function is provided to draw the bitmap used to replace the cursor. As such, DrawCursor is called twice: first using the WHITENESS argument to blank the old bitmapped image, and second, after updating the position, using the SRCCOPY argument to draw the new bitmapped image.

As you should observe when executing the Animate2 demo program, however, the image placement/replacement process used is not entirely satisfactory, particularly when the cursor bitmap overlies another image or anything except a plain white background (that is, when the bitmapped image interacts with another image).

The WHITENESS and SRCCOPY arguments used are predefined BitBlt (raster) operations defining how the graphic-device interface (GDI) combines the bitmapped pixels with the pixels in the existing image. But, while the two operations demonstrated do work, after a fashion, they are neither ideal for this task nor optimal for all tasks in general.

Of the total of 256 ternary raster operations that are defined for BitBlt and StretchBlt operations, only 14 of these have predefined labels. The remaining 242 operations are referenced only by value but are defined, together with details on each operation, in Chapter 11 of Borland's *Windows API Reference Guide*.

Unfortunately, it is difficult to decide which operation types are best-suited for a specific application and circumstance. For example, the SCRAND operation works by combining source and destination pixels using the Boolean AND operator. Alternately, a choice that might be explored is the SCRINVERT operation, which uses the Boolean XOR operator to combine source and destination pixels. The advantage in this operation is twofold: first, the existing background is not entirely overwritten, and second, repeating the drawing operation erases the original. The drawback is that the source bitmap (for this type of operation) needs to be an inversion of the desired display because, after XORing with a white background, whites in the bitmap become blacks, blacks do nothing (that is, act transparent), and colors are inverted (becoming their complements).

The ideal operator, perhaps, might be one that emulates cursor operations by drawing only pixels which are set, treating background pixels as transparent and, most importantly, preserving the background. Unfortunately, however, there is no defined ROP operation with all of these characteristics; the mouse cursor manages this feat by using a combination of two bitmaps, one image, and one screen background, but it lacks the two desired elements of having a definable size and multiple colors.

Even though there is no single operation providing this capability, if desired, a function can be created to provide a full-color and fully sizable bitmap cursor. However, while the implementation of such a color cursor (for Windows) is left as an exercise for the reader, a few hints will be offered.

▸ Include a provision to store the background image only for the area which the color cursor will overlie.

▸ Either create the cursor bitmap as an inversion of the desired image or invert the bitmapped image before pasting it onto the screen.

▸ Create a second bitmap to act as a mask, defining areas which the cursor bitmap should not overwrite.

▸ Combine the saved screen area, the mask, and the cursor images to produce the desired screen appearance.

▸ Use the saved screen image to restore the screen when the cursor is erased before repositioning.

And there you have it: the recipe for a full-color and fully sizable cursor. Granted, it is not an easy task to implement, but if this is what is actually needed, it is not an impossible task either.

THE ANIMATE1 AND ANIMATE2 APPLICATIONS

The Animate1 and Animate2 applications, whose code appears at the end of this chapter and which are included on the disk bound with this book, were written as demonstrations of two different approaches to simple animation.

The Animate1 program uses a series of cursor images to animate the flipped hourglass and the sands running through the glass. The capture cursor is a simple ring with which to encircle the target images before pressing the mouse button to catch the falling balls (Figure 11.2A).

While any of the hourglass cursors are active, notice that the cursor position cannot be moved away from the bottom-center of the game window—a provision which is made quite easily by continuously resetting the cursor position. Once the cursor is released, however, notice also that the cursor shape changes anytime the cursor moves outside of the client window, a provision that is handled by Windows and not by the application.

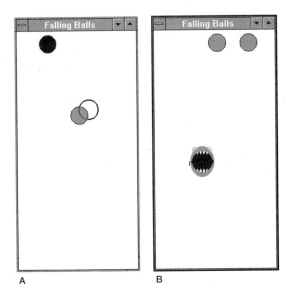

A   B

Figure 11.2: The Animate1 and Animate2 demos

The drawbacks to the Animate1 program are minor, if not all obvious. The first is that the animated images are monochromatic and not particularly attractive. And the second, as has already been pointed out, is that the size of the cursor image is fixed and cannot be enlarged beyond 32-by-32 pixels.

The third and last flaw is also the least obvious and is not always visible. Sometimes the cursor images, while loading from the resource segment of the executable file, are distorted, resulting in a temporary aberration in the display. The source of this specific flaw is not easily determined but, likewise, it is a minor flaw and does not occur with any regularity; and, since this is not a particularly useful approach to animation, it shouldn't present any serious concern.

The Animate2 demo (Figure 11.2B) is considerably more sophisticated than Animate1, although still falling short of the optimum even for such a simple game. In this version, instead of playing with cursor images, the cursor has been replaced with a blank cursor that is tracked by a 16-color bitmapped image.

The alternative to having a blank cursor is to hide the cursor. But, because the cursor position continues to be tracked—even when hidden—this alternative imposes no additional programming constraints.

There are two principal advantages to Animate2: the use of colors and the freedom from size restrictions imposed by cursor images. There's also a third advantage resulting in part from the first two: the smoothness with which the images progress during the flipping of the hourglass and the running of the sands.

Of course, there is one disadvantage. The visual interactions between the bitmapped image cursor and the background screen fall somewhat short of what might be desired. This last, however, can be overcome with additional provisions to emulate conventional cursor/screen interactions (or, more accurately, to improve on these).

SUMMARY

While the Animate1 and Animate2 demo programs do show simple animation techniques, true animation with any degree of sophistication requires not only a great deal of work but also more computing speed than is generally available in a personal computer.

What is more important, as has been demonstrated here, is how timer processes are implemented and used, and how the mouse (cursor) is used interactively for processes other than standard control purposes.

In future chapters, bitmapped images and mouse interactions will be used further in applications that are more practically oriented and which are more in line with the physical capabilities of the hardware and software.

PROGRAM LISTING OF ANIMATE1.C

```
//======================================//
//              Amimate1.C              //
//            Cursor Animation          //
//======================================//

#include <windows.h>
#include <string.h>
#include <stdlib.h>
#include <time.h>
#include <stdio.h>
#include <dir.h>
#include <bwcc.h>         // include bwcc.lib in project file
#include "animate1.h"

struct tagBalls {  POINT pt;
                   int   iRadius;
                   int   iStat;
                   int   Color;  } Balls[3];
char * HrGls[12] =
```

```
                { "GLASS_00", "GLASS_01", "GLASS_02",
                  "GLASS_03", "GLASS_04", "GLASS_05",
                  "GLASS_06", "GLASS_07", "GLASS_08",
                  "GLASS_09", "GLASS_10", "GLASS_11" };
char * Flip[9] =
                { "FLIP_00",  "FLIP_01",  "FLIP_02",
                  "FLIP_03",  "FLIP_04",  "FLIP_05",
                  "FLIP_06",  "FLIP_07",  "FLIP_08"  };

char    szAppName[]  = "Animate1";
WORD    ActiveTimer, Sands;
short   aBall;
HANDLE  hInst;
HCURSOR hCursor;

int EndMsg( char *Message )
{
   MessageBox( GetFocus(), Message, "End Game",
               MB_ICONASTERISK | MB_OK );
   return(0);
}

void ResetTimer( HWND hwnd )
{
   BOOL  Done;
   int   i;

   Done = TRUE;
   randomize();
   for( i=0; i<3; i++ )
      if( Balls[i].iStat == Waiting ) Done = FALSE;
   if( Done )
   {
      PostMessage( hwnd, WM_COMMAND, IDM_ENDGAME, NULL );
      return;
   }
   ActiveTimer = SetTimer( hwnd, InitTimer,
                           FlipTime, NULL );
}

void DropBall( HWND hwnd )
{
   BOOL  Done;

   do
   {
```

```
         Done = FALSE;
         aBall = random(3);
         if( Balls[aBall].iStat == Waiting ) Done = TRUE;
      }
   while( !Done );
   Balls[aBall].iStat = Falling;
   ActiveTimer =
      SetTimer( hwnd, RunTimer,
                FallTime * (random(5)+3), NULL );
}

void KillBall( HWND hwnd )
{
   KillTimer( hwnd, ActiveTimer );
   ActiveTimer = 0;
   MessageBeep( NULL );
   Balls[aBall].iStat = Dead;
   Balls[aBall].pt.x = -20;
   Balls[aBall].pt.y = -20;
   aBall = -1;
}

void CatchBall( HWND hwnd )
{
   int  Which = aBall;

   KillBall( hwnd );
   Balls[Which].iStat = Caught;
   ResetTimer( hwnd );
}

long FAR PASCAL WndProc( HWND hwnd,   WORD msg,
                         WORD wParam, LONG lParam )
{
   static   POINT    nPt, cPt;
   static   HBRUSH   hBrush[3];
   PAINTSTRUCT       ps;

   FARPROC  lpProc;
   RECT     pRect;
   HDC      hdc;
   BOOL     Match;
   char     szBuff[30];
   int      i, j, Count;

   switch( msg )
```

```
      {
      case WM_CREATE:
         SetClassWord( hwnd, GCW_HCURSOR,
            LoadCursor( hInst, HrGls[11] ) );
         aBall = -1;
         for( i=0; i<3; i++ )
         {
            Balls[i].pt.x = ( WinWidth / 4 ) * ( i + 1 );
            Balls[i].pt.y = 20;
            Balls[i].iRadius = 14;
            Balls[i].iStat = Waiting;
            do
            {
               Match = FALSE;
               Balls[i].Color = random(16);
               for( j=0; j<i; j++ )
                  if( Balls[i].Color == Balls[j].Color )
                     Match = TRUE;
            }
            while( Match );
            hBrush[i] =   CreateSolidBrush(
               PALETTEINDEX( Balls[i].Color ) );
         }
         ResetTimer( hwnd );
         break;

      case WM_COMMAND:
         switch( wParam )
         {
            case IDM_ENDGAME:
               Count = 0;
               for( i=0; i<3; i++ )
                  if( Balls[i].iStat == Caught ) Count++;
               sprintf( szBuff,
                       "Results: %d of 3 caught",
                       Count );
               EndMsg( szBuff );
               PostMessage( hwnd, WM_DESTROY, 0L, 0L );
               break;
            case IDM_ABOUT:
               lpProc = MakeProcInstance( AboutProc,
                                          hInst );
               DialogBox( hInst, "ABOUT", hwnd, lpProc );
               FreeProcInstance( lpProc );
               break;
         }
```

```
        return(Ø);

    case WM_PAINT:
        hdc = BeginPaint( hwnd, &ps );
        for( i=Ø; i<3; i++ )
        {
            SelectObject( hdc, hBrush[i] );
            Ellipse( hdc,
                        Balls[i].pt.x-Balls[i].iRadius,
                        Balls[i].pt.y-Balls[i].iRadius,
                        Balls[i].pt.x+Balls[i].iRadius,
                        Balls[i].pt.y+Balls[i].iRadius );
        }
        EndPaint( hwnd, &ps );
        return(Ø);

    case WM_LBUTTONDOWN:
        cPt.x = LOWORD( lParam );
        cPt.y = HIWORD( lParam );
        if( ( abs( Balls[aBall].pt.x - cPt.x ) < 6 ) &&
            ( abs( Balls[aBall].pt.y - cPt.y ) < 6 ) )
        {
            pRect.left   = Balls[aBall].pt.x - 2Ø;
            pRect.top    = Balls[aBall].pt.y - 2Ø;
            pRect.right  = Balls[aBall].pt.x + 2Ø;
            pRect.bottom = Balls[aBall].pt.y + 2Ø;
            CatchBall( hwnd );
        }
        InvalidateRect( hwnd, &pRect, TRUE );
        MessageBeep( NULL );
        break;

    case WM_TIMER:
        switch( wParam )
        {
            case InitTimer:
                SetClassWord( hwnd, GCW_HCURSOR,
                    LoadCursor( hInst, Flip[Sands] ) );
                nPt.x = WinWidth / 2;
                nPt.y = WinHeight - 5Ø;
                ClientToScreen( hwnd, &nPt );
                SetCursorPos( nPt.x, nPt.y );
                Sands++;
                if( Sands >= 9 )
                {
                    MessageBeep( NULL );
```

```
                KillTimer( hwnd, ActiveTimer );
                ActiveTimer = FALSE;
                Sands = 0;
                ActiveTimer =
                    SetTimer( hwnd, StartTimer,
                              SandTime, NULL );
            }
            break;

    case StartTimer:
        SetClassWord( hwnd, GCW_HCURSOR,
            LoadCursor( hInst, HrGls[Sands] ) );
        nPt.x = WinWidth / 2;
        nPt.y = WinHeight - 50;
        ClientToScreen( hwnd, &nPt );
        SetCursorPos( nPt.x, nPt.y );
        Sands++;
        if( Sands >= 12 )
        {
            MessageBeep( NULL );
            KillTimer( hwnd, StartTimer );
            ActiveTimer = FALSE;
            Sands = 0;
            SetClassWord( hwnd, GCW_HCURSOR,
                LoadCursor( hInst, "CATCHER" ) );
            DropBall( hwnd );
        }
        break;

    case RunTimer:
        pRect.left   = Balls[aBall].pt.x - 30;
        pRect.top    = Balls[aBall].pt.y - 30;
        pRect.right  = Balls[aBall].pt.x + 30;
        pRect.bottom = Balls[aBall].pt.y + 30;
        nPt.y = Balls[aBall].pt.y + random(5);
        nPt.x = Balls[aBall].pt.x + (5-random(11));
        nPt.x = max( nPt.x, 20 );
        nPt.x = min( nPt.x, WinWidth-20 );
        Balls[aBall].pt.x = nPt.x;
        Balls[aBall].pt.y = nPt.y;
        InvalidateRect( hwnd, &pRect, TRUE );
        if( Balls[aBall].pt.y >= ( WinHeight-40 ) )
        {
            KillBall( hwnd );
            ResetTimer( hwnd );
        }
```

```
                break;
            }
            break;

        case WM_DESTROY:
            if( ActiveTimer ) KillTimer( hwnd, ActiveTimer );
            for( i=0; i<3; i++ ) DeleteObject( hBrush[i] );
            PostQuitMessage(0);
            return(0);
    }
    return( DefWindowProc( hwnd, msg, wParam, lParam ) );
}

#pragma argsused

int PASCAL WinMain( HANDLE hInstance,
                    HANDLE hPrevInstance,
                    LPSTR  lpszCmdParam,
                    int    nCmdShow )
{
    HWND        hwnd;
    MSG         msg;
    WNDCLASS    wc;
    int         i;

    if( ! hPrevInstance )
    {
        wc.hInstance      = hInstance;
        wc.lpfnWndProc    = WndProc;
        wc.cbClsExtra     = 0;
        wc.cbWndExtra     = 0;
        wc.lpszClassName  = szAppName;
        wc.hIcon          = LoadIcon( hInstance, szAppName );
        wc.lpszMenuName   = (LPSTR) szAppName;
        wc.hCursor        = LoadCursor( NULL, IDC_ARROW );
        wc.hbrBackground  = GetStockObject( WHITE_BRUSH );
        wc.style          = CS_HREDRAW | CS_VREDRAW;
        RegisterClass( &wc );
    }
    hInst = hInstance;

    hwnd = CreateWindow( szAppName, "Falling Balls",
            WS_OVERLAPPEDWINDOW | WS_CLIPCHILDREN,
            WinOrgX, WinOrgY, WinWidth, WinHeight,
            0L, 0L, hInst, 0L  );
    ShowWindow(   hwnd, nCmdShow );
```

```
         UpdateWindow( hwnd );
         while( GetMessage( &msg, NULL, 0, 0 ) )
         {
            TranslateMessage( &msg );
            DispatchMessage(  &msg );
         }
         return( msg.wParam );
      }


      ;================;
      ;  Animate1.DEF  ;
      ;================;

      NAME          Animate1

      DESCRIPTION   "Animation One Program"
      EXETYPE       WINDOWS
      STUB          "WINSTUB.EXE"
      CODE          PRELOAD MOVEABLE DISCARDABLE
      DATA          PRELOAD MOVAEBLE MULTIPLE
      HEAPSIZE      1024
      STACKSIZE     8192
      EXPORTS       WndProc


      //================//
      //   Animate1.H   //
      //================//

      #define IDM_ENDGAME     200

      //=== window size and position ===============================
      #define WinOrgX    50
      #define WinOrgY    50
      #define WinWidth   200
      #define WinHeight  400

      //=== timer id numbers =======================================
      #define InitTimer   1
      #define StartTimer  2
      #define RunTimer    3

      //=== clock speeds ===========================================
      #define FlipTime   25
      #define SandTime   100
      #define FallTime   5
```

```
//=== status of balls ================================
#define Waiting    1
#define Falling    2
#define Caught     3
#define Dead       4
```

PROGRAM LISTING OF ANIMATE2.C

```
//====================================//
//              Animate2.C            //
//           Bitmap Animation         //
//====================================//

#include <windows.h>
#include <string.h>
#include <stdlib.h>
#include <time.h>
#include <stdio.h>
#include <dir.h>
#include <bwcc.h>          // include bwcc.lib in project file
#include "animate2.h"

#define MaxSands 14
#define MaxFlips  9

struct tagBalls {  POINT pt;
                   int   iRadius;
                   int   iStat;
                   int   Color;  } Balls[3];

char * HrGls[MaxSands] =
   { "GLASS_00", "GLASS_01", "GLASS_02", "GLASS_03",
     "GLASS_04", "GLASS_05", "GLASS_06", "GLASS_07",
     "GLASS_08", "GLASS_09", "GLASS_10", "GLASS_11",
     "GLASS_12", "GLASS_13"  };

char * Flip[MaxFlips] =
   { "FLIP_01",  "FLIP_02",  "FLIP_03",  "FLIP_04",
     "FLIP_05",  "FLIP_06",  "FLIP_07",  "FLIP_08",
     "FLIP_09"  };

char * Bite[3] = { "OPENBITE", "HITSBITE", "MISSBITE" };

char    ActiveBM[10], szAppName[]  = "Animate2";
BYTE    ActiveTimer, Sands;
POINT   nPt, ptCursor, ptReserve;
```

```
short    aBall;
HANDLE   hInst;
HBITMAP  hCurBm;
BOOL     bStatic;
HBRUSH   hBrush[3];

int EndMsg( char *Message )
{
   MessageBox( GetFocus(), Message, "End Game",
               MB_ICONASTERISK | MB_OK );
   return(0);
}

#pragma argsused

void ResetTimer( HWND hwnd )
{
   BOOL  Done;
   int   i;

   Done = TRUE;
   randomize();
   for( i=0; i<3; i++ )
      if( Balls[i].iStat == Waiting ) Done = FALSE;
   if( Done )
   {
      PostMessage( hwnd, WM_COMMAND, IDM_ENDGAME, NULL );
      return;
   }
   InvalidateRect( hwnd, NULL, TRUE );
   ActiveTimer = SetTimer( hwnd, InitTimer,
                           FlipTime, NULL );
}

void DropBall( HWND hwnd )
{
   BOOL  Done;

   do
   {
      Done = FALSE;
      aBall = random(3);
      if( Balls[aBall].iStat == Waiting ) Done = TRUE;
   }
   while( !Done );
   Balls[aBall].iStat = Falling;
```

```
   ActiveTimer =
       SetTimer( hwnd, RunTimer,
                 FallTime * (random(5)+3), NULL );
}

void KillBall( HWND hwnd )
{
   KillTimer( hwnd, ActiveTimer );
   ActiveTimer = Ø;
   MessageBeep( NULL );
   Balls[aBall].iStat = Dead;
   Balls[aBall].pt.x = -2Ø;
   Balls[aBall].pt.y = -2Ø;
   aBall = -1;
}

void CatchBall( HWND hwnd )
{
   int   Which = aBall;

   KillBall( hwnd );
   Balls[Which].iStat = Caught;
   ResetTimer( hwnd );
}

BOOL DrawBitmap( HWND hwnd, LPSTR lpName,
                 int   xPos, int   yPos )
{
   HBITMAP hBm;
   HDC     hdc, hdcMem;
   BITMAP  bm;

   if( !( hBm = LoadBitmap( hInst, lpName ) ) )
      return( FALSE );
   hdc = GetDC( hwnd );
   hdcMem = CreateCompatibleDC( hdc );
   SelectObject( hdcMem, hBm );
   SetMapMode( hdcMem, GetMapMode( hdc ) );
   GetObject( hBm, sizeof(BITMAP), (LPSTR) &bm );
   BitBlt( hdc,
           xPos-(bm.bmWidth/2),
           yPos-(bm.bmHeight),
           bm.bmWidth, bm.bmHeight,
           hdcMem, Ø, Ø, SRCCOPY );
   ReleaseDC( hwnd, hdc );
   DeleteDC( hdcMem );
```

```
        DeleteObject( hBm );
        return( TRUE );
    }


    void DrawCursor( HWND hwnd, POINT ptCursor, DWORD dwRop )
    {
        HDC     hdc, hdcMem;
        BITMAP  bmCur;

        hdc = GetDC( hwnd );
        hdcMem = CreateCompatibleDC( hdc );
        SelectObject( hdcMem, hCurBm );
        SetMapMode( hdcMem, GetMapMode( hdc ) );
        GetObject( hCurBm, sizeof(BITMAP), (LPSTR) &bmCur );
        BitBlt( hdc,
                ptCursor.x - (bmCur.bmWidth/2),
                ptCursor.y - (bmCur.bmHeight/2),
                bmCur.bmWidth, bmCur.bmHeight,
                hdcMem, 0, 0, dwRop );
        ReleaseDC( hwnd, hdc );
        DeleteDC( hdcMem );
    }


    BOOL InitCursor( HWND hwnd, POINT ptCursor, LPSTR lpName )
    {
        if( !( hCurBm = LoadBitmap( hInst, lpName ) ) )
            return( FALSE );
        DrawCursor( hwnd, ptCursor, SRCCOPY );
        bStatic = FALSE;
        return( TRUE );
    }


    void ClearCursor( HWND hwnd, POINT ptCursor )
    {
        DrawCursor( hwnd, ptCursor, WHITENESS );
        DeleteObject( hCurBm );
        ptCursor.x = WinWidth / 2;
        ptCursor.y = WinHeight - 50;
        ClientToScreen( hwnd, &ptCursor );
        SetCursorPos( ptCursor.x, ptCursor.y );
        bStatic = TRUE;
        InvalidateRect( hwnd, NULL, TRUE );
    }


    long FAR PASCAL WndProc( HWND hwnd,   WORD msg,
                             WORD wParam, LONG lParam )
```

```c
{
    PAINTSTRUCT ps;
    FARPROC     lpProc;
    RECT        pRect;
    HDC         hdc;
    BOOL        Match;
    char        szBuff[30];
    int         i, j, Count;

    switch( msg )
    {
        case WM_CREATE:
            bStatic = TRUE;
            sprintf( ActiveBM, "%s", HrGls[14] );
            SetClassWord( hwnd, GCW_HCURSOR,
                LoadCursor( hInst, "NCursor" ) );
            ptReserve.x = WinWidth / 2;
            ptReserve.y = WinHeight - 50;
            aBall = -1;
            for( i=0; i<3; i++ )
            {
                Balls[i].pt.x = ( WinWidth / 4 ) * ( i + 1 );
                Balls[i].pt.y = 20;
                Balls[i].iRadius = 14;
                Balls[i].iStat = Waiting;
                do
                {
                    Match = FALSE;
                    Balls[i].Color = random(16);
                    for( j=0; j<i; j++ )
                        if( Balls[i].Color == Balls[j].Color )
                            Match = TRUE;
                }
                while( Match );
                hBrush[i] =   CreateSolidBrush(
                    PALETTEINDEX( Balls[i].Color ) );
            }
            ResetTimer( hwnd );
            break;

        case WM_COMMAND:
            switch( wParam )
            {
                case IDM_ENDGAME:
                    ptReserve.x = WinWidth / 2;
                    ptReserve.y = 50;
```

```
            ClientToScreen( hwnd, &ptCursor );
            SetCursorPos( ptCursor.x, ptCursor.y );
            for( i=0, Count=0; i<3; i++ )
                if( Balls[i].iStat == Caught ) Count++;
            if( Count )
                sprintf( ActiveBM, "%s", Bite[1] );
            else
                sprintf( ActiveBM, "%s", Bite[2] );
            InitCursor( hwnd, ptReserve, ActiveBM );
            sprintf( szBuff,
                    "Results: %d of 3 caught",
                    Count );
            EndMsg( szBuff );
            PostMessage( hwnd, WM_DESTROY, NULL, NULL );
            break;
    }
    return(0);

case WM_PAINT:
    hdc = BeginPaint( hwnd, &ps );
    for( i=0; i<3; i++ )
    {
        SelectObject( hdc, hBrush[i] );
        Ellipse( hdc,
                Balls[i].pt.x-Balls[i].iRadius,
                Balls[i].pt.y-Balls[i].iRadius,
                Balls[i].pt.x+Balls[i].iRadius,
                Balls[i].pt.y+Balls[i].iRadius );
    }
    EndPaint( hwnd, &ps );
    if( bStatic )
        DrawBitmap( hwnd, ActiveBM,
                    ptReserve.x, ptReserve.y );
    else
        DrawCursor( hwnd, ptReserve, SRCCOPY );
    return(0);

case WM_MOUSEMOVE:
    if( !bStatic )
    {
        DrawCursor( hwnd, ptReserve, WHITENESS );
        GetCursorPos( &ptCursor );
        ScreenToClient( hwnd, &ptCursor );
        DrawCursor( hwnd, ptCursor, SRCCOPY );
        ptReserve = ptCursor;
    }
```

```
        break;

case WM_LBUTTONDOWN:
    ptCursor.x = LOWORD( lParam );
    ptCursor.y = HIWORD( lParam );
    if( ( abs(Balls[aBall].pt.x-ptCursor.x) < 6 ) &&
        ( abs(Balls[aBall].pt.y-ptCursor.y) < 6 ) )
    {      // cursor has hit target
        pRect.left   = Balls[aBall].pt.x - 20;
        pRect.top    = Balls[aBall].pt.y - 20;
        pRect.right  = Balls[aBall].pt.x + 20;
        pRect.bottom = Balls[aBall].pt.y + 20;
        CatchBall( hwnd );
        GetCursorPos( &ptCursor );
        ScreenToClient( hwnd, &ptCursor );
        bStatic = TRUE;
        ClearCursor( hwnd, ptCursor );
        ptReserve.x = WinWidth / 2;
        ptReserve.y = WinHeight - 50;
        ptCursor = ptReserve;
        ClientToScreen( hwnd, &ptCursor );
        SetCursorPos( ptCursor.x, ptCursor.y );
        ResetTimer( hwnd );
    }
    InvalidateRect( hwnd, &pRect, TRUE );
    MessageBeep( NULL );
    break;

case WM_TIMER:
    switch( wParam )
    {
        case InitTimer:      // flip hourglass
            sprintf( ActiveBM, "%s", Flip[Sands] );
            DrawBitmap( hwnd, ActiveBM,
                        ptReserve.x, ptReserve.y );
            Sands++;
            if( Sands >= MaxFlips )      // flip is finished
            {
                MessageBeep( NULL );
                KillTimer( hwnd, ActiveTimer );
                ActiveTimer = FALSE;
                Sands = 0;
                ActiveTimer =      // start sands falling
                    SetTimer( hwnd, StartTimer,
                              SandTime, NULL );
            }
```

```
      break;

  case StartTimer:      // handle falling sands
     sprintf( ActiveBM, "%s", HrGls[Sands] );
     DrawBitmap( hwnd, ActiveBM,
                    ptReserve.x, ptReserve.y );
     Sands++;
     if( Sands >= MaxSands )      // keep going
     {
        MessageBeep( NULL );
        KillTimer( hwnd, StartTimer );
        ActiveTimer = FALSE;
        Sands = 0;
        ptCursor = ptReserve;
        ClientToScreen( hwnd, &ptCursor );
        SetCursorPos( ptCursor.x, ptCursor.y );
        sprintf( ActiveBM, "%s", Bite[Sands] );
        InitCursor( hwnd, ptReserve, ActiveBM );
        DropBall( hwnd );      // time to drop ball
     }
     break;

  case RunTimer:      // handle falling ball
     pRect.left   = Balls[aBall].pt.x - 20;
     pRect.top    = Balls[aBall].pt.y - 20;
     pRect.right  = Balls[aBall].pt.x + 20;
     pRect.bottom = Balls[aBall].pt.y + 20;
     nPt.y = Balls[aBall].pt.y + random(5);
     nPt.x = Balls[aBall].pt.x + (5-random(11));
     nPt.x = max( nPt.x, 20 );
     nPt.x = min( nPt.x, WinWidth-20 );
     Balls[aBall].pt.x = nPt.x;
     Balls[aBall].pt.y = nPt.y;
     if( Balls[aBall].pt.y >= ( WinHeight-40 ) )
     {      // ball hits bottom
        GetCursorPos( &ptCursor );
        ScreenToClient( hwnd, &ptCursor );
        ClearCursor( hwnd, ptCursor );
        KillBall( hwnd );
        ptReserve.x = WinWidth / 2;
        ptReserve.y = WinHeight - 50;
        ptCursor = ptReserve;
        ClientToScreen( hwnd, &ptCursor );
        SetCursorPos( ptCursor.x, ptCursor.y );
        ResetTimer( hwnd );
     }
```

```
                else
                    InvalidateRect( hwnd, &pRect, TRUE );
                break;
            }
            break;

        case WM_DESTROY:
            if( ActiveTimer ) KillTimer( hwnd, ActiveTimer );
            for( i=0; i<3; i++ ) DeleteObject( hBrush[i] );
            PostQuitMessage(0);
            return(0);
    }
    return( DefWindowProc( hwnd, msg, wParam, lParam ) );
}


#pragma argsused

int PASCAL WinMain( HANDLE hInstance,
                    HANDLE hPrevInstance,
                    LPSTR  lpszCmdParam,
                    int    nCmdShow )
{
    HWND        hwnd;
    MSG         msg;
    WNDCLASS    wc;
    int         i;

    if( ! hPrevInstance )
    {
        wc.hInstance      = hInstance;
        wc.lpfnWndProc    = WndProc;
        wc.cbClsExtra     = 0;
        wc.cbWndExtra     = 0;
        wc.lpszClassName  = szAppName;
        wc.hIcon          = LoadIcon( hInstance, szAppName );
        wc.lpszMenuName   = (LPSTR) szAppName;
        wc.hCursor        = LoadCursor( NULL, IDC_ARROW );
        wc.hbrBackground  = GetStockObject( WHITE_BRUSH );
        wc.style          = CS_HREDRAW | CS_VREDRAW;
        RegisterClass( &wc );
    }
    hInst = hInstance;

    hwnd = CreateWindow( szAppName, "Falling Balls",
                WS_OVERLAPPEDWINDOW | WS_CLIPCHILDREN,
                WinOrgX, WinOrgY, WinWidth, WinHeight,
```

```
              ØL, ØL, hInst, ØL  );
      ShowWindow(    hwnd, nCmdShow );
      UpdateWindow( hwnd );
      while( GetMessage( &msg, NULL, Ø, Ø ) )
      {
         TranslateMessage( &msg );
         DispatchMessage(  &msg );
      }
      return( msg.wParam );
}


;===============;
;  Animate2.DEF  ;
;===============;

NAME         Animate2

DESCRIPTION  "Animation Two Program"
EXETYPE      WINDOWS
STUB         "WINSTUB.EXE"
CODE         PRELOAD MOVEABLE DISCARDABLE
DATA         PRELOAD MOVEABLE MULTIPLE
HEAPSIZE     1Ø24
STACKSIZE    8192
EXPORTS      WndProc


//===============//
//   Animate2.H  //
//===============//

#define IDM_ENDGAME      2ØØ

//=== window size and position ============================
#define WinOrgX    5Ø
#define WinOrgY    5Ø
#define WinWidth   2ØØ
#define WinHeight  4ØØ

//=== timer id numbers ====================================
#define InitTimer   1
#define StartTimer  2
#define RunTimer    3

//=== clock speeds ========================================
#define FlipTime    25
#define SandTime    1ØØ
```

```
#define FallTime    5

//=== status of balls =====================================
#define Waiting     1
#define Falling     2
#define Caught      3
#define Dead        4
```

Interactive Images

IDENTIFYING REGIONS AND ENCLOSURES

SUMMARY

PROGRAM LISTING OF MAPDEMO.C

Chapter

12

A major element—and a major problem—in many graphics programs is identifying a location as the point where an event such as a mouse click occurred. On the one hand, this is simple because the mouse-click event messages, such as WM_LBUTTONDOWN or WM_MBUTTONDBLCKL, are accompanied by the mouse coordinates in the lParam argument. However, difficulty can arise in deciding where the mouse click occurred in relation to a displayed bitmap or some other region defined on the screen but not necessarily defined by a series of bounding coordinates.

As an example, Figure 12.1 shows three shapes representing possible screen areas. At the left, the first shape or region displayed could be defined by using a half-dozen coordinate pairs—one pair for each of the six vertices. At the same time, a mouse event occurring within the bounded region could be identified by testing the area as two rectangular regions.

The center region illustrated is both simpler, having only four vertices, and more complex, because the boundary consists of diagonal rather than rectangular sides. In this case, an entire series of tests would be required to calculate where the edges lie in relation to the mouse-click event.

The third region, at the right, is the most complex of all and would require, following conventional processes, a relatively large number of coordinates describing the convolutions followed by the area's outline.

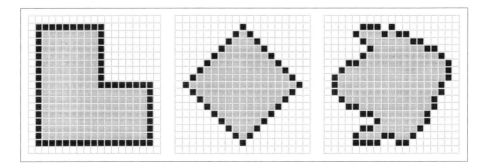

Figure 12.1: Three bounded regions

IDENTIFYING REGIONS AND ENCLOSURES

Still, with the exception of simple outlines and custom recognition algorithms tailored for each specific type, an entirely different approach to identifying regions and enclosures is desirable. As such, there are a variety of algorithms that could be used for this purpose.

The first of these is a mathematical method of identifying the inside (or outside) of a closed region. This method can be adapted to decide—assuming one is inside a selected border—whether the region intersects a single known point identifying the region. And the second is simply a recursive process that tests every point within a region—halting at boundaries, of course—until locating a single known point.

But there are also simpler methods, two of which will be demonstrated by the MapDemo program presented in this chapter. They can be used as generalized search or locate algorithms for both regularly and irregularly defined regions.

The first process, demonstrated by the MapDemo program using the USMAP01 bitmap, relies on the fact that each region within the map (each state) possesses a uniquely identifiable color. Figure 12.2 shows an example displaying the 48 contiguous United States with Alaska and Hawaii inserted at the lower-left.

The MapDemo program contains a lookup table that matches the color used for each state with the name of the state; the color choices themselves are arbitrary. Obviously, this approach has a few limitations, including being limited to use on systems with capacities greater than 16 colors. Overall, it is a practical and useful method of identifying a large number of irregular regions. Furthermore, in Chapter 13, a similar approach will be demonstrated with images which were generated from business data instead of preconstructed bitmaps.

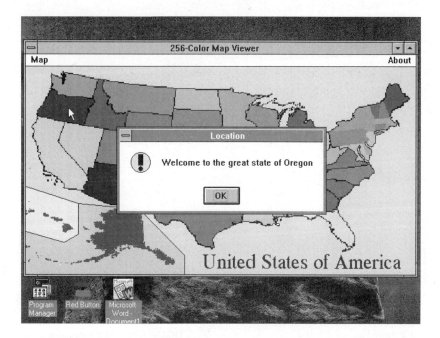

Figure 12.2: MapDemo showing USMAP01

NOTE. The upper New England states (which appear relatively small in the US-MAP01 bitmap) are displayed separately in the USMAP02 bitmap and are used to demonstrate a second area-identification algorithm. The USMAP02 image can be selected either by clicking on the upper New England states in USMAP01 or through the Map menu.

COLOR MATCHING AS AN ID PROCESS

Within the MapDemo program, while the USMAP01 bitmap is displayed, a WM_LBUTTONDOWN event message calls the ColorCheckMap function, passing three parameters: the window handle (*hwnd*) and the two mouse-click coordinates derived from the lParam argument accompanying the mouse-button event message.

```
case WM_LBUTTONDOWN:
    ...
        ColorCheckMap( hwnd, LOWORD( lParam ),
                             HIWORD( lParam ) );
    ...
    return(0);
```

The mouse click x-coordinate is contained in the low word of lParam while the high word reports the y-axis coordinate.

Outwardly, the ColorCheckMap function is a simple process, but operating under Windows it requires a bit of finessing. (Under MS-DOS, a similar algorithm is somewhat easier to implement simply by not requiring context-matching and palette-color conversions, although the end results are the same.)

```
void ColorCheckMap( HWND hwnd, WORD xCoord, WORD yCoord )
{
   HDC    hdc;
   DWORD  RColor;
   WORD   SColor;
   int    i;

       ...
   hdc = GetDC( hwnd );
   RColor = GetPixel( hdc, xCoord, yCoord ) | 0x02000000;
   ReleaseDC( hwnd, hdc );
```

The GetPixel function returns a DWORD value containing the RGB color value of the selected pixel in the form 0x00rrggbb. However, while this is the color of the pixel itself, the data that identifies the several states consists of the simpler palette indexes, not their RGB equivalents. Therefore, the value returned by GetPixel is immediately converted to a palette-relative RGB value using the form 0x**02**rrggbb.

After a palette-relative RGB value is retrieved, the next task is to match this color value to the bitmap's palette, retrieving the palette index. To accomplish this, the first requirement is to lock the pointer to the global palette information (*pGLP*) and to lock a handle to a logical palette (*hGPal*) before calling the CreatePalette function to temporarily re-create the bitmap palette.

```
   GlobalLock( hGLP );
   GlobalLock( hGPal );
           // lock and create palette for reference
   hGPal = CreatePalette( pGLP );
   if( hGPal == NULL ) ErrorMsg( "Palette not found" );
           // get palette index for comparison
   SColor = GetNearestPaletteIndex( hGPal,
                      (COLORREF) RColor );
           // unlock everything but don't delete palette
   GlobalUnlock( hGLP );
   GlobalUnlock( hGPal );
```

Finally, after the palette is created (or re-created), the GetNearestPaletteIndex function returns the palette index value as SColor. Of course, before finishing, the two memory locks on the global and re-created palettes should be released. Neither, however, should be freed from memory, since they may be needed again.

Once the palette index is available, a pair of simple loop processes is all that's required to identify the corresponding state—or, in the case of the upper New England states, to display the USMAP02 bitmap.

```
for( i=0; i<12; i++ )
   if( SColor == NewEngland[i] )
          // if any New England state, switch maps
      PostMessage( hwnd, WM_COMMAND, IDM_MAP2, 0L );
for( i=0; i<StateColors; i++ )
   if( SColor == CState[i].Color )
      LocationMsg( CState[i].State );
MessageBeep(NULL);
}
```

Once the state or area is identified, a variety of other responses could be implemented, as elaborately or as simply as desired. In this case, however, a simple pop-up dialog box is used, identifying the state selected with a welcome message.

Last, the data matching states and colors are provided by a simple structure listing these by name and palette index. An abbreviated sample follows:

```
ColorState CState[StateColors] =
{  "Arizona",        2,  "New Mexico",       7,
   "Oklahoma",       9,  "Georgia",        11,
   "Oregon",        12,  "Colorado",       13,
   "Missouri",      15,  "South Carolina", 16,
   "Texas",         17,  "Hawaii",         18,
   . . .
```

USING THE DRUNKARD'S WALK ALGORITHM

A second algorithm for identifying any region, but particularly useful for identifying irregular regions, is the drunkard's walk algorithm, titled thus because the search pattern follows a trace reminiscent of an inebriated and staggering pedestrian. (It is likewise known as Brownian motion as exhibited by microscopic particles subject to thermal agitation.)

Where a drunkard (or a microscopic particle) simply continues indefinitely, however, the drunkard's walk algorithm executes a test after each staggering step to determine if it has reached an identifiable point, halting when such an encounter occurs. These target points, of course, are assigned locations that are within each enclosed region and that uniquely identify the region.

The drunkard's walk algorithm begins at the point indicated by the mouse click and proceeds in any arbitrary direction until a boundary is reached, a random instruction instigates a change in direction, or the drunkard's search reaches a target coordinate identifying the enclosed region.

In the first case—on reaching a boundary as identified either by a change in color or by encountering a specific, preselected border color—the drunkard's path simply bounces or reverses, retracing itself until the second instance forces a new direction or, ultimately, the path intersects an identifiable point.

In the second instance, a pseudo-random generator initiates a change in direction, on average, every ten steps. Granted, of course, one chance out of eight will ensure that this change is not a change at all, but the overall effect is to trace paths with an average length of about ten steps (or pixels, in this case) between changes in direction. Figure 12.3 shows the same three regions illustrated previously, but this time with a drunkard's walk trace that ends upon intersecting the desired target coordinates (shown as a small box outline).

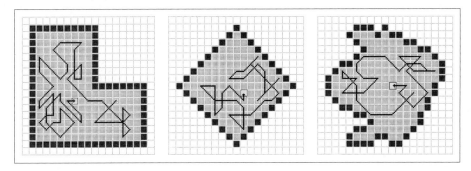

Figure 12.3: The drunkard's walk search

Implementing the drunkard's walk search algorithm is relatively simple. Like the ColorCheckMap function, it is called with three arguments: the window handle and the x and y coordinates reported by the mouse-click event message.

```
void CoordCheckMap( HWND hwnd, WORD xCoord, WORD yCoord )
{
    BOOL   Done = FALSE, Reverse;
    HDC    hdc;
    WORD   i;
    int    j, k, x, y;

    ...
    randomize();
    hdc = GetDC( hwnd );
    x = random(3)-1;
    y = random(3)-1;
```

Initially, CoordCheckMap retrieves the device-context handle for the window displaying the bitmap and selects a step direction (x,y) with each in the range −1..1. Since these are used to increment the *xCoord* and *yCoord* values, the result is a search track beginning in one of eight compass directions.

Before the search is initiated, however, the first step is to check the present coordinates against a loop testing all of the identified coordinate pairs. Rather than requiring a perfect hit on the target coordinates, however, the actual test accepts any point that is within ten pixels of the target (total offset on both axes). Since the target locations are nominally located somewhere near the centers of the regions identified, a close hit is sufficient; requiring a precise hit would simply slow identification.

```
do
{
   for( i=0; i<AllCoords; i++ )
   {
      if( ( abs( xCoord - Coord[i].xPos ) +
            abs( yCoord - Coord[i].yPos ) ) < 10 )
      {
         if( i < StateCoords )
               LocationMsg( Coord[i].State );
         else PostMessage( hwnd, WM_COMMAND,
                           IDM_MAP1, 0L );
         Done = TRUE;
      } }
```

Because this is a case of horseshoes—that is, close *does* count—an exact match is not required and the search is simplified by not requiring a precise hit. Instead, if the current coordinates are within a total of ten units of the target coordinates, a match is simply assumed. In other cases, of course, a closer or looser match might be appropriate, with the algorithm adjusted accordingly, but the present range is adequate for current purposes.

State coordinate pairs in the MapDemo program are identified, together with the appropriate state name, as a simple structure table, thus:

```
CoordState Coord[AllCoords] =
{  "Connecticut",   267, 208,  "Delaware",      202, 311,
   ...
   "RETURN",         14, 337,  "RETURN",        331, 290,
   "RETURN",        122,  81  };
```

In addition to the state coordinates, three area coordinates are provided that do not fall within a specific state: one below the upper New England states and two in the blank areas surrounding these states. Intersecting any of these three sends the application back to the USMAP01 display.

Alternately, until a match is found, the next test is to determine whether the bitmap borders have been reached.

```
Reverse = FALSE;
if( ( xCoord >= bmWidth-1 ) || ( xCoord <= 1 ) ||
    ( yCoord >= bmHeight-1 ) || ( yCoord <= 1 ) )
   Reverse = TRUE;
```

If for any reason the search is approaching the bitmap border, the Boolean Reverse flag is set and subsequently will reverse the search direction. Without this provision, the usual result under Windows is a system application error, which often trashes the system memory as well.

Next, as long as the search remains away from the bitmap borders, a second loop pair executes a check of the immediate vicinity, searching for pixels identifying a border encounter and again reversing direction if a border is encountered.

```
else
   for( j=-1; j<2; j++ )
      for( k=-1; k<2; k++ )
         if( GetPixel( hdc, xCoord + j,
                            yCoord + k ) == Border )
            Reverse = TRUE;
```

A simple, straight-ahead check could be executed, but it would have one fairly simple, if not obvious, flaw. Stated plainly, the flaw is that narrow borders can leak through either single-pixel gaps or diagonal leaks, both of which are illustrated in Figure 12.4.

In Figure 12.4, the left and bottom of the irregular figure have been altered to remove any diagonally permeable flaws. On the right, however, a single gap shows a search trace escaping, while a second search trace escapes through a diagonal pore. Both of these flaws—as well as the need for extra care in "sealing" borders—are prevented by the broad area checking in the preceding code.

Finally, if any of the preceding tests have set the Reverse flag, both the x and y increment variables are inverted by multiplying by -1.

```
if( Reverse )
{   x *= -1;
    y *= -1;  }
else
if( ! random(10) )
{   x = random(3)-1;
    y = random(3)-1;  }
```

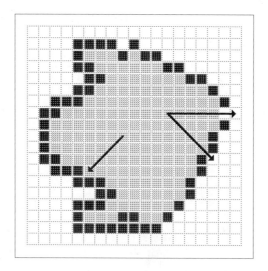

Figure 12.4: Leaky borders using the drunkard's walk algorithm

Alternately, if no reverse condition has been encountered, a simple random test uses a 1-to-10 chance to change the search direction—again, randomly.

Last, the present *x* and *y* incremental values are added to the *xCoord* and *yCoord* values before the *do..while* loop continues.

```
        xCoord += x;
        yCoord += y;
    }
    while( !Done );
    ReleaseDC( hwnd, hdc );
    return;
}
```

The drunkard's walk algorithm is not, however, without an occasional short-coming. Stuart Ozer, who is the technical reviewer for this book, has reported finding a starting point on Cape Cod from which the algorithm required ten minutes or more to identify Massachusetts. Such a flaw could be blamed on the geometry of the search versus the boundary configuration, or it could be simple chance produced by bad luck in the pseudo–random number sequence directing the search.

At the same time, however, there are two factors that tend to prevent such occurrences: a natural human tendency to click on some point roughly near the center of any area (as opposed to human perversity in selecting bottlenecked regions), and an innate tendency of the algorithm and odds to quickly execute an escape from such regions.

Of course, a third guard also can be provided by selecting an extra coordinate point within such a region. See the provisions for New York and Long Island (in the program code) for an example.

DIRECT COORDINATE SEARCHES

While it may appear odd or even inefficient, the drunkard's walk algorithm is overall a very fast method for determining a regional location. There is, however, one alternative that, on first consideration, sometimes appears more efficient: simply search the coordinate list for the coordinate pair closest to the starting point, and then look for a border between the two points.

The reasons for this second step are simple but are best illustrated by an example. Consider the states of Pennsylvania and New Jersey and assume that the coordinate pairs for each are located, approximately, at Altoona (Pennsylvania) and East Brunswick (New Jersey), each location being roughly at the center of the state. However, a mouse click in the region of Philadelphia (Pennsylvania) would not select the Altoona coordinates as nearest because the East Brunswick coordinates (in New Jersey) are considerably closer.

Of course, searching for a border between the initial point and the closest target would identify the problem and could proceed with a second search for the next closest coordinates, and so on. But the search for a border is almost as time-consuming as a simple drunkard's walk and, also relevant, harder to program reliably.

CONVOLUTED AND DISCONTINUOUS MAP REGIONS

As an alternative to the single border-crossing question, suppose that the located coordinate set was correct—that is, lay in the same state or region as the mouse click—but a straight line between the origin and the coordinate points has to cross two borders.

Sound unlikely? It isn't. For example, look at Figure 12.5 (following) where the state of Maryland (at the bottom of the map) is virtually split in two by the Chesapeake Bay. At the same time, Long Island and the mainland portion of the state of New York are technically all one region but, physically, are two separate areas on the map. In this instance, neither of the algorithms discussed (the drunkard's walk or closest points with border-crossing tests) is adequate.

The solution for discontinuous areas, as used in the MapDemo program, is fairly simple: provide two coordinate sets for New York, one on Long Island, and one on the mainland.

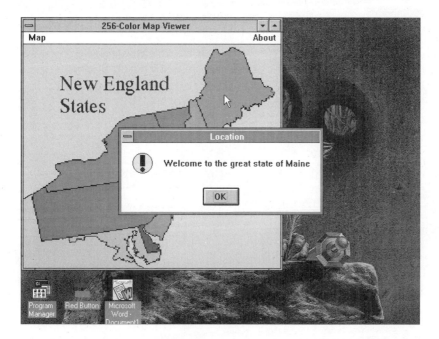

Figure 12.5: The New England region map

THE DRUNKARD'S WALK VERSUS A RECURSIVE SEARCH

A second alternative to the drunkard's walk algorithm is a recursive search algorithm. This algorithm begins, from the initial coordinates, by initiating a recursive search. For example, it might search to the left and both down and up, with each point searched initiating a further recursive search in the same directions, unless a border or the target is reached. If this first search direction pair fails, the second search is initiated to the right following the same pattern.

As an example, a recursive search beginning at point 100,100 calls itself recursively, first with the coordinates for the point to the immediate left, 99,100, and then, after that call returns, with the point immediately below at 100,101. Both of these calls, however, initiate their own recursive calls, with the test at 99,100 testing 98,100 and 99,101 . . . both of which, again, make their own recursive calls, which in turn, make further recursive calls . . . and so on, ad infinitum.

Of course, this would not be a truly infinite recursion, since each recursive call searches both for the target location and for a boundary point, returning if/when either is found. But even with finite recursion, the number of active recursions does increase geometrically (1, 2, 4, 8, 16, and so on). And at the same time, each recursion requires its own register values to be pushed onto the stack, leading very quickly to stack overflow—unless, of course, the recursive procedure is very carefully designed (and sometimes even then it's a problem).

On the other hand, a well-designed recursive search has the advantage of being absolutely certain. It will find the desired target location even if it has to check absolutely every location within the region.

Still, for all its certainty, a recursive search is not necessarily any faster than a drunkard's walk search, while it consumes considerably more of the system's resources.

At its worst, the drunkard's walk algorithm is sometimes a bit slower, but only rarely and randomly so. In general, it tends to be faster as well as more efficient in overall usage of both memory resources and, most important under Windows, CPU time.

On the basis of simple aesthetics, the drunkard's walk algorithm is far more satisfying to the soul (the programmer's, at least, if such is not granted to the machine) than the stolidly pedestrian recursive search. After all, getting there is half the fun . . . isn't it?

SUMMARY

While the MapDemo program employed bitmapped images together with predefined color and coordinate tables, neither is a requirement for using the algorithms demonstrated—only choices to simplify the demonstration.

In Chapter 13, further applications for both algorithms will be suggested, using reference colors or coordinates which are generated "on the fly." Again, these will be suggestions only, not limitations, because the two principal algorithms demonstrated are applicable and useful in a virtually unlimited variety of circumstances.

Also, as an incidental note, while recursive processes have been somewhat "praised with faint damns," for present purposes, at least, this should not sour you entirely on recursive processes. In many cases, a good recursive process is not only the best solution but the only solution—as in a variety of fill algorithms and other painting processes.

PROGRAM LISTING OF MAPDEMO.C

```c
//=======================//
//        MAPDEMO.C      //
//  256-Color Map Viewer //
//=======================//

#include <windows.h>
#include <stdlib.h>
#include <stdio.h>
#include <conio.h>
#include <string.h>
#include <alloc.h>
#include <bwcc.h>                // include bwcc.lib in project
#include "mapdemo.h"

#define StateColors  45
#define StateCoords  12
#define AllCoords    StateCoords+3
#define Border       0x00000000

HANDLE        hInst;                // application hInstance
DWORD         bmImgSize, bmScanWidth;
WORD          bmBitCount, bmWidth, bmHeight;
BOOL          bReadColor;
HANDLE        hInst, hGLP;
HBITMAP       hGBM  = NULL;
HPALETTE      hGPal = NULL;
LPLOGPALETTE  pGLP  = NULL;

typedef struct { char *State;
                 int  Color;  } ColorState;

typedef struct { char *State;
                 int  xPos;
                 int  yPos;   } CoordState;

int NewEngland[12] =
{  60,  61,  65,  67,  69,  70,
   72,  76,  80, 151, 153, 185  };

ColorState CState[StateColors] =
{  "Arizona",         2,      "New Mexico",      7,
   "Oklahoma",        9,      "Georgia",        11,
   "Oregon",         12,      "Colorado",       13,
   "Missouri",       15,      "South Carolina", 16,
   "Texas",          17,      "Hawaii",         18, // 10
```

```
        "Virginia",      21,    "Arkansas",     23,
        "Nebraska",      24,    "Illinois",     27,
        "Mississippi",   29,    "Louisana",     35,
        "Ohio",          39,    "California",   40,
        "Florida",       41,    "Idaho",        52, // 20
        "Michigan",      56,    "North Carolina", 59,
        "Kansas",        62,    "Washington",   65,
        "Wisconsin",     68,    "West Virginia", 71,
        "Minnesota",     74,    "Kentucky",     77, // 30
        "Iowa",          79,    "Nevada",       81,
        "Tennessee",     83,    "Utah",        109,
        "South Dakota", 114,    "North Dakota", 121,
        "Montana",      142,    "Alabama",     158, // 40
        "Alaska",       180,    "Wyoming",     189,
        "Indiana",      194,    "Alaska",      248,
        "Hawaii",       250   };               // 45

CoordState Coord[AllCoords] =
{   "Connecticut",   267, 208,  "Delaware",      202, 311,
    "Maine",         330,  86,  "Maryland",      148, 305,
    "Massachusetts", 279, 184,  "New Hampshire", 276, 144,
    "New Jersey",    209, 253,  "New York",      181, 178,
    "New York",      258, 237,  "Pennsylvania",  119, 256,
    "Rhode Island",  300, 201,  "Vermont",       238, 132,
    "RETURN",         14, 337,  "RETURN",        331, 290,
    "RETURN",        122,  81 };

#pragma argsused

BOOL FAR PASCAL About( HWND hDlg,   WORD msg,
                       WORD wParam, LONG lParam )
{
    switch( msg )
    {
        case WM_INITDIALOG: return( TRUE );
        case WM_COMMAND:
          switch( wParam )
          {
            case IDOK: EndDialog( hDlg, TRUE );
                       return( TRUE );
            default: return( TRUE );
        }      }
    return( FALSE );
}


void LocationMsg( char *State )
```

```
{
    char szBuff[80];

    sprintf( szBuff,
             "Welcome to the great state of %s", State );
    MessageBox( GetFocus(), szBuff, "Location",
                MB_ICONEXCLAMATION | MB_OK );
    return;
}

int ErrorMsg( char *Message )
{
    MessageBox( GetFocus(),   Message, "Error!",
                MB_ICONQUESTION | MB_OK );
    return(0);
}

int ReadBitmap( HWND hwnd, char *szFName )
{
    BITMAPFILEHEADER     bmFH;
    LPBITMAPINFOHEADER pBmIH;
    LPBITMAPINFO        pBmInfo;
    RGBQUAD     FAR    * pRGB;
    BYTE       huge   * pBits;
    HDC        hdc;
    HANDLE     hBM, hBmInfo, hBmIH;
    HBITMAP    hBitmap;
    HPALETTE   hOldPal, hNewPal;
    WORD       PalSize;
    int        hFile;
    char       szBuff[64];
    LPSTR      lpBits;
    int        i, j, CRes = 256;
    LONG       GetBytes, ReadBytes, BytesLeft;

//=== clean up any existing memory objects ==============
    if( hGBM ) GlobalFree( (HANDLE) hGBM );
    if( hGPal ) GlobalFree( (HANDLE) hGPal );
    if( hGLP ) GlobalFree( hGLP );
    bmWidth = bmHeight = bmImgSize = bmScanWidth = 0;
//=== open file =========================================
    hFile = _lopen( szFName, OF_READ );
    if( hFile == -1 )
    {
        sprintf( szBuff, "Can't open %s", szFName );
        return( ErrorMsg( szBuff ) );
```

```
        }
    //=== read bitmap header ==============================
        SetCursor( LoadCursor( NULL, IDC_WAIT ) );
        _lread( hFile, (LPSTR) &bmFH,
                sizeof(BITMAPFILEHEADER) );
        if( bmFH.bfType != 0x4D42 )   // if type isn't "BF" ...
            return( ErrorMsg( "Not a bitmap image" ) );
    //=== read bitmap info header =========================
        hBmIH = GlobalAlloc( GMEM_FIXED,
                        sizeof(BITMAPINFOHEADER ) );
        pBmIH = (LPBITMAPINFOHEADER) GlobalLock( hBmIH );
        _lread( hFile, (LPSTR) pBmIH,
                sizeof(BITMAPINFOHEADER) );
        if( (WORD) pBmIH->biBitCount != 8 ) // 2^8 colors = 256
            return( ErrorMsg( "Not a 256 color bitmap"));
        if( (DWORD) pBmIH->biCompression != BI_RGB )
            return( ErrorMsg("Compressed images not accepted"));
        PalSize = pBmIH->biClrUsed * sizeof(RGBQUAD);
        GlobalUnlock( hBmIH );
    //=== read palette info into bitmap info ==============
        hBmInfo = GlobalAlloc( GHND, PalSize +
                        sizeof(BITMAPINFOHEADER) );
        pBmInfo = (LPBITMAPINFO) GlobalLock( hBmInfo );
        pBmInfo->bmiHeader = *pBmIH;
        GlobalFree( hBmIH );          // free old memory handle
    //=== save size data for this image ===================
        bmWidth    = LOWORD( pBmInfo->bmiHeader.biWidth );
        bmHeight   = LOWORD( pBmInfo->bmiHeader.biHeight );
        //  note width and height saved as WORD, not DWORD
        bmBitCount = (WORD)  pBmInfo->bmiHeader.biBitCount;
        bmImgSize  = (DWORD) pBmInfo->bmiHeader.biSizeImage;
        bmScanWidth = (DWORD) bmWidth;
        while( bmScanWidth % sizeof(WORD) ) bmScanWidth++;
                            // must be an even WORD size !!!
    //=== if image size not in header, calculate size ========
        if( pBmInfo->bmiHeader.biSizeImage == 0 )
        {
            bmImgSize = ( ( ( ( bmWidth * bmBitCount ) +
                        31 ) / 32 ) * 4 ) * bmHeight;
            pBmInfo->bmiHeader.biSizeImage = bmImgSize;
        }
    //=== now read the palette information ================
        if( _lread( hFile, (LPSTR) pBmInfo->bmiColors,
                PalSize ) != PalSize )
        {
            GlobalUnlock( hBmInfo );
```

```
      GlobalFree( hBmInfo );
      pBmInfo = NULL;
      return( ErrorMsg( "Palette read error" ) );
   }
//=== allocate space for bitmap palette ==================
   pRGB = pBmInfo->bmiColors;
      //=================================================//
      // check for short palette indicated by biClrUsed //
      //=================================================//
   if( pBmInfo->bmiHeader.biClrUsed )
      CRes = pBmInfo->bmiHeader.biClrUsed;
   if( hGLP != NULL ) GlobalFree( hGLP );
   hGLP = GlobalAlloc( GHND, sizeof(LOGPALETTE) +
            ( ( CRes - 1 ) * sizeof(PALETTEENTRY) ) );
   pGLP = (LPLOGPALETTE) GlobalLock( hGLP );
               // allocate and lock memory for palette
   pGLP->palNumEntries = CRes;        // fill in size and
   pGLP->palVersion    = 0x0300;      // version (3.0)
   for( i=0; i<CRes; i++ )            // convert colors
   {
      pGLP->palPalEntry[i].peRed   = pRGB[i].rgbRed;
      pGLP->palPalEntry[i].peGreen = pRGB[i].rgbGreen;
      pGLP->palPalEntry[i].peBlue  = pRGB[i].rgbBlue;
      pGLP->palPalEntry[i].peFlags = 0;
   }
   hNewPal = CreatePalette( pGLP );
   GlobalUnlock( hGLP );
//=== now retrive actual image information ===============
   hBM = GlobalAlloc( GHND, bmImgSize );
   BytesLeft = ReadBytes = bmImgSize;
   pBits = (BYTE huge *) GlobalLock( hBM );
   while( BytesLeft > 0 )
   {
      if( BytesLeft > 32767L ) GetBytes = 32768L;
                        else GetBytes = BytesLeft;
         //=============================================//
         // limit block reads to 32K to avoid crossing //
         // segment boundary when calling _lread       //
         //=============================================//
      if( (WORD) _lread( hFile, (LPSTR) pBits,
                     (WORD) GetBytes ) != GetBytes )
         if( ReadBytes <= 0 ) break; else return( FALSE );
      pBits += GetBytes;
      ReadBytes -= GetBytes;
      BytesLeft -= GetBytes;
   }
```

```
        _lclose( hFile );
   //=== make new palette active ==========================
        hdc = GetDC( GetFocus() );
        hOldPal = SelectPalette( hdc, hNewPal, FALSE );
        RealizePalette( hdc );
   //=== create DIB Bitmap ================================
        lpBits = GlobalLock( hBM );
        hBitmap = CreateDIBitmap( hdc,
              (LPBITMAPINFOHEADER) &pBmInfo->bmiHeader,
                                   CBM_INIT,
                                   lpBits,
                    (LPBITMAPINFO) pBmInfo,
                                   DIB_RGB_COLORS );
        GlobalUnlock( hBM );
        if( hBitmap != NULL )
        {
           if( hGBM )                      // if old bitmap
              DeleteObject( hGBM );        //    delete same ...
           hGBM = hBitmap;                 // save global handle
           if( hGPal )                     // if old palette
              DeleteObject( hGPal );       //    delete same ...
           hGPal = hNewPal;                // save global handle
        } else ErrorMsg( "Bitmap failed" );
   //=== discard global memory object =====================
        if( hOldPal ) SelectPalette( hdc, hOldPal, FALSE );
        ReleaseDC( GetFocus(), hdc );
        GlobalUnlock( hBmInfo );
        GlobalFree( hBmInfo );
        pBmInfo = NULL;
        GlobalFree( hBM );
        SetCursor( LoadCursor( NULL, IDC_ARROW ) );
        InvalidateRect( hwnd, NULL, TRUE );
        return(0);
   }


   //=== use color matching for the USMAP01 image ===========

   void ColorCheckMap( HWND hwnd, WORD xCoord, WORD yCoord )
   {
        HDC    hdc;
        DWORD  RColor;
        WORD   SColor;
        int    i;

        char   szBuff[20];
```

```c
   if( ( xCoord >= ( bmWidth - 1  ) ) ||
       ( yCoord >= ( bmHeight - 1 ) ) )
   {
      MessageBeep(NULL);
      ErrorMsg( "Point selected must\n"
                "be within map bounds" );
      return;
   }
   hdc = GetDC( hwnd );
   RColor = GetPixel( hdc, xCoord, yCoord ) | 0x02000000;
            // need RGB palette-relative color value
   ReleaseDC( hwnd, hdc );
   GlobalLock( hGLP );
   GlobalLock( hGPal );
            // lock and create palette for reference
   hGPal = CreatePalette( pGLP );
   if( hGPal == NULL ) ErrorMsg( "Palette not found!" );
            // get palette index for comparison
   SColor =  GetNearestPaletteIndex( hGPal,
                        (COLORREF) RColor );
         // unlock everything but don't delete palette
   GlobalUnlock( hGLP );
   GlobalUnlock( hGPal );
   for( i=0; i<12; i++ )
      if( SColor == NewEngland[i] )
            // if any New England state, switch maps
         PostMessage( hwnd, WM_COMMAND, IDM_MAP2, 0L );
   for( i=0; i<StateColors; i++ )
      if( SColor == CState[i].Color )
         LocationMsg( CState[i].State );
   MessageBeep(NULL);
}


//=== use drunkard's walk algorithm and coordinate =======
//=== matching for the USMAP02 image ====================

void CoordCheckMap( HWND hwnd, WORD xCoord, WORD yCoord )
{
   BOOL  Done = FALSE, Reverse;
   HDC   hdc;
   WORD  i;
   int   j, k, x, y;
   char  szError[80];

   if( ( xCoord >= ( bmWidth - 1  ) ) ||
       ( yCoord >= ( bmHeight - 1 ) ) )
```

```
    {
       MessageBeep(NULL);
       ErrorMsg( "Point selected must\n"
                 "be within map bounds" );
       return;
    }
    randomize();
    hdc = GetDC( hwnd );
    x = random(3)-1;
    y = random(3)-1;
    do
    {
       for( i=0; i<AllCoords; i++ )
       {
          if( ( abs( xCoord - Coord[i].xPos ) +
                abs( yCoord - Coord[i].yPos ) ) < 10 )
          {
             if( i < StateCoords )
                 LocationMsg( Coord[i].State );
             else PostMessage( hwnd, WM_COMMAND,
                               IDM_MAP1, 0L );
             Done = TRUE;
       }  }
       Reverse = FALSE;
       if( ( xCoord >= bmWidth-1  ) || ( xCoord <= 1 ) ||
           ( yCoord >= bmHeight-1 ) || ( yCoord <= 1 ) )
          Reverse = TRUE;
       else
          for( j=-1; j<2; j++ )
             for( k=-1; k<2; k++ )
                if( GetPixel( hdc, xCoord+j,
                                   yCoord+k ) == Border )
                   Reverse = TRUE;
       if( Reverse )
       {  x *= -1;
          y *= -1;    }
       else
       if( ! random(10) )
       {  x = random(3)-1;
          y = random(3)-1;    }
       xCoord += x;
       yCoord += y;
    }
    while( !Done );
    ReleaseDC( hwnd, hdc );
    return;
```

```
}

void ResizeWindow( HWND hwnd )
{
    RECT   rMajor, rMinor;
    int    wWidth, wHeight;

    GetWindowRect( hwnd, &rMajor );
    GetClientRect( hwnd, &rMinor );
    wWidth  = ( rMajor.right - rMajor.left ) -
              ( rMinor.right - rMinor.left ) +
                bmWidth;
    wHeight = ( rMajor.bottom - rMajor.top ) -
              ( rMinor.bottom - rMinor.top ) +
                bmHeight;
    MoveWindow( hwnd, 0, 0, wWidth, wHeight, TRUE );
}

long FAR PASCAL WndProc( HWND hwnd,   WORD msg,
                         WORD wParam, LONG lParam )
{
    FARPROC       lpProc;             // pointer to dialog box
    HMENU         hMenu;
    HDC           hdc, hdcMem;
    PAINTSTRUCT   ps;
    HBITMAP       hBMOld;
    HPALETTE      hPalOld;

    switch( msg )
    {
      case WM_CREATE:
          PostMessage( hwnd, WM_COMMAND, IDM_MAP1, NULL );
          return(0);

      case WM_COMMAND:
          switch( wParam )
          {
            case IDM_MAP1:
                ReadBitmap( hwnd, "USMAP01.BMP" );
                bReadColor = TRUE;
                ResizeWindow( hwnd );
                break;
            case IDM_MAP2:
                ReadBitmap( hwnd, "USMAP02.BMP" );
                bReadColor = FALSE;
                ResizeWindow( hwnd );
```

```
                break;
           case IDM_ABOUT:
               lpProc = MakeProcInstance( About, hInst );
               DialogBox( hInst, "ABOUT", hwnd, lpProc );
               FreeProcInstance( lpProc );
               break;
           case IDM_EXIT:
               PostMessage( hwnd, WM_CLOSE, 0, 0L );
               break;
           default: break;
       }
       return(0);

   case WM_LBUTTONDOWN:
       if( bReadColor )
           ColorCheckMap( hwnd, LOWORD( lParam ),
                                HIWORD( lParam ) );
       else
           CoordCheckMap( hwnd, LOWORD( lParam ),
                                HIWORD( lParam ) );
       return(0);

   case WM_PAINT:
       hdc = BeginPaint( hwnd, &ps );
       if( hGBM )
       {
           hdcMem = CreateCompatibleDC( hdc );
           hBMOld = SelectObject( hdcMem, hGBM );
           if( hGPal )
               hPalOld =
                   SelectPalette( hdc, hGPal, FALSE );
           BitBlt( hdc, 0, 0, bmWidth, bmHeight,
                   hdcMem, 0, 0, SRCCOPY );
           if( hGPal )
           {
               SelectPalette( hdc, hPalOld, FALSE );
               DeleteObject( hGPal );
           }
           SelectObject( hdcMem, hBMOld );
           DeleteObject( hGBM );
           DeleteDC( hdcMem );
       }
       EndPaint( hwnd, &ps );
       return(0);

   case WM_DESTROY:
```

```
        if( hGBM ) GlobalFree( (HANDLE) hGBM );
        if( hGPal ) GlobalFree( (HANDLE) hGPal );
        if( pGLP ) GlobalFree( (HANDLE) pGLP );
        PostQuitMessage(0);
        return(0);
    }
    return( DefWindowProc( hwnd, msg, wParam, lParam ) );
}

#pragma argsused

int PASCAL WinMain( HANDLE hInstance,
                    HANDLE hPrevInstance,
                    LPSTR  lpszCmdParam, int nCmdShow )
{
    static char szAppName[] = "MapDemo";
    HWND        hwnd;
    MSG         msg;
    WNDCLASS    wc;

    if( ! hPrevInstance )
    {
        wc.hInstance     = hInstance;
        wc.lpfnWndProc   = WndProc;
        wc.cbClsExtra    = 0;
        wc.cbWndExtra    = 0;
        wc.lpszClassName = szAppName;
        wc.hIcon         = LoadIcon( hInstance, szAppName );
        wc.lpszMenuName  = (LPSTR) szAppName;
        wc.hCursor       = LoadCursor( NULL, IDC_ARROW );
        wc.hbrBackground = GetStockObject( WHITE_BRUSH );
        wc.style         = CS_HREDRAW | CS_VREDRAW;
        RegisterClass( &wc );
    }
    else GetInstanceData( hPrevInstance,
                          (PSTR) szAppName, 10 );
    hInst = hInstance;               // global instance handle
    hwnd = CreateWindow( szAppName, "256-Color Map Viewer",
                         WS_OVERLAPPEDWINDOW,
                         CW_USEDEFAULT, CW_USEDEFAULT,
                         CW_USEDEFAULT, CW_USEDEFAULT,
                         NULL, NULL, hInstance, NULL );
    ShowWindow(   hwnd, nCmdShow );
    UpdateWindow( hwnd );
    while( GetMessage( &msg, NULL, 0, 0 ) )
    {
```

```
        TranslateMessage( &msg );
        DispatchMessage(  &msg );
    }
    return( msg.wParam );
}


;===========================;
;  MapDemo.DEF              ;
;  module definition file   ;
;===========================;

NAME          MapDemo
DESCRIPTION   "View 256-Color Map Images"
EXETYPE       WINDOWS
STUB          "WINSTUB.EXE"
CODE          PRELOAD MOVEABLE DISCARDABLE
DATA          PRELOAD MOVEABLE MULTIPLE
HEAPSIZE      1024
STACKSIZE     8192
EXPORTS       WndProc
              About


//=======================//
// MAPDEMO.H             //
//=======================//

#define  IDM_MAP1     101   // US map
#define  IDM_MAP2     102   // NE map
#define  IDM_EXIT     103
#define  IDM_ABOUT    104
```

Bitmaps in Business Applications

A SIMPLE LINE GRAPH

ADDING BITMAPS TO A LINE GRAPH

MATCHING BITMAPS TO THE DISPLAY
ENVIRONMENT

BAR GRAPHS

PIE GRAPHS

ADDING AN INTERACTIVE ELEMENT

USING GRAPHS IN NONBUSINESS
APPLICATIONS

SUMMARY

PROGRAM LISTING OF BUSGRAPH.C

PROGRAM LISTING OF PIEGRAPH.C

Chapter

13

While bitmapped images are often perceived as a standard element belonging to video games—even though, as you have seen, Windows is not the optimal environment for video gaming—the images can be applied in a wide variety of applications. One commonly overlooked area is applying bitmaps in business applications. Bitmaps can be used to dress up a data report, to highlight categories in a list of products, to display logos and trademarks, or as illustrated here, to turn a plain-vanilla business graph into something which is, at a minimum, visually more attractive if not necessarily financially more attractive.

As an example, this chapter includes four business graphs plotted from the same data set, drawn respectively as a simple line graph, a line graph with bit-mapped images, a bar graph, and last, an interactive pie graph. These four graphs are generated by the BusGraph and PieGraph demo programs appearing at the end of this chapter and on the program disk accompanying this volume.

A SIMPLE LINE GRAPH

In Figure 13.1, the annual profits report (for a small, fictitious company) compares four categories over a four-year period. Each category is delineated in a different color and identified by labels at the origin of each graph line. At the far left, vertical increments are identified and the annual periods appear across the bottom of the graph.

This simple business graph requires relatively little programming to create. In brief, all that is really necessary is

1 A loop to create and label the horizontal scale lines

2 A nested loop to draw and label the graph lines

3 A loop to write the year labels across the bottom

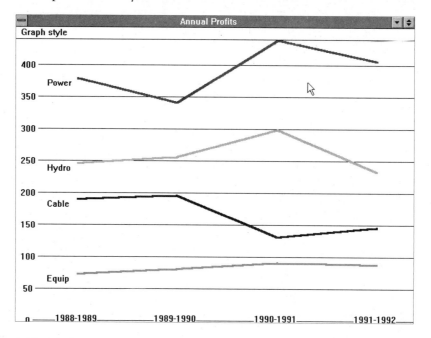

Figure 13.1: A simple business graph

In practice, however, the process is slightly more complicated than the outlined description. The real first step is setting up the window (device-context handle) appropriate for the task. Normally, as you will recall, an application window uses text coordinates with the origin at the upper-left, increasing down and right.

For graphs, however, the conventions demand an origin at the lower-left—not upper-left—with values increasing to the top and right. Obviously, a business graph can be drawn without changing the default coordinates and/or origins by calculating points as an offset using the vertical screen (window) size and then plotting the result relative to the upper-left origin point. And, in MS-DOS, this is essentially what is done.

But, since Windows provides flexibility in both respects, it now becomes easier to begin by establishing a coordinate system that fits the graph layout rather than trying to match the data to an inverted layout.

The task of setting up the device-context-handle orientation and extent is handled in the WndProc function, in response to the WM_PAINT message.

```
case WM_PAINT:
   hdc = BeginPaint( hwnd, &ps );
   for( i=0, MaxVal=0; i<4; i++ )
      for( j=0; j<4; j++ )
         MaxVal = max( MaxVal, Profits[i][j] );
   OrgDc = SaveDC( hdc );
   SetMapMode(     hdc, MM_ANISOTROPIC );
   SetWindowExt(   hdc, cxWnd,  MaxVal );
   SetViewportExt( hdc, cxWnd, -MaxVal );
   GetClientRect(  hwnd, &rect );
   SetWindowOrg(   hdc, -20,    MaxVal );
```

The WM_PAINT response begins by calculating MaxVal to determine what vertical extent will be needed. Then it sets the map mode as anisotropic before setting the window and viewport extents by using MaxVal. Notice, however, that while the window and viewport extents are equal in magnitude, they are opposite in sign, ensuring that values increase from bottom to top. At the same time, the window origin is set at the lower-left (with a slight horizontal offset).

Next, a series of horizontal lines are drawn and labeled to show the vertical increments, and the horizontal dimension is divided to provide the required annual increments (*cxStep*).

```
for( i=-1; i<MaxVal; i+= 50 )
{
   MoveTo( hdc, -20,   i );
   LineTo( hdc, cxWnd, i );
   TextOut( hdc, -20, i+(cyChr/2), szBuff,
            sprintf( szBuff, "%5d ", i+1 ) );
}
cxStep = cxWnd / 4;
switch( GraphType )
{
   case gSimple:  CreateLineGraph( hdc );
                  break;
   case gLine:    CreateLineGraph( hdc );
                  PasteLineBitmaps( hdc );
                  break;
   case gBar:     CreateBarGraph( hdc );
                  break;
```

```
        }
        RestoreDC( hdc, OrgDc );
        EndPaint( hwnd, &ps );
        return(0);
```

Last, depending on the type of graph selected, one or two subprocedures are called to create the actual graph: one to create the graph itself and, optionally, a second to add bitmapped images.

For a simple line graph, only the CreateLineGraph is needed. It contains three provisions: labels placed at the beginning of each graph line, the graph lines themselves, and the year labels across the bottom.

```
void CreateLineGraph( HDC hdc )
{
    HPEN    hPen, hOldPen;
    char    szBuff[30];
    int     i, j;

    for( i=0; i<4; i++ )
       TextOut( hdc, 30, Profits[i][0],
                Labels[i], strlen( Labels[i] ) );
    for( i=0; i<4; i++ )
    {
        hPen = CreatePen( PS_SOLID, 3, cColor[i+1] );
        hOldPen = SelectObject( hdc, hPen );
```

Initially, after the line label is printed, the CreatePen function is called to select a different color for each category line and, at the same time, to set the line thickness to 3, rather than to the usual 1.

After creating the pen, the next step is to set a starting position by using the MoveTo function. Notice particularly that the coordinates used are in standard Cartesian format relative to a lower-left origin; no provisions are made to translate the point relative to an upper-left origin.

```
        MoveTo( hdc, cxStep/2, Profits[i][0] );
        for( j=1; j<4; j++ )
           LineTo( hdc, j*cxStep+cxStep/2,
                   Profits[i][j] );
        SelectObject( hdc, hOldPen );
        DeleteObject( hPen );
    }
```

Once the line origin is established, the actual line is drawn by using the LineTo function in a simple loop with no requirement for further calls to the MoveTo function. Instead, each LineTo call establishes a new current position that is used as the origin for the next call to LineTo.

The final step is writing the year labels across the bottom. The CreateLine-Graph function is now finished.

```
for( i=0; i<4; i++ )
    TextOut( hdc, i * cxStep + cxStep / 2 -
             strlen( szYear[i] ) * cxChr / 2,
             10, szYear[i],   strlen(szYear[i]) );
}
```

ADDING BITMAPS TO A LINE GRAPH

While the line graph illustrated in Figure 13.1 is adequate for showing comparative information, in this modern computerized era, it is also rather dull and lacking in flash. Therefore, to add a little interest (as well as to make the display more palatable to CEOs) the simple line graph can be enhanced by using bitmapped images at the year points on each line.

Figure 13.2 shows a line graph with bitmapped images added for each category.

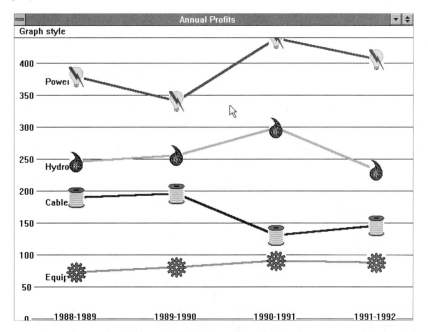

Figure 13.2: A line graph with bitmaps

Creating this second line graph is relatively simple. It requires little more than calling the PasteLineBitmaps function to load each bitmapped image in turn and then to loop through the same points used to plot each line, but this time pasting a bitmapped image over the line.

The PasteLineBitmaps function begins by creating a compatible device-context handle (in memory) with a mapping mode to match the active display map mode.

```
void PasteLineBitmaps( HDC hdc )
{
    BITMAP   bm;
    HBITMAP  hBm, hBmOld;
    HDC      hdcMem;
    int      i, j;

    hdcMem = CreateCompatibleDC( hdc );
    SetMapMode( hdcMem, GetMapMode( hdc ) );
    for( i=0; i<4; i++ )
    {
        if( !( hBm = LoadBitmap( hInst, Labels[i] ) ) )
            break;
        hBmOld = SelectObject( hdcMem, hBm );
        GetObject( hBm, sizeof(BITMAP), (LPSTR) &bm );
```

By this time, the LoadBitmap, SelectObject, and GetObject functions should be familiar from previous examples. They are used simply to copy the bitmapped images from the resource segment of the executable code into the memory context.

Once the bitmap is loaded, a loop is used to copy each image from the memory context to the display. Notice that there is a provision included to offset the bitmap origin by half the bitmap height and width, thus centering the bitmap on the coordinates.

```
        for( j=0; j<4; j++ )
            BitBlt( hdc,
                    j * cxStep + (cxStep - bm.bmWidth)/2,
                    Profits[i][j] - bm.bmHeight/2,
                    bm.bmWidth, bm.bmHeight,
                    hdcMem, 0, 0, SRCCOPY );
        SelectObject( hdcMem, hBmOld );
        DeleteObject( hBm );
    }
    DeleteDC( hdcMem );
    return;
}
```

There's one further provision included that requires a brief mention here. When each bitmap is loaded—even though there is no previous bitmap in use—the *hBmOld* variable receives a handle returned by the SelectObject call. And, before calling DeleteObject to discard the selected bitmap, *hBmOld* is used to deselect the current bitmap by selecting the saved bitmap.

The reason?

Plain and simple: Failure to include this provision results in a memory violation and, generally, leaves the Windows DeskTop in an unstable and very undesirable state.

MATCHING BITMAPS TO THE DISPLAY ENVIRONMENT

In previous examples, bitmapped images were simply drawn (or captured) exactly as they were intended to be displayed. In this example, however, there's an additional twist to be taken into account: The display environment has been inverted with values increasing from bottom to top instead of top to bottom.

However, because the display environment is inverted, the bitmaps also need to be inverted to display correctly, as shown in Figure 13.3. These four images, which are taken from the Resource Workshop bitmap editor, can be compared with the display images in Figure 13.2. Of course, the second bitmap (Equipment), being symmetrical, requires no inversion.

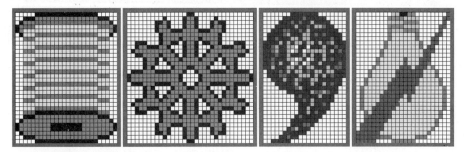

Figure 13.3: Four inverted bitmapped images

In other circumstances, as when importing images that were captured from other screens or were obtained from independent sources or from scanners, various utilities such as ZSoft's PhotoFinish can be used to flip the bitmapped images before importing them into a resource file. Or, if necessary, existing bitmaps can be exported from resource files (that is, saved as .BMP images), flipped, or otherwise altered outside of your resource editor, and then imported again.

OR USE THE ALTERNATIVE APPROACH

It is said that "Even Jove nods," and it was Stuart Ozer (programmer and technical reviewer for this book) who pointed out that, while the BitBlt function could not be used to invert a bitmap, the StretchBlt function is perfectly capable of either horizontal or vertical inversion.

Thus, the PasteLineBitmaps function in BusGraph.C can be rewritten to replace the BitBlt API call with the StretchBlt API call, thus:

```
StretchBlt( hdc,
            j * cxStep + (cxStep - bm.bmWidth)/2,
            Profits[i][j] + bm.bmHeight/2,
            bm.bmWidth, -bm.bmHeight,
            hdcMem,
            0, 0, bm.bmWidth, bm.bmHeight,
            SRCCOPY );
```

Also, the CreateBarGraph function can be rewritten in like fashion, with both revisions supporting uninverted bitmaps.

The advantages, of course, in using bitmaps without requiring inversion are that these bitmaps can be used in a variety of display contexts and that no special tools or utilities are required to create the bitmaps.

Bar graphs

The third graph type demonstrated here is a simple, two-dimensional bar graph with the optional addition of bitmaps identifying the categories, as illustrated in Figure 13.4.

In essence, bar graphs are no more complicated than line graphs. The only principal differences appear in the spacing and the arrangement of the graphic elements (vertical bars replace horizontal lines). Other than this, the similarities are greater than the differences.

The following listing shows the heart of the CreateBarGraph subprocedure:

```
void CreateBarGraph( HDC hdc )  // , int MaxVal )
{
   ...
   for( j=0; j<4; j++ )
   {
      hPen = CreatePen( PS_SOLID, 1, cColor[j+9] );
      hBrush = CreateSolidBrush( cColor[j+1] );
      hOldPen = SelectObject( hdc, hPen );
      hOldBrush = SelectObject( hdc, hBrush );
      for( i=0; i<4; i++ )
         Rectangle( hdc,
            cxOfs+j*cxBar+i*cxBlock,      // x-origin
```

```
        0,                          // y-origin
        cxOfs+(j+1)*cxBar+i*cxBlock, // width
        Profits[j][i] );            // height
  SelectObject( hdc, hOldPen );
  DeleteObject( hPen );
  SelectObject( hdc, hOldBrush );
  DeleteObject( hBrush );
}
```

Of course, after the rectangles are drawn, the task of adding the year labels across the bottom and drawing the bitmapped images remains, but except for spacing, these tasks are simply duplicates of the processes shown earlier.

More relevant is the fact that flat, two-dimensional bar graphs, with or without bitmapped graphics, fall somewhat short of the graph standards offered by many contemporary programs such as Quattro Pro, Excel, and Lotus 1-2-3. While the DOS versions of both TC++ and BC++ offer 3-D bar capabilities, no similar feature is offered directly through the Windows API functions. Still, even if a 3-D bar feature is not directly supported, similar provisions could be created by combining the Rectangle function demonstrated with the Polygon function to add a side and top. Alternatively, the PolyPolygon function could be used by itself to draw a 3-D bar in a single step.

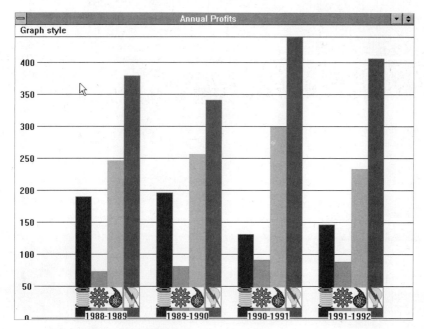

Figure 13.4: A bar graph with bitmaps

For optimal effects, however, combining the Rectangle and Polygon functions is probably better, since this would permit drawing the top and side of the bar by using a darker shading than the front or using a patterned fill to heighten the illusion of depth.

Last, one further possibility is to replace the bars themselves with stacked icons. This could conceivably be done by using the StretchBlt function to vertically (or horizontally) size one or more bitmaps to fit the required bar height, or by stacking unresized bitmaps (using BitBlt) and truncating the uppermost bitmap to fit the vertical height. These latter possibilities are not demonstrated but are left as an exercise, if desired, for the reader.

PIE GRAPHS

The fourth type of business graph illustrated is the pie graph shown in Figure 13.5. Unlike the line and bar graphs, the pie graph shows only one year's data, providing a comparison between categories instead of—in these examples—between years.

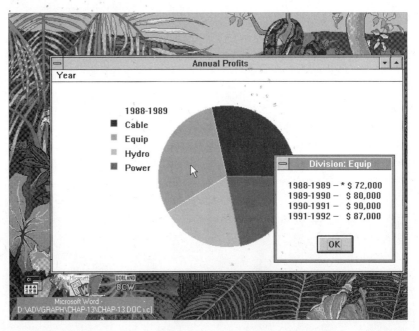

Figure 13.5: An interactive pie graph

Creating a pie graph is relatively simple, with the principal requirement—drawing the pie sections—provided by the Windows API PieGraph function. However, unlike the previous graph examples, where subprocedures were used to provide different styles, PieGraph is handled entirely within the WndProc function in response to the WM_PAINT message.

But, before anything is drawn for a pie graph, the individual magnitudes of the pie sections have to be converted into fractions of the whole (that is, slices).

```
case WM_PAINT:
    TVal[0] = 0;
    for( i=0; i<4; i++ )
        TVal[i+1] = TVal[i] + Profits[Year][i];
```

In this fashion, the original values for the 1988–1989 period, which were 189, 72, 245, and 378, become a scalar sequence—0, 189, 261, 506, 884—which will be used, presently, to calculate the beginning and ending angles for each pie section.

But, before creating pie sections, the device-context handle requires setup. Previously, an anisotropic mapping mode was used with the x-axis and y-axis set to quite different ranges. For pie graphs, however, the usual expectation is that the overall pie graph will be round; therefore, the isotropic mapping mode is used and the viewport origin is set at the center of the screen.

```
hdc = BeginPaint( hwnd, &ps );
OrgDc = SaveDC( hdc );          // save original DC
SetMapMode(     hdc, MM_ISOTROPIC );
SetWindowExt(   hdc,     400,       400 );
SetViewportExt( hdc,   cxWnd,   -cyWnd );
SetViewportOrg( hdc, cxWnd/2, cyWnd/2 );
                // set map mode and extent for display
```

After the mapping mode is set, several routine steps (selecting colors, and creating color labels and color blocks) are omitted from the present sample code. The next important step, within the *for* loop, is creating each of the pie sections.

In addition to the device-context handle, calling the Pie function requires several parameters, beginning with four coordinates describing a rectangle or a square that encloses the entire pie figure. If the coordinates describe a rectangle rather than a square, the resulting ellipse will be oval rather than circular.

The size, *Radius*, has been set arbitrarily but could, optionally, be a function of the total magnitude of the component values as when several pie graphs are combined in one display.

```
Radius = 150;
for( i=0; i<4; i++ )
```

```
{
   ...      // set color label
   ...      // set colors for block and pie graph
   ...      // create color block
   ...      // draw pie graph section
   Pie( hdc, -Radius, Radius, Radius, -Radius,
       (int)( Radius * cos( PI2 *
               TVal[i] / TVal[4]) ),
       (int)( Radius * sin( PI2 *
               TVal[i] / TVal[4]) ),
       (int)( Radius * cos( PI2 *
               TVal[i+1] / TVal[4]) ),
       (int)( Radius * sin( PI2 *
               TVal[i+1] / TVal[4]) ) );
   ...      // reset pen and brush objects
}
```

The final four parameters, represented here by formulas rather than constants or variables, provide two pairs of x and y coordinates. Each coordinate set describes a point, relative to the center of the ellipse, while the edges of each pie section are drawn as a line from the center through the point indicated.

Note, however, that the points used are not required to lie on the radius. They only determine the angle of the line, not the extent of the line nor the position of the arc describing the circumference.

ADDING AN INTERACTIVE ELEMENT

While graphs are an integral part of modern business—or so it has seemed since the first Phoenician merchants sailed the Mediterranean—graphs also have been inherently dull . . . despite multitudinous efforts to add interest or amusement to what are simply static displays, whether they be on paper, a computer screen, or clay tablets. Unfortunately, there are no miracle cures for inherently dull material, but it is possible, with a computer display, to add some degree of flexibility to a graph display. At the very least, some flexibility is better than nothing.

Toward this end, the PieGraph program introduces a simple interactive element, allowing the user to click the mouse button on any of the pie sections to display comparative figures (as shown in Figure 13.5) for the selected category.

The coding for this example should be familiar from previous examples. It consists simply of checking the color of the pie section and then displaying a message box with the figures for that category. But the point in hand is not how the interaction was provided—since other graph displays might well require other handling provisions—but that interactive effects are possible and can be used to enhance the presentation of otherwise dull information.

Which effects, or alternate displays, should be used can only be determined by the requirements of your application, but in like fashion, the possibilities are also open. Thus, to offer one example, a graph display might include provisions to select two or more categories to be given a comparison display in a pop-up window. Or, instead of displaying figures as shown in the example, a bar graph might be popped up to compare the annual figures for the selected category.

Of course, the example used is quite simple. A real application might respond to mouse selection by displaying a breakdown within the category, a projection of future sales versus costs, or anything else dear to an accountant's heart.

Using graphs in nonbusiness applications

If the preceding leads you to surmise a personal disenchantment with accounting in general, please remember that tastes do differ, and what one individual finds boring, another may find fascinating. All of this is preface to a reminder that business graphs can be used for purposes more interesting than the intricacies of higher finance.

For example, since the principal topic is graphics, a bar graph is perfect for displaying a histogram of the color distribution within an image. In similar fashion, a small pie graph can be adapted as a "cat's-eye" meter displaying the progress of a task by the degree and rate at which the "eye" closes or opens. The same timing information could also be provided by a horizontal bar graph within a box, with the box showing the total range and the bar showing the completed portion of the task or any other proportional element.

Of course, these few hints have probably already suggested a myriad of other possibilities—and probably some of these are better than the suggestions offered. In any case, the point remains that business graph elements, including a myriad of forms that have not been mentioned here, can be applied to a wide variety of types of information. And, at the same time, most any of these can also—with a little ingenuity—include interactive elements and, thereby, enhance a variety of applications.

Summary

While business graphs are not the soul of excitement for everyone, they do remain a stock element in business presentations, as well as a valid means of presenting information in forms more readily recognizable than plain columns of figures. And, in the end, the convenience of visual recognition is the real reason for using graphs for data presentation in the first place.

Thus, when necessary or useful, by all means use graphs, but at the same time, these do not necessarily only need to be static displays or confined to one form. Instead, feel free to have fun.

PROGRAM LISTING OF BUSGRAPH.C

```
//=====================//
//     BusGraph.C      //
// Business Graphics   //
//=====================//

#include <windows.h>
#include <string.h>
#include <stdlib.h>
#include <time.h>
#include <stdio.h>
#include <dir.h>
#include <bwcc.h>         // include bwcc.lib in project file
#include "busgraph.h"

enum    gTypes { gSimple, gLine, gBar } GraphType;
enum    pTypes { Cable = 101, Equip, Hydro, Power  };
char *  Labels[4] = { "Cable", "Equip", "Hydro", "Power" };
char *  szYear[4] = { "1988-1989", "1989-1990",
                      "1990-1991", "1991-1992" };
int     cxWnd, cxStep, cxChr, cyChr,
        Profits[4][4] = { 189, 195, 130, 145,
                           72,  80,  90,  87,
                          245, 255, 298, 232,
                          378, 340, 438, 405  };
static COLORREF cColor[8] =
   { RGB(   0,   0,   0 ),  RGB(   0,   0, 255 ),
     RGB(   0, 255,   0 ),  RGB(   0, 255, 255 ),
     RGB( 255,   0,   0 ),  RGB( 255,   0, 255 ),
     RGB( 255, 255,   0 ),  RGB( 255, 255, 255 ) };

char    szAppName[] = "BusGraph";
HANDLE hInst;

void CreateLineGraph( HDC hdc )
{
   HPEN    hPen, hOldPen;
   char    szBuff[30];
```

```
    int     i, j;

//=== print labels at line origins ========================
    for( i=0; i<4; i++ )
        TextOut( hdc, 30, Profits[i][0],
                    Labels[i], strlen( Labels[i] ) );
//=== draw graph lines ====================================
    for( i=0; i<4; i++ )
    {
        hPen = CreatePen( PS_SOLID, 3, cColor[i+1] );
        hOldPen = SelectObject( hdc, hPen );
        MoveTo( hdc, cxStep/2, Profits[i][0] );
        for( j=1; j<4; j++ )
            LineTo( hdc, j*cxStep+cxStep/2,
                    Profits[i][j] );
        SelectObject( hdc, hOldPen );
        DeleteObject( hPen );
    }
//=== print year labels at bottom =========================
    for( i=0; i<4; i++ )
        TextOut( hdc, i * cxStep + cxStep / 2 -
                    strlen( szYear[i] ) * cxChr / 2,
                    10, szYear[i],   strlen(szYear[i]) );
}


void PasteLineBitmaps( HDC hdc )
{
    BITMAP  bm;
    HBITMAP hBm, hBmOld;
    HDC     hdcMem;
    int     i, j;

    hdcMem = CreateCompatibleDC( hdc );
    SetMapMode( hdcMem, GetMapMode( hdc ) );
    for( i=0; i<4; i++ )
    {
        if( !( hBm = LoadBitmap( hInst, Labels[i] ) ) )
            break;
        hBmOld = SelectObject( hdcMem, hBm );
        GetObject( hBm, sizeof(BITMAP), (LPSTR) &bm );
        for( j=0; j<4; j++ )
            BitBlt( hdc,
                    j * cxStep + (cxStep - bm.bmWidth)/2,
                    Profits[i][j] - bm.bmHeight/2,
                    bm.bmWidth, bm.bmHeight,
                    hdcMem, 0, 0, SRCCOPY );
```

```
            SelectObject( hdcMem, hBmOld );
            DeleteObject( hBm );
        }
        DeleteDC( hdcMem );
        return;
    }

    void CreateBarGraph( HDC hdc ) // , int MaxVal )
    {
        BITMAP  bm;
        HBITMAP hBm, hBmOld;
        HDC     hdcMem;
        HPEN    hPen, hOldPen;
        HBRUSH  hBrush, hOldBrush;
        int     i, j, cxBar, cxBlock, cxOfs;

        cxBar = cxWnd / 24;
        cxBlock = cxBar * 5;
        cxOfs = cxBar * 3;
    //=== create vertical bars ===============================
        for( j=0; j<4; j++ )
        {
            hPen = CreatePen( PS_SOLID, 1, cColor[j+9] );
            hBrush = CreateSolidBrush( cColor[j+1] );
            hOldPen = SelectObject( hdc, hPen );
            hOldBrush = SelectObject( hdc, hBrush );
            for( i=0; i<4; i++ )
                Rectangle( hdc,
                          cxOfs + j * cxBar + i * cxBlock,      // x-origin
                          0,                                     // y-origin
                          cxOfs + (j+1) * cxBar + i * cxBlock, // width
                          Profits[j][i] );                       // height
            SelectObject( hdc, hOldPen );
            DeleteObject( hPen );
            SelectObject( hdc, hOldBrush );
            DeleteObject( hBrush );
        }
    //=== print year labels at bottom =========================
        for( i=0; i<4; i++ )
            TextOut( hdc, cxOfs + i * cxBlock + cxBar * 2 -
                    strlen( szYear[i] ) * cxChr / 2,
                    10, szYear[i],   strlen(szYear[i]) );
    //=== optional: add bitmaps to vertical bars =============
        hdcMem = CreateCompatibleDC( hdc );
        SetMapMode( hdcMem, GetMapMode( hdc ) );
        for( j=0; j<4; j++ )
```

```c
        {
        if( !( hBm = LoadBitmap( hInst, Labels[j] ) ) )
            break;
        hBmOld = SelectObject( hdcMem, hBm );
        GetObject( hBm, sizeof(BITMAP), (LPSTR) &bm );
        for( i=0; i<4; i++ )
            BitBlt( hdc, cxOfs + i * cxBlock + j * cxBar +
                    0.5 * cxBar - bm.bmWidth/2,
                    bm.bmHeight/2, bm.bmWidth, bm.bmHeight,
                    hdcMem, 0, 0, SRCCOPY );
        SelectObject( hdcMem, hBmOld );
        DeleteObject( hBm );
        }
    DeleteDC( hdcMem );
    return;
}

long FAR PASCAL WndProc( HWND hwnd,   WORD msg,
                         WORD wParam, LONG lParam )
{
    PAINTSTRUCT ps;
    HDC         hdc, OrgDc;
    char        szBuff[30];
    int         i, j, Count, MaxVal = 0;
    TEXTMETRIC  tm;
    RECT        rect;

    switch( msg )
    {
        case WM_CREATE:
            GraphType = gSimple;
            hdc = GetDC( hwnd );
            SelectObject( hdc,
                GetStockObject( SYSTEM_FIXED_FONT ) );
            GetTextMetrics( hdc, &tm );
            cxChr = tm.tmAveCharWidth;
            cyChr = tm.tmHeight;
            ReleaseDC( hwnd, hdc );
            break;

        case WM_SIZE:
            cxWnd = LOWORD( lParam );
            break;

        case WM_COMMAND:
            switch( wParam )
```

```
        {
            case IDM_SIMPLE:
                GraphType = gSimple;
                InvalidateRect( hwnd, NULL, TRUE );
                break;
            case IDM_LINE:
                GraphType = gLine;
                InvalidateRect( hwnd, NULL, TRUE );
                break;
            case IDM_BAR:
                GraphType = gBar;
                InvalidateRect( hwnd, NULL, TRUE );
                break;
        }
        return(0);

    case WM_PAINT:
        hdc = BeginPaint( hwnd, &ps );
        for( i=0, MaxVal=0; i<4; i++ )
            for( j=0; j<4; j++ )
                MaxVal = max( MaxVal, Profits[i][j] );
        OrgDc = SaveDC( hdc );
        SetMapMode(     hdc, MM_ANISOTROPIC );
        SetWindowExt(   hdc, cxWnd,  MaxVal );
        SetViewportExt( hdc, cxWnd, -MaxVal );
        GetClientRect(  hwnd, &rect );
        SetWindowOrg(   hdc, -20,    MaxVal );
        for( i=-1; i<MaxVal; i+= 50 )
        {
            MoveTo( hdc, -20,   i );
            LineTo( hdc, cxWnd, i );
            TextOut( hdc, -20, i+(cyChr/2), szBuff,
                    sprintf( szBuff, "%5d ", i+1 ) );
        }
        cxStep = cxWnd / 4;
        switch( GraphType )
        {
            case gSimple:  CreateLineGraph( hdc );
                           break;
            case gLine:    CreateLineGraph( hdc );
                           PasteLineBitmaps( hdc );
                           break;
            case gBar:     CreateBarGraph( hdc );
                           break;
        }
        RestoreDC( hdc, OrgDc );
```

```
            EndPaint( hwnd, &ps );
            return(0);

        case WM_DESTROY:
            PostQuitMessage(0);
            return(0);
    }
    return( DefWindowProc( hwnd, msg, wParam, lParam ) );
}


#pragma argsused

int PASCAL WinMain( HANDLE hInstance,
                    HANDLE hPrevInstance,
                    LPSTR  lpszCmdParam,
                    int    nCmdShow )
{
    HWND        hwnd;
    MSG         msg;
    WNDCLASS    wc;

    if( ! hPrevInstance )
    {
        wc.hInstance      = hInstance;
        wc.lpfnWndProc    = WndProc;
        wc.cbClsExtra     = 0;
        wc.cbWndExtra     = 0;
        wc.lpszClassName  = szAppName;
        wc.hIcon          = LoadIcon( hInstance, szAppName );
        wc.lpszMenuName   = (LPSTR) szAppName;
        wc.hCursor        = LoadCursor( NULL, IDC_ARROW );
        wc.hbrBackground  = GetStockObject( WHITE_BRUSH );
        wc.style          = CS_HREDRAW | CS_VREDRAW;
        RegisterClass( &wc );
    }
    hInst = hInstance;

    hwnd = CreateWindow( szAppName, "Annual Profits",
             WS_OVERLAPPEDWINDOW | WS_CLIPCHILDREN,
             CW_USEDEFAULT, CW_USEDEFAULT,
             CW_USEDEFAULT, CW_USEDEFAULT,
             0L, 0L, hInst, 0L  );
    ShowWindow(   hwnd, nCmdShow );
    UpdateWindow( hwnd );
    while( GetMessage( &msg, NULL, 0, 0 ) )
    {
```

```
        TranslateMessage( &msg );
        DispatchMessage(  &msg );
    }
    return( msg.wParam );
}


;===============;
;  BusGraph.DEF  ;
;===============;

NAME        BusGraph

DESCRIPTION  "Business Graphics Demo"
EXETYPE     WINDOWS
STUB        "WINSTUB.EXE"
CODE        PRELOAD MOVEABLE DISCARDABLE
DATA        PRELOAD MOVEABLE MULTIPLE
HEAPSIZE    1024
STACKSIZE   8192
EXPORTS     WndProc


//===============//
//   BusGraph.H    //
//===============//

#define IDM_SIMPLE 100    // graph types
#define IDM_LINE   101
#define IDM_BAR    102
#define IDM_PIE    103
```

Program listing of PieGraph.C

```
//===================//
//     PieGraph.C      //
//  Business Graphics  //
//===================//

#include <windows.h>
#include <string.h>
#include <stdlib.h>
#include <time.h>
#include <math.h>
#include <stdio.h>
#include <dir.h>
#include <bwcc.h>          // include bwcc.lib in project file
#include "piegraph.h"
```

```
#define  PI2 ( 3.14159 * 2.0 )

enum   gTypes { gSimple, gLine, gBar } GraphType;
enum   pTypes { Cable = 101, Equip, Hydro, Power  };
char * Labels[4] = { "Cable", "Equip", "Hydro", "Power" };
char * szYear[4] = { "1988-1989", "1989-1990",
                     "1990-1991", "1991-1992" };
int    cxWnd, cyWnd, cxStep, cxChr, cyChr,
       Profits[4][4] = { 189, 195, 130, 145,
                          72,  80,  90,  87,
                         245, 255, 298, 232,
                         378, 340, 438, 405  };
static COLORREF cColor[8] =
   { RGB(   0,   0,   0 ),  RGB(   0,   0, 255 ),
     RGB(   0, 255,   0 ),  RGB(   0, 255, 255 ),
     RGB( 255,   0,   0 ),  RGB( 255,   0, 255 ),
     RGB( 255, 255,   0 ),  RGB( 255, 255, 255 ) };

char    szAppName[] = "PieGraph";
int     Year, iRadius;
HANDLE  hInst;

void ReportMsg( HWND hwnd, char * Label, char * Text )
{
   char szBuff[20];

   sprintf( szBuff, "%s sales", Label );
   MessageBox( GetFocus(), Text, szBuff,
               MB_ICONEXCLAMATION | MB_OK );
   return;
}

long FAR PASCAL WndProc( HWND hwnd,   WORD msg,
                         WORD wParam, LONG lParam )
{
   PAINTSTRUCT ps;
   HDC         hdc, OrgDc;
   HPEN        hPen, hOrgPen;
   HBRUSH      hBrush, hOrgBrush;
   char        szBuff[180];
   int         i, j, Count, TVal[5];
   COLORREF    RColor;
   TEXTMETRIC  tm;
   RECT        rect;
```

```
switch( msg )
{
    case WM_CREATE:
        Year = 0;
        hdc = GetDC( hwnd );
        SelectObject( hdc,
            GetStockObject( SYSTEM_FIXED_FONT ) );
        GetTextMetrics( hdc, &tm );
        cxChr = tm.tmAveCharWidth;
        cyChr = tm.tmHeight;
        ReleaseDC( hwnd, hdc );
        break;

    case WM_SIZE:
        cxWnd = LOWORD( lParam );
        cyWnd = HIWORD( lParam );
        break;

    case WM_COMMAND:
        switch( wParam )
        {
            case IDM_1989:  case IDM_1990:
            case IDM_1991:  case IDM_1992:
                Year = wParam - IDM_1989;
                break;
        }
        InvalidateRect( hwnd, NULL, TRUE );
        return(0);

    case WM_LBUTTONDOWN:
        hdc = GetDC( hwnd );
        RColor = GetPixel( hdc, LOWORD(lParam),
                                HIWORD(lParam) );
        ReleaseDC( hwnd, hdc );
        for( i=0; i<4; i++ )
            if( ( RColor == cColor[i+1] ) ||
                ( RColor == cColor[i+9] ) )
            {
                sprintf( szBuff, "Comparative Profits\n"
                    "%10s ... %3d,000%c\n"
                    "%10s ... %3d,000%c\n"
                    "%10s ... %3d,000%c\n"
                    "%10s ... %3d,000%c",
                    szYear[0], Profits[i][0],
                        (Year==0)?'*':' ',
                    szYear[1], Profits[i][1],
```

```
                     (Year==1)?'*':' ',
               szYear[2], Profits[i][2],
                   (Year==2)?'*':' ',
               szYear[3], Profits[i][3],
                   (Year==3)?'*':' ' );
            ReportMsg( hwnd, Labels[i], szBuff );
            MessageBeep( NULL );
        }
    return(0);

case WM_PAINT:
    for( i=0, TVal[0]=0; i<4; i++ )
        TVal[i+1] = TVal[i] + Profits[Year][i];
    iRadius = 150;
    hdc = BeginPaint( hwnd, &ps );
    OrgDc = SaveDC( hdc );
    SetMapMode(    hdc, MM_ISOTROPIC );
    SetWindowExt(  hdc, 400,    400 );
    SetViewportExt( hdc, cxWnd,  -cyWnd );
    SetViewportOrg( hdc, cxWnd/2, cyWnd/2 );
                // set map mode and extent for display
    GetClientRect(  hwnd, &rect );
    TextOut( hdc, -250, cyChr*10, szBuff,
            sprintf( szBuff, "%d", Year+1989 ) );
    for( i=0; i<4; i++ )
    {
        hPen = CreatePen( PS_SOLID, 1, cColor[i+9] );
        hOrgPen = SelectObject( hdc, hPen );
        hBrush = CreateSolidBrush( cColor[i+1] );
        hOrgBrush = SelectObject( hdc, hBrush );
        Rectangle( hdc, -250 - cyChr*2,
                    (4-i)*cyChr*2, -250,
                    (4-i)*cyChr*2 - cyChr*2 );
        TextOut( hdc, -250 + cxChr,
                    cyChr*2*(4-i),   szBuff,
                sprintf( szBuff, "%s", Labels[i] ) );

        Pie( hdc, -iRadius, iRadius, iRadius, -iRadius,
            (int)( iRadius *
                cos( PI2 * TVal[i] / TVal[4] ) ),
            (int)( iRadius *
                sin( PI2 * TVal[i] / TVal[4] ) ),
            (int)( iRadius *
                cos( PI2 * TVal[i+1] / TVal[4] ) ),
            (int)( iRadius *
                sin( PI2 * TVal[i+1] / TVal[4] ) ) );
```

```
                SelectObject( hdc, hOrgPen );
                DeleteObject( hPen );
                SelectObject( hdc, hOrgBrush );
                DeleteObject( hBrush );
            }
            RestoreDC( hdc, OrgDc );
            EndPaint( hwnd, &ps );
            return(0);

        case WM_DESTROY:
            PostQuitMessage(0);
            return(0);
    }
    return( DefWindowProc( hwnd, msg, wParam, lParam ) );
}


#pragma argsused

int PASCAL WinMain( HANDLE hInstance,
                    HANDLE hPrevInstance,
                    LPSTR  lpszCmdParam,
                    int    nCmdShow )
{
    HWND        hwnd;
    MSG         msg;
    WNDCLASS    wc;

    if( ! hPrevInstance )
    {
        wc.hInstance     = hInstance;
        wc.lpfnWndProc   = WndProc;
        wc.cbClsExtra    = 0;
        wc.cbWndExtra    = 0;
        wc.lpszClassName = szAppName;
        wc.hIcon         = LoadIcon( hInstance, szAppName );
        wc.lpszMenuName  = (LPSTR) szAppName;
        wc.hCursor       = LoadCursor( NULL, IDC_ARROW );
        wc.hbrBackground = GetStockObject( WHITE_BRUSH );
        wc.style         = CS_HREDRAW | CS_VREDRAW;
        RegisterClass( &wc );
    }
    hInst = hInstance;

    hwnd = CreateWindow( szAppName, "Annual Profits",
             WS_OVERLAPPEDWINDOW | WS_CLIPCHILDREN,
             CW_USEDEFAULT, CW_USEDEFAULT,
```

```
            CW_USEDEFAULT, CW_USEDEFAULT,
            0L, 0L, hInst, 0L  );
    ShowWindow(   hwnd, nCmdShow );
    UpdateWindow( hwnd );
    while( GetMessage( &msg, NULL, 0, 0 ) )
    {
        TranslateMessage( &msg );
        DispatchMessage(  &msg );
    }
    return( msg.wParam );
}


;=================;
;  PieGraph.DEF  ;
;=================;

NAME        PieGraph

DESCRIPTION "Business Graphics Demo"
EXETYPE     WINDOWS
STUB        "WINSTUB.EXE"
CODE        PRELOAD MOVEABLE DISCARDABLE
DATA        PRELOAD MOVEABLE MULTIPLE
HEAPSIZE    1024
STACKSIZE   8192
EXPORTS     WndProc


//=================//
//   PieGraph.H   //
//=================//

#define IDM_1989   1989    // year selections
#define IDM_1990   1990
#define IDM_1991   1991
#define IDM_1992   1992
```

Graphic Simulations

Chapter 14

O ver the past decade, computers have revolutionized more of our world than most people are aware of. Granted, many people have heard of using computers to study fluid dynamics (aero- and hydro-dynamics), weather patterns, engineering structures, and even the design of new computer chips, but these are only a few of the areas where computers have changed (often almost beyond recognition) the traditional arts, crafts, and sciences. A complete list of affected areas would be a large book of its own—and would be out-of-date long before it could be published.

The computer revolution, however, is not the present topic. Instead, the current subject is an area that was not revolutionized but that simply did not exist (with a few exceptions) prior to the advent of the computer.

The area in question?

Simply phrased: *graphic simulations*, or more accurately, the mathematical simulation of dynamic systems in general, including both physical and non-physical systems.

In ages B.C. (before computers), the problem was quite simple: Without computers, the sheer volume of calculations ruled out simulating even the simplest of systems unless a measurable physical analog could be employed. In some cases, there were alternatives. Physical erosion was relatively simple to study by using a slanted box of sand and a water source. Minimal route mapping problems were solved by using soap films. (The same solution was also applied to certain nonphysical connectivity problems.) And many ballistic and navigational problems were attacked by using electronic (and some physical) analog systems.

As for more general simulations, however, the Life program introduced in Chapter 4 was roughly the practical limit for an unaided human. (Before computers, Life was played with paper and pencils by students who might better have spent their time studying.)

Advancing beyond the three simple rules governing the Life program—and expanding beyond what is, essentially, a very small universe—the complexity of the calculations as well as the number of calculations required for most simulations have simply overwhelmed both human patience and practical capacities. Granted, some few individuals have accomplished prodigious feats of cogitation and calculation, such as the compiling of the Rudolphine Tables (Kepler) or calculating the trigonometric logarithms (Napier), but these have always been exceptions as well as monumental endeavors. (The Aztec calendar might also qualify but it was probably a group effort.)

Thus, for the most part, simulations of any complexity have waited for the advent of our newest and most powerful tool: the computer. And using this newest tool, we are now able to study—through simulation—systems which previously could only be theorized about.

All of this says nothing about the accuracy of our simulations, but it does permit testing our theories against actual performance—which is, itself, a tremendous step forward. Therefore, if your theory holds that playing to fill an inside straight is better than folding on the sixth card, you can create a simulation to test this theory faster and more cheaply than testing the theory at Saturday night poker games. (Of course, this question also can be settled by probability theory without requiring simulation, but. . . .)

Graphics in simulations

While simulations do not necessarily require graphics—and, in some cases, would be slowed down by graphics—we also have a very human desire to see what is happening rather than to read about it afterwards.

As an example, the Forest demo program (which appears in full at the end of this chapter, as well as on the accompanying program disk) displays a small universe where some 10,000 acres of trees are simulated. The simulation begins with bare ground that is randomly seeded with 100 starting trees.

As the simulation progresses, the various wooded areas grow, age, and propagate, spreading trees to new areas. Of course, if this were all, the mini-universe would simply fill with trees until there was no bare ground left—an easily calculated result requiring no simulation, just a calculation of the average time required to fill the forest.

This simulation, however, is not so limited. Instead, as the tree population within a defined area ages, eventually the trees die, rot, and leave a new plot of bare ground. At the same time, in emulation of the real world, the simulated forest is subject to fires. Once a fire starts, it spreads. The older trees are easiest to ignite and changing wind patterns affect the spread of the fire.

Overall, the simulation would tell us almost as much if its only output were a statistical report listing the forested acres for each year. But almost as much is not the same as seeing it happen because, by being able to watch the forest grow, burn, and reseed, we gain understanding of two new and very important elements: the patterns of growth and death, and the way changing parameters affect not only the end results but the patterns themselves.

NOTE. If you have any doubts about the relative importance of simple statistical results versus patterns, as an extreme example, consider any fractal algorithm. In fractal calculations such as the Henon Attractor or the Malthusian equation (another famous simulation) statistical results reveal nothing, while the patterns, which are visible only when plotted graphically, reveal everything.

CREATING THE FOREST COSMOS

The Forest program demonstrates the creation of a synthetic cosmos whose reality is governed by a relative few and easily defined rules. By intention, the Forest exists as a shadow, mimicking reality without requiring the complexity of rules (natural laws) that govern what we familiarly consider reality.

Instead, the complex interactions of our reality have been replaced by simpler shadow rules that can be manipulated, compressed, and studied so that we might—by analogy and experimentation—better understand the complexities of reality.

Thus, instead of modeling the growth and complexity of individual trees (along with weather patterns, soil composition, and a thousand other factors) and repeating this for the thousands of trees composing each acre of our map, we simplify all of these into a few statistical rules representing an acre of forest rather than the trees composing the forest.

In this fashion, instead of being unable to see the forest for the trees, we are now able to look at the forest as an entity while ignoring the trees themselves.

CREATING A DYNAMIC (MEMORY) COSMOS

The forest exists in a cosmos consisting of a scant 10,000 units (100 by 100) that, for convenience only, are nominally referred to as acres. Because this is a simple simulation, the essential status for each unit is stored in an array of BYTE.

Two arrays are used for convenience, permitting the second array to be updated by reference to the first and then replace the first array. In this fashion, the first array, which holds the prior status, is not affected by changes that could produce recursive effects.

At the same time, there is also a limitation. The maximum possible array is limited in size to 64k (a limitation imposed by MS-DOS/Windows). This, in turn, restricts the size and complexity of our simulation.

Of course, using multiple arrays is one method of circumventing the 64k limit. A file written to a RAM disk is a second method. But, regardless, the limitation remains an inconvenience and should be taken into account when designing simulations.

CONDITIONS AND RULES OF THE COSMOS

The Forest cosmos is governed by a series of relatively simple rules. While the rules are stated here verbally, the actual rules are numerical algorithms provided within the program.

- The Forest cosmos begins as bare ground and is randomly seeded, initially, with 100 plantings.

- On subsequent cycles (years), these plantings age as shown by changing colors.

- After a minimum of five cycles, the forest plots are well-developed enough to propagate and, if adjacent plots are bare, may seed those areas, initiating new growth.

- Old growth acres—arbitrarily those over 11 years old—are susceptible to natural death: A simple simulation provides for old age and other causes. As with natural forests, however, this is a minor element and affects approximately 1 percent of the forest.

- Fire, however, is a major effect in the Forest cosmos, just as it is a major effect in real-world forests. For simplicity, only one fire can start during any cycle—minor fires are not simulated—but a fire may spread to adjacent acreage.

- Fires die out when their fuel is exhausted but they are also affected by winds (direction and wind speed).

- Fires can spread only to mature acreage. Young plots are not affected (under the assumption that young trees are scattered and little deadwood is available to fuel a major burn).

Given these relatively simple rules, the Forest cosmos simulates the same growth and death patterns exhibited by real-world forests. And a correspondence in patterns is the hallmark by which a simulation is tested.

BOUNDARY (LIMIT) PROBLEMS

While not all simulations are subject to boundary problems, any simulation that re-creates or models a subset of a larger reality is subject to a boundary problem in one form or another.

In Chapter 9, one form of boundary problem was discussed where transformations left a one-pixel border around the image. While this border data was included in calculating transformations for adjacent pixels, because these pixels did not themselves have a complete complement of neighbors, they were not included in the transformed image.

Alternately, in Chapter 4, the Life program avoided a similar problem by wrapping or closing the simulated cosmos. In Life, what appeared to be a two-dimensional, planar universe was, more accurately, a toroidal surface in which the left edge of the display was contiguous with the right and the top edge with the bottom.

Although a toroidal surface is not commonly encountered in our universe— at least, not as a planetary surface (with the exception of the world built by Niven's Protector)—this is a popular method of avoiding boundary problems in simulations.

A second method, popular in the physical universe, involves using a spherical surface, but this is somewhat more difficult to simulate in computer memory and requires considerably more processing and calculation.

There is a third possible method: the use of algorithms to simulate the effects of areas outside of the actual boundaries, but this approach is, again, unnecessarily complicated and computation intensive when not required.

Thus, for most simulations, the toroidal universe provides the simplest approach and the fastest computational results. And if your simulated cosmos is a volume rather than a plane, such as a fluid or gaseous volume, this same practice can be extended to create a hyper-toroid in a cybernetically four-dimensional space.

CREATING A CLOSED, UNBOUNDED COSMOS

Had I been present at the creation, I might have offered the creator much valuable advice.

—remark attributed to Alphonso the YYs

The practice of creating, or simulating, a closed but unbounded cosmos in cyberspace is both simple and complex.

On the simple side, because the data describing a simulation is stored in one or more arrays or matrices, the primary consideration, using the toroidal surface model, is to test all coordinate references (that is, references to array data) and to provide adjustments for references that fall outside the array limits, thus wrapping the index back into the array from the "other side."

On the complex side, while simple rectilinear offsets are easily converted, operations involving vectors, angles, or curves are not always easily handled. When operations of this or similar type are necessary, the simplest approach is to use a separate matrix where the operation can be carried out without crossing a boundary, and then to map the results—using whatever offsets and adjustments are necessary—into the simulation space.

In spatial terms, the most important element, obviously, is to ensure that all operations that wrap across an array boundary are correctly adjusted for the wrap. While failure can have strange and interesting results, these are not always easily identified or, necessarily, recognized.

USING COLORS IN SIMULATIONS

One principal characteristic of graphic simulations is the use of color to make information clear. In many cases, commonly referred to as false-color imaging, color assignments are arbitrary and have no real-world relation to the source or the data.

For example, false-color imaging is commonly used in astronomy to "translate" radio-frequency images into a visual presentation. The translation involved can use several different forms, including using color to represent intensities, radio frequencies, densities, or even gravitational gradations—none of which have any direct correspondence to the visual spectrum.

A second format uses mapping colors that are chosen to represent approximate analogs of the data. An example of this latter approach is used in the Forest.C demo program, where bare ground is represented by browns, various stages of forest growth by greens, fires and embers by reds, and ashy ground by grays.

In some cases, a third approach (combining both representational-color and false-color coding) is also used, but this approach generally involves switching between display formats: showing first one information set and then another.

An example of a switched display could be created by adding one or more alternates to the Forest.C program to show simulated rainfall patterns, temperature profiles, species of vegetation, insect populations, terrain elevations, detailed wind patterns, or soil composition characteristics. (While none of these factors are included in the present demonstration program, they are possible extensions to the present simulation.)

In Forest.C, a palette of 16 colors has been defined, beginning with two representing bare ground (light brown and dark brown), 10 shades of green for trees of various ages, and light red and dark red for fire and embers, respectively. Finally, a dark gray is used to represent freshly burnt, ashy ground, and a third brown for bare ground left by a fire.

The palette colors are defined in Forest.H as RGB values, each with a corresponding integer constant as a convenient identifier. (Note that these latter elements are for the programmer's convenience only . . . but then, what's more important?)

However, while RGB values are defined for each color, this palette is never activated for the device-context handle. Instead, while the RGB colors are referenced as drawing colors, Windows is allowed to dither the existing default palette colors in drawing the simulation map. The decision to permit dithering instead of activating the color palette is arbitrary, but even on SVGA systems, it shows how a similar display would appear on standard EGA or VGA systems. Figure 14.1 shows the defined colors as dithered color bars.

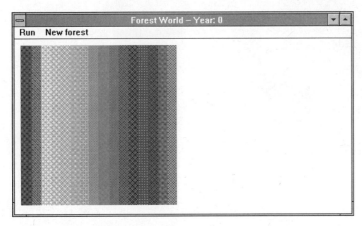

Figure 14.1: Sixteen colors as a dithered display

The alternative—activating the defined palette colors—is left as an exercise for the reader but has been demonstrated numerous times in preceding examples.

OPERATING A SIMULATION

Deciding how to set up a simulation is the first step and coding the simulation is the second. But both of these require provisions for a variety of circumstances.

As an example, Figure 14.2 shows the Forest cosmos some 74 years after seeding and 38 days into a major burn-off. The present burn (illustrated) began somewhere near the lower-right corner of the display and, initially spread northwest under the influence of moderate winds. At this point, the simulated wind is from the south and, at a strength of 5 (on a scale of 2 to 5), fairly strong. A short time after the displayed snapshot, the winds shifted to the north and remained steady long enough to block further spread.

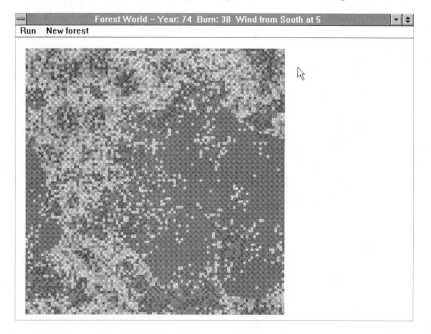

Figure 14.2: The Forest World display

All of these events, of course, resulted from a pseudorandom number sequence but provided a faithful emulation of the patterns of growth and burn-off that have been observed in natural forests.

Initiating the cosmos   The first provision is to set the initial conditions for the simulation. In the Forest demo, this is done in two steps; the first in response to the WM_CREATE message.

```
case WM_CREATE:
    randomize();
    ActiveTimer = NULL;
    sprintf( szBuff, szCaption, nYears );
```

```
    SetWindowText( hwnd, szBuff );
    for( i=0; i<GRID; i++ )          // init world as
        for( j=0; j<GRID; j++ )      // bare ground
            Acres[i][j] = random(2);
    return(0);
```

The *randomize()* function, of course, ensures that new initial conditions (that is, a new pseudorandom number sequence) are used each time the program is run. The second provision, the double loop, sets the world to a random mixture of the two browns.

Within the program, both shades of brown are treated simply as bare ground without differentiation. In a more elaborate program, however, the two browns could be used as different conditions: either as dry and wet soils or as different elevations. For the present, however, two shades of brown are not as dull as a single uniform color.

The second stage of initialization occurs only when the New forest option is selected from the menu. It begins by resetting *nYears* to zero and by seeding 100 random locations, setting the corresponding array elements as *iNewGrowth*.

```
        case IDM_RESEED:
            randomize();
            nYears = 0;
            for( i=0; i<100; i++ )
                Acres[random(GRID)][random(GRID)] =
                    iNewGrowth;
            EnableMenuItem( GetMenu(hwnd),
                        IDM_STOPTIMER, MF_ENABLED );
            PostMessage( hwnd, WM_COMMAND,
                        IDM_STARTGROWTH, 0L );
            InvalidateRect( hwnd, NULL, FALSE );
            break;
    }
    return(0);
```

The pull-down Run menu has two options, Start and Stop, both of which are initially disabled (grayed-out). After the forest is seeded, the Stop option is re-enabled, a message is posted to start the ID_GROWTH timer, and, last, the InvalidateRect function is called to repaint the window.

Variable time   After the initial conditions for a simulation are set (your cosmos is created), normally the next step is to initiate a sequence of events. In some simulations, plotting fractal algorithms, for example, it is the end result that is important. This type of process is normally carried out as quickly as possible.

More commonly, however, simulations are executed at some regular process rate—ideally, a rate fast enough to prevent boredom but slow enough to permit us to observe how the simulation is developing.

Generally, for macro simulations, this is compressed time for the simple reason that no one is interested in waiting a year to see a simulation complete a forest's growth cycle. There are, however, equally valid simulations where time is expanded to permit the examination of events that normally happen too fast for conventional observation.

In the Forest.C demo, two different (compressed) time rates are used, each controlled by a system timer.

Initially, forest growth is simulated at 1 year = 1 second with a one-second timer stepping through the growth cycle. Thus, at one-second intervals, the ID_GROWTH timer sends a WM_TIMER message to the WndProc procedure, in response to which a number of events are initiated.

```
case WM_TIMER:
    switch( wParam )
    {
        case ID_GROWTH:
            sprintf( szBuff, szCaption, nYears++ );
            SetWindowText( hwnd, szBuff );
            AgeWorld();
            PropagateTrees();
```

The first response is to update the window caption, displaying the current year (the years since the initial seeding) before calling the AgeWorld procedure to cycle the forest through a year's growth.

The next step, PropagateTrees, calls a subprocedure to seed new areas from existing growth. In this simulation, three factors control the rate of spread of the forest: first, the age of the existing growth (within each plot); second, quite arbitrarily, selection of a single plot within a range of three plots in any direction; and third, whether the target plot is fertile soil (in this case, any bare ground).

All of these factors could be variables or could be changed arbitrarily to experiment with new environmental conditions, but the present settings serve as good foundation for a forest simulation.

The growth and seeding operations are executed by writing new values to a copy of the original data array, ensuring that the new conditions do not overwrite the existing conditions that are used to generate the new ones. However, because of this separation of present and future, the StepForest() procedure is called to copy the future status back to the present array.

In the current simulation, the potential conflicts between the present and future states of the forest are minimal, and the second array could be simply disposed of with all operations carried out in a single array. In other simulations, however, not only may duplicate arrays be essential, but circumstances may require several arrays to store not only present and future but also different data types which may be constants (such as terrain) or may contain factors affecting larger areas (such as rainfall).

```
StepForest();
InitBurns( hwnd );
InvalidateRect( hwnd, NULL, FALSE );
break;
```

After the current state of the forest is updated, the InitBurns() procedure is called to simulate potential forest fires.

```
void InitBurns( HWND hwnd )
{
    int  i, j, x, y, NoChance = 20;

    x = random( GRID );
    y = random( GRID );
    if( random(iOldGrowth+NoChance) <= Acres[x][y] )
    {
```

Again, a couple of arbitrary conditions have been established. First, only one fire can be started in any year. Second, any fire that does start completely burns out the affected plot (that is, no plots are partially burned). Third, a constant, NoChance, has been included to adjust the chances for a burn to start.

As before, all of these factors, including the algorithm, can be changed or can include variables to adjust conditions for various ignition potentials.

Assuming that a burn is initiated, another simulation sequence is initiated, beginning by setting *nDays* to zero and setting an initial wind direction.

```
    nDays = 0;
    nWind = random(4);
    Acres[x][y] = iBurning;
    PostMessage( hwnd, WM_COMMAND, IDM_STOPGROWTH, 0L );
    PostMessage( hwnd, WM_COMMAND, IDM_STARTBURNS, 0L );
}   }
```

Last, to initiate the actual burn simulation sequence, the first timer (ID_-GROWTH) is turned off and a second timer (ID_FIRES) is turned on.

Incidentally, because two separate timers are involved here and because the Start and Stop menu options are intended to operate either of these independently, a set of internal message procedures is used to trigger these options indirectly rather than directly.

After the ID_FIRES timer has been turned on, all subsequent WM_TIMER messages carry the ID_FIRES identifier and are used to control the new simulation sequence.

Because the burn events are an important departure from the normal growth pattern, the MessageBeep function is used to call attention to change. Also, the global *nWind* wind direction is allowed to change at random intervals before calling the TrackFire subprocedure.

```
case ID_FIRES:
    MessageBeep( NULL );
    if( ! random(4) ) nWind = random(4);
    if( ! TrackFire() )
    {
        PostMessage( hwnd, WM_COMMAND,
                     IDM_STOPBURNS, ØL );
        PostMessage( hwnd, WM_COMMAND,
                     IDM_STARTGROWTH, ØL );
    }
    InvalidateRect( hwnd, NULL, FALSE );
    break;
}
return(Ø);
```

The TrackFire() procedure accomplishes two tasks. First, it ensures that existing fires do burn out to embers and then to ashy ground. Second, it provides a means for fire to spread to new areas.

The first provision (ensuring that existing fires burn out) is governed by a fairly simple algorithm that allows fires to sustain a long burn initially but, after the fires have been burning, causes later burns to develop swiftly and last only briefly.

The second provision (spreading fires) is affected by three factors. The first two, wind direction and wind speed, are relatively obvious, while the third is simply a provision to ensure that young acreage does not burn off (under the assumption that young acreage has not yet had time to develop easily ignited deadwood).

As long as any burn areas remain—either actively burning or in embers—TrackFire() returns TRUE, sustaining the burn cycle for another period (day). Once all fires have been extinguished (or burned out), the TrackFire() procedure returns FALSE (0). At this point, the burn sequence is finished and two PostMessage calls turn off the ID_FIRES timer and turn on the ID_GROWTH timer, returning the simulation to the normal growth cycle… at least, until the next fire starts.

SIMULATION DESIGN

In the preceding description of the Forest.C program, as you should realize, the processes involving the growth of a forest have been greatly simplified. For example, no provisions have been made to account for rainfall or, during burn phases, for rains limiting fire spread or even extinguishing existing fires.

In like fashion, no provisions have been made for seasonal variations such as wet springs or dry summers or for longer-term climatic variations. Similarly, only a single generic species of tree is included, with no other plant life present and with no insect damage or disease damage simulated.

Furthermore, even if all of the preceding elements were included in the simulation, this would still be a very simplified cosmos.

The relevant point here is simply that any simulation must be restricted— to a greater or lesser degree—if only to allow the computer to handle it in a reasonable time and with reasonable memory requirements.

Still, simplifying a simulation does not necessarily mean that the results must be simplified. Likewise, since the objective is to model reality, there is certainly every reason that the results of the simulation should not be simple.

The problem, of course, is threefold:

- ▶ To decide which elements in reality are essential to the simulation

- ▶ To develop algorithms which mathematically mimic reality

- ▶ To present the results of the computation in a format that will show what is happening

Because the Forest World program was designed solely to demonstrate a graphic simulation and to serve as an example, many elements reflecting reality that also would have increased the complexity of the program were omitted. Instead, two principal factors were chosen: first, propagation rates and patterns for the development of the forest, and second, fires to destroy older growth and make room for additional new growth.

At the same time, a minor provision was included to cause older growth to die off without burning, but—as can be seen in older, wetland forests—without burns, a forest tends toward a steady-state climax forest composed almost entirely of older growth.

Given these two principal factors, the resulting simulation (in terms of burn-off and regrowth patterns) still tends to mimic the patterns observed in natural forests quite accurately—which, as an initial objective, is exactly what is desired.

EXTENDING A SIMULATION

Once a basic simulation is operating with a satisfactory degree of validity (that is, operations correspond fairly faithfully to reality) further extensions can be added to simulate additional factors such as disease, insect damage, and rainfall. The advantage of a simulation is that any of these additional factors, or any combination of additional factors, can be tested, varied, and tested again to observe how changes in various parameters affect the progress of the overall simulation.

As an example, even the simplified Forest.C program could be used to study the various cutting patterns and their effects on the recovery and long-term sustained-yield management for a real forest.

Of course, for real validity, there are other factors that should be included in the simulation: principally, elevation and erosion effects, rainfall, and, not least, the effects of leftover debris from cutting operations and how this might affect the spread of fires. Other factors that affect the overall health of a forest, such as insect infestation and disease, might be simply ignored as irrelevant during the suggested tests.

Alternately, if some validity is found for these latter factors—perhaps cutting debris provides a locus for the insect population to breed—then the model requires these factors also to be included. Or, more likely, the model may show effects that were not anticipated, such as debris in newly cut areas affecting how fires spread through the remaining forest.

In any case, the real value of a simulation is to reveal how processes occur, how elements interact, or where and how patterns appear within a system.

MECHANICAL SIMULATIONS

While the Forest.C simulation demonstrated interactions in a living system (a forest) mechanical systems are also a popular subject for modeling. At the same time, while CAD systems are commonly thought of as design utilities, an integral part of mechanical design is simulating how mechanical elements interact.

After all, if a set of gears is going to jam when two driven mechanical arms unexpectedly attempt to pass through the same volume of space, it's considerably cheaper to discover the flaw in an electronic simulation than after tooling up to begin production—or even after building a physical model.

At the same time, granted, mechanical modeling could be carried out without any accompanying visual elements. After all, it should be faster to calculate how two gears mesh than to draw the two gears on-screen and to repeatedly redraw them as they turn, right?

Absolutely right; if that was all that there was to consider. But what about that movement arm driven by the gearing that, in another few seconds of arc, will attempt to pass through one of several mechanical supports? These supports, of course, are static and weren't included in the calculated motions—a small oversight, true, but also one which the real universe is not likely to duplicate.

Instead of attempting to calculate where every point belonging to every element (both static and dynamic) may potentially interact with some other point, it is simpler to draw the various elements, redrawing each as often as necessary, and allow the best processor of all—the human eye and brain—to spot potential conflicts.

SIMULATING THEORETICAL REALITIES

Physical realities, whether living systems or mechanical constructs, offer their own physical appearances as a basis for graphic simulations. Other systems, which may be theoretical or nonphysical, however, do not offer quite the same convenience; instead they require imagination and artistry in deciding how to display their information.

As an example, not only can the operations of a computer chip be simulated by a computer program, they often are—particularly during the design process for a new chip. During such a design process, there are two quite different elements that are taken into consideration: the physical layout and the electronic layout of the chip.

Of these, the physical layout of the chip is relatively simple: How many circuits can be fabricated within a given area of silicon?

The electronic layout, however, not only is more complex but also is affected directly by the physical layout. In this respect, considerations include the signal path between different elements and therefore the signal time between two components, how the components interact electronically, what leakage currents, and what capacitive effects have to be accounted for, and—far from least—how the various components function cybernetically.

So, how is a system this complex simulated? And how is the simulation shown graphically?

In the first case no single simulation, graphic or otherwise, is going to suffice (except, possibly, for a very simple chip), simply because of the level of physical complexity in contemporary monolithic ICs. Instead, referring strictly to the physical layout, small portions of the chip might be simulated on-screen. Or, for an overview, color-coded areas might represent repetitive circuit areas or areas dedicated to some specific function.

The electronic functions, however, are not even this easily coded and would probably require several different simulations and several different displays to handle different elements. As one example, a histogram might be used to show signal-path times for different elements; remember, with today's high-speed chips, even the paths required for clock pulses can be critical, and more than one engineer has vainly expressed a wish for faster electricity.

Still other elements are not even this easily displayed. Thus, in many cases, instead of attempting to show the simulations directly, only the results of simulations are shown.

Computer chip designs and other electronic circuitry are only one area involving nonphysical simulations while there are others, still valid, which have even less connection to traditional physical reality. Some, for example, are simply constructs of our own observation.

As an example, consider simulating population growth patterns using the Malthusian equation,

$$P_{n+1} = R * P_n * (1 - P_n)$$

where R represents the growth rate for successive generations.

Okay, population grows linearly, doesn't it? So, do you think a simple line graph should be appropriate for this equation? If the whole suggestion sounds like a loaded question . . . you're right, it is.

First, after a half-dozen initial steps, the equation given is anything but linear. And second, this particular simulation will yield results unlike anything you might normally expect. In fact, the Malthusian equation is a member of a loose group of formulas that are referred to as "strange attractors" because of the curves generated from what individually appear to be scattered points.

NOTE. To experiment with the Malthusian equation, one convenient method is to plot successive points (P_n and P_{n+1}) as x and y coordinate pairs. After a few thousand generations, the resulting plots will begin to show an interesting curve. Next, by varying the growth rate, R—try the range from 2.3 to 3.8—a single curve becomes an interesting group of curves, complete with inflection and bifurcation points.

The point, of course, is not that this specific equation produces an interesting simulation but that simulations can show interesting results that would not be visible by simply examining columns of numbers.

In other cases, such as plotting radiation-intensity patterns from a broadcast antenna—or reception sensitivity for a receiver—the results are lobes or, in other instances, landscapes ranging from smoothly undulating hills and valleys to fields of jagged peaks and crevasses.

Regardless of the source of the data plotted or the algorithms used for a simulation, the visual presentation is not simply a gimmick to impress, but a very useful tool to allow use of our own most sensitive tools: color eyesight, superior image processing and unequaled pattern recognition.

SPEEDING UP FLOATING-POINT CALCULATIONS

One problem often encountered in executing simulations is slow processing caused by repetitive floating-point calculations. In some cases, floating-point operations simply cannot be avoided; when such is the circumstance, the only solution is a math coprocessor.

But, in other cases, even when fractional interim values are desired or needed, these can be derived using integer rather than floating-point operations by the simple expedient of limiting accuracy to what is needed.

For example, suppose that an algorithm that is called repeatedly (several thousand times per simulation cycle) needs to calculate a radial distance using *pi*. Since the result of the calculation will be typecast as an integer and used as an index to a data array, however, the calculation does not need to be carried out to 10 or 12 decimal places—or even to three or four places. Therefore, instead of using a floating-point value for *pi* such as 3.14159, the calculations can be carried out as integer operations (which are faster) by using the value 402 (*pi * 128*) and then dividing the result by shifting seven places to the right.

The bit-shift operation is fast—considerably faster than any decimal division—and the entire process is appreciably faster than floating-point operations, while achieving the same end result.

USING THE VIRTUAL SCREEN AS MEMORY

A second area that poses more than a little inconvenience in simulations is the 64k size limit imposed on data arrays under both MS-DOS and Windows. While multiple arrays provide one means of circumventing this limitation and, under MS-DOS, an XMS driver can be used to write larger arrays directly in extended memory (above the 1Mb mark); likewise, neither is particularly convenient.

NOTE. This is also a continuing reason for Unix/Xenix being a popular environment for simulations and may prove to be one of the strengths of OS/2 Version 2. Alternately, Windows NT is also rumored to provide a flat memory environment, finally overcoming a hang-up that should never have been established in the first place.

The good news is that, within MS-DOS and Windows systems, there is one area where an array of flat memory lacking the 64k limit can be found. The bad news is that there are limitations on how it can be used—sometimes stringent limitations.

The memory area in question is, of course, the video memory, which, on an SVGA system using a 640-by-480-pixel display, forms a continuous array of some 300k, some five times larger than normal array limitations. Alternately, as a 1,024-by-768 display, the possible array size more than doubles to 768k.

The drawback is twofold: first, that anything written to this data area directly affects the display itself, and second, that both read and write operations (using *GetPixel* / *SetPixel* under Windows or *getpixel* / *putpixel* under MS-DOS) are somewhat slower than other memory accesses. And the advantage, obviously, is that the display does not have to be rewritten to show changes in the simulation data.

Still, when appropriate, accessing the video memory as a data buffer is permissible and, if the palette colors are carefully assigned, can be quite advantageous. (Note that under Windows, the GetPixel and SetPixel API calls do not actually access the physical video memory directly, but they still act as if they did, which is all that's really required.)

If you would like to experiment in this area, the Forest.C program can be adapted to use pixel operations instead of the present mapped rectangles. Don't forget to make the defined palette colors active before using GetPixel to read the data from the virtual screen and SetPixel to write changes to the virtual screen.

Oh, yes, remember that GetPixel returns an RGB value, not the palette index that it retrieved from memory. The RGB value will need to be reconverted to get the appropriate palette index identifier. For this, use the techniques demonstrated in Chapter 12 in the MapDemo program.

SUMMARY

There is some justification for the attitude that video graphics are designed for two purposes: pretty pictures and video games. After all, editors and text processors got along fine for years without graphics, spreadsheets likewise, modem

communications still have little real use for graphics, and aside from typesetting, the only real applications that absolutely require graphics are… yep…
video games and pretty pictures.

As you have seen, however, graphic simulations are one of the few other
areas where video graphics accomplish a task that simply cannot be handled in
any other fashion.

At the same time, graphic simulations are far more than simply pretty pictures (particularly as "pretty" is secondary, at best). Instead, graphic simulations present information in an active, visual format that is, quite simply, the
optimal interface format between our desktop (or portable) computers and
our internal pattern processing and recognition facilities.

Since, unlike Shakespeare's Shylock, a computer hath not eyes—nor the
dedicated parallel preprocessors necessary to use them—the obvious solution
is the graphical interface supplied by computer graphic simulations. If these
are also fun in the bargain, simply consider it a bonus.

PROGRAM LISTING OF FOREST.C

```
//=======================//
//       Forest.C        //
//   Simulation Example  //
//=======================//

#include <windows.h>
#include <string.h>
#include <stdlib.h>
#include <time.h>
#include "forest.h"

static COLORREF cColor[16] =
    {  DampSoil,   DrySoil,     //  0,  1
       NewGrowth,  Green1,      //  2,  3
       Green2,     Green3,      //  4,  5
       Mature,     Green4,      //  6,  7
       Green5,     Green6,      //  8,  9
       Green7,     OldGrowth,   // 10, 11
       Burning,    Embers,      // 12, 13
       BurnOut,    Bare    };   // 14, 15

#define  szCaption  "Forest World -- Year: %d"
#define  GRID  100
#define  xOfs  4
#define  yOfs  4
```

```
BYTE    Acres[GRID][GRID], NewAC[GRID][GRID], ActiveTimer;
int     nYears = 0, nDays, nWind;
HANDLE  hInst;

int CheckPos( int nPos )
{
   if( nPos < 0 )    nPos += GRID;
   if( nPos >= GRID ) nPos -= GRID;
   return( nPos );
}

void AgeWorld()
{
   int  i, j;

   for( i=0; i<GRID; i++ )
     for( j=0; j<GRID; j++ )
     {
        NewAC[i][j] = Acres[i][j];
        switch( Acres[i][j] )
        {
           case iNewGrowth:
           case iGreen1:   case iGreen2:
           case iGreen3:   case iMature:
           case iGreen4:   case iGreen5:
           case iGreen6:   case iGreen7:
              if( ! random(5) )
                 NewAC[i][j] = Acres[i][j] + 1;    break;
           case iOldGrowth:
              if( ! random(199) )
                 NewAC[i][j] = iBare;              break;
           case iBurning: NewAC[i][j] = iEmbers;  break;
           case iEmbers:  NewAC[i][j] = iBurnOut; break;
           case iBurnOut: NewAC[i][j] = iBare;    break;
           case iBare:
              NewAC[i][j] = iDampSoil + random(2); break;
}      }   }

void PropagateTrees()
{
   int  i, j, x, y;

   for( i=0; i<GRID; i++ )
     for( j=0; j<GRID; j++ )
        if( ( NewAC[i][j] >= iMature ) &&
```

```
                ( NewAC[i][j] < iBurning ) &&
                ( random(3) ) )
            {
               x = CheckPos( i + ( random(7) - 3 ) );
               y = CheckPos( j + ( random(7) - 3 ) );
               if( ( NewAC[x][y] == iDampSoil ) ||
                   ( NewAC[x][y] == iDrySoil  ) ||
                   ( NewAC[x][y] == iBare     ) )
                  NewAC[x][y] = iNewGrowth;
}        }

void StepForest()
{
   int  i, j;

   for( i=0; i<GRID; i++ )
      for( j=0; j<GRID; j++ )
         Acres[i][j] = NewAC[i][j];
}


void InitBurns( HWND hwnd )
{
   int  i, j, x, y, NoChance = 20;

   x = random( GRID );
   y = random( GRID );
   if( random(iOldGrowth+NoChance) <= Acres[x][y] )
   {
      nDays = 0;
      nWind = random(4);
      Acres[x][y] = iBurning;
      PostMessage( hwnd, WM_COMMAND, IDM_STOPGROWTH, 0L );
      PostMessage( hwnd, WM_COMMAND, IDM_STARTBURNS, 0L );
}    }


void IgniteTrees( int xPos, int yPos )
{
   xPos = CheckPos( xPos );
   yPos = CheckPos( yPos );
   if( ( Acres[xPos][yPos] >= iGreen1 ) &&
       ( Acres[xPos][yPos] <= iOldGrowth ) &&
       ( Acres[xPos][yPos] > random(iOldGrowth+2) ) )
      Acres[xPos][yPos] = iBurning;
}


int TrackFire()
```

```
{
   static int  i, j, x, y, Burns, WindSpeed;
   char        szBuff[80], szWind[6];

   WindSpeed = random(4)+2;
   Burns = 0;
   switch( nWind )
   {
      case 0: strcpy( szWind, "North" ); break;
      case 1: strcpy( szWind, "West" );  break;
      case 2: strcpy( szWind, "South" ); break;
      case 3: strcpy( szWind, "East" );
   }
   sprintf( szBuff,
            "Forest World -- Year: %d  Burn: %d"
            "  Wind from %s at %d",
            nYears, ++nDays, szWind, WindSpeed );
   SetWindowText( GetFocus(), szBuff );
   switch( nWind )
   {
      case 0:      // wind from North
         SetWindowText( GetFocus(), szBuff );
         for( j=GRID-1; j>=0; j-- )
            for( i=GRID-1; i>=0; i-- )
            {
               if( ( Acres[i][j] == iBurning ) ||
                   ( Acres[i][j] == iEmbers  ) )
               {
                  Burns++;
                  for( y=1; y<WindSpeed; y++ )
                     for( x=-y; x<=y; x++ )
                        IgniteTrees( i+x, j+y );
               }
               if( Acres[i][j] == iEmbers )
                  Acres[i][j] = iBurnOut;
               if( ( nDays > random(20)+5 ) &&
                   ( Acres[i][j] == iBurning ) )
                  Acres[i][j] = iEmbers;
            }
            break;

      case 1:     // wind from West
         for( i=GRID-1; i>=0; i-- )
            for( j=GRID-1; j>=0; j-- )
            {
               if( ( Acres[i][j] == iBurning ) ||
```

```
                        ( Acres[i][j] == iEmbers  ) )
                {
                  Burns++;
                  for( x=1; x<WindSpeed; x++ )
                    for( y=-x; y<=x; y++ )
                      IgniteTrees( i+x, j+y );
                }
                if( Acres[i][j] == iEmbers )
                  Acres[i][j] = iBurnOut;
                if( ( nDays > random(20)+5 ) &&
                    ( Acres[i][j] == iBurning ) )
                  Acres[i][j] = iEmbers;
            }
        break;

case 2:     // wind from South
    for( j=0; j<GRID; j++ )
      for( i=0; i<GRID; i++ )
        {
            if( ( Acres[i][j] == iBurning ) ||
                ( Acres[i][j] == iEmbers  ) )
                {
                  Burns++;
                  for( y=1; y<WindSpeed; y++ )
                    for( x=-y; x<=y; x++ )
                      IgniteTrees( i-x, j-y );
                }
                if( Acres[i][j] == iEmbers )
                  Acres[i][j] = iBurnOut;
                if( ( nDays > random(20)+5 ) &&
                    ( Acres[i][j] == iBurning ) )
                  Acres[i][j] = iEmbers;
            }
        break;

case 3:     // wind from East
    for( i=0; i<GRID; i++ )
      for( j=0; j<GRID; j++ )
        {
            if( ( Acres[i][j] == iBurning ) ||
                ( Acres[i][j] == iEmbers  ) )
                {
                  Burns++;
                  for( x=1; x<WindSpeed; x++ )
                    for( y=-x; y<=x; y++ )
                      IgniteTrees( i-x, j-y );
```

```
            }
            if( Acres[i][j] == iEmbers )
               Acres[i][j] = iBurnOut;
            if( ( nDays > random(20)+5 ) &&
                ( Acres[i][j] == iBurning ) )
               Acres[i][j] = iEmbers;
      }           }
   return( Burns );  // is anything still burning?
}

#pragma argsused

long FAR PASCAL WndProc( HWND hwnd,   WORD msg,
                         WORD wParam, LONG lParam )
{
   static int   i, j, xPos, yPos;
   char         szBuff[64];
   HDC          hdc, hdcInfo;
   HMENU        hMenu;
   HBRUSH       hBrush[16], hOldBrush;
   RECT         rect;
   PAINTSTRUCT  ps;
   FARPROC      lpProc;

   switch( msg )
   {
      case WM_CREATE:
         randomize();
         ActiveTimer = NULL;
         sprintf( szBuff, szCaption, nYears );
         SetWindowText( hwnd, szBuff );
         for( i=0; i<GRID; i++ )         // init world as
            for( j=0; j<GRID; j++ )      // bare ground
               Acres[i][j] = random(2);
         return(0);

      case WM_COMMAND:
         switch( wParam )
         {
            case IDM_STARTTIMER:
               EnableMenuItem( GetMenu(hwnd),
                            IDM_STARTTIMER, MF_GRAYED );
               EnableMenuItem( GetMenu(hwnd),
                            IDM_STOPTIMER, MF_ENABLED );
               switch( ActiveTimer )
               {
```

```
        case ID_GROWTH:
            PostMessage( hwnd, WM_COMMAND,
                            IDM_STARTGROWTH, 0L );
            break;
        case ID_FIRES:
            PostMessage( hwnd, WM_COMMAND,
                            IDM_STARTBURNS, 0L );
            break;
    }
    break;

case IDM_STOPTIMER:
    EnableMenuItem( GetMenu(hwnd),
                    IDM_STOPTIMER,  MF_GRAYED );
    EnableMenuItem( GetMenu(hwnd),
                    IDM_STARTTIMER, MF_ENABLED );
    switch( ActiveTimer )
    {
        case ID_GROWTH:
            PostMessage( hwnd, WM_COMMAND,
                            IDM_STOPGROWTH, 0L );
            break;
        case ID_FIRES:
            PostMessage( hwnd, WM_COMMAND,
                            IDM_STOPBURNS, 0L );
            break;
    }
    break;

case IDM_STARTGROWTH:
    SetTimer( hwnd, ID_GROWTH, 1000, NULL );
    ActiveTimer = ID_GROWTH;
    break;

case IDM_STOPGROWTH:
    KillTimer( hwnd, ID_GROWTH );
    break;

case IDM_STARTBURNS:
    SetTimer( hwnd, ID_FIRES, 500, NULL );
    ActiveTimer = ID_FIRES;
    break;

case IDM_STOPBURNS:
    KillTimer( hwnd, ID_FIRES );
    break;
```

```
                    case IDM_RESEED:
                       randomize();
                       nYears = 0;
                       for( i=0; i<100; i++ )
                       {
                          xPos = random(GRID);
                          yPos = random(GRID);
                          Acres[xPos][yPos] = iNewGrowth;
                          rect.left = xPos + xOfs;
                          rect.right = rect.left + 1;
                          rect.top = yPos + yOfs;
                          rect.bottom = rect.top + 1;
                       }
                       EnableMenuItem( GetMenu(hwnd),
                                  IDM_STOPTIMER, MF_ENABLED );
                       PostMessage( hwnd, WM_COMMAND,
                                  IDM_STARTGROWTH, 0L );
                       InvalidateRect( hwnd, NULL, FALSE );
                       break;
                 }
                 return(0);

          case WM_PAINT:
             hdc = BeginPaint( hwnd, &ps );
             GetClientRect( hwnd, &rect );
             SetMapMode( hdc, MM_ISOTROPIC );
             SetWindowOrg( hdc, 0, 0 );
             SetWindowExt( hdc, (110*GRID)/rect.right,
                                (110*GRID)/rect.bottom );
             SetViewportExt( hdc, GRID, GRID );
             for( i=0; i<16; i++ )
                hBrush[i] = CreateSolidBrush( cColor[i] );
             for( i=0; i<GRID; i++ )
                for( j=0; j<GRID; j++ )
                {
                   SetRect( &rect, i+xOfs,   j+yOfs,
                                   i+xOfs+1, j+yOfs+1 );
                   FillRect( hdc, &rect, hBrush[Acres[i][j]]);
                }
             for( i=0; i<16; i++ )
                DeleteObject( hBrush[i] );
             EndPaint( hwnd, &ps );
             return(0);

          case WM_TIMER:
```

```c
            switch( wParam )
            {
               case ID_GROWTH:
                  sprintf( szBuff, szCaption, nYears++ );
                  SetWindowText( hwnd, szBuff );
                  AgeWorld();
                  PropagateTrees();
                  StepForest();
                  InitBurns( hwnd );
                  InvalidateRect( hwnd, NULL, FALSE );
                  break;

               case ID_FIRES:
                  MessageBeep( NULL );
                  if( ! random(4) ) nWind = random(4);
                  if( ! TrackFire() )
                  {
                     PostMessage( hwnd, WM_COMMAND,
                                  IDM_STOPBURNS, ØL );
                     PostMessage( hwnd, WM_COMMAND,
                                  IDM_STARTGROWTH, ØL );
                  }
                  InvalidateRect( hwnd, NULL, FALSE );
                  break;
            }
            return(Ø);

         case WM_DESTROY:
            PostMessage( hwnd, WM_COMMAND,
                         IDM_STOPTIMER, ØL );
            PostQuitMessage(Ø);
            return(Ø);
   }
   return( DefWindowProc( hwnd, msg, wParam, lParam ) );
}

#pragma argsused

int PASCAL WinMain( HANDLE hInstance,
                    HANDLE hPrevInstance,
                    LPSTR  lpszCmdParam, int nCmdShow )
{
   char     szAppName[] = "FOREST";
   HWND     hwnd;
   MSG      msg;
   WNDCLASS wc;
```

```
   if( ! hPrevInstance )
   {
      wc.hInstance     = hInstance;
      wc.lpfnWndProc   = WndProc;
      wc.cbClsExtra    = 0;
      wc.cbWndExtra    = 0;
      wc.lpszClassName = szAppName;
      wc.hIcon         = LoadIcon( hInstance, szAppName );
//====================================================//
//    wc.hIcon        = NULL;                          //
//  if a null icon is assigned, the territory becomes  //
//  the map and the icon appears as a miniature of the //
//  Forest World display                               //
//====================================================//
      wc.lpszMenuName  = (LPSTR) szAppName;
      wc.hCursor       = LoadCursor( NULL, IDC_ARROW );
      wc.hbrBackground = GetStockObject( WHITE_BRUSH );
      wc.style         = CS_HREDRAW | CS_VREDRAW;
      RegisterClass( &wc );
   }
   hInst = hInstance;
   hwnd = CreateWindow( szAppName, "Forest Simulation",
                        WS_OVERLAPPEDWINDOW,
                        CW_USEDEFAULT, CW_USEDEFAULT,
                        CW_USEDEFAULT, CW_USEDEFAULT,
                        NULL, NULL, hInstance, NULL  );
   ShowWindow(   hwnd, nCmdShow );
   UpdateWindow( hwnd );
   while( GetMessage( &msg, NULL, 0, 0 ) )
   {
      TranslateMessage( &msg );
      DispatchMessage(  &msg );
   }
   return( msg.wParam );
}


;============================
;  Forest.DEF
;============================

NAME          Forest

DESCRIPTION   "Forest Simulation"
EXETYPE       WINDOWS
STUB          "WINSTUB.EXE"
```

```
CODE            PRELOAD MOVEABLE DISCARDABLE
DATA            PRELOAD MOVEABLE MULTIPLE
HEAPSIZE        1024
STACKSIZE       8192
EXPORTS         WndProc



//=============//
//   Forest.H   //
//=============//

#define   IDM_STARTTIMER     101    // MENU ITEM
#define   IDM_STOPTIMER      102    // MENU ITEM
#define   IDM_STARTGROWTH    103    // NON-MENU
#define   IDM_STOPGROWTH     104    // NON-MENU
#define   IDM_STARTBURNS     105    // NON-MENU
#define   IDM_STOPBURNS      106    // NON-MENU
#define   IDM_RESEED         107    // MENU ITEM


#define   ID_GROWTH            1    // GROWTH TIMER
#define   ID_FIRES             2    // BURN TIMER


#define   DampSoil   RGB( 0x60, 0x40, 0x20 ) // DAMP SOIL
#define   iDampSoil    0
#define   DrySoil    RGB( 0x75, 0x50, 0x00 ) // DRY SOIL
#define   iDrySoil     1
#define   NewGrowth  RGB( 0x90, 0xFF, 0x90 ) // YOUNG GROWTH
#define   iNewGrowth   2
#define   Green1     RGB( 0x75, 0xFF, 0x75 )
#define   iGreen1      3
#define   Green2     RGB( 0x60, 0xFF, 0x60 )
#define   iGreen2      4
#define   Green3     RGB( 0x45, 0xFF, 0x45 )
#define   iGreen3      5
#define   Mature     RGB( 0x30, 0xFF, 0x30 ) // MATURE TREES
#define   iMature      6
#define   Green4     RGB( 0x00, 0xF0, 0x00 )
#define   iGreen4      7
#define   Green5     RGB( 0x00, 0xC0, 0x00 )
#define   iGreen5      8
#define   Green6     RGB( 0x00, 0x90, 0x00 )
#define   iGreen6      9
#define   Green7     RGB( 0x00, 0x70, 0x00 )
#define   iGreen7     10
#define   OldGrowth  RGB( 0x10, 0x50, 0x00 ) // OLD GROWTH
```

```
#define iOldGrowth  11
#define  Burning    RGB( 0xFF, 0x10, 0x10 ) // HOT FIRE
#define iBurning    12
#define  Embers     RGB( 0x70, 0x30, 0x30 ) // EMBERS
#define iEmbers     13
#define  BurnOut    RGB( 0x60, 0x60, 0x40 ) // ASHES
#define iBurnOut    14
#define  Bare       RGB( 0x70, 0x70, 0x30 ) // ASHY GROUND
#define iBare       15
```

Super VGA (SVGA) Graphics For MS-DOS and Windows

W ith falling prices and new, more sophisticated applications demanding more sophisticated color, Super VGA video cards are rapidly becoming the new standard, replacing conventional VGA video cards
just as VGA supplanted the earlier EGA and CGA standards. Unfortunately,
however, neither MS-DOS nor Windows yet provide complete support for
SVGA graphics capabilities.

In Chapter 4 the problems involved in installing original equipment manufacturers' SVGA drivers were mentioned but, even after the appropriate drivers
are in use, there is another area where applications must make special provisions before being truly SVGA-compatible: color palettes.

Where earlier video standards are supported—under both MS-DOS and
Windows—thus far, no standardized provisions have been made in support of
the SVGA 256-color palettes. By default, of course, the SVGA video modes do
use the existing 16-color MS-DOS VGA palette and the 20-color Windows palette but, in either case, the defaults provided less than 10 percent of the possible
palette colors.

Obviously, in many cases, the default colors will be adequate and no further
provisions required and, in other cases, such as displaying images, the necessary palette colors are supplied within the image file itself. There are still applications, however, for which neither of the preceding apply and, therefore, one
or more custom palettes must be supplied.

Also, while customizing individual palette entries has been demonstrated—
for a Windows application, at least—nothing has been said yet about creating
entire palettes or about creating SVGA palettes for MS-DOS applications.

And, although this book has been primarily about Windows graphics, as you may have noticed in Chapter 14 when using the Forest.C demo, some applications are not ideally suited for Windows and can still be better executed under MS-DOS.

Furthermore, because MS-DOS remains important but has been secondary thus far in this book, this section will begin with MS-DOS examples for SVGA palette handling before adapting these examples to a Windows application.

SVGA HARDWARE AND SOFTWARE REQUIREMENTS

Obviously, SVGA video features cannot be used without the appropriate hardware (an SVGA video board and a compatible monitor).

There is also, however, a second requirement: an SVGA video driver. In general, OEM sources (video card manufacturers) supply SVGA video drivers for compatibility with major applications such as Windows, Ventura Publisher, Lotus, and AutoCad. At the same time little, if any, support is provided for application developers, although some sources may include limited document files or occasional code samples.

Happily, application developers do not necessarily need the complicated support drivers required by so many finished, commercial applications. For generic use, Borland International supplies an SVGA driver (SVGA256.BGI) while several independent sources, such as Thomas Design's ISVGA256 driver package (available on CompuServe), provide alternative drivers together with additional documentation and some interesting code examples.

SVGA FOR MS-DOS

The examples provided here are written for the SVGA256.BGI driver and expect a 320-by-200, 640-by-400 or 640-by-480-pixel display supporting a 256-color palette.

NOTE. No provision is included to support higher-resolution SVGA modes such as 800-by-600 pixels and 1,024-by-768 pixels.

Ideally, the MS-DOS demo program is written for the 640-by-480-pixel display mode, although the Windows counterpart example (SVGA_WIN.C) is less limited. Both demonstration programs create and display four 256-color palettes in two formats: a 16-by-16 grid array and a bull's-eye target (256 concentric circles using a progression of colors). The first example, SVGA_DOS, also demonstrates how an application loads and uses a nonstandard driver—a feature that, under Windows, is still required but is accomplished in a different fashion, outside of the SVGA_WIN example.

INSTALLING AN SVGA DRIVER (MS-DOS ONLY)

The SVGA_DOS program, in place of the usual *initgraph* function call, begins with a more explicit InitSVGAGraphics() call—calling a custom initialization function defined in the SVGA.I include file, as follows.

```
void InitSVGAGraphics()
{
    int   gdriver = DETECT, gmode;

    installuserdriver( "SVGA256", DetectSVGA );
    checkerrors();
    initgraph( &gdriver, &gmode,
             "F:\\BC\\BGI\\" );      // where is SVGA.BGI ?
    checkerrors();
    setaspectratio( 10000, 10000 );  // 1:1 aspect ratio
}
```

Borland C/C++ (or Turbo C or Turbo Pascal) makes provisions for third-party video drivers through the *installuserdriver* function that is called with two parameters: the name of the desired driver and an optional mode-detection function. Unlike most C-language or Windows functions, however, instead of testing the return value, a separate call to a *checkerrors()* function is used to test for an error result.

After installing an OEM or third-party driver, the *initgraph* function is called in the customary fashion and, last, *setaspectratio* is called to insure a 1-to-1 aspect ratio.

The DetectSVGA function, very loosely, is the counterpart of Borland's autodetect feature but, in this example, the response is determined by a define statement at the beginning of the SVGA_DOS program:

```
#define  SVGA640x480
```

In this example, the DetectSVGA function itself is simply a series of *#ifdef* statements:

```
int  huge  DetectSVGA()
{
#ifdef SVGA320x200
    return( 0 );                     //  320 x 200 x 256
#endif
#ifdef SVGA640x400
```

```
    return( 1 );                          //  640 x 400 x 256
#endif
#ifdef SVGA640x480
    return( 2 );                          //  640 x 480 x 256
#endif
#ifdef SVGA800x600
    return( 3 );                          //  800 x 600 x 256
#endif
#ifdef SVGA1024x768
    return( 4 );                          // 1024 x 768 x 256
#endif
};
```

In other circumstances, the Detect____ function may actually execute system tests to determine hardware capabilities.

After installing an SVGA (or any other) driver, all further graphics function calls are executed in the same fashion as any other graphics mode, with the exception of provisions explicit to the new driver, such as color range (palette size) and pixel resolution. At the same time, mode and system query functions, such as *getmaxx* or *gettextcolor*, can be expected to return values appropriate for the new graphics driver and active mode.

MS-DOS VERSUS WINDOWS COLOR SPECIFICATIONS

In previous examples, for Windows applications, color palette entries were defined by three byte values; one byte each setting the red, green, and blue color values, each with an individual value from 0 to 255.

For the MS-DOS SVGA palette settings, a similar format is used with the palette structure defined as an array of 256 unsigned *char* triplets. But, for the MS-DOS version, there is a difference because, even while these are essentially byte values representing RGB settings, here the individual color settings are limited to a 0 to 63 range—a six-bit value versus an eight-bit value.

Obviously, there is a discrepancy here but, visually, palettes defined by using full eight-bit values (under Windows) cannot be distinguished from palettes defined by using six-bit values (under MS-DOS). Thus, the only real difference is that palette creation functions for Windows generate the same values as MS-DOS palette creation functions, but shift the results left two bits to produce the equivalent result.

THE SCALED PALETTE

The first of these, the scaled palette, allocates 32 palette entries each to shades of red, blue, green, yellow, cyan, and magenta while the remaining 64 shades are reserved for a range of black to gray to white. In effect, the scaled palette replaces each of the conventional 16 palette entries with a range of 16 shades (red and light red together are replaced by 32 shades of red ranging from virtually black to the brightest red). Figure 15.1 shows the scaled palette (reproduced as grays) with the bull's-eye pattern overlying the color grid.

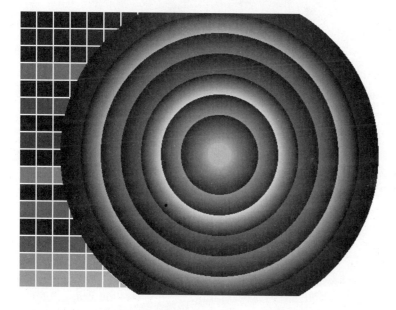

Figure 15.1: A scaled 256-color palette

The SetScaledPalette procedure (MS-DOS version) is found in the SVGA.I include file, together with the RGB, Hue, Saturation, Intensity (HSI), and gray palette procedures.

THE RGB PALETTE

The second 256-color palette, arbitrarily titled an RGB palette, weights the color assortment in favor of the three primary colors (red, green, and blue) and black through white, while the secondary colors (cyan, magenta, and yellow) are also represented but with a narrower assortment of shades. Figure 15.2 shows the RGB palette, again with the bull's-eye pattern overlying the color grid.

The scaled and RGB palettes are similar both in definition and range with the only real difference being the weight given to the primary (RGB) hues over the secondary (CMY) colors.

At the same time, a variety of other palettes can be created, by using essentially the same tool set, to suit special purposes or special applications.

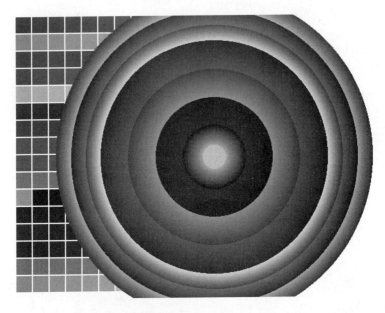

Figure 15.2: An RGB 256-color palette

For example, both the scaled and RGB palettes consist only of three groups—grays, primary colors, and secondary color hues—but provide a range of varying intensities in each. In both palettes, the grays consist of varying intensities of balanced red, green, and blue, producing white when all three are at maximum intensity. At the same time, the three primary color ranges consist of varying intensities of pure red, pure green, or pure blue while the secondary (or complementary) colors consist of varying intensities of balanced color pairs—that is, green and blue (cyan), red and green (yellow), or red and blue (magenta).

But, while this may initially appear to offer a useful variety of colors, for a painting program, for instance, either selection would be quite limiting because no mixed colors are provided, such as browns, mauves, golds, gray-greens, purples, pastels, off-whites or any of the thousands of other colors that are expressed as varying combinations (not balanced) of two or three of the RGB primaries.

Although all of these possible palettes are generated in essentially the same fashion, a 256-color palette is not large enough to contain substantial ranges of all possible hues. This limitation is also a principal reason for the development of 24-bit video boards.

Still, even if and when 24-bit video becomes the standard, it will not supplant the use of palettes in many applications; it will only make palettes more popular with provisions for switching between, for example, a palette of primary and secondary color, a palette of pastel hues, a palette of earth tones, and so forth.

Last, while the two preceding palette algorithms can be used, with modification, to create any desired colors, there are two other principal palette algorithms that deserve attention: the HSI and gray palettes.

THE HSI PALETTE

The third palette example uses a different approach to generate colors, employing an algorithm and method known as HSI, or **H**ue, **S**aturation, **I**ntensity.

The 256-color HSI palette begins with a set of 16 grays (ranging from black to white) before getting down to the real task of generating four intensity levels, three saturation levels within each intensity level, and 20 hues for each saturation level for a total of 240 colors to complete the palette entries.

```
for( X=0; X<3; X++ )
{                        // four intensities
   I = (double)( ( X + 2.0 ) / 4.0 );
   for( Y=0; Y<2; Y++ )
   {                     // three saturation levels
      S = (double)( ( Y + 2.0 ) / 3.0 );
      for( Z=0; Z<19; Z++ ) // 20 hues
      {                  // H,S,I between 0 and 1
         H = (double)( Z / 20.0 );
         Hsi2Rgb( H, S, I, Index++ );
} } }                        // calc and store as R, G, B
```

HSI color values consist of fractions—values in the range 0.0 through 1.0 with a triplet (1.0,1.0,1.0), the rough equivalent of an RGB (0xFF, 0xFF, 0xFF). But, before an HSI color can be used as a palette entry, the fractional values are passed to the Hsi2Rgb function for conversion.

```
void Hsi2Rgb( double H, double S, double I, int Index )
{
   double    T, Rv, Gv, Bv;

   T  = (double)( 2.0 * PI * H );
   Rv = (double)( 1.0 + S * sin( T - 2.0 * PI / 3.0 ) );
   Gv = (double)( 1.0 + S * sin( T ) );
   Bv = (double)( 1.0 + S * sin( T + 2.0 * PI / 3.0 ) );
   T  = (double)( 63.999 * I / 2.0 );
   PalBuff[Index][0] = (int)( Rv * T );
   PalBuff[Index][1] = (int)( Gv * T );
   PalBuff[Index][2] = (int)( Bv * T );
}
```

The result (as shown in Figure 15.3) is a series of mixed colors that progress in intensity and hue. The order in which the colors are generated (within the palette) can be altered by changing the order of the three loops in the SetHSIPalette function or by changing the Index values passed to the Hsi2Rgb function.

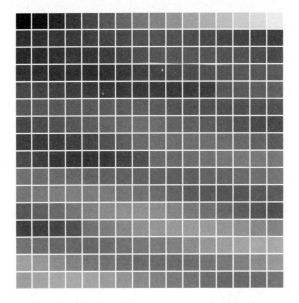

Figure 15.3: An HSI palette

While most applications will find either the preceding scaled or RGB palettes or the following gray-scale palette more useful than the ordering in the HSI palette, hue, saturation, intensity ordering is used by some systems (particularly photography and dye-stuffs) simply because its color-generation algorithm matches the system's physical (chemical or hardware) characteristics.

THE GRAY PALETTE

The fourth palette illustrated (Figure 15.4), is a gray-scale palette—that is, while the individual hues are defined as RGB values, for each palette entry, the three color values are equal (balanced), varying only in overall intensity (ergo, grays).

Granted, color is the most common display format but there are still circumstances where only varying degrees of black and white are practical (for example, most printer systems) and a gray palette, even on a color monitor, is the most practical method of designing for the final output.

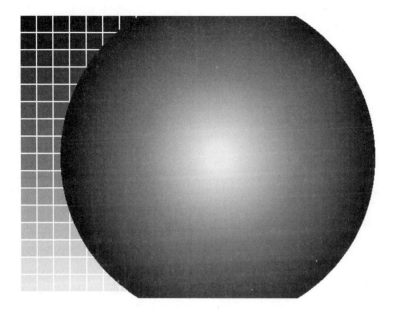

Figure 15.4: A palette of grays

THE VGASETALLPALETTE FUNCTION

After setting palette colors, under MS-DOS, the new palette is written to the video board by calling the VGASetAllPalette function, which, in turn, calls interrupt 10h, function 10h, and subfunction 12h to set multiple palette entries. The *bx* register provides the index of the first palette entry to be loaded while the *cx* register gives the number of palette entries to be replaced.

```
void VGASetAllPalette( SVGAPalette *PBuf )
{
   struct REGPACK reg;

   reg.r_ax = 0x1012;        // set entire color palette
   reg.r_bx = 0;
   reg.r_cx = 256;           // entries in palette
   reg.r_es = FP_SEG( PBuf ); // seg address of pal struct
   reg.r_dx = FP_OFF( PBuf ); // ofs address of pal struct
   intr( 0x10, &reg );
}
```

Last, before calling interrupt 10h, the *ex* and *dx* registers are loaded with the segment and offset addresses of the palette structure.

In like fashion, individual palette entries or smaller groups of palette entries can be changed by assigning the appropriate values in the *bx* and *cx* registers.

The SVGA_WIN program

The SVGA_WIN.C program provides the Windows equivalent of the SVGA_-DOS application, generating the same four palette variations. There are, however, a couple of important differences between the two versions.

First, as mentioned previously, where MS-DOS expects (and accepts) six-bit values for the red, green and blue color specifications, Windows expects eight-bit values (to conform to 24-bit true-color image standards). Therefore, while the same algorithms are employed in both versions, in the Windows version, the resulting RGB values have been shifted left two places, changing these from six-bit to eight-bit values with the two least significant bits as zeros.

Because, for all practical purposes (those involving the human eye) the two least significant bits in a color specification do not produce a distinguishable color difference, the differences between the six-bit and eight-bit RGB specifications are a distinction without relevance. (In like fashion, it is questionable whether Windows actually uses the two least significant bits in the absence of a true-color, 24-bit per pixel, video card.)

The second principal difference is how Windows handles 256-color palettes. As you will notice when executing the SVGA_WIN application, unlike the SVGA_DOS application, the last 20 palette entries shown will appear as black rather than whatever palette colors were assigned to the LPLOGPALETTE structure.

What has happened here, in effect, is that Windows has reserved the first 20 palette entries for the default palette colors, shifting the newly assigned palette entries to begin with the hardware's (video card's) palette entry 20.

Further, when the application accesses what it believes to be a 256-color palette, it is actually accessing a 236-color palette with an index offset of 20. As a result, all operations attempting to use palette entries 236 through 255 are actually accessing entries 256 through 275, and since these entries do not exist, they appear as black.

Figure 15.5, following, shows the scaled palette produced by SVGA_WIN. Contrasting this with Figure 15.1, produced by the MS-DOS version, notice both the black center of the bull's-eye target and the black palette grids at the lower-left, both of which are produced by the missing 20 palette entries.

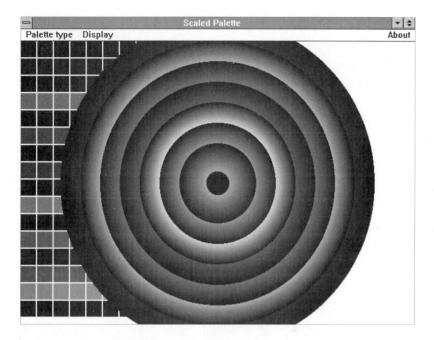

Figure 15.5: A scaled palette displayed by SVGA_WIN

In the eventuality that you actually need the full 256 SVGA colors for an application palette, rather than using the CreatePalette function to set up a new logical palette, the AnimatePalette function can be used to replace palette entries in the existing palette.

Like the MS-DOS interrupt function detailed previously, the AnimatePalette function accepts parameters for the starting palette index and the number of palette entries to be changed—thus permitting the replacement of selected palette elements without affecting the entire palette. As an added bonus, palette entries changed using AnimatePalette take effect immediately without requiring an update (repaint) of the application's window.

At the same time, of course, you need to be careful not to attempt to overwrite the 20 stock palette entries because doing so will affect other application's displays.

16-, 24-, AND 32-BIT COLOR IMAGES

Several previous mentions have been made of palette-independent, or true-color, image formats, generally as references to 24-bits-per-pixel images. Instead of defining image pixels by palette indexes (byte, nibble, or binary) where accompanying palettes provide the actual color definitions, in 24-bits-per-pixel images each pixel is identified by a full RGB color specification (eight bits each for the red, green, and blue values).

While this type of image format is still relatively new, it also is becoming increasingly common. But, until this format becomes standard, there also will be a real need to provide conversions from true-color to palette-based formats. Incidentally, this need also means creating a custom palette to fit the image.

One caveat is appropriate here: Although high-resolution images can be converted to limited palettes such as 16-color VGA, the results are hardly worth the trouble. At best, the image after conversion has a rather cartoon-like quality and, at worst, is unrecognizable. Therefore, the following algorithm suggestions will assume a minimal configuration of 256-color SVGA.

Caveat aside, regardless of the format of the source image—16, 24 or 32 bits per pixel—creating a custom palette follows essentially the same procedure and begins by stepping through the image to prepare a histogram or frequency table of the existing colors within the image.

For a 16-bit image, the existing pixel values are used precisely as is to create a table (or linked list or binary tree) of 16-bit colors. For 24- or 32-bit images, conversion can be simplified by ignoring the two or three least significant bits of each of the R, G, or B color values—thus building a smaller histogram concentrating on the important, most significant bits in each color.

Remember, the camera and computer can distinguish (or manufacturers claim they can) between color values that, to the human eye, have no differences and, for conversion to 256-color palettes, differences that cannot be distinguished are hardly worth the trouble of preservation attempts—particularly when other, more important color information will be subsumed anyway.

Now, although an array of records might, at first, appear to be the ideal method of building the histogram information, whether you're operating under MS-DOS or Windows, that old familiar 64k data element limit is quite likely to interfere. Instead, a pointer-linked list or even a binary tree structure offers a valid alternative without causing concern over data limits.

Once the histogram information is complete, the next step is to decide which colors should be used to build the palette. The simplest approach is to select the highest frequency colors and to build a palette consisting of them.

A second, somewhat more elegant approach, is to run back through the histogram with two criteria: first, eliminate all color values with a frequency below a selected threshold and, second, find color-value pairs which lie close together in absolute value, eliminating the lower-frequency instance. This approach continues until the color tree has been reduced to a maximum of 256 entries, which are then used to build the palette.

This second approach has the primary advantage of producing a better spread of colors by eliminating both those that are infrequent and those that are closely duplicated. The problem using this approach is to decide where the low-frequency cut-off should occur and to balance increasing color spread against the loss of important color elements.

A third variation, similar to gray-scale conversion, is to assign relative weights to the red, green, and blue values and to have the weights varying according to the image subject matter. For images of roses, for example, reds might be given a higher weight than greens and blues while, for sapphires, blues would be the important element or, for oceanographic images, reds might be minimized and both greens and blues given the principal weight.

A fourth, also specialized, approach involves creating a gray-scale image for SVGA display. For this last purpose, however, there is no need to create a color histogram. Instead, conversion can begin by creating a palette of 256 shades of gray and then proceed to the final step of mapping the image pixels—by gray-intensity values—to the output format.

Regardless of the approach, after creating the custom palette, the final step involves a second pass through the original image data, replacing the true-color pixel values with the closest equivalent palette-based index—and, of course, writing the results either as an appropriate image file format or directly to the display.

NOTE. For a Windows version, the GetNearestPaletteIndex function can be used to identify the existing palette entry that is the closest match to the new RGB value, greatly simplifying the process of mapping the image to the new palette.

SUMMARY

Even though Windows is an important programming environment, thus far it is not the final answer to all application requirements, nor is it likely—at least in the near future—to totally replace the MS-DOS operating system. At the same time, while neither MS-DOS nor Windows has yet provided true support for SVGA capabilities, 256-color-palette capabilities do provide an important tool (especially for the majority of us who cannot yet afford true-color systems) for many applications including painting and imaging programs and simulations.

On the other hand, although computer displays are rapidly moving toward the newest true-color standards, even when true color is common, palettes will still be an important element of many applications. They provide a more convenient (and faster) method for color selection than defining all colors individually via scroll bar or other controls.

Also, until true-color systems are standard, there will be a need for converting images from 24-bit (or higher) standards to formats supported by commonly available (six- and eight-bit) hardware.

The last 15 chapters have covered most of the important elements of graphics programming in Windows. But, because of limitations of space, time, and the author's skills, not all possible elements of Windows graphics have been covered. Thus, a world of possibilities remain for development, subject only to the limits of your imagination and programming skills.

So have fun, happy hacking, and the best of luck.

Program listing of SVGA_DOS.C

```c
//==============================//
//         SVGA_DOS.C           //
// DOS version SVGA Palettes    //
// include GRAPHICS.LIB         //
// library before compiling     //
//==============================//

#include <stdio.h>
#include <stdlib.h>
#include <conio.h>
#include <graphics.h>

#define  SVGA640x480

#include "svga.i"

int  BlockSize = 30;

void Comment1( char * szCaption, int iColor )
{
   setviewport( getmaxx()-150, 0, getmaxx(), 100, 1 );
   clearviewport();
   setviewport( 0, 0, getmaxx(), getmaxy(), 1 );
   settextjustify( RIGHT_TEXT, TOP_TEXT );
   setcolor( iColor );
   outtextxy( getmaxx(), 10, szCaption );
   outtextxy( getmaxx(), 35, "press any key" );
   outtextxy( getmaxx(), 50, "for bull's-eye" );
   outtextxy( getmaxx(), 65, "palette" );
```

```
}

void Comment2( char * szCaption, int iColor )
{
    setviewport( getmaxx()-150, 0, getmaxx(), 100, 1 );
    clearviewport();
    setviewport( 0, 0, getmaxx(), getmaxy(), 1 );
    settextjustify( RIGHT_TEXT, TOP_TEXT );
    setcolor( iColor );
    outtextxy( getmaxx(), 10, szCaption );
    outtextxy( getmaxx(), 35, "Return for" );
    outtextxy( getmaxx(), 50, "next palette" );
    outtextxy( getmaxx(), 65, "or Escape" );
    outtextxy( getmaxx(), 80, "to exit" );
}

void DrawBlockPalette()
{
    int i, j, k;

    for( i=0; i<16; i++ )
       for( j=0; j<16; j++ )
       {
           setcolor( j + i * 16 );
           for( k=0; k<BlockSize; k++ )
              line( BlockSize * j,
                    BlockSize * i + k,
                    BlockSize * ( j + 1 ) - 2,
                    BlockSize * i + k - 2 );
    }      }

void DrawTargetPalette()
{
    int  xCen, yCen, i;

    rectangle( 0, 0, getmaxx(), getmaxy() );
    xCen = getmaxx()/2;
    yCen = getmaxy()/2;
    for( i=0; i<256; i++ )
    {
        setcolor( 256-i );
//=== for transparent moire patterns, disable following ==
        if( i < 255 )
        {
            circle( xCen, yCen+1, i );
            circle( xCen+1, yCen, i );
```

```
        }
//=========================================================
        circle( xCen, yCen, i );
}   }

int  main()
{
    int   i, j, x, y, CVal, Done, PaletteStep = 0;
    char  szPalStr[20];

    InitSVGAGraphics();
    BlockSize = getmaxy() / 16;
    do
    {
        clearviewport();
        switch( PaletteStep )
        {
            case 0:  SetScaledPalette();
                     strcpy( szPalStr, "Scaled Palette" );
                     CVal = 0xFF ;
                     break;
            case 1:  SetRGBPalette();
                     strcpy( szPalStr, "RGB Palette" );
                     CVal = 0xFF;
                     break;
            case 2:  SetHSIPalette();
                     strcpy( szPalStr, "HSI Palette" );
                     CVal = 0x0F;
                     break;
            case 3:  SetGrayPalette();
                     strcpy( szPalStr, "Gray Palette" );
                     CVal = 0xFF;
                     break;
        }
        DrawBlockPalette();
        Comment1( szPalStr, CVal );
        Done = ( getch() == '\x1B' );
        if( !Done )
        {
            Comment2( szPalStr, CVal );
            DrawTargetPalette();
            Done = ( getch() == '\x1B' );
        }
        PaletteStep++;
        if( PaletteStep == 4 ) PaletteStep = 0;
    } while( ! Done );
```

```
    closegraph();
    return(0);
}
```

Program listing of SVGA.I

```
//========================================//
//   SVGA.I -- used by SVGA_DOS.C         //
//   supplies palette and init functions  //
//========================================//

#include <dos.h>
#include <math.h>
#include <graphics.h>

#define  PI      3.14159

typedef  unsigned  char  SVGAPalette[256][3];

SVGAPalette    PalBuff;
static int     SelectMode = 2;

void VGASetAllPalette( SVGAPalette *PBuf )
{
    struct REGPACK reg;

    reg.r_ax = 0x1012;          // set entire color palette
    reg.r_bx = 0;
    reg.r_cx = 256;             // entries in palette
    reg.r_es = FP_SEG( PBuf ); // seg address of pal struct
    reg.r_dx = FP_OFF( PBuf ); // ofs address of pal struct
    intr( 0x10, &reg );
}

void SetGrayPalette()
{
    int i, j;

    for( i=0; i<64; i++ )
        for( j=0; j<4; j++ )
            PalBuff[i*4+j][0] =
            PalBuff[i*4+j][1] =
            PalBuff[i*4+j][2] = i;
    VGASetAllPalette( &PalBuff );
}
```

```
void SetScaledPalette()
{
   int i, j, k;

   for( i=0,j=0; i<32; i++,j+=2 )          // Blue
   {
      PalBuff[i][2] = j;
      PalBuff[i][0] = PalBuff[i][1] = 0;
   }
   for( i=32,j=0; i<96; i++,j+=2 )         // Cyan
   {
      PalBuff[i][0] = 0;
      PalBuff[i][1] = PalBuff[i][2] = j;
   }
   for( i=64,j=0; i<96; i++,j+=2 )         // Magenta
   {
      PalBuff[i][1] = 0;
      PalBuff[i][0] = PalBuff[i][2] = j;
   }
   for( i=96,j=0; i<128; i++,j+=2 )        // Red
   {
      PalBuff[i][0] = j;
      PalBuff[i][1] = PalBuff[i][2] = 0;
   }
   for( i=128,j=0; i<160; i++,j+=2 )       // Yellow
   {
      PalBuff[i][2] = 0;
      PalBuff[i][0] = PalBuff[i][1] = j;
   }
   for( i=160,j=0; i<192; i++,j+=2 )       // Green
   {
      PalBuff[i][1] = j;
      PalBuff[i][0] = PalBuff[i][2] = 0;
   }
   for( i=192,j=0; i<256; i++,j++ )        // Grays & Whites
      PalBuff[i][0] = PalBuff[i][1] =
      PalBuff[i][2] = j;
   VGASetAllPalette( &PalBuff );
}

void SetRGBPalette()
{
   int i;

   for( i=0; i<24; i++ )
   {
```

```
      PalBuff[i][1]    = PalBuff[i][2] = 2*(i+8);
      PalBuff[i][0]    = 0;                    // Cyan
      PalBuff[i+24][0] = PalBuff[i+24][2] = 2*(i+8);
      PalBuff[i+24][1] = 0;                    // Magenta
      PalBuff[i+48][0] = PalBuff[i+48][1] = 2*(i+8);
      PalBuff[i+48][2] = 0;                    // Yellow
   }
   for( i=0; i<45; i++ )
   {
      PalBuff[i+72][1]  = PalBuff[i+72][2]  = 0;
      PalBuff[i+72][0]  = i+19;               // Red
      PalBuff[i+116][0] = PalBuff[i+116][2] = 0;
      PalBuff[i+116][1] = i+19;               // Green
      PalBuff[i+160][0] = PalBuff[i+160][1] = 0;
      PalBuff[i+160][2] = i+19;               // Blue
   }
   for( i=0; i<48; i++ )                       // Grays &
      PalBuff[i+204][0] =                      // Whites
      PalBuff[i+204][1] =
      PalBuff[i+204][2] = (int)( i * 64 / 48 );
   PalBuff[255][0] =
   PalBuff[255][1] =
   PalBuff[255][2] = 0xFF;
   VGASetAllPalette( &PalBuff );
}

void Hsi2Rgb( double H, double S, double I, int Index )
{
   double    T, Rv, Gv, Bv;

   T  = (double) ( 2.0 * PI * H );
   Rv = (double) ( 1.0 + S * sin( T - 2.0 * PI / 3.0  ) );
   Gv = (double) ( 1.0 + S * sin( T ) );
   Bv = (double) ( 1.0 + S * sin( T + 2.0 * PI / 3.0 ) );
   T  = (double) ( 63.999 * I / 2.0 );
   PalBuff[Index][0] = (int) ( Rv * T );
   PalBuff[Index][1] = (int) ( Gv * T );
   PalBuff[Index][2] = (int) ( Bv * T );
}

void SetHSIPalette()
{
   double  H, S, I;
   int     X, Y, Z, Index;

   for( Z=0; Z<=15; Z++ )        // create gray scale
```

```
            PalBuff[Z][0] =
            PalBuff[Z][1] =
            PalBuff[Z][2] = Z * 4;
      Index = 16;                    // create HSI spectrum
      for( X=0; X<=3; X++ )          // four intensities
      {
         I = (double)( ( X + 2.0 ) / 4.0 );
         for( Y=0; Y<=2; Y++ )       // three saturations
         {
            S = (double)( ( Y + 2.0 ) / 3.0 );
            for( Z=0; Z<=19; Z++ )   // 20 hues
            {                        // H,S,I between 0 and 1
               H = (double) ( Z / 20.0 );
               Hsi2Rgb( H, S, I, Index++ );
      } } }                          // calc and store R, G, B
      VGASetAllPalette( &PalBuff );
}


int  huge  DetectSVGA()
{
#ifdef SVGA320x200
   return( 0 );                         //  320 x 200 x 256
#endif
#ifdef SVGA640x400
   return( 1 );                         //  640 x 400 x 256
#endif
#ifdef SVGA640x480
   return( 2 );                         //  640 x 480 x 256
#endif
#ifdef SVGA800x600
   return( 3 );                         //  800 x 600 x 256
#endif
#ifdef SVGA1024x768
   return( 4 );                         // 1024 x 768 x 256
#endif
};


void checkerrors()
{            // check for and report any graphics errors
   int errorcode;

   errorcode = graphresult();     // get results of last
   if( errorcode != grOk )        // graphics operation
   {
      printf( "Graphics error: %s\n",
            grapherrormsg(errorcode) );
```

```
        printf( "Press any key to halt:" );
        getch();
        exit(1);
} }

void InitSVGAGraphics()
{
    int   gdriver = DETECT, gmode;

    installuserdriver( "SVGA256", DetectSVGA );
    checkerrors();
    initgraph( &gdriver, &gmode,
              "F:\\BC\\BGI\\" );     // where is SVGA.BGI ?
    checkerrors();
    setaspectratio( 10000, 10000 );  // 1:1 aspect ratio
}
```

PROGRAM LISTING OF SVGA_WIN.C

```
//===================================//
//          SVGA_WIN.C               //
//  Windows Version SVGA Palettes    //
//===================================//

#include <windows.h>
#include <alloc.h>
#include <dos.h>
#include <math.h>
#include <stdio.h>
#include <stdlib.h>
#include <conio.h>
#include "svga_win.h"

#define  PI    3.14159

HANDLE        hInst;               // application hInstance
HPALETTE      hPalOld, hPal = NULL;
LPLOGPALETTE  lPal;
int           Grid, Sphere;

#pragma argsused

BOOL FAR PASCAL About( HWND hDlg,   WORD msg,
                       WORD wParam, LONG lParam )
{
    switch( msg )
```

```
   {
      case WM_INITDIALOG: return( TRUE );
      case WM_COMMAND:
         switch( wParam )
         {
            case IDOK: EndDialog( hDlg, TRUE );
                       return( TRUE );
            default: return( TRUE );
   }        }
   return( FALSE );
}

void SetGrayPalette()
{
   int i, j;

   for( i=0; i<256; i++ )
      lPal->palPalEntry[i].peRed =
      lPal->palPalEntry[i].peGreen =
      lPal->palPalEntry[i].peBlue = i;
}

void SetScaledPalette()
{
   int i, j, k;

   for( i=0,j=0; i<32; i++,j+=8 )                 // blues
   {
      lPal->palPalEntry[i].peBlue = j;
      lPal->palPalEntry[i].peRed =
      lPal->palPalEntry[i].peGreen = 0;
   }
   for( i=32,j=0; i<96; i++,j+=8 )                // cyan
   {
      lPal->palPalEntry[i].peRed = 0;
      lPal->palPalEntry[i].peGreen =
      lPal->palPalEntry[i].peBlue = j;
   }
   for( i=64,j=0; i<96; i++,j+=8 )                // magenta
   {
      lPal->palPalEntry[i].peGreen = 0;
      lPal->palPalEntry[i].peRed =
      lPal->palPalEntry[i].peBlue = j;
   }
   for( i=96,j=0; i<128; i++,j+=8 )               // red
   {
```

```
        lPal->palPalEntry[i].peRed = j;
        lPal->palPalEntry[i].peGreen =
        lPal->palPalEntry[i].peBlue = 0;
    }
    for( i=128,j=0; i<160; i++,j+=8 )             // yellow
    {
        lPal->palPalEntry[i].peBlue = 0;
        lPal->palPalEntry[i].peRed =
        lPal->palPalEntry[i].peGreen = j;
    }
    for( i=160,j=0; i<192; i++,j+=8 )             // green
    {
        lPal->palPalEntry[i].peGreen = j;
        lPal->palPalEntry[i].peRed =
        lPal->palPalEntry[i].peBlue = 0;
    }
    for( i=192,j=0; i<256; i++,j+=4 )             // grays &
        lPal->palPalEntry[i].peRed =              // whites
        lPal->palPalEntry[i].peGreen =
        lPal->palPalEntry[i].peBlue = j;
}

void SetRGBPalette()
{
    int i;

    for( i=0; i<24; i++ )
    {
        lPal->palPalEntry[i].peGreen =            // Cyan
        lPal->palPalEntry[i].peBlue  = 8*(i+8);
        lPal->palPalEntry[i].peRed   = 0;
        lPal->palPalEntry[i+24].peRed =           // Magenta
        lPal->palPalEntry[i+24].peBlue = 8*(i+8);
        lPal->palPalEntry[i+24].peGreen = 0;
        lPal->palPalEntry[i+48].peRed =           // Yellow
        lPal->palPalEntry[i+48].peGreen = 8*(i+8);
        lPal->palPalEntry[i+48].peBlue = 0;
    }
    for( i=0; i<45; i++ )
    {
        lPal->palPalEntry[i+72].peGreen  =        // Red
        lPal->palPalEntry[i+72].peBlue  = 0;
        lPal->palPalEntry[i+72].peRed   = 4*(i+19);
        lPal->palPalEntry[i+116].peRed =          // Green
        lPal->palPalEntry[i+116].peBlue = 0;
        lPal->palPalEntry[i+116].peGreen = 4*(i+19);
```

```
         lPal->palPalEntry[i+160].peRed   =            // Blue
         lPal->palPalEntry[i+160].peGreen = 0;
         lPal->palPalEntry[i+160].peBlue  = 4*(i+19);
      }
   for( i=0; i<48; i++ )
      lPal->palPalEntry[i+204].peRed   =
      lPal->palPalEntry[i+204].peGreen =
      lPal->palPalEntry[i+204].peBlue  =
                                    (int)( i * 256 / 48 );
   lPal->palPalEntry[255].peRed   =
   lPal->palPalEntry[255].peGreen =
   lPal->palPalEntry[255].peBlue  = 0xFF;
}


void Hsi2Rgb( double H, double S, double I, int Index )
{
   double    T, Rv, Gv, Bv;

   T  = (double) ( 2.0 * PI * H );
   Rv = (double) ( 1.0 + S * sin( T - 2.0 * PI / 3.0 ) );
   Gv = (double) ( 1.0 + S * sin( T ) );
   Bv = (double) ( 1.0 + S * sin( T + 2.0 * PI / 3.0 ) );
   T  = (double) ( 63.999 * I / 2.0 );
   lPal->palPalEntry[Index].peRed   = (int)( Rv * T * 4 );
   lPal->palPalEntry[Index].peGreen = (int)( Gv * T * 4 );
   lPal->palPalEntry[Index].peBlue  = (int)( Bv * T * 4 );
}


void SetHSIPalette()
{
   double  H, S, I;
   int     X, Y, Z, Index;

   for( Z=0; Z<=15; Z++ )          // create gray scale
      lPal->palPalEntry[Z].peRed   =
      lPal->palPalEntry[Z].peGreen =
      lPal->palPalEntry[Z].peBlue  = Z * 16;

   Index = 16;                     // create HSI spectrum
   for( X=0; X<=3; X++ )           // four intensities
   {
      I = (double) ( ( X + 2.0 ) / 4.0 );
      for( Y=0; Y<=2; Y++ )        // three saturations levels
      {
         S = (double) ( ( Y + 2.0 ) / 3.0 );
         for( Z=0; Z<=19; Z++ )  // 20 hues
```

```
          {                              // H,S,I between 0 and 1
             H = (double) ( Z / 20.0 );
             Hsi2Rgb( H, S, I, Index++ );
} } } }                                  // calc and store R, G, B

long FAR PASCAL WndProc( HWND hwnd,    WORD msg,
                         WORD wParam, LONG lParam )
{
   FARPROC        lpProc;              // pointer to dialog box
   HMENU          hMenu;
   HDC            hdc, hdcMem;
   HPEN           hOldPen, hPen;
   HBRUSH         hOldBrush, hBrush;
   RECT           rect;
   PAINTSTRUCT    ps;
   unsigned int   BlockSize, xCen, yCen, i, j;

   switch( msg )
   {
      case WM_CREATE:
         lPal = (LPLOGPALETTE)
                 farmalloc( sizeof(LOGPALETTE) +
                            sizeof(PALETTEENTRY) * 256 );
         lPal->palVersion = 0x300;
         lPal->palNumEntries = 256;
         for( i=0; i<256; i++ )
         {
            lPal->palPalEntry[i].peRed =
            lPal->palPalEntry[i].peGreen =
            lPal->palPalEntry[i].peBlue = 0;
            lPal->palPalEntry[i].peFlags = PC_RESERVED;
         }
         Grid = Sphere = TRUE;
         PostMessage( hwnd, WM_COMMAND, IDM_SCALED, 0L );
         return(0);

      case WM_COMMAND:
         switch( wParam )
         {
            case IDM_SCALED:
               SetScaledPalette();
               SetWindowText( hwnd, "Scaled Palette" );
               InvalidateRect( hwnd, NULL, TRUE );
               break;
            case IDM_RGB:
               SetRGBPalette();
```

```
            SetWindowText( hwnd, "RGB Palette" );
            InvalidateRect( hwnd, NULL, TRUE );
            break;
        case IDM_HSI:
            SetHSIPalette();
            SetWindowText( hwnd, "HSI Palette" );
            InvalidateRect( hwnd, NULL, TRUE );
            break;
        case IDM_GRAY:
            SetGrayPalette();
            SetWindowText( hwnd, "Gray Palette" );
            InvalidateRect( hwnd, NULL, TRUE );
            .break;
        case IDM_GRID:
            if( Grid )
            {
                Grid = FALSE;
                CheckMenuItem( GetMenu(hwnd), IDM_GRID,
                        MF_BYCOMMAND | MF_UNCHECKED );
                Sphere = TRUE;
                CheckMenuItem( GetMenu(hwnd),
                            IDM_SPHERE,
                        MF_BYCOMMAND | MF_CHECKED );
                InvalidateRect( hwnd, NULL, TRUE );
            }
            else
            {
                Grid = TRUE;
                CheckMenuItem( GetMenu(hwnd), IDM_GRID,
                        MF_BYCOMMAND | MF_CHECKED );
                InvalidateRect( hwnd, NULL, FALSE );
            }
            break;
        case IDM_SPHERE:
            if( Sphere )
            {
                Sphere = FALSE;
                CheckMenuItem( GetMenu(hwnd),
                            IDM_SPHERE,
                        MF_BYCOMMAND | MF_UNCHECKED );
                Grid = TRUE;
                CheckMenuItem( GetMenu(hwnd), IDM_GRID,
                        MF_BYCOMMAND | MF_CHECKED );
                InvalidateRect( hwnd, NULL, TRUE );
            }
            else
```

```
            {
                Sphere = TRUE;
                CheckMenuItem( GetMenu( hwnd ),
                            IDM_SPHERE,
                        MF_BYCOMMAND | MF_CHECKED );
                InvalidateRect( hwnd, NULL, FALSE );
            }
            break;
        case IDM_ABOUT:
            lpProc = MakeProcInstance( About, hInst );
            DialogBox( hInst, "ABOUT", hwnd, lpProc );
            FreeProcInstance( lpProc );
            break;
        default: break;
        }
        return(0);

case WM_PAINT:
    hdc = BeginPaint( hwnd, &ps );
    GetClientRect( hwnd, &rect );
    BlockSize =
            (int)( ( rect.bottom - rect.top ) / 16 );
    xCen = (int)( ( rect.right - rect.left ) / 2 );
    yCen = (int)( ( rect.bottom - rect.top ) / 2 );
    hPal = CreatePalette( lPal );
    hPalOld = SelectPalette( hdc, hPal, FALSE );
    RealizePalette( hdc );
    if( Grid )
        for( i=0; i<16; i++ )
            for( j=0; j<16; j++ )
            {
                hPen = CreatePen( PS_SOLID, 1,
                        PALETTEINDEX( j + i * 16 ) );
                hOldPen = SelectObject( hdc, hPen );
                hBrush = CreateSolidBrush(
                        PALETTEINDEX( j + i * 16 ) );
                hOldBrush = SelectObject( hdc, hBrush );
                Rectangle( hdc,
                        BlockSize*j,
                        BlockSize*i,
                        BlockSize*(j+1)-2,
                        BlockSize*(i+1)-2 );
                SelectObject( hdc, hOldPen );
                DeleteObject( hPen );
                SelectObject( hdc, hOldBrush );
                DeleteObject( hBrush );
```

```
                }
            if( Sphere )
                for( i=0; i<256; i++ )
                {
                    hPen = CreatePen( PS_SOLID, 1,
                                      PALETTEINDEX(255-i) );
                    hOldPen = SelectObject( hdc, hPen );
//=== for transparent moire patterns, disable following ==
                    if( i < 255 )
                    {
                        Arc( hdc, xCen-i, yCen-i+1,
                                  xCen+i, yCen+i+1,
                                  0, 0, 0, 0 );
                        Arc( hdc, xCen-i+1, yCen-i,
                                  xCen+i+1, yCen+i,
                                  0, 0, 0, 0 );
                    }
//=========================================================
                    Arc( hdc, xCen-i, yCen-i,
                              xCen+i, yCen+i, 0, 0, 0, 0 );
                    SelectObject( hdc, hOldPen );
                    DeleteObject( hPen );
                }
            SelectPalette( hdc, hPalOld, FALSE );
            DeleteObject( hPal );
            DeleteDC( hdcMem );
            EndPaint( hwnd, &ps );
            return(0);

        case WM_DESTROY:
            farfree( lPal );
            PostQuitMessage(0);
            return(0);
    }
    return( DefWindowProc( hwnd, msg, wParam, lParam ) );
}


#pragma argsused

int PASCAL WinMain( HANDLE hInstance,
                    HANDLE hPrevInstance,
                    LPSTR  lpszCmdParam, int nCmdShow )
{
    static char szAppName[] = "SVGA_WIN";
    HWND        hwnd;
    MSG         msg;
```

```
        WNDCLASS    wc;

        if( ! hPrevInstance )
        {
            wc.hInstance     = hInstance;
            wc.lpfnWndProc   = WndProc;
            wc.cbClsExtra    = Ø;
            wc.cbWndExtra    = Ø;
            wc.lpszClassName = szAppName;
            wc.hIcon         = LoadIcon( hInstance, szAppName );
            wc.lpszMenuName  = (LPSTR) szAppName;
            wc.hCursor       = LoadCursor( NULL, IDC_ARROW );
            wc.hbrBackground = GetStockObject( WHITE_BRUSH );
            wc.style         = CS_HREDRAW | CS_VREDRAW;
            RegisterClass( &wc );
        }
        else GetInstanceData( hPrevInstance,
                              (PSTR) szAppName, 1Ø );
        hInst = hInstance;              // global instance handle
        hwnd = CreateWindow( szAppName, "SVGA Palette Viewer",
                            WS_OVERLAPPEDWINDOW,
                            CW_USEDEFAULT, CW_USEDEFAULT,
                            CW_USEDEFAULT, CW_USEDEFAULT,
                            NULL, NULL, hInstance, NULL );
        ShowWindow(   hwnd, nCmdShow );
        UpdateWindow( hwnd );
        while( GetMessage( &msg, NULL, Ø, Ø ) )
        {
            TranslateMessage( &msg );
            DispatchMessage(  &msg );
        }
        return( msg.wParam );
}


;===========================;
;  SVGA_WIN.DEF             ;
;  module definition file   ;
;===========================;

NAME          SVGA_WIN

DESCRIPTION   "SVGA 256-Color Palettes"
EXETYPE       WINDOWS
STUB          "WINSTUB.EXE"
CODE          PRELOAD MOVEABLE DISCARDABLE
DATA          PRELOAD MOVEABLE MULTIPLE
```

```
HEAPSIZE    1024
STACKSIZE   8192
EXPORTS     WndProc
            About


//==================//
//   SVGA_WIN.H     //
//==================//
#define IDM_SCALED 101
#define IDM_RGB    102
#define IDM_HSI    103
#define IDM_GRAY   104

#define IDM_GRID   105
#define IDM_SPHERE 106

#define IDM_ABOUT  107
```

APPENDIX A:
GRAPHIC AND APPLICATION
UTILITIES FOR WINDOWS
PROGRAMMERS

This appendix describes several utilities of interest to Windows programmers. Included are descriptions of application resource editors, ZSoft's graphics preparation program PhotoFinish, and image-compression utilities.

APPLICATION RESOURCE EDITORS

Programmers using both Windows version 3.0 and version 3.1 have enjoyed considerable support from a variety of sources, particularly in the form of high-level application generators and application-creation utilities. Originally, Windows programmers designing dialog boxes, menus, and other application accessories depended on the Resource Compiler in Microsoft's Software Development Kit (SDK) to compile and link resource scripts, which were essentially ASCII text scripts detailing how menus, dialog boxes, or other pop-up resources should appear.

Happily, however, such idiot work is increasingly being left to the appropriate idiot—the computer, rather than the programmer—with resource-creation facilities permitting interactive, on-screen resource design instead of laboriously written, compiled, linked, tested, and rewritten scripts.

Two of the principal interactive resource editors are Borland's Resource Workshop and Whitewater's Resource Toolkit, each described in the following sections.

BORLAND'S RESOURCE WORKSHOP

Borland's Resource Workshop—distributed with both BCW for Windows and Turbo Pascal for Windows—provides a selection of utilities for creating Windows application resources. Principal resource types include accelerators, bitmaps, cursors, icons, fonts, menus, and string tables.

Accelerators are key combinations pressed to perform a task in an application. They substitute for menu commands and, like menu commands, create WM_COMMAND or WM_SYSCOMMAND messages.

Bitmaps, including cursors and icons, are generated by a simple bitmap editor. While Resource segment bitmaps are limited to 64k, larger images may be more easily prepared using, for example, the PaintBrush utility and then imported to the application resource via the Resource Workshop.

Dialog resources were described briefly in Chapters 2 and 3; they include everything from message dialogs to radio-button dialogs, edit entry dialogs, and pull-down list boxes. Next to the icon editor, the dialog editor may be your most frequently used resource editor.

Fonts are collections of data used to present individual characters on the screen (or printer). A resource font contains data describing a character collection as well as the information required to draw the individual characters. Note: Although Windows supports both raster fonts (bitmapped images) and outline fonts (vectored fonts), the Resource Workshop only supports raster fonts. The font editor can also be used to create picture fonts, small bitmaps that are grouped together and drawn using text rather than image functions. Also, unlike bitmaps, pictures fonts are limited to monochrome images.

Menu resources are probably thoroughly familiar to you by now, and need little explanation or description. However, although menus (unlike most resources) can be created quite conveniently from scripts, the menu editor is almost as convenient and sometimes faster.

String tables are resource tables used to hold prompts, error messages, or other text strings displayed by the application. Defining strings of text as a separate resource makes it easy to edit the text without changing your source code. It also makes it easier to translate your program into international languages.

In addition to the utility editors described, the Resource Workshop includes provisions to create custom-defined resource types—a provision which was previously supported only by Microsoft's SDK.

The Resource Workshop also provides the custom control buttons illustrated in Chapter 2 (Figure 2.1). Be aware, however, that applications using these particular control buttons will not function on other systems unless the Borland Windows Custom Controls Dynamic Link Library (BWCC.DLL) is present.

NOTE. When BCW is installed, the BWCC.DLL is installed in the \WINDOWS\ SYSTEM subdirectory. As with all DLL resources, only one copy of the Dynamic Link Library is required, no matter how many applications may make use of these resources.

WHITEWATER RESOURCE TOOLKIT (WRT)

The Whitewater Resource Toolkit (WRT) was distributed with earlier versions of BCW, predating Borland's Resource Workshop, and is now available as a separate utility. While the WRT duplicates most of the editor features supplied by the Resource Workshop (accelerator, bitmap, cursor, dialog, icon, menu, and string table), WRT also supplies two very important features lacking from the Resource Workshop.

Where Borland's Resource Workshop has no provisions for assigning mnemonic identifiers to resource elements—aside from using the Windows Notepad to prepare a .H text file or (shudder) working with .RC resource scripts—the WRT is somewhat more intelligently arranged and includes two important provisions:

First, when editing menu or dialog resources, WRT permits (almost insists on) opening a .H header file.

Second, while defining a menu resource (for example), both numerical values and mnemonic symbols can be entered. Alternatively, the include editor can be used to add mnemonic symbols to the header file, after which either values or symbols can be used while preparing the resource.

Figure A.1 shows the WRT after loading the BUSGRAPH.RES resource file and selecting the menu resource for editing.

Figure A.1 shows four windows, beginning in the background at the upper-left with the WRT resource manager. Still at the top but to the right, the Menu editor appears with the BusGraph menu editor. Below and in the foreground, the Header editor appears with the BUSGRAPH.H header file. Finally, to the lower-left and partially obscured, the Test Menu window offers precisely what the name suggests.

If you are developing any serious Windows applications using more than the simplest of menus and dialogs, the Whitewater Resource Toolkit is almost indispensable—or at the least, it's a very desirable convenience.

Whitewater Resource Toolkit
The Whitewater Group, Inc.
1800 Ridge Avenue
Evanston, IL 60201
(708) 328-3800

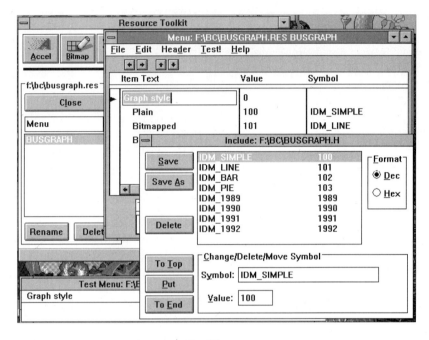

Figure A.1: The Whitewater Resource Toolkit

Graphics preparation with PhotoFinish

A variety of paint programs are available for Windows, with varying degrees of sophistication. For general use, the Microsoft Windows PaintBrush application distributed with Windows is satisfactory, but for more elaborate graphics, a number of very sophisticated paint programs have been appearing, both commercially and as shareware.

Of course, if you have a favorite and familiar paint program that has been ported to Windows or that has introduced a Windows version, then well and good—stick with the tried and true. But if not, you may want to consider ZSoft's PhotoFinish. PhotoFinish supports all video resolutions from black and white through 16-color EGA/VGA (which includes Windows's 20-color palette), 256-color VGA, and 24-bit true color.

Perhaps equally important, PhotoFinish is capable of emulating both 256- and 24-bit colors on standard EGA/VGA systems (using dithering). And on SVGA systems, PhotoFinish can emulate 24-bit colors (with or without dithering, depending on color range and image size). At the same time, PhotoFinish provides excellent gray-scale conversion either for gray-format images or for printing color images on black-and-white devices. In addition, PhotoFinish offers the option of using either its own halftones or the printer's halftones for printing and for scaling.

> **NOTE.** Although using the printer's halftones is recommended in most cases, this is not an indictment of PhotoFinish's halftones, simply recognition of the fact that, if a device supports its own halftones, these will generally produce a better appearance.

Other features supported by PhotoFinish include tools for equalizing the dynamic range of colors within an image, image sharpening using edge-detection algorithms, blending and smoothing tools, special-effects filters, and palette-creation capabilities. At the same time, PhotoFinish provides image file conversion, supporting .PCX, .TIF, .GIF, .BMP, .TGA, .MSP, and .EPS formats together with on-line help, multiple undo levels, and multiple views of a single image.

Also, for those using scanners, PhotoFinish provides direct scanner control for most flatbed and hand-held scanners as well as for many video capture cards. Image capture, depending on the image device, supports black-and-white, gray-scale, and color (up to 24-bits-per-pixel) scans.

ZSoft also includes a screen-capture program, ZCapture, which is compatible with all Windows screen formats (including, importantly, SVGA).

Nothing's perfect, of course, and PhotoFinish has a few regrettable shortcomings. It lacks any curve-capable tools (either circles or bezier curves), and although images can be enlarged and scrolled, it lacks facilities to select (for cut and paste) areas larger than the current display. Still, for photo-realistic artwork, PhotoFinish is excellent, offering features not found in conventional "paint" programs.

PhotoFinish
ZSoft Corporation
Department PF
450 Franklin Road, Suite 100
Marietta, GA 30067
(800) 444-4780
(404) 428-0008
(404) 427-1150 (fax)

IMAGE COMPRESSION

Graphics image files tend to require quite a lot of disk storage, certainly more than most other types of data files—this is inherent in the nature of the information. Even with increasing hard-drive capacities and higher-density removable storage media, images still present problems in transport, either via floppy disk or via telephone link. So until both media densities and modem speeds increase, there will be a need for image-compression facilities, several of which are detailed in the following sections.

> **NOTE.** Although the new 3.5-inch magnetic-optical disks from Teac, at 128Mb per disk and with true random access, are ideal for transporting large collections of images, at present, the high costs of both the disk drives and the media itself are somewhat prohibitive.

ZSOFT'S ZPACK FILE-COMPRESSION UTILITY

Included with ZSoft's PhotoFinish is the ZPack file-compression utility. While nominally designed for compression and decompression of image files, ZPack can be used with all file types.

ZPack provides file list boxes with mouse-click selection, permitting almost as much convenience as, for example, XTree Pro (which is DOS only). Compression varies according to the source-file type, providing, on average, about 70 percent compression (exact file-compression percentage varies greatly, depending on image size, detail, and color range).

PKZIP COMPRESSION

The PKZIP format, available as a public-domain utility, is another popular image file-compression utility. PKZIP and PKUNZIP are operated as command-line utilities but can also be accessed via a variety of file-selection utilities. Again, compression ranges vary but average about 70 percent (3:1) for .PCX, .BMP, and .TIF images. PKZIP is available from CompuServe, GEnie, Prodigy, and other BBS services.

LOSSY VERSUS LOSSLESS IMAGE COMPRESSION

There are two drawbacks in using most conventional compression utilities: First, compression ratios are generally limited to a maximum of roughly 3:1, and second, these utilities cannot conveniently be integrated with other applications.

Following are descriptions of three compression utilities created specifically for images. They have varying compression capabilities with, appropriately, varying loss levels.

Also, while the following three compression utilities use varying compression algorithms and processes, all offer both stand-alone or application-integrated operation via C-language libraries (licensing requirements vary).

These compression/decompression facilities were tested in consideration for an application requiring extremely high color fidelity and image resolution. Images were captured using a high-resolution, 3-chip CCD (Charge Coupled

Device) video camera (Hitachi Z-1) with a 60mm macro lens and custom optical adapter, together with T-TOOLS TTGRAB (.TGA R/G/B format) and custom fiber-optic lighting. Images were displayed on Sony CPD-1302 monitors with original and decompressed images compared side by side. Effects were judged by visual appearance, not on a pixel-by-pixel basis.

ALICE JPEG image compression   The ALICE JPEG image compression system is compatible with most popular image file types, supporting both color and gray-scale images. Both hardware and software only versions are offered, boasting compression ratios from 5:1 to 50:1 for .TGA, .TIF, .PCX, .GIF, .EPS, .BMP, .DIB, and .VIA formats and version compatibility for DOS, Windows, OS/2, and UNIX systems. In addition, the ALICE JPEG system supports hardware accelerators and offers integration libraries in both Microsoft C and Borland C.

ALICE JPEG
Telephoto Communications, Inc.
11722 Sorrento Valley Road, Suite D
San Diego, CA 92121-1084
(619) 452-0903
(619) 792-0075 (fax)

LeadView image compression   Like the ALICE JPEG system, the LeadView image-compression system is supported by both hardware and software-only versions. Compression algorithms used permit varying compression factors (up to 255:1) and support .BIN, .BMP, .GIF, .PCX, .TGA, .TIF, and .VIA image formats. Also, while the LeadView system extends beyond the JPEG compression standards, the LeadView implementation is compatible with JPEG compression and the JFIF and JTIFF interchange file formats as well as supporting most video drivers.

   LeadView requires MS-DOS (3.0 or later) and recommends an 80386 system with 2Mb of RAM. Tested on 80386 and 80486 systems, image compression and decompression rates—using software only—were quite satisfactory, ranging from 15 to 25 seconds each to compress .4Mb .TGA images (16-bit-per-pixel) with excellent image quality at compression ratios up to 25:1. Higher compression ratios are possible, but at 50:1 restoration quality was judged unsatisfactory for the application being considered.

   Two enhanced versions of LeadView are also available but were not tested. The first, LeadView Turbo, provides significant speed enhancements for both compression and decompression with software compression times of 8 to 10 seconds.

The second, LeadView 255, offers hardware compression/decompression with compression times of less than 1 second.

LeadView
Lead Technologies, Inc.
8701 Mallard Creek Road
Charlotte, NC 28262
(704) 549-5532
(704) 548-8161 (fax)

Iterated Systems fractal compression   Iterated Systems's Fractal Transform Compression offers a quite different approach to image compression. Where most compression algorithms depend on identifying sequences of bits in an image, which can be compressed by encoding as a tag, the Fractal Transform Compression process (FTC)—discovered in 1988 by Michael Barnsley—derives a series of fractal algorithms that recreate the image with varying degrees of fidelity.

Again, the Fractal Transform process is a variable-loss process with the degree of loss proportional to the degree of compression. For example, working with 16-bit .TGA images, source images roughly 400k in size were compressed to 30k (13:1 compression) with virtually no discernible image loss after restoration. At 20k (20:1 compression), only minimal image losses were visible on restoration. However, at 12k (33:1 compression), images became grainy, showing losses both in detail and color resolution, although the resulting quality may well have remained acceptable for other application types. Images compressed at ratios higher than 33:1, on decompression, were judged unacceptable for the application under consideration.

There are two drawbacks, however: First, even with an Fractal Transform Compression board, image compression is relatively slow, requiring anywhere from seconds to a minute or two per image. Software compression, lacking the dedicated processors, is slower. Second, FTC boards are priced out of range for general use (in the thousands of dollars at the time this book was written).

The advantages are also twofold: In general, higher degrees of compression are available than with other systems. Second, Fractal Image Format (FIF) decompression—requiring software only—is relatively fast (1 to 3 seconds, rather than minutes, even for 24-bit per pixel color images).

Fractal Transform Compression
Iterated Systems, Inc.
5550-A Peachtree Parkway, Suite 650
Norcross, GA 30092
(404) 840-0633

APPENDIX B:
ABOUT THE ACCOMPANYING DISK

This appendix describes the files on the disk accompanying this volume, arranged here according to the chapter where each appears and with brief notes about each program. Preferably, before use, these files should be copied to your hard disk; they may be located in any directory or subdirectory desired.

Note that no .EXE files are included, since these can be created as needed. Also, because .RES resource files are used, no .RC resource scripts, .ICO icon files, or other separate resource files are included or required. These last, however, may be prepared if desired using either the Borland Resource Workshop or Whitewater's Resource Toolkit (see Appendix A).

Unfortunately, since .PRJ project files include drive and path specifications which probably would not conform to your specific drive and path settings, you will need to create your own project files using the BCW Integrated Development Environment editor. While doing so, don't forget to include the BWCC-.LIB library in the project (located in the \BORLANDC\LIB subdirectory).

Figure B.1 shows 20 of the sample programs in a Windows group where they were collected for testing.

All files on this disk have been tested and checked thoroughly. In the event errors are found, first check your compiler settings and, second, check the program listings against the listings in the book. If this does not solve the problem, please notify the author (c/o Ziff-Davis Press). Insofar as practical, please include any relevant details.

Figure B.1: Example programs shown as a Windows group

Chapter 1: Creating a Windows Program

WINHELLO.C Introductory Windows program following traditional
WINHELLO.DEF C/C++ examples
WINHELLO.RES

Chapter 2: Windows Messages and Child Processes

DIALOG1.C Windows dialogs and messages
DIALOG1.DEF
DIALOG1.H
DIALOG1.RES

Chapter 4: Graphics Systems

WINMODES.C   Windows mapping modes

WINMODES.DEF

WINMODES.H

WINMODES.RES

LIFE.C   Isotropic and anisotropic mapping

LIFE.DEF

LIFE.H

LIFE.RES

Chapter 5: Identifying System Graphics Capabilities

DC.C   Device context information providing information on
                    video and printer device capabilities
DC.DEF

DC.H

DC.RES

Chapter 6: Colors and Color Palettes

COLOR1.C   Shows default color palette (20 colors)

COLOR1.DEF

COLOR1.RES

COLOR2.C   Demonstrates color dithering

COLOR2.DEF

COLOR2.RES

COLOR3.C   Demonstrates palette color creation

COLOR3.DEF

COLOR3.H

COLOR3.RES

CHAPTER 7: GRAPHICS UTILITIES

CAPTURE1.C   Demonstrates screen capture and display modes using

CAPTURE1.DEF   BitBlt and StretchBlt

CAPTURE1.H

CAPTURE1.RES

CAPTURE2.C   Combines screen capture with file save capabilities

CAPTURE2.DEF   (.BMP format)

CAPTURE2.H

CAPTURE2.RES

CHAPTER 8: ALTERNATIVE IMAGE FORMATS

VIEWPCX.C   Image file display using .PCX format

VIEWPCX.DEF

VIEWPCX.H

VIEWPCX.RES

PCXHEAD.I   Include file with .PCX header definition

Chapter 9: Image Enhancement

SHADES.C
SHADES.DEF
SHADES.H
SHADES.RES

Demonstrates edge detection algorithms for conversion of images to image maps

Chapter 10: Printing Graphics

GRAYIMG.C
GRAYIMG.DEF
GRAYIMG.H
GRAYIMG.RES

Converts color image to gray-scale format with output to printer

Chapter 11: Cursors, Bitmaps, and Image Animations

ANIMATE1.C
ANIMATE1.DEF
ANIMATE1.H
ANIMATE1.RES

Simple animation using multiple cursor images

ANIMATE2.C
ANIMATE2.DEF
ANIMATE2.H
ANIMATE2.RES

Simple animation using bitmap images

CHAPTER 12: INTERACTIVE IMAGES

MAPDEMO.C	Interactive application demonstrating identification of irregular regions using color ID and using drunkard's walk search algorithm
MAPDEMO.DEF	
MAPDEMO.H	
MAPDEMO.RES	
USMAP01.BMP	Images required by the MapDemo application
USMAP02.BMP	

CHAPTER 13: BITMAPS IN BUSINESS APPLICATIONS

BUSGRAPH.C	Line and bar graph displays using bitmaps
BUSGRAPH.DEF	
BUSGRAPH.H	
BUSGRAPH.RES	
PIEGRAPH.C	Interactive pie graph displays
PIEGRAPH.DEF	
PIEGRAPH.H	
PIEGRAPH.RES	

CHAPTER 14: GRAPHIC SIMULATIONS

FOREST.C	Simulating a forest environment using the screen display
FOREST.DEF	
FOREST.H	
FOREST.RES	

Chapter 15: Super VGA Graphics for DOS and Windows

SVGA_DOS.C   Using SVGA and SVGA palettes under DOS

SVGA.I   SVGA initialization and palette functions

SVGA_WIN.C   Using SVGA and SVGA palettes under Windows

SVGA_WIN.DEF

SVGA_WIN.H

SVGA_WIN.RES

Other Files

TGA2VGA.CPP   Example program for TGA to SVGA conversion

TGA.H   TARGA image header definition

GINI.PCX   Sample images for use with ViewPCX, Shades, GrayImg

HELLO.BMP   applications, and so on

IGUANA.BMP

MODERN.BMP

MODERN2.BMP

YODO_2.BMP

INDEX

■ TO RECEIVE 3½-INCH DISK(S)

The Ziff-Davis Press software contained on the $5\frac{1}{4}$-inch disk(s) included with this book is also available in $3\frac{1}{2}$-inch (720k) format. If you would like to receive the software in the $3\frac{1}{2}$-inch format, please return the $5\frac{1}{4}$-inch disk(s) with your name and address to:

Disk Exchange
Ziff-Davis Press
5903 Christie Avenue
Emeryville, CA 94608

■ END-USER LICENSE AGREEMENT